AF819588

Recommended by **Teachers**
Trusted by **Toppers**

# All in One®

# PSYCHOLOGY
## Class 12

**EVERYTHING YOU NEED TO SCORE**

- Simplified Theory
- NCERT & Other Important Questions
- CBQs; MCQs, A-R, Case Based
- Board Questions Upto 2025
- Sample Question Papers

**CBSE Exams 2026**

Recommended by **Teachers**
Trusted by **Toppers**

# All in One

# PSYCHOLOGY
## Class 12

**EVERYTHING YOU NEED TO SCORE**

- Simplified Theory
- NCERT & Other Important Questions
- CBQs; MCQs, A-R, Case Based
- Board Questions Upto 2025
- Sample Question Papers

**CBSE Exams 2026**

*Authors*
Chanda Singh

arihant
SUCCESS AND NOTHING LESS

arihant
SUCCESS AND NOTHING LESS

## ARIHANT PRAKASHAN
(School Division Series)



卐 ADMINISTRATIVE & PRODUCTION OFFICES

*Regd. Office*

'Ramchhaya' 4577/15, Agarwal Road, Darya Ganj, New Delhi -110002
Tele: 011- 47630600, 43518550; Fax: 011- 23280316

卐 *Head Office*

Kalindi, TP Nagar, Meerut (UP) - 250002, Tel: 0121-7156203, 7156204

卐 SALES & SUPPORT OFFICES

Agra, Ahmedabad, Bengaluru, Bareilly, Chennai, Delhi, Guwahati, Hyderabad, Jaipur, Jhansi, Kolkata, Lucknow, Nagpur & Pune.

*PO No : TXT-XX-XXXXXXX-X-XX*

Published By Arihant Publications (India) Ltd.

For further information about the books published by Arihant, log on to www.arihantbooks.com or e-mail at info@arihantbooks.com

Follow us on

卐 PRICE ₹350.00

**PRODUCTION TEAM**

| | | |
|---|---|---|
| *Publishing Managers*<br>Mahendra Singh Rawat & Keshav Mohan | *Cover Designer*<br>Rakesh Rawat | *Inner Designer*<br>Ankit Tyagi |
| *Project Head*<br>Manju | *Page Layouting*<br>Lalit Chaprana | *Proof Reader*<br>Bhawna Madhrey |

# Index *cum* Study Planner

# One Book- Endless Features

## *to Help you Succeed*

**Complete Theory in Each Chapter**

Each chapter has Complete, Easy to Understand and Simplified theory covering latest syllabus and rationalised NCERT Textbook. Theory is developed in such a way that it is suitable for all types of learners.

**01**

**CHAPTER**

One of the most popular psychological attributes which has been of interest to psychologists is intelligence. People differ from each other in their ability to understand complex ideas, adapt to environment, learn from experience, engage in various forms of reasoning and to overcome obstacles.

**YOUR STUDY GOALS**

1.1 Individual Differences in Human Functioning

1.2 Assessment of Psychological Attributes

**YOUR PRACTICE GOAL**

- Objective Type Questions (30 Qs ; MCQs, A-R)
- Subjective Questions (30 VSAs, 35 SAs, 4 LAs, 3 Case Based)

### Variations in Psychological Attributes

#### 1.1 Individual Differences in Human Functioning

- Individual variations are common in all species and these variations add colour and beauty to nature.
- People differ in physical traits such as height, weight, strength and hair colour.
- They also vary in psychological traits like intelligence, creativity, dominance and sociability.
- Each person has a unique combination of traits, that makes them distinct

### NCERT Folder

**1. How do psychologist characterise and define intelligence?**

**Ans.** Every psychologist characterises and defines intelligence in their own way

- **Alfred Binet** was one of the first psychologists who worked on intelligence and defined intelligence as 'the ability to judge well, understood well and reason well'.
- **Wechsler**, whose intelligence tests are most widely used, understood intelligence in term of its functionality i.e. its value for adaptation to environment. According to him, intelligence is the global and aggregate capacity of an individual to think rationally, act purposefully and to deal effectively with her/his environment.
- **Gardner** and **Sternberg** suggested that an intelligent individual not only adapts to the environment but also actively modifies or shape it. Thus, intelligence has certain attributes like mentally alert and quick, sense of humour and understanding according to psychologists.

**2. To what extent is our intelligence the result of heredity (nature) and environment (nurture)? Discuss.**

**Ans.** Intelligence is a product of complex interaction of heredity (nature) and environment (nurture). There are various examples which show that intelligence is the result of heredity and environment. We can explain it in the following ways

- The evidence for hereditary influences on intelligence comes mainly from studies on twins and adopted children. The intelligence of identical twins almost correlate who grow up together.
- Twins separated early in childhood show considerable similarity in their intellectual personality and behavioural characteristics.
- The evidence of adopted children shows that children's intelligence is more similar to their biological rather than adoptive parents.
- With respect to the role of environment, studies have reported that as children grew in age, their intelligence level tends to move closer to that of their adoptive parents.
- Children from disadvantaged homes adopted into families with higher socio-economic status exhibit a large increase in their intelligence scores.
- Environmental deprivation lowers intelligence, while rich nutrition, good family background, and quality schooling increases intelligence.
- Intelligence is a product of complex interaction of heredity (nurture) and environment (nurture). Heredity sets a range within which an individual's development is actually shaped by the support and opportunities of the environment.

**3. Explain briefly the multiple intelligence identified by Gardner.**

*Or* **Explain briefly the multiple intelligences identified by Howard Gardner with the help of examples.** CBSE 2024 C

**Ans.** Howard Gardner proposed the theory of multiple intelligences, which includes

(i) **Linguistic Intelligence** It refers to an ability to use language effectively and flexibly to express one's thinking and understand others, for example, writers, poets.

(ii) **Logical-Mathematical Intelligence** It refers an ability to analyse and solve problems. It includes person who can think logically and critically, for example, mathematicians, scientists and Nobel Prize winners.

(iii) **Musical Intelligence** It refers to an ability to perceive, manipulate and create musical patterns, for example, musicians.

(iv) **Spatial Intelligence** It refers to an ability involved in forming, using and transforming mental images. The person included in this intelligence can easily represent the spatial world in mind for example, pilots, architects, sculptors etc.

(v) **Bodily-kinesthetic Intelligence** It refer to an ability to use the body for expression, for example, athletes, dancers, actors etc.

(vi) **Interpersonal Intelligence** It refers to an ability to understand the motives, feelings and behaviours of other people, for example, psychologist, politicians, counselors etc.

(vii) **Intrapersonal Intelligence** It refers to the knowledge of one's internal strengths and limitations and using that knowledge to effectively relate to others, for examples, philosophers and spiritual leaders.

(viii) **Naturalistic Intelligence** It refers to the complete knowledge of our relationship with the natural world. It is useful in recognising the beauty of different species of flora and fauna for example, hunters, farmers, zoologists etc.

**Quick Test 1**

1. What do individual differences in human functioning refer to?
2. What physical traits contribute to individual differences?
3. Which psychological traits show individual differences?
4. What are the two types of psychological assessments?
5. What is the purpose of psychological assessment?
6. What are the domains of psychological attributes?

**Quick Test**

A set of 4-6 Questions given in between the text, helps students to remain connected with the text while studying. They can instantly assess themselves for their understanding.

**NCERT Folder**

Complete explanations of all the questions of NCERT Exercises.

# One Book- Endless Features

*to Help you Succeed*

**Exam Pattern Questions**

Exam Pattern Questions have all types of questions; Objective Type Questions, VSA, SA, LA Type Questions and Case Based Questions

## Exam Pattern Questions

### Objective Type Questions

**Multiple Choice Questions (MCQs)**

1. Who among the following was the first person that devised systematic tests to measure intelligence test?
   (a) Terman (b) Binet (c) Thorudike (d) Wechsler
2. The structure of intellect model was proposed by
   (a) Spearman (b) Thurstone
   (c) Guilford (d) Thorudike
3. Ability to use past experiences creatively to solve novel problems is known as
   (a) musical intelligence
   (b) interpersonal intelligence
   (c) experiential intelligence
   (d) contextual intelligence
4. ......... and performance tests help reduce the cultural bias usually associated with intelligence tests. CBSE SQP Term I 2021
   (a) Non-verbal (b) Group
   (c) Individual (d) Verbal

10. Howard Gardner has proposed many types of intelligences except ...... . CBSE SQP Term I 2021
    (a) linguistic (b) creative
    (c) intrapersonal (d) interpersonal
11. Which of the following best describes the nature of creativity tests where there are no specified answers to questions or problems, allowing for freedom to use one's imagination and express it in original ways? CBSE 2025
    (a) Divergent (b) Convergent (c) Analytical (d) Structured
12. Helen took a/an ...... test which indicated that she could excel in typing and highlighted it in her resume while looking for jobs.
    (a) multiple aptitude (b) specialised aptitude
    (c) interest (d) achievement
13. If a person has the skill of understanding the motives, feelings and behaviour of other people, he/she is said to have

## SELF ASSESSMENT TEST

**Objective Answer Types Questions**

1. Information processing approach to intelligence is represented in the
   (a) multiple intelligence (b) triarchic theory
   (c) one-factor theory (d) two-factor theory
2. Entrepreneurial competence refers to
   (a) respect for social order (b) self-exposure
   (c) discrimination (d) commitment
3. Which of the following is true about individual differences in human functioning?
   (a) Everyone is identical in terms of intelligence and creativity.
   (b) People differ in both physical and psychological traits.
   (c) Individual differences only occur in physical traits.
   (d) Individual differences do not affect behaviour.
4. What is the main purpose of psychological assessment?
   (a) To measure an individual's physical traits only.
   (b) To predict future behaviour and identify necessary interventions.
   (c) To assess only intelligence and aptitude.
   (d) To judge a person's moral values.

**Sample Question Papers**

To make students practice of examination in real sense, there are 3 Sample Question Papers at the end. All these Sample Questions Papers are exactly prepared on the latest syllabus & pattern of examination.

**Self Assessment Test**

Complete Test of chapter in Exam format.

## SAMPLE QUESTION PAPER 1

A Highly Simulated Sample Question Paper for CBSE Class XII

### PSYCHOLOGY

**General Instructions**

- All questions are compulsory except where internal choice has been given.
- Question Nos. 1-14 in Section A carry 1 mark each.
- Question Nos. 15-19 in Section B are Very Short Answer Type-I questions carrying 2 marks each. Answer to each question should not exceed 30 words.
- Question Nos. 20-23 in Section C are Short Answer Questions Type-II carrying 3 marks each. Answer to each question should not exceed 60 words.
- Question Nos. 24-27 in Section D are Long Answer Type I questions carrying 4 marks each. Answer to each question should not exceed 120 words.
- Question Nos. 28-29 in Section E are Long Answer Type question carrying 6 marks. Answer to this question should not exceed 200 words.
- Question Nos. 30–33 in Section F are based on two cases given. Answer to each one-mark question should not exceed 20 words. Answer to each two-mark question should not exceed 30 words.

**Time : 3 hours** **Max. Marks : 70**

1. Which of the following personalites gave the conecpt of logotheraphy? (1)
   (a) Victor Frankl (b) Sigmund Freud
   (c) Ivan Pavlov (d) Carl Rogers

(a) Emotionally Intelligent Person
(b) Emotionally Creative Person
(c) Powerful Influential Person
(d) Socially Influential Person

4. Sam is 19-year old athletic built ambitious swimmer. He has been selected for upcoming

# Latest Course *Structure*

## UNIT 1 Variations in Psychological Attributes

The topics in this unit are:

1. Introduction
2. Individual Differences in Human Functioning
3. Assessment of Psychological Attributes
4. Intelligence
5. Psychometric Theories of Intelligence, Information Processing Theory: Attention-arousal and Simultaneous Successive Model of Intelligence, Triarchic Theory of Intelligence, Planning, Theory of Multiple Intelligences
6. Individual Differences in Intelligence
7. Culture and Intelligence
8. Emotional Intelligence
9. Special Abilities: Aptitude: Nature and Measurement
10. Creativity

## UNIT II Self and Personality

The topics in this unit are:

1. Introduction
2. Self and Personality
3. Concept of Self
4. Cognitive and Behavioural Aspects of Self
5. Culture and Self
6. Concept of Personality
7. Major Approaches to the Study of Personality
    - Type Approaches
    - Trait Approaches
    - Psychodynamic Approach and Past Freudian Approaches
    - Behavioural Approach
    - Cultural Approach
    - Humanistic Approach
8. Assessment of Personality
    - Self-report Measures
    - Projective Techniques
    - Behavioural Analysis

## UNIT III Meeting Life Challenges

The topics in this unit are:

1. Introduction
2. Nature, Types and Sources of Stress
3. Effects of Stress on Psychological Functioning and Health
   - Stress and Health
   - General Adaptation Syndrome
   - Stress and Immune System
   - Lifestyle
4. Coping with Stress
   - Stress Management Techniques
5. Promoting Positive Health and Well-being
   - Life Skills
   - Positive Health

## UNIT IV Psychological Disorders

The topics in this unit are

1. Introduction
2. Concepts of Abnormality and Psychological Disorders
   - Historical Background
3. Classification of Psychological Disorders
4. Factors Underlying Abnormal Behaviour
5. Major Psychological Disorders
   - Anxiety Disorders
   - Obsessive-Compulsive and Related Disorders
   - Trauma-and Stressor-Related Disorders
   - Somatic Symptom and Related Disorders
   - Dissociative Disorders
   - Depressive Disorder
   - Bipolar and Related Disorders
   - Schizophrenia Spectrum and Other Psychotic Disorders
   - Neurodevelopmental Disorders
   - Disruptive, Impulse-Control and Conduct Disorders
   - Feeding and Eating Disorders
   - Substance Related and Addictive Disorders

## UNIT V Therapeutic Approaches

The topics in this unit are

1. Nature and Process of Psychotherapy
   - Therapeutic Relationship
2. Types of Therapies
   - Behaviour Therapy
   - Cognitive Therapy
   - Humanistic-Existential Therapy
   - Alternative Therapies
   - Factors Contributing to Healing in Psychotherapy
   - Ethics in Psychotherapy
3. Rehabilitation of the Mentally Ill

## UNIT VI Attitude and Social Cognition

The topics in this unit are

1. Introduction
2. Explaining Social Behaviour
3. Nature and Components of Attitudes
4. Attitude Formation and Change
   - Attitude Formation
   - Attitude Change
   - Attitude-Behaviour Relationship
5. Prejudice and Discrimination
6. Strategies for Handling Prejudice

## UNIT VII Social Influence and Group Processes

The topics in this unit are

1. Introduction
2. Nature and Formation of Groups
3. Type of Groups
4. Influence of Group on Individual Behaviour
   - Social Loafing
   - Group Polarisation

## PRACTICAL

A. Development of Case Profile:Using appropriate methods like interview, observation and psychological tests.

B. Test administration: Students are required to administer and interpret five psychological tests related to various psychological attributes like intelligence, aptitude, attitude, personality, etc.

C. In Practical examination, the student will be required to administer and interpret two psychological tests.

Distribution of Marks:

| | |
|---|---|
| • Practical File and Case Profile | 10 Marks |
| • Viva Voce (Case Profile and Two Practical) | 05 Marks |
| • Two Tests (5 Marks for conduct of practicals and 10 Marks for report writing) | 15 Marks |
| **Total** | **30 Marks** |

# 01 CHAPTER

One of the most popular psychological attributes which has been of interest to psychologists is Intelligence. People differ from each other in their ability to understand complex ideas, adapt to environment, learn from experience, engage in various forms of reasoning and to overcome obstacles.

**▼ YOUR STUDY GOALS**



**▼ YOUR PRACTICE GOAL**

- Objective Type Questions (30 Qs ; MCQs, A-R)
- Subjective Questions (30 VSAs, 35 SAs, 4 LAs, 3 Case Based)

# Variations in Psychological Attributes

## 1.1 Individual Differences in Human Functioning

- Individual variations are common in all species and these variations add colour and beauty to nature.
- People differ in physical traits such as height, weight, strength and hair colour.
- They also vary in psychological traits like intelligence, creativity, dominance and sociability.
- Each person has a unique combination of traits, that makes them distinct.
- Psychologists study individual differences to understand the reasons behind variations in behaviour and traits.
- Some psychologists believe personal traits shape behaviour, while others argue that situational factors play a larger role.
- The concept of situationism suggests that behaviour is influenced by the situations and circumstances individual's encounter.
- In certain situations, individuals with different traits may respond in similar ways due to the powerful influence of the environment.
- The situationist perspective views human behaviour relatively more as a result of influence of external factors.

## 1.2 Assessment of Psychological Attributes

- Psychological attributes cover simple things like how fast someone reacts to a stimulus (reaction time) and broader concepts like happiness.
- Assessment involves measuring and evaluating these attributes using scientific methods. It can be types categorised into following
  - (i) **Formal Assessment** Objective, standardised, organised psychologists are trained in making formal assessment.
  - (ii) **Informal Assessment** It varies from case to case/assessor to assessor; open to subjective interpretation.
- Psychologists use formal assessments to reliably evaluate psychological attributes.
- Assessment helps predict future behaviour, such as leadership style based on dominance.
- Interventions can be made if the predicted behaviour is not desirable.
- The attribute chosen for assessment depends on the specific purpose, like assessing intellectual abilities for academic improvement or personality traits for social adjustment.
- Psychological assessments systematically evaluate abilities, behaviours and personal qualities to understand and predict behaviour.

### Some Domains of Psychological Attributes

- Psychological attributes are complex and have many dimensions, like a box with length, width and height.
- To fully understand a person, we need to look at how they think, feel, and interact in different areas, such as cognitive, emotional and social.
- Following are the attributes that are categorised based on variety of tests used in psychological literature

| Domains | Definition | Assessment Purpose |
|---|---|---|
| Intelligence | The global capacity to understand the world, think rationally, and use resources effectively. | Intelligence tests predict cognitive performance in educational settings. |
| Aptitude | An individual's potential for acquiring skills, indicating what a person can achieve with appropriate training and environment. | Aptitude tests forecast future performance based on inherent potential, such as mechanical or language skills. |
| Interest | An individual's preferences for engaging in specific activities over others. | Interest assessments help identify suitable subjects or courses for career satisfaction. |
| Personality | The relatively enduring characteristics that distinguish one individual from another. | Personality tests evaluate unique traits to explain behaviour and predict future actions, such as dominance or emotional stability. |
| Values | Enduring beliefs about ideal behaviour that guide actions and judgements about oneself and others. | Value assessments identify dominant values (political, religious, social or economic) that influence decision making. |

## Methods used for Psychological Assessment

Various methods are used for psychological assessment. Some important methods and their features are described below

| Assessment Method | Key Features |
|---|---|
| Psychological Test | ▪ Assessment of an individual's mental and/or behavioural characteristics.<br>▪ Developed to assess various psychological attributes (e.g. intelligence, aptitude).<br>▪ Widely used for clinical diagnosis, guidance, personnel selection, placement and training.<br>▪ Includes both objective tests and projective tests and objective tests primarily used for personality assessment. |
| Interview | ▪ Involves one-to-one interaction to gather information.<br>▪ Used in various contexts such as counselling, sales surveys, employee selection and journalistic interviews.<br>▪ Allows for a personal understanding of the respondent's thoughts and feelings. |
| Case Study | ▪ An in-depth examination of an individual's psychological attributes and history within their psychosocial and physical environment.<br>▪ Commonly used by clinical psychologists.<br>▪ Can draw insights from the lives of notable individuals.<br>▪ Based on data from interviews, observations, questionnaires and psychological tests. |
| Observation | ▪ Utilises systematic, organised and objective procedures to record natural behavioural phenomena in real time.<br>▪ Effective for studying specific interactions (e.g., mother-child interactions).<br>▪ Challenges include limited control over the situation and potential subjective interpretations by the observer. |
| Self-Report | ▪ A method where individuals provide factual information about themselves, including opinions and beliefs.<br>▪ Information can be collected via interviews, questionnaires, psychological tests or personal diaries.<br>▪ Offers insights directly from the individual about their experiences and perceptions. |

### Quick Test 1

1. What do individual differences in human functioning refer to?
2. What physical traits contribute to individual differences?
3. Which psychological traits show individual differences?
4. What are the two types of psychological assessments?
5. What is the purpose of psychological assessment?
6. What are the domains of psychological attributes?

## 1.3 Intelligence

- Intelligence is a key concept used to understand individuals differences. It also provides insight into how people adapt their behaviour to their environment they live in.
- The psychological notion of intelligence differs from the commonsense understanding. When observing an intelligent person, attributes like mental alertness, quick learning and the ability to understand relationships are often noticed.
- According to the Oxford Dictionary, intelligence is defined as the power of perceiving, learning, understanding and knowing.
- **Alfred Binet**, one of the first psychologists to work on intelligence, defined it as the ability to judge well, understand well and reason well.

- **Wechsler,** whose intelligence tests are widely used, viewed intelligence in terms of its functionality, emphasising its value for adaptation to the environment. He defined intelligence as the global and aggregate capacity of an individual to think rationally, act purposefully and deal effectively with the environment.
- Other psychologists, such as **Gardner** and **Sternberg**, expanded on this view, suggesting that an intelligent individual not only adapts to the environment but also actively modify or shape it.
- The concept of intelligence has evolved over time, and its understanding continues to develop through various important theories.

## Approaches/Theories to Study Intelligence

Theories of intelligence can be classified into two main categories psychometric/structural approaches and information-processing approaches.

| Category | Definition | Key Features |
|---|---|---|
| 1. Psychometric Approach | Intelligence is an aggregate of cognitive abilities measured by standardised tests. | Emphasises quantifying intelligence using a single index (e.g., IQ) to assess cognitive capabilities.<br>**Alfred Binet's** created the first intelligence test to identify children needing educational assistance. |
| 2. Information Processing Approach | Focuses on how individuals process information and the cognitive functions of intelligence. | Highlights problem-solving reasoning over test based on intelligence measurement.<br>Aims to understand mental processes that characterise, such as attention, memory and information retrieval. |

### Uni-Factor Theory of Intelligence (Binet)

- **Alfred Binet** was the first psychologist to formalise the concept of intelligence in terms of mental operations.
- **Binet's** theory of intelligence was simple and focused on distinguishing more intelligent individuals from less intelligent ones.
- He conceptualised intelligence as a single set of abilities for solving any problem in an individual's environment.
- This idea became known as the Uni or One-Factor Theory of Intelligence, suggesting intelligence was uniform and applicable to all tasks.
- However, this theory was later disputed when data from **Binet's** test, showed that intelligence could not be explained by single factor.

### Two-Factor Theory of Intelligence (Spearman In 1927)

- In 1927, **Charles Spearman** proposed the two-factor theory of intelligence using factor analysis.
- He demonstrated that intelligence consists of two components a general factor (g-factor) and specific factors (s-factors).
- The g-factor represents mental operations common to all types of intellectual performances.
- The s-factors refer to specific abilities that are unique to certain individuals complementing the g-factor.
- For example, individuals excelling in fields such as singing, architecture, science or athletics possess both the g-factor and specialised s-factors.
- These s-factors, enable individuals to excel in their respective areas of expertise, while the g-factor underlies overall cognitive performance across tasks.

## Primary Mental Abilities

- Louis Thurstone proposed the theory of primary mental abilities, which suggests that intelligence is composed of seven distinct and relatively independent abilities.
- These seven primary abilities are
  - (i) **Verbal Comprehension** Grasping meaning of words, concepts and ideas.
  - (ii) **Numerical Abilities** The capacity for speed and accuracy in numerical and computational skills.
  - (iii) **Spatial Relations** The skill to visualise patterns and forms.
  - (iv) **Perceptual Speed** The ability to quickly perceive details.
  - (v) **Word Fluency** The flexibility and fluency in using words.
  - (vi) **Memory** Accurately recalling information.
  - (vii) **Inductive Reasoning** The skill to derive general rules from facts.
- Under the theory of primary mental abilities, two models were proposed i.e. *Hierarchical Model* and *Intellectual Model by Arthur Jensen* and *JP Guilford*, respectively.

1. **Arthur Jensen's Hierarchical Model of Intelligence**

   This model divides intelligence into two levels: Level I and Level II.
   - (i) Level I Associative learning (similar output to input, such as in rote learning and memory).
   - (ii) Level II Cognitive competence (higher-order skills that transform the input to produce an effective output, emphasising reasoning and problem-solving).

2. **J.P. Guilford's Structure of Intellect Model**

   This model classifies intellectual traits across three dimensions are operations, contents and products.
   - (i) **Operations** The processes of cognition, memory recording, memory retention, divergent production (creative thinking), convergent production (logical reasoning) and evaluation.
   - (ii) **Contents** The type of information used in intellectual operations, which includes visual (images), auditory (sounds), symbolic (letters, numbers), semantic (words) and behavioural (attitudes, behaviours).
   - (iii) **Products** The forms in which processed information is represented, such as units, classes, relations, systems, transformations and implications.

- **Guilford's** (1988) model contains 180 cells (6 operations $\times 5$ contents $\times 6$ products) and each cell represents a unique intellectual factor or ability, with some cells containing multiple factors.
- These theories reflect the psychometric approach, emphasising the measurement of cognitive abilities and their role in human behaviour.

### Quick Test 2

1. Who introduced the uni-factor theory of intelligence?
2. What are the two approaches to studying intelligence?
3. What are the two levels in Arthur Jensen's Hierarchical Model of Intelligence?
4. What are the seven primary mental abilities proposed by Thurstone?
5. How does J.P. Guilford's Structure of Intellect Model classify intellectual traits?

# Theory of Multiple Intelligence

## Howard Gardner's Theory of Multiple Intelligences

- Gardner proposed that intelligence is not a single unified entity, but consist of multiple distinct types of intelligences.
- Each intelligences operates independently, meaning excelling in one does not imply similar ability in others.
- These intelligences often interact and collaborate to solve complex problems.
- His theory was based on the study of highly talented individuals with exceptional abilities in specific areas.
- Gardner identified eight types of intelligence. These are

1. **Linguistic Intelligence**
   - The ability to use language effectively for communication and expression.
   - Persons high on this intelligence are 'word-smart', i.e. they are sensitive to different shades of word meanings, are articulate and can create linguistic images in their mind. e.g. poets and writers.
2. **Logical-Mathematical Intelligence**
   - The capacity for logical thinking, critical analysis and solving complex problems.
   - Individuals strong in this intelligence excel in abstract reasoning and manipulating symbols, such as numbers, e.g. scientists and Nobel laureates.
3. **Spatial Intelligence**
   - The ability to form, use and transform mental images of spatial relationships.
   - People with high spatial intelligence can visualise and manipulate patterns or spaces. e.g. pilots, sculptors, architects and surgeons.
4. **Musical Intelligence**
   - The ability to produce, create and manipulate musical rhythms and patterns.
   - Those with strong musical intelligence are highly sensitive to sounds and vibrations and can compose or interpret music effectively. e.g. musicians, composers and singers.
5. **Bodily-Kinaesthetic Intelligence**
   - The ability to use the body or parts of it in a skilled, flexible and creative way.
   - This intelligence is prominent in people who use their physical abilities for performance, crafting or problem-solving. e.g. athletes, dancers, actors and surgeons.
6. **Interpersonal Intelligence**
   - The ability to understand and respond to the feelings, motives and behaviours of others.
   - Those with strong interpersonal intelligence build comfortable relationships and deeply understand others. e.g. psychologists, counsellors, politicians and social workers.
7. **Intrapersonal Intelligence**
   - The ability to understand one's own emotions, motives and desires.
   - People with high intrapersonal intelligence have deep self-awareness and use it to manage their lives effectively. e.g. philosophers and spiritual leaders.
8. **Naturalistic Intelligence**
   - The ability to recognise, categorise and understand the natural world, including plants, animals and environmental patterns.
   - Those with naturalistic intelligence are attuned to nature and are skilled in identifying and interacting with natural features. e.g. hunters, botanists, zoologists and bird watchers.
   - **Gardner's** theory highlights the diverse nature of human abilities, stressing that different individuals excel in different forms of intelligence depending on their strengths and areas of interest.

## Triarchic Theory of Intelligence

- This theory was proposed by Robert Sternberg in 1985.
- He views intelligence as "the ability to adapt, to shape and select environment to accomplish one's goals and those of society and culture".
- According to this theory, there are three basic types of intelligence i.e. componential, experiential and contextual.

### 1. Componential Intelligence

- Also known as analytical intelligence, it involves analysing information to solve problems.
- Individuals high in componential intelligence excel at thinking analytically and critically, contributing to academic success.
- It consists of three components
  - (i) **Knowledge Acquisition Component** Responsible for learning and acquiring the methods to perform tasks.
  - (ii) **Meta-Component** Involves higher-order planning determining actions and how to execute them.
  - (iii) **Performance Component** Focuses on the actual execution of tasks and problem-solving.

### 2. Experiential Intelligence

- Also referred to as creative intelligence, it involves using past experiences in innovative ways to solve new problems.
- It is demonstrated through creative performance and originality.
- Individuals with high experiential intelligence can integrate diverse experiences to make new discoveries and inventions.
- Excelling at identifying crucial information in various situations.

### 3. Contextual Intelligence

- Also known as practical intelligence, it involves the ability to navigate everyday environmental demands.
- Often described as 'street smartness' or 'business sense'.
- Individuals high in contextual intelligence adapt easily to their current environments, select more favourable environments or modify their surroundings to meet their needs. Contributing to overall life success.

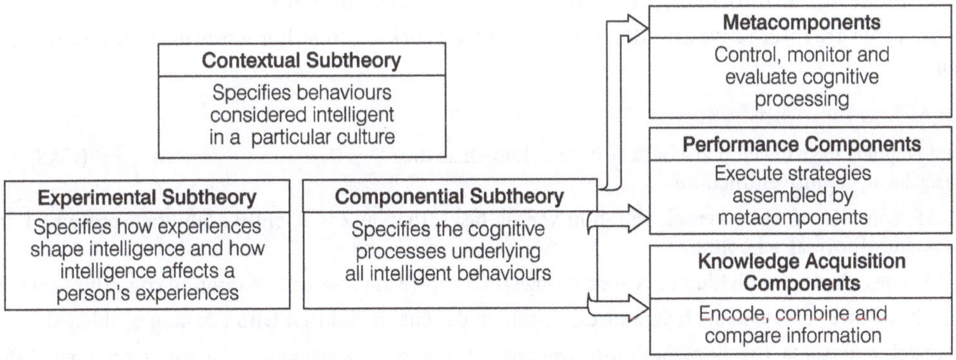


▲ *Elements of Triarchic Theory of Intelligence*

## PASS Model of Intelligence

- Planning, Attention-Arousal and Simultaneous Successive (PASS) Model of intelligence was developed by *J.P. Das,* Jack Naglieri and Kirby in 1994.
- This model posits that intellectual activity involves the interdependent functioning of three neurological systems, which are referred to as the functional units of the brain.
- These functional units are responsible for arousal/attention, coding or processing and planning.

### Arousal/Attention

- Arousal is fundamental to any behaviour as it helps individuals attend to stimuli and process information.
- An optimal level of arousal directs focus to relevant aspects of a problem.
- Both excessive and insufficient arousal can hinder attention.
- For example, when a teacher informs students about an upcoming test, it triggers arousal that helps them focus on the specific chapters to study.
- This arousal compels students to concentrate on reading, learning and revising the relevant material.

### Simultaneous and Successive Processing

**Simultaneous Processing** Occurs when individuals perceive relationships among various concepts and integrate them into a meaningful pattern. For example, In Raven's Progressive Matrices (RPM) test, a design is presented with a missing part and the task is to choose one of the six options that best completes the design.

**Successive Processing** It involves remembering information in a serial order, where recalling one piece of information leads to other e.g. learning digits, alphabets and multiplication tables.

### Planning

- This is an essential feature of intelligence. After the information is attended to and processed, planning is activated.
- If a plan fails work, it is modified to suit the task or situation.
- For example, To prepare for a test, you set goals, plan study time, get clarifications if needed, you may have to think of other ways to meet your goals.
- The PASS processes operate on a knowledge base developed either formally (through reading, writing and experimenting) or informally, (by learning from the environment).
- These processes are interactive and dynamic in nature, working together while each maintaining distinct function.

#### Cognitive Assessment System (CAS)

- Das and Naglieri have developed a battery of tests known as the Cognitive Assessment System[1] (CAS), which measures basic cognitive functions.
- The CAS consists of both verbal and non-verbal tasks that assess cognitive abilities presumed to be independent of formal schooling.
- The CAS is designed for individuals between the ages of 5 and 18 and evaluates a range of cognitive functions.
- The results of these assessments help address cognitive deficits in children with learning problems.
- This model represents the information-processing approach to intelligence, focusing on how different cognitive processes.

1 Cognitive Assessment System A battery of tests designed to measure the four PASS processes (Planning, Attention, Simultaneous and Successive processing).

**Individual Differences in Intelligence : Intelligence Interplays of Nature and Nurture**

- The study of individual differences in intelligence explores the interaction between heredity (nature) and environment (nurture).
- Evidence for hereditary influences on intelligence comes from twins and adoption studies.
- Identical twins reared together show a high correlation in intelligence, around 0.90, indicating strong hereditary factors.
- Twins separated early in childhood still show considerable similarity in intellectual, personality and behavioural characteristics, which suggests a genetic influence.
- Identical twins raised apart show an intelligence correlation of 0.72, while fraternal twins raised together have a correlation of around 0.60.
- The intelligence correlation between siblings raised together is about 0.50 and between siblings raised apart, it drops to approximately 0.25.
- Studies on adopted children demonstrate that their intelligence is more closely related to their biological parents than to their adoptive parents, further emphasising the role of genetics.
- Children from disadvantaged homes adopted into families with higher socio-economic status tend to show a significant increase in their intelligence scores, highlighting the impact of the environmental impact.
- Environmental deprivation can lower intelligence, while factors like good nutrition, supportive family backgrounds and quality schooling boost intelligence.
- Research suggests that as adopted children grow older, their intelligence levels tend to become more similar to that of their adoptive parents, illustrating environmental influences over time.
- Psychologists generally agree that intelligence is a result of a complex interplay between heredity and environment.

## Assessment of Intelligence

- In 1905, Alfred Binet and Theodore Simon made the first formal attempt to measure intelligence.
- In 1908, they introduced the concept of Mental Age (MA), which is a measure of a person's intellectual development compared to people of the same age group.
- A mental age of 5 means a child's performance on an intelligence test is equivalent to the 5-year-olds.
- Chronological Age (CA) refers to biological age from birth. A bright child's MA is greater than their CA, whereas a dull child's MA is lower than their CA.
- Binet and Simon defined **mental retardation**[2] as an MA two years below CA.
- In 1912, William Stern, a German psychologist, introduced the concept of **Intelligence Quotient (IQ)**[3], which is calculated as IQ = (MA/CA) × 100.
- The number 100 is used to avoid decimals, and when MA equals CA, IQ is 100. If MA is higher than CA, IQ is more than 100 and if MA is lower than CA, IQ is less than 100.
- The average IQ score in the population is 100, regardless of age.
- IQ scores are distributed in such a way that most people's scores fall in the middle range, while few have very high or very low scores.
- The frequency distribution of IQ scores tends to follow a bell-shaped curve, known as the normal curve, which is symmetrical around the mean value.
- The mean IQ score is 100, with people scoring between 90-110 having normal intelligence.
- Individuals with IQs below 70 indicate 'intellectual disability', while IQs above 130 suggest exceptional talents.

---

2 **Mental Retardation** It is characterised by sub-average intellectual functioning along with varying degrees of deficits in adaptive behaviour.

3 **Intelligence Quotient (IQ)** An index derived from standardised intelligence tests that indicates the ratio of mental age to chronological age.

- One practical use of intelligence tests is to identify people at the extremes of intellectual functioning.
- About 2% of the population have IQs above 130, and a similar percentage have IQs below 70.
- People with IQs above 130 are referred to as intellectually gifted, and those with IQs below 70 are termed intellectually disabled.

**IQ Classifications**

| IQ Range | Descriptive Label | Percentage in Population |
|---|---|---|
| Above 130 | Very superior | 2.2% |
| 120-130 | Superior | 6.7% |
| 110-119 | High average | 16.1% |
| 90-109 | Average | 50.0% |
| 80-89 | Low average | 16.1% |
| 70-79 | Borderline | 6.7% |
| Below 70 | Intellectually disabled | 2.2% |

### Quick Test 3

1. How many types of intelligences are identified in Gardner's theory?
2. What are the three types of intelligence in Sternberg's triarchic theory?
3. What does componential intelligence focus on in Sternberg's triarchic theory?
4. What are the components of the PASS model of intelligence?
5. How does the concept of arousal relate to attention in intelligence?
6. What is the role of environmental factors in the development of intelligence?

## Variations of Intelligence

### 1. Intellectual Deficiency

- Children with intellectual deficiency are referred to as 'intellectually disabled'.
- The American Association on Mental Deficiency (AAMD) defines intellectual disability as 'significantly sub-average general intellectual functioning' combined with deficits in adaptive behaviour, manifesting during the developmental period.
- This definition highlights three key features
  - (i) Sub-average intellectual functioning (IQ below 70).
  - (ii) Deficits in adaptive behaviour, referring to the ability to interact independently.
  - (iii) These deficits must occur during the developmental period (ages 0-18).
- Individuals with intellectual disability vary in their abilities, ranging from those who can be trained to work with special attention to those who require lifelong institutional care.
- The average IQ in the population is 100, and IQ figures help categorise the levels of intellectual disability.

- The different levels of intellectual deficiency are

| Level | IQ Range | Characteristics |
|---|---|---|
| Mild | 55 to 70 | ▪ Development is slower than peers.<br>▪ Can Function independently with minimal supervision.<br>▪ Capable of holding jobs and maintaining families. |
| Moderate | 35-40 to 50-55 | ▪ Lag behind peers in language and motor skills.<br>▪ Can be trained in self-care and basic social skills.<br>▪ Require moderate supervision for daily tasks. |
| Severe | 20-25 to 35-40 | ▪ Severe delays in developmental skills.<br>▪ Require extensive supervision and training for basic tasks. |
| Profound | Below 20-25 | ▪ Incapable of indepentent functioning.<br>▪ Need constant care throughout life.<br>▪ Severe limitations in all areas of development. |

- As the level of disability increases, the difficulties in language, motor skills, and independence become more pronounced, and individuals need greater supervision and support in daily life.

## Intellectual Giftedness

- Intellectually gifted individuals demonstrate higher performance due to their exceptional potential.
- In 1925, Lewis Terman began studying gifted individuals by following about 1500 children with IQs of 130 and above to examine the relationship between intelligence, occupational success and life adjustment.
- The terms 'talent' and 'giftedness' are distinct, giftedness refers to exceptional general ability, across various areas. While talent refers to exceptional ability in a specific field, such as spiritual, social or aesthetic domains and highly talented individuals are often called 'prodigies'.
- Psychologists suggest that from a teacher's perspective, giftedness depends on a combination of high ability, high creativity and high commitment.
- Gifted children exhibit early signs of intellectual superiority, including
  - Larger attention span and strong recognition memory.
  - Preference for novelty and sensitivity to changes in the environment.
  - Early development of language skills.
- Giftedness should not be equated solely with academic excellence, as athletes with superior psychomotor abilities are also considered gifted.
- Key characteristics of gifted children include
  - Advanced logical thinking, questioning, and problem-solving abilities.
  - High speed in processing information.
  - High intrinsic motivation and self-esteem.
  - Independent thinking and preference for solitary activities.
- Identifying giftedness is not limited to intelligence tests. Other methods include, teachers' judgement, school achievement records, parent interviews and peer and self-assessments.
- Gifted children need special attention and educational programmes beyond regular classrooms to fully develop their potential.
- These educational programmes may include life enrichment activities aimed at sharpening skills in productive thinking, planning, decision-making and communication.

## Types of Intelligence Tests

| Classification | Description |
| --- | --- |
| **1. Based on Administration Procedure** | |
| Intelligence tests can be categorised based on how they are administered. | |
| Individual Tests | Administered to one person at a time. |
| | Requires personal interaction and sensitivity to the subject's feeling between the test administrator and the subject. |
| | Subjects respond verbally, in writing or by manipulating objects as per the tester's instructions. |
| Group Tests | Administered to multiple individuals simultaneously. |
| | Do not allow for familiarity with the subject's emotional states or individual expressions. |
| | Responses are typically written, often in a multiple-choice format. |
| **2. Based on Nature of Test Items** | |
| Intelligence tests can be categorised based on the type of items used in the test. | |
| Verbal Tests | Require verbal responses either orally or in written form. |
| | Only for literate individuals who can read and write. |
| Non-Verbal Tests | Use pictures or illustrations instead of words. |
| | An example is Raven's Progressive Matrices (RPM), where subjects select figures to complete patterns. |
| Performance Tests. | Require subjects to manipulate objects and materials to complete tasks. |
| | Do not rely on written or spoken language. |
| | Example Kohs' Block Design Test, where subjects arrange blocks to create specific designs. |
| **3. Cultural Considerations** | |
| Culture-Fair Tests | Applied meaningfully to all cultures. |
| | Culturally appropriate, ensuring no discrimination against individuals from different cultures. |
| | Some questions do not require language, making them accessible to a wider audience. |
| | Non-verbal and performance tests reduce cultural bias typically associated with verbal tests. |
| Culture-Biased Tests | It is nearly impossible to design an intelligence test that is meaningful across all cultures. |
| | Many intelligence tests exhibit a bias toward the culture in which they were developed; these are termed culture-biased tests. |
| | Tests developed in America and Europe often reflect an urban and middle-class cultural ethos. |
| | As a result, educated middle-class white subjects tend to perform well on culture-biased tests. |
| | The items included in culture-biased tests may not respect or acknowledge the cultural perspectives of individuals from Asia and Africa. |
| | Furthermore, the norms for these tests are usually derived from Western cultural groups, which can disadvantage test-takers from other backgrounds. |

**Some Tests Developed in India**

| Verbal Tests | Performance Tests |
|---|---|
| CIE Verbal Group Test of Intelligence by Uday Shankar | CIE Non-verbal Group Test of Intelligence |
| Group Test of General Mental Ability by S. Jalota | Bhatia's Battery of Performance Tests |
| Group Test of Intelligence by Prayag Mehta | Draw-a-Man Test by Pramila Pathak |
| The Bihar Test of Intelligence by S.M. Mohsin | Adaptation of Wechsler Adult Performance Intelligence Scale by R. Ramalingaswamy |
| Group Test of Intelligence by Bureau of Psychology, Allahabad | |
| Indian Adaptation of Stanford-Binet Test (Third Edition) by S.K. Kulshrestha | |
| Test of General Mental Ability (Hindi) by M.C. Joshi | |

## Intelligence Testing in India

- S.M. Mohsin pioneered an intelligence test in Hindi.
- The National Council of Educational Research and Training (NCERT) has documented various Indian tests. Critical reviews of Indian tests are published in the form of handbooks.
- The National Library of Educational and Psychological Tests (NLEPT) has released handbooks on intelligence, aptitude, personality, attitudes and interests.
- Among these tests, Bhatia's Battery of Performance Tests gained considerable popularity in the 1930s.
- C.H. Rice standardised Binet's test in Urdu and Punjabi.
- Around the same time, Mahalanobis made efforts to standardise Binet's test in Bengali.
- Indian researchers developed norms for several Western tests, like Raven's Progressive Matrices (RPM), Wechsler Adult Intelligence Scale (WAIS), Alexander's Passalong, Cube Construction and Kohs' Block Design.
- Long and Mehta prepared a Mental Measurement Handbook that listed 103 tests of intelligence available in India across various languages.
- Since the publication of this handbook, numerous tests have been either developed or adapted from Western cultures.
- The NLEPT continues to document and disseminate of intelligence tests in India.

### Quick Test 4

1. What is intellectual deficiency defined as according to the American Association on Mental Deficiency (AAMD)?
2. What are the IQ ranges for mild, moderate, severe, and profound intellectual deficiencies?
3. What does intellectual giftedness signify?
4. What are some key characteristics of intellectually gifted children?
5. How are intelligence tests classified based on administration procedures?
6. Name two intelligence tests developed in India for verbal and performance testing.

## 1.4 Culture And Intelligence

- A major characteristic of intelligence is its ability to help individuals adapt to their environment.
- The cultural environment provides a context in which intelligence can develop.
- Vygotsky, a Russian psychologist, argued that culture offers a social context for growth and understanding.
- In less technologically developed societies, social and emotional skills related to interpersonal relationships are highly valued.
- Conversely, in technologically advanced societies, personal achievement based on reasoning and judgement abilities.
- Many theorists have traditionally viewed intelligence as attributes specific to the individual, disregarding their cultural background.
- Unique cultural features have begun to be represented in theories of intelligence.
- Sternberg's notion of contextual or practical intelligence suggests that intelligence is a product of culture.
- Vygotsky also believed that cultures, like individuals, grow and influence intellectual development.
- According to Vygotsky, while elementary mental functions are universal, the operation of higher mental functions such as problem-solving and thinking is largely shaped by culture.
- Technologically advanced societies adopt child-rearing practices that promote skills such as generalisation, abstraction, speed, minimal movements and mental manipulation among children.
- These societies encourage behaviours that can be classified as technological intelligence, with individuals excelling in attention, observation, analysis, performance, speed and achievement orientation.
- Intelligence tests developed in Western cultures specifically seek to measure these skills in individuals.
- In many Asian and African societies, technological intelligence is not as highly valued.
- Some non-Western societies value self-reflection and collectivistic orientation.

### Intelligence in the Indian Tradition

- Unlike technological intelligence, intelligence in the Indian tradition can be termed integral intelligence, emphasising connectivity with the social and world environment.
- Indian thinkers view intelligence from a holistic perspective, where equal attention is given to both cognitive and non-cognitive processes and their integration.
- The Sanskrit word 'buddhi' represents intelligence and encompasses a broader scope than the Western concept of intelligence.
- According to J.P. Das, buddhi includes various skills such as mental effort, determined action, feelings, and opinions, along with cognitive competencies like knowledge, discrimination, and understanding.
- Among other aspects, buddhi represents the self knowledge informed by conscience, will and desire.
- Unlike Western views, which primarily focus on cognitive parameters, the following competencies are identified as facets of intelligence in the Indian tradition
  - (i) **Cognitive Capacity** This includes sensitivity to context, understanding, discrimination, problem-solving and effective communication.
  - (ii) **Social Competence** This involves respect for social order, commitment to elders, the young and the needy, concern for others and the ability to recognise others' perspectives.
  - (iii) **Emotional Competence** This encompasses self-regulation and selfmonitoring of emotions, honesty, politeness, good conduct and selfevaluation.
  - (iv) **Entrepreneurial Competence** This includes commitment, persistence, patience, hard work, vigilance and goal-directed behaviours.

## Emotional Intelligence

- The notion of emotional intelligence expands the concept of intelligence beyond the intellectual sphere and acknowledges that intelligence encompasses emotions.
- It alligns with the Indian tradition emphasising the importance of emotional aspects.
- Emotional intelligence consists of a set of skills that underlie the accurate appraisal, expression and regulation of emotions.
- It represents the feeling side of intelligence, indicating that having a high IQ and strong academic records alone is not sufficient for success in life.
- The concept of emotional intelligence was first introduced by Salovey and Mayer, who defined it as "the ability to monitor one's own and others' emotions, to discriminate among them, and to use the information to guide one's thinking and actions."
- Emotional Quotient (EQ) is used to express emotional intelligence, analogous to how IQ is used to express intellectual intelligence.
- In simple terms, emotional intelligence refers to the ability to process emotional information accurately and efficiently.
- Emotional intelligence is gaining increasing attention from educators, particularly for supporting students dealing with external stresses.
- Programmes aimed at improving students' emotional intelligence have been shown to have beneficial effects on their academic achievement, promoting cooperation and reducing antisocial behaviour.
- Such programmes encourage cooperative behaviour and help reduce antisocial activities among students.

## Characteristics of Emotionally Intelligent Persons

- They perceive and are sensitive to their own feelings and emotions.
- They perceive and are sensitive to various types of emotions in others by observing their body language, voice tone, and facial expressions.
- They relate their emotions to their thoughts, ensuring that they take emotions into account while solving problems and making decisions.
- They can control and regulate their emotions and expressions when dealing with themselves and others to achieve harmony and peace.

# 1.5 Special Abilities

## Aptitude-Nature and Measurement

- Aptitude refers to an individual's special abilities in a specific field, indicating their capacity to acquire knowledge or skills through training.
- It is a combination of characteristics that predicts how well an individual might perform in a particular area after proper training.
- Aptitude helps in forecasting an individual's future performance, as people with similar intelligence can differ significantly in acquiring specific skills.
- Success in any field requires both aptitude and interest.

### Aptitude Test

Aptitude test is available in two forms

(i) **Independent (Specialised) Aptitude Test** Clerical Aptitude, Mechanical Aptitude, Numerical aptitude and Typing aptitude are such type of tests.

(ii) **Multiple (Generalised) Aptitude Test** It exists in the form of test batteries, which measure aptitude in several separate but homogeneous areas.

- Differential Aptitude Test (DAT), the General Aptitude Test Battery (GATB) and the Armed Services Vocational Aptitude Battery (ASVAB) are well known aptitude test batteries.
- It consists of eight independent subtests which are as follows

(i) Verbal Reasoning
(ii) Numerical Reasoning
(iii) Abstract Reasoning
(iv) Clerical Speed and Accuracy
(v) Mechanical Reasoning
(vi) Space Relations
(vii) Spelling
(viii) Language Usage

- JM Ojha has developed an Indian adaptation of DAT. Several other aptitude tests have been developed in India for measuring scientific, scholastic, literary, clerical and teaching aptitude.

### Quick Test 5

1. What is emphasized in non-Western societies in terms of intelligence?
2. How is intelligence defined in the Indian tradition according to J.P. Das?
3. What are the four facets of intelligence identified in the Indian tradition?
4. Who first introduced the concept of emotional intelligence?
5. What are the two forms of aptitude tests?
6. Name any two examples of aptitude test batteries.
7. How many independent subtests are included in aptitude tests?

## 1.6 Creativity

- Creativity refers to the ability to produce novel, appropriate ideas, objects and problem solutions.
- It involves thinking in unique ways to come up with original solutions, inventions or innovations.
- Variations in creativity exist across individuals, just as there are differences in psychological attributes like intelligence, aptitude and personality.
- Some individuals, such as **Tagore, Einstein, CV Raman** and **Ramanujan**, have made outstanding contributions in their respective fields, reflecting their high levels of creativity.
- Research suggests that children begin developing their imagination in early childhood, often expressing creativity through physical activities and non-verbal ways. As intellectual abilities grow creativity can be expressed verbally.
- Variations in creativity can be explained by the complex interaction of heredity and environment. Heredity sets the limits of creative potential, while environmental factors stimulate its development.

## Creativity and Intelligence

- In the 1920s, **Terman** discovered that individuals with high IQs were not necessarily creative and creative ideas could emerge from people with average IQs.
- Research shows that both high and low levels of creativity can be found in highly intelligent children as well as those of average intelligence.
- There is a positive relationship between creativity and intelligence. All creative acts require a minimum ability to acquire knowledge and a capacity to comprehend, retain and retrieve information.
- A high level of intelligence alone does not guarantee creativity.

### Creativity Test

- Creativity tests assess variations in an individual's potential for creativity. These tests are open-ended, allowing individuals the freedom to use their imagination and express it in original ways.
- Creativity tests involve divergent thinking, measuring the ability to generate a variety of ideas and explore multiple solutions.
- Investigators have developed creativity tests in different areas such as literary and scientific creativity to assess specific domains.
- Notable psychologists who have developed creativity tests include Guilford, Torrance, Khatena, Wallach and Kogan, Paramesh, Baqer Mehdi and Passi.
- Each creativity test follows a standardised procedure and includes a complete manual and interpretation guide to ensure proper administration and analysis.

### Intelligence Test

- Intelligence tests are close-ended and focus on measuring abilities that involve convergent thinking.
- These tests, focus on finding correct solution often assessing abilities such as memory, logical reasoning, and analytical skills.
- The primary focus of intelligence tests is on determining right answers, leaving little room for the expression of spontaneity, originality or imagination.
- Unlike creativity tests, intelligence tests emphasise structured problem-solving rather than generating multiple ideas or novel solutions.

### Quick Test 6

1. Which two factors explain variations in creativity?
2. What relationship exists between creativity and intelligence?
3. What type of thinking is measured in creativity tests?
4. Which psychologists are notable for developing creativity tests?
5. What do intelligence tests focus on?
6. How do intelligence tests differ from creativity tests?

# NCERT Folder

**1. How do psychologist characterise and define intelligence?**

**Ans.** Every psychologist characterises and defines intelligence in their own way

- **Alfred Binet** was one of the first psychologists who worked on intelligence and defined intelligence as 'the ability to judge well, understood well and reason well'.
- **Wechsler,** whose intelligence tests are most widely used, understood intelligence in term of its functionality i.e. its value for adaptation to environment. According to him, intelligence is the global and aggregate capacity of an individual to think rationally, act purposefully and to deal effectively with her/his environment.
- **Gardner** and **Sternberg** suggested that an intelligent individual not only adapts to the environment but also actively modifies or shape it. Thus, intelligence has certain attributes like mentally alert and quick, sense of humour and understanding according to psychologists.

**2. To what extent is our intelligence the result of heredity (nature) and environment (nurture)? Discuss.**

**Ans.** Intelligence is a product of complex interaction of heredity (nature) and environment (nurture). There are various examples which show that intelligence is the result of heredity and environment. We can explain it in the following ways

- The evidence for hereditary influences on intelligence comes mainly from studies on twins and adopted children. The intelligence of identical twins almost correlate who grow up together.
- Twins separated early in childhood show considerable similarity in their intellectual personality and behavioural characteristics.
- The evidence of adopted children shows that children's intelligence is more similar to their biological rather than adoptive parents.
- With respect to the role of environment, studies have reported that as children grew in age, their intelligence level tends to move closer to that of their adoptive parents.
- Children from disadvantaged homes adopted into families with higher socio-economic status exhibit a large increase in their intelligence scores.
- Environmental deprivation lowers intelligence, while rich nutrition, good family background, and quality schooling increases intelligence.
- Intelligence is a product of complex interaction of heredity (nurture) and environment (nurture). Heredity sets a range within which an individual's development is actually shaped by the support and opportunities of the environment.

**3. Explain briefly the multiple intelligence identified by Gardner.**

*Or* **Explain briefly the multiple intelligences identified by Howard Gardner with the help of examples. CBSE 2024 C**

**Ans.** Howard Gardner proposed the theory of multiple intelligences, which includes

(i) **Linguistic Intelligence** It refers to an ability to use language effectively and flexibly to express one's thinking and understand others, for example, writers, poets.

(ii) **Logical-Mathematical Intelligence** It refers an ability to analyse and solve problems. It includes person who can think logically and critically, for example, mathematicians, scientists and Nobel Prize winners.

(iii) **Musical Intelligence** It refers to an ability to perceive, manipulate and create musical patterns, for example, musicians.

(iv) **Spatial Intelligence** It refers to an ability involved in forming, using and transforming mental images. The person included in this intelligence can easily represent the spatial world in mind for example, pilots, architects, sculptors etc.

(v) **Bodily-kinesthetic Intelligence** It refer to an ability to use the body for expression, for example, athletes, dancers, actors etc.

(vi) **Interpersonal Intelligence** It refers to an ability to understand the motives, feelings and behaviours of other people, for example, psychologist, politicians, counselors etc.

(vii) **Intrapersonal Intelligence** It refers to the knowledge of one's internal strengths and limitations and using that knowledge to effectively relate to others, for examples, philosophers and spiritual leaders.

(viii) **Naturalistic Intelligence** It refers to the complete knowledge of our relationship with the natural world. It is useful in recognising the beauty of different species of flora and fauna for example, hunters, farmers, zoologists etc.

**4. How does the triarchic theory help us to understand intelligence?**

**Ans.** Triarchic theory was proposed by Robert Sternberg in 1985. He views intelligence as the ability to adapt, to shape and select the environment to accomplish one's goals and the goals of society and culture.

According to this theory, there are three basic types of intelligence i.e. componential, experiential and contextual.

(i) **Componential Intelligence/Analytical Intelligence** It is the analysis of information to solve problems. Persons included in this type of intelligence think analytically and critically and succeed in schools. It has three components

(a) **Knowledge Acquisition** It is responsible for learning and acquisition of the ways of doing things.

(b) **Meta or Higher Order Component** It involves planning and concerning what to do and how to do it.

(c) **Performance Component** It involves actually doing things.

(ii) **Experiential/Creative Intelligence** It is involved in using past experiences creatively to solve novel problems. It is an ability to integrate different experiences in an original way to make new discoveries and inventions. Persons included in this types of intelligence quickly find out which information is crucial in a given situation.

(iii) **Contextual /Practical Intelligence** It is the ability to deal with environmental demands encountered on a daily basis. It may be called 'street smartness' or 'business sense'.

Persons with this type of intelligence easily adapt to their present environment or select a more favourable environment than their current environment and modify the environment to fit their needs. Therefore, they turn out to be successful in life.

**5. "Any intellectual activity involves the independent functioning of three neurological systems." Explain with reference to PASS model.**

**Ans.** The PASS model was given by JP Das, Jack Naglieri and Kirby in 1994. According to this model, intellectual activity involves the interdependent functioning of three neurological systems, called functional units of the brain. These PASS processes operate on a knowledge base developed either formally (by reading, writing and experimenting) or informally from the environment. These processes are interactive and dynamic in nature yet each has its own distinctive function.

**Arousal/Attention** State of arousal is basic to any behaviour, as it helps us in attending to stimuli. It enables a person to process information. An optimal level of arousal focuses our attention to the relevant aspects of a problem. Too much or too little arousal would interfere with attention.

**Simultaneous and Successive Processing** Simultaneous processing takes place when you perceive the relations among various concepts and integrate them into a meaningful pattern for comprehension. Successive processing takes place when you remember all the information serially so that the recall of one leads to the recall of another. Learning of digits, alphabets, multiplication tables, etc are examples of successive processing.

**Planning** It allows us to think of the possible courses of action, implement them to reach a target and evaluate their effectiveness. If a plan does not work, it is modified to suit the requirements of the task or situation.

**6. Are there cultural differences in the conceptualisation of intelligence?**

**Ans.** Yes, there are cultural differences in the conceptualisation of intelligence. The cultural environment provides a context for intelligence to develop.

**Culture and Intelligence**

(i) A person's intelligence is likely to be tuned by cultural parameters like customs, beliefs, attitudes, and achievements in art and literature. Many theorists have regarded intelligence as attributes specific to the person without regard to their cultural background.

(ii) According to Sternberg, intelligence is a product of culture. Vygotsky also believed that cultures, like individuals, have a life of their own; they grow and change, and in the process specify what will be the end-product of successful intellectual development.

**Technological Intelligence**

(i) Technological intelligence is found in technologically advanced societies. Skills of generalisation and abstraction, speed, minimal moves, and mental manipulation are promoted among children.

(ii) These societies promote a type of behaviour, which can be called technological intelligence. In these societies, persons are well-versed in skills of attention, observation, analysis, performance, speed, and achievement orientation.

(iii) Technological intelligence is not valued much in many Asian and African societies. The qualities and skills regarded as intelligent actions in non-Western cultures are sharply different. Contrary to technological intelligence, intelligence in the Indian tradition can be termed as integral intelligence.

Indian thinkers view intelligence from a holistic perspective where equal attention is paid to cognitive and non-cognitive processes as well as their integration.

**7. What is IQ? How do psychologists classify people on the basis of their IQ scores?**

**Ans.** William Stern, a German psychologist, gave the concept of Intelligence Quotient (IQ) in 1912. IQ refers to mental age divided by chronological age, and multiplied by 100.

$$IQ = \frac{MA}{CA} \times 100$$

The number 100 is used as a multiplier to avoid the decimal point. IQ scores are distributed in the population in such a way that the scores of most people tend to fall in the middle range of the distribution. Only a few people have either very high or very low scores. The mean IQ score in a population is 100.

People with IQ scores in the range of 90–110 have normal intelligence. Those with IQ below 70 are suspected to have mental retardation, while persons with IQ above 130 are considered to have exceptional talents.

**8. How can you differentiate between verbal and performance tests of intelligence?**

**Ans.** There are various types of intelligence. They may be fully verbal, fully non-verbal or fully performance based.

**Verbal Test** These test require subjects to give verbal responses either orally or in a written form. It can be administered only to literate people.

Some verbal test developed in INDIA are

- CIE Verbal Group Test of Intelligence by Uday Shankar.
- Group Test of General Mental Ability by S Jalota.
- Group Test of Intelligence by Prayag Mehta.
- The Bihar Test of Intelligence by SM Mohsin.
- Group Test of Intelligence by Bureau of Psychology, Allahabad.
- Indian Adaptation of Stanford-Binet Test (Third Edition) by SK Kulshrestha.
- Test of General Mental Ability (Hindi) by M.C. Joshi.

Performance Tests These tests require subjects to manipulate objects and other materials to perform a task. Written language is not necessary for answering the items. For example, Kohs' Block Design Test contains a number of wooden blocks. The subject is asked to arrange the blocks within a time period to produce a given design. A major advantage of performance tests is that they can be easily administered to persons from different cultures.

Some Performance tests developed in India are

- CIE Non-verbal Group Test of Intelligence.
- Bhatia's Battery of Performance Tests.
- Draw-a-Man Test by Pramila Pathak.
- Adaptation of Wechsler Adult Performance Intelligence Scale by R Ramalingaswamy.

**9. All persons do not have the same intellectual capacity. How do individuals vary in their intellectual ability? Explain.**

**Ans.** It is true that all persons do not have the same intellectual capacity, it differs from person to person. Some are exceptionally bright and some are below average. In IQ tests only a few people have either very high or very low scores. The frequency distribution for the IQ scores tends to approximate a bell-shaped curve, called the normal curve.

There are two forms of variation in the Intellectual ability of individuals

(i) **Intellectual Deficiency** There are children who face enormous difficulty in learning even very simple skills. Those children who have intellectual deficiency are termed as mentally challenged or mentally retarded. There is wide variation among the mentally deficient.

The American Association on Mental Deficiency (AAMD) views mental retardation as sub-average general intellectual functioning. Such person deficits in adaptive behaviour during the developmental period.

(ii) **Intellectual Giftedness** The study of intellectually gifted individuals was started in 1925 by Levis Terman to examine the relationship of intelligence to occupational success and life adjustment.

Giftedness from the teacher's point of view depends on a combination of high ability, high creativity and high commitment. Gifted children show early signs of intellectual superiority. Even during infancy and early childhood, they show longer attention span, good recognitive memory, preference for novelty, sensitivity to environmental changes and early appearance of language skills.

**10. Which of the two, IQ or EQ, do you think would be more related to success in life and why?**

**Ans.** IQ or intelligence quotient, is a number derived from a standardised intelligence test. On the original IQ tests, scores were calculated by dividing the individual's mental age by his or her chronological age and then multiplying that number by 100. IQ represents abilities such as visual and spatial processing, knowledge of the world, fluid reasoning, working memory and short-term memory and quantitative reasoning.

EQ (Emotional Quotient) is a measure of a person's level of emotional intelligence. This refers to a person's ability to perceive, control, evaluate, and express emotions. EQ is centered on abilities such as identifying emotions, evaluating feeling of others, controlling one's own emotions, perceiving feeling of others and using emotions to facilitate social communication.

IQ is still recognised as an important element of success, particularly when it comes to academic achievement. People with high IQs typically do well in school, often earn more money, and tend to be healthier in general.

The concept of emotional intelligence has had a strong impact in a number of areas, including the business world. Many companies now mandate emotional intelligence training and utilise EQ tests as part of the hiring process.

Research has found that individuals with strong leadership potential also tend to be more emotionally intelligent, suggesting that a high EQ is an important quality for business leaders and managers to have. Hence, EQ would be more related to success in life.

**11. How is 'aptitude' different from 'interest' and 'intelligence'? How is aptitude measured?**

**Ans.** Psychological attributes are categorised on the basis of varieties of tests used in psychological literature. Aptitude, Interest, and Intelligence are some important psychological attributes.

- **Aptitude** Aptitude refers to an individual's natural ability or potential in a specific area of activity. It is a combination of traits that indicates an individual's capacity to acquire specific knowledge or skills after training. Aptitude reflects an individual's underlying potential for acquiring skills. Aptitude tests are used to predict an individual's ability to succeed in a given field when provided with the right environment and training.
- **Interest** Interest refers to an individual's preference for engaging in certain activities over others. Knowledge of one's interests can help in making choices that promote life satisfaction and improve job performance.
- **Intelligence** Intelligence is the global capacity to understand the world and solve problems. Intelligence tests provide a measure of a person's general cognitive competence, including the ability to learn from schooling.

For example, students with low intelligence may not perform well in school related exams, but their success in life is not solely determined by their intelligence test scores.

In order to be successful in a particular field, a person must have both aptitude and interest measurement of aptitude.

**Measurement of Aptitude** We assess aptitude with the help of selected tests. These aptitude tests are available in two forms

(i) Independent (Specialised) Aptitude Tests Clerical Aptitude, Mechanical Aptitude, Numerical Aptitude, and Typing Aptitude are independent aptitude tests.

(ii) Multiple (Generalised) Aptitude Tests Multiple Aptitude Tests exist in the form of test batteries, which measure aptitude in several separate but homogeneous areas. Differential Aptitude Tests (DAT), the General Aptitude Tests Battery (GATB), and the Armed Service Vocational Aptitude Battery (ASVAB) are well-known aptitude test batteries. Among these, DAT is most commonly used in educational settings.

**12. How is creativity related to intelligence?**

**Ans.** There is a positive relationship between creativity and intelligence. All creative acts require some minimum ability to acquire knowledge and capacity to comprehend, retain, and retrieve. Creative writers, for example, need facility in dealing with language.

The artist must understand the effect that will be produced by a particular technique of painting, a scientist must be able to reason and so on. Hence, a certain level of intelligence is required for creativity but beyond that intelligence does not correlate well with creativity.

A person who has the ability to learn faster and reproduce accurately may be considered intelligent more than creative unless she/he devises new ways of learning and doing.

In 1920s, Terman found that persons with high IQ were not necessarily creative. At the same time, creative ideas could come from persons who did not have a very high IQ.

It can be concluded that creativity can take many forms. Some may have more of intellectual attributes, others may have more of attributes associated with creativity.

# Exam Pattern Questions

## Objective Type Questions

### Multiple Choice Questions (MCQs)

**1. Who among the following was the first person that devised systematic tests to measure intelligence test?**

(a) Terman (b) Binet (c) Thorudike (d) Wechsler

**2. The structure of intellect model was proposed by**

(a) Spearman (b) Thurstone
(c) Guilford (d) Thorudike

**3. Ability to use past experiences creatively to solve novel problems is known as**

(a) musical intelligence
(b) interpersonal intelligence
(c) experiential intelligence
(d) contextual intelligence

**4. ......... and performance tests help reduce the cultural bias usually associated with intelligence tests.** CBSE SQP Term I 2021

(a) Non-verbal (b) Group
(c) Individual (d) Verbal

**5. Howard Gardner's theory of intelligence is known as**

(a) Theory of Primary Mental Abilities
(b) Theory of Multiple Intelligences
(c) Triarchic theory
(d) Two-factor theory

**6. Information processing approach to intelligence is**

(a) multiple Intelligences theory
(b) triarchic theory
(c) one-factor theory
(d) two-factor theory

**7. ......... involves seeking information from a person on a one-to-one basis.** CBSE SQP Term I 2021

(a) Case study (b) Self-Report
(c) Interview (d) Psychological test

**8. Giftedness from the teachers' point of view depends on a combination of .......... .** CBSE SQP Term I 2021

(a) high ability, high creativity, high commitment
(b) high ability, high creativity, high cooperation
(c) high ability, high commitment, high talent
(d) high ability, high creativity, high dependence

**9. A hierarchial model of intelligence consisting of abilities operating at two level was proposed by**

(a) J.P. Guilford (b) Charles Spearman
(c) Arthur Jensen (d) Howard Gardner

**10. Howard Gardner has proposed many types of intelligences except ....... .** CBSE SQP Term I 2021

(a) linguistic (b) creative
(c) intrapersonal (d) interpersonal

**11. Which of the following best describes the nature of creativity tests where there are no specified answers to questions or problems, allowing for freedom to use one's imagination and express it in original ways?** CBSE 2025

(a) Divergent (b) Convergent (c) Analytical (d) Structured

**12. Helen took a/an ...... test which indicated that she could excel in typing and highlighted it in her resume while looking for jobs.**

(a) multiple aptitude (b) specialised aptitude
(c) interest (d) achievement

**13. If a person has the skill of understanding the motives, feelings and behaviour of other people, he/she is said to have**

(a) interpersonal intelligence (b) intrapersonal intelligence
(c) linguistic intelligence (d) social intelligence

**14. Sternberg's experiential intelligence includes** CBSE 2019

(a) the ability to learn from past events
(b) the ability to manipulate people's opinions
(c) creative problem solving
(d) basic academic skills

**15. Intelligence Quotient (IQ) refers to** CBSE Term I 2021

(a) chronological age divided by mental age and multiplied by 100.
(b) chronological age multiplied by mental age and divided by 100.
(c) mental age divided by chronological age and multiplied by 100.
(d) mental age multiplied by chronological age and result multiplied by 100.

**16. Madhu is a student who excels in remembering facts and figures but struggles when it comes to solving complex problems that require critical thinking and creativity. According to Arthur Jensen, which level of abilities does Madhu possess?** CBSE 2025

(a) Level II, associative learning
(b) Level I, cognitive competence
(c) Level I, associative learning
(d) Level II, observational learning

**17.** ...... is an exceptional general ability shown in superior performance in a wide variety of areas. **CBSE Term I 2021**

(a) Talent (b) Intelligence (c) Creativity (d) Giftedness

**18.** Vikas lags behind his peers in language and motor skills. He is trained in self-care as well as in simple social and communication skills. He also needs little supervision in everyday tasks. He is likely to be at the ......... level of intellectual disability. **CBSE Term I 2021**

(a) mild (IQs 55 to approximately 70)
(b) moderate (IQs 35-40 to approximately 50-55)
(c) severe (IQs 20-25 to approximately 35-40)
(d) profound (lQs below 20-25)

**19.** The correlation between intelligence test scores of identical twins is ......... **CBSE SQP Term I 2021**

I. higher when they are raised together than when they are raised apart.
II. greater than that for fraternal twins raised together.
III. lower than that for any other blood relatives.
IV. the same whether they are reared together or apart.

Codes

(a) I and III (b) I and II
(c) III and IV (d) I and IV

**20.** Abdul realises that intelligence tests are of several types. Which of the following is/are a correct explanation/explanations of the types of tests that he can use to assess intelligence? **CBSE Term I 2021**

I. On the basis of their administration procedure, they can be categorised as either culture-fair or culture-biased.
II. They can also be classified as either verbal or performance tests on the basis of the nature of items used.
III. Depending upon the extent to which an intelligence test favours one culture over another, it can be judged as either individual or group tests.
IV. Abdul can choose a test depending on the purpose. This can be individual, group, verbal, non-verbal or performance test.

Codes

(a) I, II and III (b) Only III (c) III and IV (d) II and IV

**21.** Angel is high on the ability to think analytically and critically. Therefore, she performs well in academics. She is most likely to possess the following **CBSE Term I 2021**

(i) Contextual intelligence, i.e. the analysis of information to solve problems.
(ii) Componential intelligence, which has three components, each serving a different function.
(iii) Experiential intelligence, which is the knowledge acquisition component.
(iv) Meta or a higher-order component, which involves planning about what to do and how to do it.
(v) Performance component, which involves actually doing things.

Codes

(a) I, II, IV and V (b) I, III, IV and V
(c) II, III and V (d) II, IV and V

**22.** Jasleen is high on critical thinking and can manipulate symbols to solve numerical problems. She is also high on the ability to understand one's own feelings, motives and desires. Which of the following intelligences are displayed by Jasleen? **CBSE SQP 2022-23**

I. Spatial II. Logical-mathematical
III. Interpersonal IV. Intrapersonal

Codes

(a) I and II (b) II and III
(c) I and III (d) II and IV

**23.** Sangeeta is a counsellor. She interacts with the client and seeks information from the client on one-to-one basis. She is using ......... as a method of assessment. **CBSE SQP 2024**

(a) self-report (b) observation
(c) psychological test (d) interview

**24.** Raghav was told by the teacher about a test which she plans to hold. This forces him to focus on reading, learning and revising the contents of the chapters. This is because of ............... . **CBSE 2024 C**

(a) arousal/attention (b) coding
(c) simultaneous processing (d) successive processing

**25.** Nirja has a mental age of 14 years with an Intelligence Quotient (IQ) of 110. What is her chronological age?

(a) 9·7 years approximately
(b) 10·7 years approximately
(c) 11·7 years approximately
(d) 12·7 years approximately

**26.** Match the following. **CBSE 2025**

| | Rearing Practices | | Correlation |
|---|---|---|---|
| 1. | Identical twins reared in different environment | I. | 0.50 |
| 2. | Fraternal twins reared together | II. | 0.60 |
| 3. | Brothers and sisters reared together | III. | 0.72 |
| 4. | Siblings reared apart | IV. | 0.25 |

| | 1, | 2, | 3, | 4 | | 1, | 2, | 3, | 4 |
|---|---|---|---|---|---|---|---|---|---|
| (a) | I, | II, | III, | IV | (b) | III, | II, | I, | IV |
| (c) | IV, | I, | III, | II | (d) | II, | IV, | I, | III |

## Assertion-Reason Questions

**Directions** (Q. Nos. 27-30) Two statements are given in the question below as Assertion (A) and Reason (R). Read the statements and choose the appropriate option.

(a) Both A and R are true and R is the correct explanation of A
(b) Both A and R are true, but R is not the correct explanation of A
(c) A is true, but R is false
(d) A is false, but R is true

**27.** **Assertion** (A) There may be many people who are academically talented but are unsuccessful in their own lives.

**Reason** (R) The source of their difficulty is lack of emotional intelligence. **CBSE SQP Term I 2021**

**28.** **Assertion** (A) Psychological tests are widely used for clinical diagnosis, guidance, personnel selection, placement and training.

**Reason** (R) Objective tests provide a standardised and reliable measure of an individual's psychological attributes. **CBSE 2025**

**29.** **Assertion** (A) Alfred Binet was the first psychologist who tried to formalise the concept of intelligence in terms of mental operations and he gave the concept of Intelligence Quotient (IQ).

**Reason** (R) Binet's one-factor theory of intelligence was rather simple as it arose from his interest in differentiating more intelligent from less intelligent individuals. **CBSE Term I 2021**

**30.** **Assertion** (A) The theory of primary mental abilities states that intelligence consists of primary abilities, each of which is relatively independent of the others.

**Reason** (R) This theory explain that intelligence consists of abilities operating at two levels, called Level I and Level II. **CBSE SQP 2024**

# Answers

1. (b) Binet
2. (c) Guilford
3. (c) experiential intelligence
4. (a) Non-verbal
5. (b) Theory of Multiple Intelligences
6. (a) multiple intelligences theory
7. (c) Interview
8. (a) high ability, high creativity, high commitment
9. (c) Arthur Jensen
10. (b) creative
11. (a) Divergent
12. (b) specialised aptitude
13. (a) interpersonal intelligence
14. (c) creative problem solving
15. (c) mental age divided by chronological age and multiplied by 100.
16. (c) Level I, associative learning
17. (d) Giftedness
18. (a) mild (IQs 55 to approximately 70)
19. (b) I and II
20. (d) II and IV
21. (d) II, IV and V
22. (d) II and IV
23. (d) interview
24. (a) arousal/attention
25. (d) 12.7 years approximately
26. (b) III, II, I, IV
27. (a) Both A and R are true and R is the correct explanation of A.
28. (a) Both A and R are true and R is the correct explanation of A
29. (d) A is false, but R is true.
30. (b) Both A and R are true, but R is not the correct explanation of A.

# Subjective Questions

## Very Short Answer Type Questions

**1. What do you understand by individual differences?**

**Ans.** Individual vary in terms of physical characteristics and psychological dimensions. According to the psychologists, individual difference refers to distinctiveness and variations among people's characteristics and behavioural patterns.

**2. What are the physical characteristics that vary between individuals?**

**Ans.** Some physical characteristics that vary between individuals are height, weight, strength, hair, etc.

**3. Define the term situationism.**

**Ans.** Situationism is the theory that situational factors, such as the environment or circumstances, have a stronger influence on an individual's behaviour than their personality traits.

**4. What is psychological assessment?**

**Ans.** Psychological assessment is a systematic testing procedure to evaluate abilities, behaviours and personal qualities of individuals.

**5. When we say, Aditya is dominant, we are referring to the degree of dominance in Aditya. Explain the types of assessment involved here.**

**Ans.** Here our assessment may be informal or formal. Formal assessment is objective, standardised and organised. On the other hand, informal assessment varies from case to case and from one assessor to another. Thus, it is open to subjective interpretations.

**6. Mention some psychological assessment methods.**

**Ans.** Some psychological assessment methods are psychological tests, interviews, case studies, observations and self reports.

**7. What is observation?**

**Ans.** It involves employing systematic, organised and objective procedures to record behavioural phenomena occurring naturally in real time. Certain phenomena such as mother-child interactions can be easily studied through observation.

**8. Define intelligence.**

**Ans.** Intelligence is a key construct employed to understand how individuals differ from one another. Psychological notion of intelligence is different from the common sensical notion of intelligence.

**9. Define the one-factor theory of intelligence.**

**Ans.** Alfred Binet conceptualised intelligence as consisting of one set of abilities which can be used for solving any or every problem in an individual's environment. This theory is known as uni-factor theory of intelligence.

**10. Explain linguistic intelligence.**

**Ans.** It is the capacity to use language fluently and flexibly to express one's thinking and understand others. Persons included in this type of intelligence are 'word-smart' i.e. they are sensitive to different shades of word meanings, can articulate and can create linguistic images in their minds.

**11. Explain naturalistic intelligence.**

**Ans.** This involves complete awareness of our relationship with the natural world. It is useful in recognising the beauty of different species of flora and fauna, and making subtle discriminations in the natural world.

**12. Explain contextual intelligence.**

**Ans.** Contextual intelligence is the ability to handle environmental demands effectively on a daily basis. It can also be described as 'street smarts' or 'business sense'.

**13. What is simultaneous and successive processing in intellectual functioning?**

**Ans.** Simultaneous processing takes place when you perceive the relations among various concepts and integrate them into a meaningful pattern for comprehension.

Successive processing takes place when you remember all the information serially so that the recall of one leads to the recall of another.

**14. Define the term mental retardation.**

**Ans.** The American Association on Mental Deficiency (AAMD) views mental retardation as significantly sub-average general intellectual functioning along with deficits in adaptive behaviour and presented during the developmental period.

**15. How are IQ scores distributed in a population?**

***Or* Classify people on the basis of IQ.**

**Ans.** The distribution of IQ scores is as follows

| IQs Range | Descriptive Label |
|---|---|
| Above 130 | Very superior |
| 120-130 | Superior |
| 110-119 | High average |
| 90-109 | Average |
| 80-89 | Low average |
| 70-79 | Borderline |
| Below 70 | Mentally challenged |

**16. A teacher notices that Neeraj, one of her class 5 students, learns new languages very easily, loves new subjects, and is very sensitive to changes in the classroom. Comment on the intellectual abilities of Neeraj.** CBSE 2025

**Ans.** Neeraj shows high intellectual abilities, including quick learning, curiosity for new knowledge and heightened sensitivity to his environment, suggesting giftedness and potential for exceptional cognitive and emotional growth.

**17. What is psychological test?**

**Ans.** It is an objective and standardised measure of an individual's mental and behavioural characteristics. These tests are widely used for the purpose of clinical diagnosis, guidance, personal selection, placement and training.

**18. Define the term buddhi.**

**Ans.** Sanskrit word *buddhi* includes skills such as mental effort, determined action, feelings and opinions alongwith cognitive competence such as knowledge, discrimination and understanding.

**19. Define emotional intelligence.**

**Ans.** Emotional Intelligence (EI) is a set of skills that underlie accurate appraisal, expression and regulation of emotions.

**20. Define the term aptitude.**

**Ans.** Aptitude refers to special abilities in a particular area of activity. It is a combination of characteristics that indicates an individual's capacity to acquire some specific knowledge or skill after training.

**21. What is situationist perspective of human behaviour?**

**Ans.** The situationist perspective views human behaviour as resulting from interaction of external and internal factors. It is product of traits and environmental factors. This approach believes that external factors play more significant role to determine individual differences.

**22. What do you mean by psychological assessment?**

**Ans.** Psychological assessment uses systematic testing procedure to evaluate abilities, behaviours and personal qualities of individuals. Our assessment may be formal or informal. Formal assessments is objective, standardised and organised. Informal assessment varies from case to case and from one assessment to another and therefore is open to subjective interpretations.

**23. What is Cognitive Assessment System (CAS)?**

**Ans.** JP Das and Naglieri have developed a battery of tests, which is known as Cognitive Assessment System (CAS). It consists of verbal as well as non-verbal tasks that measures basic cognitive functions. These are independent of schooling. This battery of test is meant for individual between 5 and 18 years of age. It is used to measure intelligence of normal as well as of children with intellectual disabilities.

**24. How Sternberg's concept of intelligence is different from other concepts?**

**Ans.** According to Sternberg, intelligence is not only adaptation, directional ability, comprehensive and self-evaluation.

It involves improving activities like shopping and selecting the environment. Sternberg emphasised that intelligence does not simply mean possessing certain abilities but also the use of these abilities in real life situations.

**25. Mention main characteristics of a bell-shaped curve.**

**Ans.** The main characteristics of a bell-shaped curve are

- Bell-shaped curve involves symmetrical distribution i.e., the left half of the curve is a mirror image of the right half.
- It is unimodel distribution.
- The value of mean, median and mode all coincide and the curve never touches the *x*-axis.
- It is symbiotic.

**26. "No two individuals are alike." Explain.**

**Ans.** Human beings distinctly differ in size, shape, appearance, reaction time and innumerable other aspects of our personality and behaviour.

Individuals differences stand for the variations and distinctiveness among individuals. It also stands for those differences which, in their totality, distinguish one individual to another.

**27. Differentiate between psychometric and information processing approaches to intelligence.**

**Ans. Psychometric Approach** considers intelligence as an aggregate of abilities. It expresses the individuals's performance in terms of a single index of cognitive abilities.

**Information Processing Approach** describes the processes that people use in intellectual reasoning and problem solving. The major focus of this approach is on how an intelligent person acts.

**28. What are the psychological dimensions of individual differences?**

**Ans.** Individuals vary along psychological dimensions which may be intelligent or dull, dominant or submissive, creative or not so creative.

**29. How individual differences are useful for the society?**

**Ans.** Individual differences are useful in following manner

(i) Individual differences make the world beautiful, purposeful and goal oriented or directed.

(ii) Different people have different needs and to satisfy the different needs different types of skills are required. That is why variability is a fact of nature which helps in adaption.

**30. Explain the term 'Assessment'.** **CBSE SQP 2024**

**Ans.** The 'Assessment' refers to systematically gathering information and data about an individual's characteristics, abilities, behaviours and other relevant factors.

The main goal of assessment is to understand and evaluate various aspects of an individual's psychological functioning, such as cognitive abilities, personality traits, emotional functioning and social skills.

**31. 'Intelligence by itself does not ensure creativity'. Do you agree with this statement? Given reasons and examples in support of your answer.** **CBSE SQP 2024**

**Ans.** Yes, intelligence does not ensure creativity as intelligence is related to learning the skill while creativity is related to generating new ideas and solutions to odd situations.

For example, to be a great chef you are required to gain knowledge about making the dish, but to be creative you are required to garnish and modify the dish according to your consumer's taste.

## Short Answer Type Questions

**1. What is case study?**

**Ans.** It is an in-depth study of the individual in terms of her/his psychological attributes and psychological history in the context of her/his psychological and physical environment. Case studies are widely used by clinical psychologists. Case studies of the lives of great people can also be highly illuminating for those willing to learn from their life experiences.

Case studies are based on data generated by different methods. For example, interviews, observation, questionnaire, psychological tests, etc.

**2. State Gardner's eight types of intelligences. Describe any one with the help of examples.**

*Or* **Mention multiple intelligence as suggested by Gardner. Explain logical mathematical intelligence.**

**Ans.** Howard Gardner proposed the theory of multiple intelligences describing eight types of intelligence which are as follows

(i) Linguistic
(ii) Logical-Mathematical
(iii) Spatial
(iv) Musical
(v) Bodily-Kinaesthetic
(vi) Interpersonal
(vii) Intrapersonal
(viii) Naturalistic

**Logical-Mathematical** It involves skills in scientific thinking and problem solving. Persons included in this type of intelligence can think logically and critically. They engage in abstract reasoning, and can manipulate symbols to solve mathematical problems. Scientists and Nobel Prize winners are likely to be strong in this component.

**3. Explain the hierarchical model of intelligence.**

**Ans.** This model was proposed by Arthur Jensen. It consists of abilities operating at two levels i.e. Level I and Level II

(i) Level I is the associative learning in which output is more or less similar to the input (e.g. rote learning and memory).

(ii) Level II, called cognitive competence involves higher-order skills, as they transform the input to produce an effective output.

**4. Briefly describe about two-factor theory.**

**Ans.** In 1927, Charles Spearman used factor analysis to propose this theory. He showed that intelligence consisted of a general factor (g-factor) and some specific factors (s-factors). G-factors include mental operations which are primary and common to all performances.

S-factors include some specific abilities which are present in some people in addition to g-factor. These specific abilities allow them to excel in their respective domains.

**5. Discuss about the structure intellectual model of intelligence.**

**Ans.** JP Guilford proposed this model which classifies intellectual traits among three dimensions

(i) **Operations** These include cognition, memory recording, memory retention, divergent production, convergent production and evaluation.

(ii) **Contents** These refer to the nature of materials or information on which intellectual operations are performed. These include visual, auditory, symbolic (e.g. letters, numbers), semantic (e.g. words) and behavioural (e.g. information about people's behaviour, attitudes, needs, etc.)

(iii) **Products** These refer to the form in which information is processed by the respondent. Products are classified into units, classes, relations, systems, transformations and implications.

**6. What are the different levels of intellectual deficiency?**

**Ans.** The different levels of intellectual deficiency are

**Mild** (IQs 55 to 70) The development of people with mild intellectual disability is typically slower than that of their peers but they can function quite independently, hold jobs and families. As the level of Intellectual disability increases, the difficulties are strongly marked.

**Moderate** (IQs 35-40 to 50-55) The people with moderate intellectual disability lag behind their peers in language and motor skills. They can be trained in self-care skills and simple social and communication skills.

**Severe** (IQs 20-25 to 35-40) and **Profound** (IQs below 20 to 25) Individuals with severe and profound intellectual disability are incapable of managing life and need constant care for their entire lives.

**7. Distinguish between verbal, non-verbal and performance tests.**

**Ans.** Differences between verbal, non-verbal and performance tests are as follows

**Verbal** It requires verbal responses in either oral or written form. It can only be administered to literate people.

**Non-Verbal** It uses pictures or illustrations as test items e.g. RPM. (Raven's Progressive Matrices Test). In this test, the subject examines an incomplete pattern and chooses a figure from the alternatives that will complete the pattern.

**Performance** It requires subjects to manipulate objects to perform a task. In this test, written language is not necessary for answering the items. It can be easily administered to persons from different cultures.

**8. Evaluate how Gardner's view of intelligence as an independent and interactive type challenges the traditional notions of a singular, unified intelligence.** **CBSE 2025**

**Ans.** Gardner's view challenges traditional ideas of intelligence by proposing multiple intelligences, for example, linguistic, spatial, interpersonal, etc., instead of a single IQ. He argues these intelligences are independent yet interact to solve problems. His approach of multiple intelligences highlights diverse talents and abilities, emphasising creativity, emotional skills, and practical knowledge, showing intelligence as a broader and more dynamic concept beyond standardised tests.

**9. Differentiate between interpersonal and intrapersonal intelligence.**

**Ans.** **Interpersonal Intelligence**

- Sensitive to understand others' behaviour.
- It is understanding the motives, feelings and the behaviour of others.
- For example, psychologists, politicians, social workers, etc.

**Intrapersonal Intelligence**

- Awareness of one's own feeling motives and desires.
- This refers to the knowledge of one's internal strengths and limitations.
- For example, philosophers, spiritual leaders.

**10. Hitakshi is a gifted child. She is good at her study, music and painting. What is the difference between talent and giftedness?**

**Ans.** Giftedness is an exceptional general ability shown in superior performance in a wide variety of areas. Hitakshi performs very well in her study and other extracurricular activities like music and paintings. She shows excellent performance in various fields. Thus, she is considered as a gifted child. Gifted children show early signs of intellectual superiority. Giftedness from the teachers' point of view depends on a combination of high ability, high creativity and high commitment.

It differs from 'Talent'. Talent is a narrower term and refers to remarkable ability in a specific field like spiritual social, aesthetic etc. The highly talented children are sometimes called 'prodigies'.

**11. Analyse the relationship between intelligence and creativity, based on Terman's research findings.** **CBSE 2025**

**Ans.** Terman's research suggests a positive relationship between intelligence and creativity, but only to a certain extent. High intelligence often supports creativity by providing problem-solving skills and knowledge. However, creativity also involves originality and divergent thinking, which are not entirely dependent on intelligence.

Thus, although intelligence helps creativity but being highly creative doesn't always require exceptional intelligence. Both are distinct but connected traits.

**12. "Individuals who are categorised as having mental retardation show significant variation in their abilities, ranging from those who can be taught to work and function with special attention, to those who cannot be trained and require institutional care throughout their lives." What are the values which can help to these mentally retarded children?** **Competency Based Que.**

**Ans.** Following values should be kept in mind while dealing with mentally retarded children

- Compassion toward children.
- Caring.
- Development of self care skills.
- Social acceptance.

**13. "No two individuals are alike." Elucidate the statement in context of the individual differences.**

**Ans.** Variation is inherent in nature and individuals are not its exception. Individual variations are common. The individual differences are in terms of physical characteristics and psychological dimensions. Physically, they are distinct in size, shape appearance and in many other aspects. Psychologically, they vary in various dimensions like intelligence and dull dominant or submissive creative or not creative, outgoing or withdrawn, etc. Thus, we can say that no two individuals are alike.

**14. You may find many people who are academically talented, but are unsuccessful in their own life. Find out the difficulty in their success. Also suggest the possible measures to improve intelligence of the person.** **Competency Based Que.**

**Ans.** Some people are talented in their academics but they experience problems in family, workplace and interpersonal relationships. According to psychologists the source of their difficulty may be a lack of emotional intelligence. Emotional intelligence is the ability to monitor one's own and others' emotions, to discriminate among them and to use the information to guide one's thinking and actions. There are various programme being run by educators which are aimed at improving student's emotional intelligence.

These programmes encourage cooperative behaviour and reduce their anti-social activities. They are useful in preparing students to face the challenges of life outside the classrooms.

**15. "Creativity is not just limited to a selected few, an ordinary person can also be creative." Illustrate this statement with suitable examples.** **Competency Based Que.**

**Ans.** Creativity is generally associated with extraordinary individual like Einstein, CV Raman, Ramanujan, etc who have made outstanding contributions in different spheres. But in recent years, our understanding of creativity has broaden. Creativity is not just limited to a selected personalities like the artist, the scientist, the poet or the inventor. An ordinary person who is engaged in simple occupation like pottery, carpentry, cooking, etc. can also be creative.

**16. Raghu and Rajiv are twins. They have been separated early in childhood. However, they both shows a considerable similarity when it comes to intelligence level. How can you explain the similarities in their intelligence?**

**Ans.** The similarities in between the twins namely Raghu and Rajiv can be explained through interplay of nature and nurture.

The hereditary influences among twins show that there is considerable similarity in intellectual, personality and behavioural characteristics with respect to their intelligence level even though they are separated early in the childhood. The intelligence of identical twins reared in different environments correlate to 0.72.

**17. Kirti is of average intelligence but is high on ability to appraise, express and regulate her emotions. Identify the intelligence that she exhibits and why it is receiving so much attention these days. Suggest some ways to enhance this kind of intelligence of students in schools.** **CBSE SQP 2022**

**Ans.** The intelligence that Kriti exhibits is emotional intelligence. It is believed that the notion of emotional intelligence broadens the concept of intelligence beyond the intellectual sphere/domain and considers that intelligence includes emotions. It builds on the concept of intelligence in the Indian tradition. The characteristics of emotionally intelligent persons are that it relates your emotions to your thoughts so that you take them into account while solving problems and taking decisions.

Receiving attention as it helps students to deal with the stresses and challenges of the outside world, benefits their academic achievements and reduces anti-social activities. Programmes that involve cooperative behaviour should be promoted in school.

**18. Describe the theory of primary mental abilities.**

**Ans** The theory of primary mental abilities was developed by Louis Thurston. It states that intelligence consists of seven primary abilities, each of which is relatively independent of the others.

These primary abilities are

- **Verbal Comprehension** It comprises grasping meaning of words, concepts, and ideas.
- **Numerical Abilities** It includes speed and accuracy in numerical and computational skills.
- **Spatial Ability** It shows visualising patterns and forms.
- **Perceptual Speed** It is the speed in perceiving details.
- **Word Fluency** It means using words fluently and flexibly.
- **Memory** It means accuracy in recalling information.
- **Inductive Reasoning** It means deriving general rules from presented facts.

**19. Ryan and Shireen are siblings brought up in the same environment. Ryan knows all the formulae in mathematics and can recall them as they are but cannot solve problems based on those formulae, whereas Shireen can use formulae to solve any kind of problem that are based on them.**

**Explain the intelligence they both exhibit. Which approach is this theory based on?** **CBSE 2023**

**Ans.** Ryan exhibits the knowledge acquisition component, which is responsible for learning and acquisition of the ways of doing things.

Shireen exhibits the performance component, which involves actually doing things.

The theory here is based on Triarchic Theory of Intelligence. It views intelligence as 'the ability to adapt, to shape and select environment to accomplish one's goals and those of one's society and culture.'

According to this theory, there are three basic types of intelligence i.e. Componential, Experiential and Contextual. Componential or Analytical Intelligence is the Analysis of Information to solve problems. Persons high on this ability think analytically and critically and succeed in schools. This intelligence has three components i.e. Knowledge acquisition component, Meta higher order component and Performance component.

**20. What is mental retardation?**

**Ans.** The children who show intellectual deficiency are termed as mentally challenged or mentally retarded. As a group, there is wide variation among the mentally deficient or retarded.

The American Association on Mental Deficiency (AAMD) views mental retardation as "significantly sub-average general intellectual functioning existing concurrently with deficits in adaptive behaviour and manifested during the developmental period".

This definition points to three basic features

(i) First, in order to be judged as mentally retarded, a person must show significantly sub-average intellectual functioning. Persons having IQ below 70 are judged to have sub-average intelligence.

(ii) The second relates to deficits in adaptive behaviour. Adaptive behaviour refers to a person's capacity to be independent and deal effectively with one's environment.

(iii) The third feature is that the deficits must be observed during the developmental period, that is between 0 and 18 years of age.

**21. Mention some characteristics of emotionally intelligent person.**

**Ans.** Following are some characteristics of emotionally intelligent persons

- Perceive and be sensitive to one's own feelings and emotions.
- Perceive and be sensitive to various types of emotions in others by noting their body language, voice and tone, and facial expressions.
- Relate your emotions to your thoughts so that you take them into account while solving problems and taking decisions.
- Understand the impact of emotions, nature and intensity.
- Control and regulate your emotions and their expressions while dealing with self and others to achieve harmony and peace.

**22. Define Giftedness. What are the characteristics of gifted children.**

**Ans.** Giftedness is exceptional general ability shown in superior performance in a wide variety of areas. Gifted children show early signs of intellectual superiority. Even during infancy and early childhood, they show larger attention span, good recognition memory, preference for novelty, sensitivity to environmental changes, and early appearance of language skills.

Some important characteristics of gifted children are

- Advanced logical thinking, questioning and problem solving behaviour.
- High speed in processing information.
- Superior generalisation and discrimination ability.
- Advanced level of original and creative thinking.
- High level of intrinsic motivation and self-esteem.
- Independent and non-conformist thinking.
- Preference for solitary academic activities for long periods.

**23. What are the ill-effects of intelligence testing by naive testers?**

**Ans.** Some of the ill-effects of intelligence testing by naive testers are as follows

- Poor performance on a test may attach a stigma to children and thereby adversely affect their performance and self-respect.
- The tests may invite discriminatory practices from parents, teachers and elders in the society.
- Administering a test biased in favour of the middle class and higher class populations may underestimate the IQ of children disadvantaged backgrounds.
- Intelligence tests do not capture creative potentialities and practical side of intelligence, and they also do not relate much to success in life. While, intelligence can be a potential factor for achievement in various spheres of life.

**24. Discuss how interplay of nature and nurture influence intelligence.**

**Ans.** Psychologist have conducted studies of adopted children, which show that children's intelligence is more similar to their biological rather than adoptive parents.

**Effect of Nurture/Environment** With respect to the role of environment, studies have reported that as children grow in age, their intelligence level tends to move closer to that of their adoptive parents. Children from disadvantaged homes adopted into families with higher socio- economic status exhibit a large increase in their intelligence scores.

There is evidence that environmental deprivation lowers intelligence, while rich nutrition, good family background, and quality schooling increases intelligence.

There is a general consensus among psychologists that intelligence is a product of complex interaction of heredity (nature) and environment (nurture). Heredity can best be viewed as something that sets a range within which an individual's development is actually shaped by the support and opportunities of the environment.

**25. Explain how PASS model helps us to understand intelligence.**

**Ans.** The PASS model has been developed by JP Das, Jack Naglieri, and Kirby (1994). According to this model, intellectual activity involves the interdependent functioning of three neurological systems, referred to functional units of brain.

These units are responsible for

- Planning
- Arousal/Attention
- Simultaneous and Successive Processing

**Planning** It is an essential feature of intelligence. Once information is processed, planning is activated. It allows us to think of the possible courses of action, implement them to reach a target, and evaluate their effectiveness.

**Arousal/Attention** State of arousal is basic to any behaviour, as it helps us in attending to stimuli. It enables a person to process information. Optimal level of arousal focuses our attention to the relevant aspects of a problem. Too much or too little arousal would interfere with attention.

**Simultaneous and Successive Processing**
Simultaneous processing takes place when you perceive the relations among various concepts and integrate them into a meaningful pattern for comprehension. For example, in Raven's Progressive Matrices (RPM) Test, a design is presented from which a part has been removed. You are required to choose one of the six options that best completes the design.

**26. Urmi is an excellent painter. She draws amazing pictures. What are the different factors that stimulate the development of creativity?** **Competency Based Que.**

**Ans.** Urmi is a creative person. Her creativity is determined both by heredity and environment. Limits of her creative potential are set by heredity. Environmental factors stimulate the development of creativity further.

How much of the creative potential can be realised and its specific form and direction is largely determined by environmental factors like motivation, commitment family support, peer influences, training opportunities, etc.

Every individual can raise his level of creative potential beyond its present level. But there is a limit, no amount of training can transform an average creative person to the level of masters in that field. A certain level of intelligence is required for creativity but beyond this intelligence does not correlate well with creativity. A high level of intelligence does not ensure that a person would certainly creative.

**27. Differentiate between culture-fair and culture-biased test.**

**Ans.** Differences between culture-fair and culture-biased tests are as follows

**Culture-fair** Psychologist have tried to develop tests that are culture-fair or culturally appropriate, i.e. one that does not discriminate against individuals belonging to different cultures.

In such tests, items are constructed in a manner that they assess experiences common to all cultures or have questions where language usage is not requirement. Non-verbal and performance tests help to reduce the cultural bias usually associated with verbal tests.

**Culture-biased** Many intelligence tests show a bias to the culture in which they are developed. Tests developed in America and Europe represent the urban and middle class cultural ethos.

Hence, educated middle class white subjects generally perform well on those tests. The items do not respect the cultural perspectives of Asia and Africa. The norms for these tests are also drawn from Western cultural groups.

**28. Differentiate between technological intelligence and integral intelligence. Elaborate the concept of intelligence in Indian tradition.**

***Or* Explain the competence of Indian notion of intelligence.**

**Ans.** **Technological Intelligence** It is found in technologically advanced societies. Skills of generalisation and abstraction, speed, minimal moves, and mental manipulation are promoted among children.

These societies promote a type of behaviour which can be called technological intelligence. In these societies, persons are well-versed in skills of attention, observation, analysis, performance, speed, and achievement orientation.

**Integral Intelligence** Technological intelligence is not as highly valued in many Asian and African societies. The qualities and skills regarded as intelligent actions in non-Western cultures are sharply different.

**Concept of Intelligence in Indian Tradition** Contrary to technological intelligence, intelligence in the Indian tradition can be termed as integral intelligence. It gives emphasis on connectivity with the social and world environment. Indian thinkers emphasise a holistic view of intelligence where equal attention is paid to cognitive and non-cognitive processes as well as their integration.

**29. Differentiate between psychological test and observation.**

**Ans.** Differences between psychological test and observation are as follows

**Psychological Test** It is an objective and standardised measure of an individual's mental and/or behavioural characteristics. Objective tests have been developed to measure all the dimensions of psychological attributes i.e. intelligence, aptitude, etc. These tests are guidance, personnel selection, placement and training. Personality is also assessed by certain projective tests.

**Observation** It involves employing systematic, organised and objective procedures to record behavioural phenomena occurring naturally in real time. For example, mother-child interactions can be easily studied through observation. However, in this method observer has little control over the situation and the reports may suffer from subjective interpretations of the observer.

**30. Angad has been a topper in class. He went to the topmost college, where he was neither sensitive to himself nor to others. This led to problems in interpersonal relationships with reference to his condition. Explain the importance of emotional intelligence in his life.** **CBSE 2020**

**Ans.** A good IQ and scholastic record is not enough to be successful in life. Angad is academically talented but is unsuccessful to build interpersonal relationship with his friends in college. Psychologists believe that the source of his difficulty is his lack of emotional intelligence.

Emotional intelligence is a set of skills that underlie accurate appraisal, expression and regulations of emotions. Psychologist Salovey and Meyer consider emotional intelligence as the ability to monitor one's own and other's emotions, to discriminate among them and to use the information to guide one's thinking and actions.

Emotional Quotient (EQ) is used to express emotional intelligence in the same way as IQ is used to express intelligence.

Emotional intelligence refers to the ability to process emotional information accurately and efficiently. But Angad lacks this intelligence which leads to his problems in interpersonal relationships.

**31. Intelligence is the interdependent functioning of three neurological system. Explain this theory.** **CBSE 2019**

**Ans.** Assessment can be formal and informal. Formal assessment is objective, standardised and organised. Whereas, informal assessment varies from case to case and from one assessor to another. Due to this variation, it is open to subjective interpretations. Psychologists are trained in making formal assessment of psychological attributes. The attribute chosen for assessment depends upon our purpose. For example, to help a weak student to perform well in examinations, we may assess her/his intellectual strengths and weaknesses. Similarly, if a person fails to adjust with members of her/his family, we may consider assessing his/her personality characteristics. Therefore, psychological assessment was a systematic testing procedure to evaluate abilities, behaviours and personal qualities of individuals.

**32. Explain Emotional Intelligence. State any two characteristics of emotionally intelligent persons.** **CBSE 2018**

**Ans.** It is believed that the notion of emotional intelligence broadens the concept of intelligence beyond the intellectual sphere and considers that intelligence includes emotions. It builds on the concept of intelligence in the Indian tradition. Emotional Intelligence (EI) is a set of skills that underlie accurate appraisal, expression and regulation of emotions.

The characteristics of emotional intelligence are

(i) Be aware and sensitive to your feelings and emotions.

(ii) Perceive and be sensitive to various types of emotions in others by noting their body language, voice and tone and facial expressions.

**33. Explain the relationship between creativity and intelligence. State the important features of creativity tests.** **CBSE 2019**

**Ans.** The relationship between creativity and intelligence is positive. All creative acts require a minimum ability to acquire knowledge and capacity to comprehend, retain and retrieve. A certain level of intelligence is necessary to be creative, but a high level of intelligence does not ensure that a person would certainly be creative. It can be concluded that creativity can take many forms and blends.

Important features of creativity tests are

- Creativity test assess variations in terms of the potential for creativity.
- They are open ended and gave freedom to a person to use its imagination and express it in original ways.
- It involves divergent thinking and assess ability to produce a variety of ideas. It also identifies relationship between unrelated things.

**34. We can see that Srikanth has the ability to adopt, shape and select the environment. Identify the theory of intelligence that would best support our understanding of Srikanth's intelligence.** **CBSE 2023**

**Ans.** According to Howard Gardner's Theory of Multiple Intelligences, Intropersonal intelligence explains Srikanth's conviction. Intrapersonal intelligence refers to the ability to understand oneself, including one's strengths, weaknesses, emotions and motivations. People with high intrapersonal intelligence are self-aware, confident and able to make decisions based on their internal sense of purpose.

Srikanth's ability to believe in his potential despite external criticism reflects strong intrapersonal intelligence.

**35. "Srikanth is standing tall living by his conviction that if the "world looks at me and says, 'Srikanth, you can do nothing, 'I look back at the world and say, I can do anything". According to Gardner's Theory of Multiple Intelligences, which kind of intelligence explains this? Discuss this intelligence in brief.** **CBSE 2023**

**Ans.** According to Gardner's Theory of Multiple Intelligences, intrapersonal intelligence explain this situation. It refers to the knowledge of one's internal strengths and limitations and using that knowledge to effectively relate to others. Persons high on this ability have finer sensibilities regarding their identity, human existence, and meaning of life.

## Long Answer Type Questions

**1. Briefly elaborate the theories related to the approach of intelligence.**

**Ans.** Several theories and approaches have been proposed by psychologists which can be broadly classified as either representing a psychometric/structural approach or an information-processing approach. Psychometric approach it considers intelligence as an aggregate of abilities. It expresses the individual's performance in terms of a single index of cognitive abilities.

**Information-Processing Approach** It describes the processes that people use in intellectual reasoning and problem solving. The major focus of this approach is on how an intelligent person acts. Information-processing approaches emphasise on studying cognitive functions underlying intelligent behaviour rather than focusing on structure of intelligence.

**Uni or One Factor Theory** Alfred Binet was the first psychologist who tried to formalise the concept of intelligence in terms of mental operations. Alfred Binet conceptualised intelligence as consisting of one similar sets of abilities which can be used for solving any or every problem in an individual's environment. This theory is known as uni or one factor theory of intelligence.

**Two-factor Theory** In 1927, Charles Spearman proposed this theory employing a statistical method called factor analysis. He showed that intelligence consisted of a general factor (g-factor) and some specific factors (s-factors). G-factor includes mental operations which are primary and common to all performances. S-factors includes some specific abilities which are present in some people in addition to g-factor.

**Theory of Primary Mental Abilities** Louis Thurnstone proposed theory of primary mental abilities. It states that intelligence consists of seven primary abilities, each of which is relatively independent of the others. These are

(i) Verbal Comprehension (ii) Numerical Abilities
(iii) Spatial Relations (iv) Perceptual Speed
(v) Word Fluency (vi) Memory
(vii) Inductive Reasoning

**2. Compare and contrast technological and integral approaches to intelligence. Also discuss the cultural factors that may influence these perspectives.** **CBSE 2025**

**Ans.** Technological approaches to intelligence focus on measuring cognitive skills through tests and algorithms, which emphasise problem-solving and logical reasoning. The technological approach allows for the development of tools that can automate complex tasks, such as in the fields of healthcare (e.g., medical diagnostics), robotics, or natural language processing. AI can handle vast amounts of data quickly and accurately, often surpassing human abilities in specific tasks.

In contrast, Integral approaches view intelligence holistically and incorporate emotions, creativity and social interactions alongside cognition. The integral approach focuses on creating a balance between intellectual and emotional well-being. It encourages individuals to grow not just intellectually but also emotionally and morally, which is critical in building well-rounded, compassionate individuals. This approach values creativity, emotional regulation, and ethical decision-making.

Cultural factors shape these perspectives. Western cultures value analytical thinking and favouring technological approaches. In contrast, Eastern cultures prioritise harmony and relationships, supporting integral approaches. Societal norms also influence the acceptance of multiple intelligences, such as musical or kinesthetic skills.

**3. Manoj and Sunil are two managers in a company. State four reasons how Manoj's higher emotional intelligence contributes to his popularity with colleagues as compared to Sunil, who lacks these qualities.** CBSE 2025

**Ans.** Manoj's higher emotional intelligence makes him more popular with colleagues because of the following reasons.

- **Better Communication** He understands others' feelings and expresses himself clearly, which builds trust. Manoj's emotional intelligence allows him to navigate social situations more effectively.
- **Conflict Resolution** He handles disagreements calmly, ensuring positive relationships. His ability to manage his emotions during stressful situations helps him prevent escalations and promotes harmony in the workplace.
- **Empathy** He listens and shows care, creating strong bonds. Manoj can empathise with his colleagues, meaning he understands and shares their feelings. Manoj can empathise with his colleagues, meaning he understands and shares their feelings. This allows him to offer support, provide constructive feedback, and show that he values their perspectives.
- **Team Motivation** He encourages and supports others, boosting teamwork and morale. Collaborative efforts allow team members to learn from each other, solve problems together, and share successes, which strengthens their commitment to the team's goals.

In contrast, Sunil lacks these qualities and he may struggle with understanding or connecting with colleagues, which leads to misunderstandings and weak relationships. This shows how emotional intelligence plays a vital role in creating a harmonious workplace.

**4. Sachin is in his infancy. Even during his infancy and early childhood, he is showing characters like larger attention span, good recognition memory, preference for novelty, sensitivity to environmental changes, and early appearance of language skills. How can you explain such child? Does it mean that he possess superior psychomotor ability as well? How will you identify such child?**

**Ans.** The children like Sachin who exhibit characters like larger attention span, good recognition memory, preference for novelty, sensitivity to environmental changes, and early appearance of language skills in their infancy or early childhood are Gifted children. Gifted children show early signs of intellectual superiority.

The mere presence of brilliant academic qualities does not mean that a child will also possess superior psychomotor ability. Each gifted student possesses different strengths, personalities and characteristics. Athletes who show superior psychomotor ability are also gifted. Some important characteristics of gifted children are

- Advanced logical thinking, questioning and problem solving behaviour.
- High speed in processing information.
- Superior generalisation and discrimination ability.
- Advanced level of original and creative thinking.
- High level of intrinsic motivation and self-esteem.
- Independent and non-conformist thinking.
- Preference for solitary academic activities for long periods.

Performance on intelligence tests is not the only measure for identifying the gifted child. Many other sources of information, such as teachers' judgement, school achievement record, parents' interviews, peer and self ratings, etc. can be used in combination with intellectual assessment for identifying the gifted children.

## Case Based Questions

**1. Read the case and answer the questions that follow.**

Mrs. Sunita is an employee of a leading MNC company in India. She has worked for past 15 years in the company. Many seniors from administration including the Branch Manager know her as a devoted and hard working employee. A new Supervisor, Mr. Anuj joins in the office and was made in-charge of the department wherein Sunita also works. He is known for having temper issues and can be insensitive toward others. At the workplace, Sunita is working on a certain project that has to be delivered in a time bound manner. One day, she received a call from her home regarding ill-health of her mother.

Consequently, she approached her Mr. Anuj asking for leave. Mr. Anuj denied the leave request citing urgency of work. Furthermore, he also told her that her work is substandard and need to be redone. Unless, she does not complete the work, she will not be granted leave. Sunita, hearing this cried in the office. On the same evening, during tea-break, the Branch Manager noted the body language of Sunita and asked if there is anything wrong. Since, the Branch Manager had lost her mother last year due to ill-health, he could relate with emotions of Sunita. Finally, becoming aware of the whole incident, the Branch Manager allowed Sunita to go on leave.

**(i) How did Sunita feel after her leave request was denied by Mr. Anuj, and what was the impact of his response on her?**

**(ii) How did the Branch Manager handle the situation once he became aware of Sunita's distress?**

**Ans.** (i) Sunita felt upset and distressed after her leave request was denied by Mr. Anuj. His response, which included criticising her work, made her emotional, leading her to cry in the office. The denial and harsh feedback added to her emotional burden, affecting her well-being, and creating a sense of helplessness.

(ii) Upon noticing Sunita's distressed body language, the Branch Manager empathised with her, understanding her emotional state due to her mother's illness. After learning about the incident with Mr. Anuj, he intervened and allowed Sunita to take the necessary leave, demonstrating compassion and providing her with the support she needed during a personal crisis.

**2. Read the case and answer the questions that follow.**

This is a story of three students Ruby, Radhika and Shankar who were enrolled in an Undergraduate Psychology Program in a University. Ruby was the admission officer's dream. She was selected for the program as she had perfect entrance test scores, outstanding grades and excellent letters of recommendation. But when it was time for Ruby to start coming up with ideas of her own, she disappointed her professors.

On the other hand, Radhika did not meet the admission officer's expectations. She had good grades but low entrance exam scores. However, her letters of recommendation described her as a creative young woman. She could design and implement research work with minimal guidance at college. Shankar ranked somewhere in between the two students. He was satisfactory on almost every traditional measure of success. But rather than falling somewhere in the middle of his class at college, Shankar proved to be an outstanding student. His strength lay in the ability to not only adapt well to the demands of his new environment but also to modify the environment to suit his needs.

**(i) How did Shankar's approach to his studies differ from Ruby and Radhika's?**

**(ii) What factors contributed to Radhika's success despite her low entrance exam scores?**

**CBSE SQP Term I 2021**

**Ans.** (i) Shankar's success was based on his ability to adapt and modify his environment to meet academic demands, showcasing flexibility and creativity. Unlike Ruby, who struggled with innovation, and Radhika, who had lower academic scores, Shankar demonstrated resilience and an adaptable approach that set him apart in his studies.

(ii) Radhika's success can be attributed to her creativity and strong problem-solving abilities. Despite her low entrance exam scores, her professors recognised her potential through positive letters of recommendation, highlighting her capability to design and implement research projects with minimal guidance, which contributed to her academic success.

**3. Read the case and answer the questions that follow.**

Indian music and dance are embedded with Indian tradition and culture from the prehistoric period. Classical dance forms of modern India have originated from ancient dance disciplines.

Narayanan Nair was a prominent 20th century Kathakali artiste. His ability to improvise on the stage by exhibiting realistic touches to facial expressions and hand gestures won him massive appreciation. He honed finer sensibilities regarding his identity and the meaning of his existence. Expression through dance also enhanced his self-awareness.

Similarly, Tirumakudalu Chowdiah played the four-stringed violin and by 1927, he became an extremely well-known violin accompanist.

When Chowdiah was a child, a scholar asked him why he looked upset. He replied, 'I feel like running away to music lessons'. The scholar convinced Chowdiah's mother to allow him to learn music and be trained under Bidaram Krishnappa.

In one of the vocal concerts of Krishnappa, Chowdiah accompanied him using his new seven-stringed violin. Krishnappa perceived that the sound emanating from the violin was louder than usual.

In those days, there was no sound amplification technology. Listeners sitting in the back rows of music halls found it difficult to hear the performance.

Therefore, Chowdiah added three more strings to the violin to amplify the sound. Krishnappa was proud of Chowdiah's accomplishment at innovating the violin.

**(i) What was Narayanan Nair's contribution to Kathakali and how did it impact his audience?**

**(ii) How did Tirumakudalu Chowdiah innovate the violin to overcome a problem faced by listeners?**

**CBSE Term I 2021**

**Ans.** (i) Narayanan Nair's contribution to Kathakali was his ability to improvise facial expressions and hand gestures, which made his performances more realistic and received widespread appreciation from the audience.

(ii) Tirumakudalu Chowdiah added three extra strings to the violin, amplifying its sound, which helped listeners in the back rows hear better during performances, compensating for the lack of sound amplification technology.

# SELF ASSESSMENT TEST

## Objective Answer Types Questions

**1.** Information processing approach to intelligence is represented in the

(a) multiple intelligence (b) triarchic theory

(c) one-factor theory (d) two-factor theory

**2.** Entrepreneurial competence refers to

(a) respect for social order (b) self-exposure

(c) discrimination (d) commitment

**3.** Which of the following is true about individual differences in human functioning?

(a) Everyone is identical in terms of intelligence and creativity.

(b) People differ in both physical and psychological traits.

(c) Individual differences only occur in physical traits.

(d) Individual differences do not affect behaviour.

**4.** What is the main purpose of psychological assessment?

(a) To measure an individual's physical traits only.

(b) To predict future behaviour and identify necessary interventions.

(c) To assess only intelligence and aptitude.

(d) To judge a person's moral values.

**5.** **Assertion** (A) Psychologists use formal assessments to reliably evaluate psychological attributes.

**Reason** (R) Formal assessments are based on scientific procedures and are designed to measure attributes like intelligence, personality and emotional stability in an objective manner.

(a) Both A and R are correct and R is the correct explanation of A.

(b) Both A and R are correct, but R is not the correct explanation of A.

(c) A is correct, but R is incorrect.

(d) A is incorrect, but R is correct

## Very Short Answer Type Questions

**1.** What do you understand by individual differences?

**2.** Define assessment.

**3.** What is aptitude?

**4.** Define self-report in your term.

**5.** What is componential intelligence?

**6.** Define spatial intelligence.

**7.** What is successive processing?

## Short Answer Type Questions

**1.** How does Arthur Jensen explain the concept of intelligence?

**2.** What are the characteristics of interpersonal intelligence?

**3.** Differentiate between aptitude, interest and intelligence.

**4.** Explain the PASS model of intelligence.

**5.** What is creativity? How it is related to intelligence?

## Long Answer Type Questions

1. What is the meaning of assessment. Describe the key features of any two methods used in psychological assessment?
2. Discuss Gardener's Theory of Multiple Intelligence with suitable examples.
3. Briefly describe the creativity test.

## Case Based Questions

**Read the case and answer the questions that follow.**

In 1905, Alfred Binet, was requested by the French government to devise a method by which students who experienced difficulty in school could be identified. Binet and his colleague, Theodore Simon, began developing questions that focused on areas not explicitly taught in schools those days, such as memory, attention skills related to problem solving. Using these questions, Binet determined which were the ones that served as the best predictors of school success.

Binet quickly realised that some children were able to answer more advanced questions than older children were generally able to answer and vice versa. Based on this observation, Binet suggested the concept of mental age or a measure of intelligence based on the average abilities of children of a certain age group.

This first intelligence test is referred to as the Binet-Simon Scale. He insisted that intelligence is influenced by many factors, it changes over time, and it can only be compared in children with similar backgrounds.

(i) Identify the approach on which the Binet-Simon Intelligence Scale is based. Discuss its features.

(ii) 'Binet quickly realised that some children were able to answer more advanced questions than older children were generally able to answer and vice versa'. Why do individuals differ in intelligence? Using examples, give reasons for your answer. **CBSE SQP 2022**

# 02
CHAPTER

# Self and Personality

Psychologists use the concept of self for knowing and evaluating an individual's behaviour. They analysed the structure and function of self and personality. By understanding self and personality we can understand our own as well as other's behaviour in diverse settings.

**YOUR STUDY GOALS**



**YOUR PRACTICE GOAL**

- Objective Type Questions (30 Qs ; MCQs, A-R)
- Subjective Type Questions (26 VSAs 31 SAs, 10 LAs, 2 Case Based)

## 2.1 Self And Personality

- Self and personality refer to the characteristic ways in which individuals define their existence.
- It is commonly observed that different people hold different ideas about themselves. These individual ideas represent a person's self.
- Additionally, people behave differently in similar situations; however, behaviour of particular person generally remains stable in different situations characterising their personality.
- Therefore, people seem to possess distinct personalities reflected in the diverse behaviours they exhibit.

## 2.2 Concept of Self

- Parents, friends, teachers and other significant people play a crucial role in shaping a child's idea of self.
- Interactions and experiences with others, and the meaning we derive from them, form the foundation of our self.
- The structure of self is adaptable and can change based on personal experiences.
- People often describe themselves through various attributes, which reflect their personal or social/cultural identities.

- Personal identity consists of traits that make a person unique compared to others. It includes one's name, qualities, capabilities and beliefs.
- Social identity includes aspects that connect a person to a social or cultural group or stem from it, such as religion, caste or region.
- These descriptions represent how people mentally conceptualise themselves.
- The concept of self refers to the totality of an individual's conscious experiences, thoughts and feelings about themselves.
- These experiences and ideas contribute to an individual's existence at both the personal and social levels.

## Self as Subject and Self as Object

- Self is viewed as subject as well as 'object'.
- This distinction suggests that the self can be understood both ways.
- When someone says, "I know who I am", they imply that the self is both a 'knower' (subject) and something that can be 'known' (object).
- As a subject (or actor), the self actively engages in understanding and knowing itself.
- As an object (or consequence), the self is observed and understood.
- This dual nature of the self–being both subject and object–is an essential aspect to remember when considering the concept of self.

## Kinds of Self

- Various kinds of self develop through our interactions with physical and socio-cultural environments.
- The first elements of self-appear when a newborn cries for milk out of hunger, initially as a reflex, which later develops into an awareness, such as 'I am hungry'.
- This biological self evolves within a socio-cultural context; for example, while one person might crave chocolate, an Eskimo might not have the same preference.
- A distinction exists between the personal self and the social self.
- The personal self focuses on one's individual needs and concerns.
- This self-place importance on individual aspects like personal freedom, responsibility, achievement and comfort.
- The social self emerges through relationships with others and highlights values such as cooperation, unity, affiliation, sacrifice, support and sharing.
- This social self-values family and social relationships and is also known as the Familial or Relational self-due to its emphasis on these bonds.

## Cognitive and Behavioural Aspects of Self

- Psychologists have shown strong interest in studying the self, leading to a deeper understanding of various self-related behavioural aspects.
- Each individual carries a sense of self—an awareness of who they are and what distinguishes them from others.
- People are generally attached to their personal and social identities and feel safe knowing these identities remain relatively stable throughout life.
- The way we perceive ourselves, including our competencies and qualities, is known as Self-concept.
- A person's self-concept tends to be overall positive or negative.
- On a more specific level, a person might view their athletic abilities positively but their academic talents negatively.

- At an even finer level, a person may have a positive self-concept in reading but a negative one in mathematics.
- Determining an individual's self-concept is challenging, and the most common method is asking the person to describe themselves.

## Self-esteem

- Self-esteem reflects our judgment of our own value or worth.
- This self-evaluation of one's value is referred to as self-esteem. Some people have high self-esteem while others may have low self-esteem.
- Research indicates that children, by age 6 to 7, typically form self-esteem in four main areas
  (i) Academic competence
  (ii) Social competence
  (iii) Physical/athletic competence
  (iv) Physical appearance
- As children grow, these areas become more refined and can combine to form a general sense of self-esteem.
- Self-esteem strongly impacts daily behaviour.
- For example, children with high academic self-esteem tend to perform better in school.
- Children with high social self-esteem are often more liked by their peers. In contrast, children with low self-esteem across all areas may exhibit anxiety, depression and even antisocial behaviour.
- Studies show that warm and positive parenting helps in the development of high self-esteem in children, as it helps them feel competent and valued.
- In contrast, children whose parents make unnecessary decisions for them may develop low self-esteem.

## Self-efficacy

- Self-efficacy is the belief in one's ability to control their own life outcomes.
- People vary in their beliefs about control over outcomes.
- Some feel their outcomes depend on their own efforts and abilities. Others attribute outcomes to luck, fate or external factors.
- High self-efficacy is shown by individuals who believe they have the necessary skills or behaviours to succeed in specific situations (e.g., passing an exam).
- The concept of self-efficacy is based on Bandura's social learning theory, which shows that behaviour is learned by observing and imitating others.
- People's beliefs in their ability to achieve and master tasks influence the types of behaviour they engage in and the level of risk they are willing to take.
- Strong self-efficacy allows individuals to create circumstances in their lives, reducing fear and encouraging proactive behaviour.
- Self-efficacy is not fixed; it can be developed over time.
- People with high self-efficacy can quit habits, such as smoking, once they decide to do so.
- Positive influences from society, parents and positive personal experiences help build a strong sense of self-efficacy by offering positive role models during a child's formative years.

## Self-regulation

- Self-regulation is the ability to organise and monitor one's own behaviour effectively.
- Individuals who can adapt their behaviour based on external demands exhibit high levels of self-monitoring.
- Many life situations require resisting situational pressures and exerting self-control.
- This control is often facilitated by will power.

- As human beings, we possess the capacity to manage our behaviour according to our desires and goals.
- People frequently choose to delay or defer the satisfaction of certain needs, a process known as self-control.
- Self-control is crucial for achieving long-term goals and maintaining focus on what is truly important.
- Indian cultural traditions offer effective strategies for developing selfcontrol, such as, fasting during rituals like vrata or roza and practicing non-attachment to worldly possessions.
- Several psychological techniques can enhance self-control and self-regulation
    - **Observation of Behaviour** This technique involves monitoring one's actions to gather information that can help, modify or strengthen certain behaviours.
    - **Self-instruction** This method entails instructing oneself on how to behave or what to do, to achieve desired behaviours.
    - **Self-reinforcement** This involves rewarding oneself for behaviours that yield positive outcomes. For example, treating oneself to a movie with friends after performing well on an exam.

## Culture and Self

- Several aspects of self are linked to the characteristic features of the culture in which an individual resides.
- An analysis of self in the Indian cultural context reveals distinct features compared to the Western cultural context.
- The most significant distinction between Indian and Western views lies in how the boundary is drawn between the self and others.

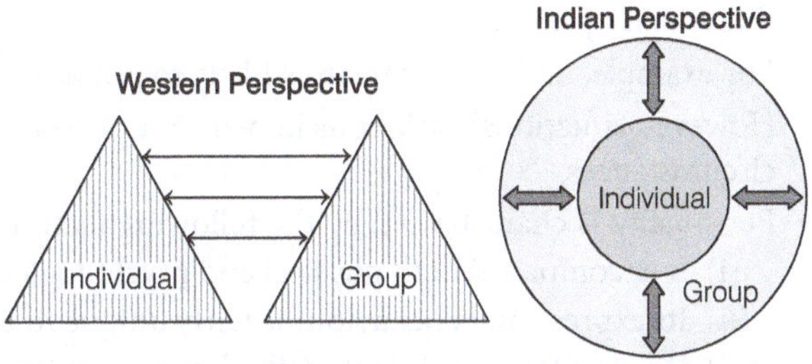

▲ *Self and Group Boundaries in Western and Indian Cultural Perspectives*

- In the Western view, this boundary appears to be relatively fixed.
- Conversely, the Indian view of self is characterised by a shifting boundary, where the self can expand to fuse with the cosmos or include others, reflecting a collective experience.
- At times, the self may withdraw and focus solely on personal needs or goals.
- The Western perspective tends to maintain clear dichotomies between self and other, man and nature, as well as subjective and objective.
- In contrast, the Indian view does not draw such clear dichotomies.
- In Western culture, the self and the group are seen as two distinct entities with clearly defined boundaries.
- Individual members of the group in Western culture maintain their individuality.
- In Indian culture, the self is typically not separated from the group; both coexist harmoniously.
- This difference leads to individualistic characteristics in many Western cultures, while many Asian cultures are characterised as collectivistic.

## 2.3 Concept of Personality

- The term 'personality' is derived from the Latin word persona, which refers to the mask used by actors in Roman theatre to change their facial appearance.
- For a layperson, personality generally refers to the physical or external appearance of an individual.
- For example, when someone is described as 'good-looking', people often assume they also have a charming personality.
- This perception of personality is based on superficial impressions, which may not be accurate.
- In psychological terms, personality refers to our characteristic ways of responding to individuals and situations.
- People often describe how they respond to various situations, using terms such as shy, sensitive, quiet, concerned or warm.
- These terms refer to different components of personality.
- Personality refers to the unique and relatively stable qualities that characterise an individual's behaviour across different situations over time.
- Consistency in behaviour, thought and emotion across situations and time periods define of an individual's personality.
- For example, an honest person is likely to remain honest regardless of the time or situation.
- However, situational variations in behaviour do occur, helping individuals adapt to their environmental circumstances.
- Personality is characterised by the following features
  - (i) It encompasses both physical and psychological components.
  - (ii) Its expression in behaviour is fairly unique to each individual.
  - (iii) Its main features do not easily change over time.
  - (iv) It is dynamic, meaning some features may change due to internal or external situational demands, making personality adaptive.
- Understanding personality helps us interact with others in realistic ways.
- For example, if a child dislikes orders, it is more effective to present a set of acceptable alternatives rather than giving direct orders.

### Quick Test 1

1. What are the two types of self?
2. What are the different cognitive and behavioural aspects of self?
3. Name some techniques of self-control.
4. What are the main components of personality?
5. What are the four features of personality?
6. How does understanding personality help in interactions?

## 2.4 Major Approaches to the Study of Personality

- Psychologists aim to understand the nature and origins of individual differences in personality.
- Observations indicate that two children from the same family can develop remarkably different personalities, evident in both physical appearance and behaviour.
- To explain behavioural differences among individuals, as well as consistencies in behaviour within an individual, various approaches and theories have been developed.
- These theories are grounded in different models of human behaviour and highlight various aspects of personality. Psychologists differentiate between type and trait approaches to personality.

## Type Approach

- The type approach seeks to understand human personality by examining broad patterns in the observed behavioural traits.
- Each behavioural pattern corresponds to a type, classifying individuals based on similarities in their behavioural traits.
- Personality types are utilised to represent expected behaviours based on observed similarities among individuals.
- Efforts to categorise individuals into specific personality types date back to ancient times.
- The Greek physician Hippocrates proposed a typology based on bodily fluids, classifying people into four types
  - (i) **Sanguine** Characterised by sociability and a cheerful disposition.
  - (ii) **Phlegmatic** Known for being calm, reliable and peaceful.
  - (iii) **Melancholic** Thoughtful, reserved and prone to sadness.
  - (iv) **Choleric** Marked by ambition, energy and leadership qualities.

### As Per Charak Samhita

- In India, the Charak Samhita, a renowned treatise on Ayurveda, classifies individuals based on three humoural elements, vata, pitta and kapha which is known as Tridosha.
- Additionally, there exists a typology based on the three gunas (qualities) known as Sattva, Rajas and Tamas.
  - (i) **Sattva guna** includes attributes such as cleanliness, truthfulness, dutifulness, detachment and discipline.
  - (ii) **Rajas guna** is characterised by intensive activity, desire for sense gratification, dissatisfaction, envy and materialistic tendencies.
  - (iii) **Tamas guna** is associated with qualities such as anger, arrogance, depression, laziness and helplessness.
- All three gunas are present in every individual to varying degrees and the dominance of one or more may lead to particular behavioural tendencies.

### As Per Sheldon

- In psychology, William Sheldon proposed typologies based on body build and temperament classifying individuals into three categories
  - (i) Endomorphic individuals are characterised as fat, soft and round, typically relaxed and sociable.
  - (ii) Mesomorphic individuals possess strong musculature and a rectangular build, exhibiting energy and courage.
  - (iii) Ectomorphic individuals are thin, long and fragile, often described as brainy, artistic and introverted.
- These body typologies are simplistic and have limited predictive value regarding individual behaviour.

### As Per Jung

- Carl Jung proposed another significant typology, dividing people into introverts and extraverts. This classification is widely recognised.
- Introverts prefer solitude, avoid social interactions, withdrawing during emotional conflicts and exhibit shyness.
- Extraverts, in contrast, are sociable and outgoing, thriving in environments that involve direct interaction with others and coping with stress by engaging in social activities.

## As Per Friedman and Rosenman

- Researchers Friedman and Rosenman classified individuals into Type A and Type B personalities.

### Type A Personalities

- Type A personalities are characterised by high motivation, impatience, sense of being short of time and a tendency to feel burdened by work.
- They often struggle to slow down and relax, making them more susceptible to health issues such as hypertension and Coronary Heart Disease (CHD).
- Studies indicate that the risk of developing CHD in Type A individuals can exceed risks from factors such as high blood pressure, high cholesterol or smoking.

### Type B Personalities

In contrast, Type B Personalities are defined by the absence of Type A traits, typically being more relaxed and less pressured.

### Type C and D Personalities

- Morris introduced the concept of Type C Personality, characterised by a predisposition to cancer.
- Individuals with this personality tend to be cooperative, unassertive and patient.
- They often suppress negative emotions, such as anger and show compliance with authority.
- More recently, a Type D Personality has been suggested, characterised by a tendency toward depression.
- Although personality typologies can be appealing, they are often overly simplistic.
- Human behaviour is highly complex and variable, making it challenging to assign individuals to specific personality types without oversimplifying their unique traits.

## Trait Approach

- The trait approach focuses on specific psychological attributes along which individuals tend to differ consistently and reliably.
- For instance, one person may exhibit less shyness, while another may display more; similarly, one individual may be less friendly, whereas another may be more sociable.
- In this context, 'shyness' and 'friendliness' are traits along which individuals can be rated based on the degree of their presence or absence.
- The interactional approach asserts that situational characteristics play a significantly influence behaviour.
- According to this perspective, individuals may behave as dependent or independent due to both internal personality traits and external rewards or threats present in specific situations.
- Research indicates that the cross-situational consistency of traits is relatively low, emphasising the impact of situational factors on behaviour.
- Behaviour can vary significantly across environment, such as markets, courtrooms, or places of worship.
- Trait approaches to personality theories focus primarily on the description and characterisation of fundamental components of personality.
- These theories aim to identify the 'building blocks' of personality by discovering various psychological attributes.
- Although human beings exhibit a wide range of psychological variations, it is feasible to categorise these attributes into a smaller number of distinct personality traits.
- The trait approach aligns closely with our everyday experiences; for instance, if person is sociable, we can reasonably assume that they will also be cooperative, friendly and helpful, engaging in behaviours that involve other social elements.

- Thus, the trait approach seeks to pinpoint the primary characteristics that define individuals.
- A trait is defined as a relatively enduring attribute or quality that distinguishes one individual from another.
- Traits encompass a spectrum of possible behaviours that can be triggered based on situational demands.
- To summarise the characteristics of traits
  - Traits are relatively stable over time.
  - They tend to be consistent across different situations.
  - The strengths and combinations of traits vary among individuals, contributing to unique differences in personality.
- Several psychologists have utilised traits to develop their own theories of personality, further expanding our understanding of this field.

## Allporti's Trait Theory

- Gordon Allport is recognised as the pioneer of the trait approach to personality.
- He proposed that individuals possess a variety of traits that are dynamic and influence behaviour.
- These traits help individuals approach different situations with similar plans and responses.
- Allport emphasised that traits integrate stimuli and responses that may otherwise appear dissimilar.
- He argued that the language people use to describe themselves and others serves as a foundation for understanding human personality.
- To identify traits, Allport analysed words from the English language that describe individuals.
- Based on his analysis, Allport categorised traits into three types—cardinal, central and secondary.

### (i) Cardinal Traits

- **Cardinal traits**[1] are highly generalised dispositions that reflect the central goals around which a person's entire life revolves.
- Examples of cardinal traits include Mahatma Gandhi's non-violence and Hitler's Nazism, which are so strongly associated with these figures that they have given rise to identities like 'Gandhian' or 'Hitlerian' traits.

### (ii) Central Traits

**Central traits**[2] are less pervasive than cardinal traits but still represent generalised dispositions, such as being warm, sincere or diligent.

These traits are often highlighted in testimonials or job recommendations.

### (iii) Secondary Traits

- Secondary traits are the least generalised characteristics of a person, such as 'likes mangoes' or 'prefers ethnic clothes'.
- While Allport acknowledged that situations can influence behaviour, he maintained that an individual's reactions depend on their traits.
- He noted that people with similar traits might express them differently in various contexts.
- Allport viewed traits as intervening variables that exist between a stimulus situation and a person's response.
- This perspective suggests that any variation in traits can lead to different responses to the same situation.

---

1 **Cardinal Traits** Key personality traits that dominate an individual's behaviour and influence their overall character, according to Allport.

2 **Central traits** General characteristics that form the foundatioin of personality but are not as dominant as cardinal traits.

## Cattell: Personality Factors

- Raymond Cattell proposed that a common structure that accounts for individual differences, determined through research and analysis.
- He employed a statistical technique known as factor analysis to uncover these common structures.
- Through his analysis, Cattell identified 16 primary or source traits that serve as the fundamental components of personality. The source traits are stable and considered the building blocks of an individual's personality. In addition to source traits, Cattell noted the presence of various surface traits that emerge from the interaction of source traits.
- He described the source traits using opposing tendencies, highlighting the complexity of personality.
- To assess personality based on his theory, Cattell developed the Sixteen Personality Factor Questionnaire (16PF), acidely used by psychologists for personality assessment.

## Eysenck's Theory

H.J. Eysenck proposed that personality could be reduced into two broad biologically and genetically based dimensions, each encompassing specific traits. These dimensions are

### Neuroticism vs. Emotional Stability

It refers to the degree to which individuals have control over their feelings. They are anxious, moody, touchy, restless and quickly lose control.

At the opposite extreme are people who are calm, even-tempered, reliable and maintain control over their emotions.

### Extraversion vs. Introversion

It refers to the degree of socially outgoingness or withdrawal. Extroverts are active, gregarious, impulsive and thrill-seeking individuals.

Introverts are passive, quiet, cautious and reserved.

### Psychoticism vs. Sociability

- It is considered to interact with the other two dimensions i.e. Neuroticism vs. Emotional stability and Extraversion vs. Introversion.
- Individuals who score high on the psychoticism dimension tend to be hostile, egocentric and antisocial.
- The Eysenck Personality Questionnaire is the test used to study these dimensions of personality.

### Five-Factor Model of Personality

**Paul Costa and Robert McCrae** identified five key personality factors, commonly referred to as the **Big Five Factors.**

(i) The first factor is Openness to Experience, which describes individuals who score high as imaginative, curious, open to new ideas, and interested in cultural pursuits. In contrast, those who score low on Openness to Experience tend to be rigid and resistant to change.

(ii) The second factor is Extraversion, which characterises people who are socially active, assertive, outgoing, talkative and fun-loving. On the opposite end of this spectrum are individuals who are shy and reserved.

(iii) The third factor is Agreeableness, which describes individuals who are helpful, cooperative, friendly, caring and nurturing. People who are low in Agreeableness may exhibit hostility and self centeredness.

(iv) The fourth factor is Neuroticism, where individuals scoring high are emotionally unstable, anxious, worried, fearful, distressed, irritable and hypertensive. In contrast, individuals on the lower end of Neuroticism are typically well-adjusted and emotionally stable.

(v) The fifth factor is Conscientiousness, characterising individuals who are achievement-oriented, dependable, responsible, prudent, hardworking and self-controlled. Those who score low in Conscientiousness tend to be impulsive and less organised.

## Quick Test 2

1 What is the focus of the type approach to studying personality?
2 Who proposed the typologies of endomorphic, mesomorphic, and ectomorphic individuals?
3 What classification of personality did Carl Jung propose?
4 What is the primary focus of the trait approach in personality studies?
5 What is defined as a relatively enduring attribute that distinguishes one individual from another?
6 What are the three types of traits identified by Gordon Allport?

## Psychodynamic Approach

- The **psychodynamic approach**[3] is a highly popular method for studying personality.
- This perspective primarily stems from the contributions of Sigmund Freud, who is considered a pioneer in the field.
- Freud was a physician who developed his theories during the course of his clinical practice.
- He used hypnosis to treat patient with physical and emotional problems.
- Through his work, Freud observed that many patients found relief by discussing their issues, often feeling better after articulating their concerns.
- Freud utilised several techniques, including free association. Free association is a method in which individuals are encouraged to openly share all thoughts, feelings and ideas that come to their mind without censorship.
- In addition to free association, Freud also employed dream analysis to explore the **unconscious**[4] aspects of personality.
- He analysed errors or slips of the tongue (often referred to as 'Freudian slips') as a means to understand underlying psychological processes.
- Overall, Freud's approach aims to uncover the complex internal dynamics that influence behaviour and personality.

### Levels of Consciousness

- Freud's theory examines the sources and consequences of emotional conflicts and how individuals cope with them.
- It conceptualises the human mind in terms of three levels of consciousness.
- The first level is the conscious, which encompasses thoughts, feelings and actions that individuals are aware of.
- The second level is the preconscious, which contains mental activity that individuals may become aware of only if they focus on it closely.
- The third level is the unconscious, which includes mental processes that individuals are unaware of.
- According to Freud, the unconscious serves as a reservoir for instinctual drives and animalistic urges.
- It also stores ideas and wishes that are hidden from conscious awareness, often because they lead to psychological conflicts.
- Many of these repressed ideas stem from sexual desires that cannot be openly expressed, leading to their suppression.
- Individuals constantly strive to find socially acceptable ways to express their unconscious impulses or to prevent them from surfacing.
- Failure to resolve these conflicts successfully can result in abnormal behaviour.

3 **Psychodynamic Approach** A psychological perspective emphasising unconscious processes and childhood experiences in shaping personality.
4 **Unconscious** The part of the mind that contains thought, memories and desires that are not currently in conscious awareness but influence behaviour.

- Analysing phenomena such as forgetting, mispronunciations, jokes and dreams can provide insight into the unconscious.
- Freud developed a therapeutic procedure known as Psychoanalysis, aiming to bring repressed unconscious material to consciousness.
- By doing so, individuals can live in a more self-aware and integrated manner.

## Structure of Personality

- According to Freud's theory, the primary structural elements of personality are three id, ego and superego.
- These elements reside in the unconscious as forces and can be inferred from people's behaviours.
- It is important to note that the id, ego and superego are concepts, not tangible physical structures. Structure of personality can be understood with the help of following table

| Element | Description | Key Characteristics |
|---|---|---|
| Id | Source of instinctual energy | It seeks immediate gratification of primitive needs |
| | | Operates on the pleasure principle |
| | | Focuses on sexual and aggressive impulses |
| | | Does not consider moral values or societal norms |
| Ego | Develops from the id to satisfy needs realstically | Operates on the reality principle |
| | | Directs the id towards more appropriate behaviours |
| | | Balances the demands of the id and supergo |
| | | Example, suggests asking for permission to grab an ice-cream cone instead of taking it impulsively |
| Superego | Represents the moral branch of personality | Guides the id and ego regarding ethical behaviour |
| | | Internalises parental authority through socialisation |
| | | Provides feelings of guilt or moral approval |
| | | Example, indicates that asking for the ice-cream cone is morally correct, avoiding feelings of guilt or anxiety. |

- Freud believed that the unconscious is composed of these three competing forces—id, ego and superego.
- In some individuals, the id is stronger than the superego, while in others, the superego dominates.
- The relative strength of the id, ego and superego determines a person's psychological stability.
- Freud also posited that the id is energised by two instinctual forces: the life instinct and the death instinct.
- He focused more on the life instinct (or sexual instinct) and paid less attention to the death instinct.
- The instinctual life force that energises the id is termed **libido**[5].
- The libido operates on the pleasure principle and seeks immediate gratification.

## Ego Defence Mechanisms

### Freud's Perspective on Anxiety

- Freud proposed that much of human behaviour reflects an attempt to deal with or escape from anxiety.
- The way the ego addresses anxiety significantly influences individual behaviour.
- Freud believed that individuals avoid anxiety mainly by developing **defence mechanisms**[6], which protect the ego from awareness of instinctual needs.
- A defence mechanism serves reduces anxiety by distorting reality.

5 **Libido** The sexual drive or desire that Freud believed is a fundamental motivating force in human behaviour.

6 **Defence Mechanisms** Psychological strategies employed by the ego to manage anxiety and protect the self from emotional pain or conflict.

- Some degree of defence against anxiety is considered normal and adaptive.
- However, excessive reliance on these mechanisms can lead to a distorted perception of reality.
- Individuals who rely heavily on these mechanisms may develop various forms of maladjustment.

### Key of Defence Mechanisms

(i) **Repression**

- Repression is regarded as the most important defence mechanism.
- In repression, anxiety-provoking thoughts or behaviours are entirely dismissed by the unconscious mind.
- When people repress a feeling or desire, they become completely unaware of that wish or desire.
- For instance, when a person says, 'I do not know why I did that', it indicates that some repressed feeling or desire is expressing itself.

(ii) **Projection**

- Projection occurs when individuals attribute their own traits or feelings to others.
- For example, someone with strong aggressive tendencies may perceive others as acting excessively towards them.

(iii) **Denial**

- Denial involves a total refusal to accept reality.
- An example of denial is someone suffering from HIV/AIDS who may entirely deny their illness.

(iv) **Reaction Formation**

- Reaction formation is a defence mechanism in which a person adopts behaviours that are opposite to their true feelings to guard against anxiety.
- A classic example is an individual with strong sexual urges who channels their energy into religious fervour.

(v) **Rationalisation**

- Rationalisation occurs when a person tries to make unreasonable feelings or behaviours appear reasonable and acceptable.
- For example, when a student performs poorly on an examination and buys a new set of pens, they may rationalise their behaviour by claiming, 'I will do much better with these pens'.

## Awareness of Defence Mechanisms

- Individuals who use defence mechanisms are often unaware that they are doing so.
- Each defence mechanism functions as a method for the ego to manage uncomfortable feelings produced by anxiety.

## Criticism of Freud's Theories

- Freud's ideas about defence mechanisms have faced scrutiny over time.
- For instance, his assertion that projection reduces anxiety and stress has not been supported by several studies.

**Stages of Personality Development**

| | Stage | Age Range | Key Features |
|---|---|---|---|
| 1. | Oral Stage | Birth to 18 months | Instincts focus on the mouth. |
| | | | The mouth is the primary pleasure-seeking center. |
| | | | Oral gratification is achieved through feeding, thumb sucking, biting and babbling. |
| | | | Basic feelings about the world are established during this stage. |
| | | | Difficulties in this stage may lead to an adult perception of the world as bitter. |
| 2. | Anal Stage | Ages 2 to 3 | Children learn to respond to societal demands. |
| | | | The primary demand from parents is control over bodily functions (urination and defecation). |
| | | | Pleasure is experienced fro bowel movements. |
| | | | This stage establishes conflict between the id and the ego and betwen childish pleasure and adult behaviour. |
| 3. | Phallic Stage | Age 4 to 5 | Focus shifts to the genitals. |
| | | | Children become aware of sex differences and parental relationships. |
| | | | Boys experience the Oedpus complex (love for mother, hostility toward father, fear of punishment). |
| | | | Resolution involves identifying with the father and modelling behaviour after him. |
| | | | Girls experience the Electra Complex (love for father, identification with mother after realising the improbability of marrying the father). |
| | | | Successful resolution leads to identification with the same-sex parent. |
| 4. | Latency Stage | Ages 7 to puberty | Period of physical growth with relatively inactive sexual urges. |
| | | | Energy is directed towards social and achievement-related activities. |
| 5. | Genital Stage | Puberty onwards | Attainment of maturity in psychosexual development. |
| | | | Previous sexuality, fears and repressed feelings are expressed again. |
| | | | Individuals learn to interact with the opposite sex in a socially and sexually mature manner. |
| | | | Excessive stress or indulgence during earlier stages may lead to fixation at a prior developmental stage. |

## Adjustment to Worldview

- Children adjust their perception of the world as they progress through developmental stages.
- Successful navigation of each stage is crucial for healthy personality development.

### Fixation

- Failure to resolve conflicts leads to fixation, where development becomes arrested.
- For example, unresolved issues during the phallic stage may result in hostility towards the same-sex parent and a skewed view of relationship.

### Regression

- Regression occurs when problems at any stage are unresolved.
- Individuals may revert to behaviours characteristic of an earlier, less mature developmental stage.
- This can manifest as childish or immature behaviour in response to stress or challenges.

## Post-Freudian Approaches

- Several theorists developed ideas after Freud, building on his foundations with new perspectives.
- These theorists, known as neo-analytic or post-Freudian, initially worked with Freud and then established unique psychoanalytic approaches.
- Neo-analytic theories differ from Freud's by placing less emphasis on sexual and aggressive drives of the id, focusing more on the ego's role in personality development.
- These theories highlight positive human qualities, such as creativity, competence and problem-solving abilities.
- Post-Freudian theories offer a comprehensive view of personality, considering both internal and external influences.

### Carl Jung: Aims and Aspirations

- Jung believed that human behaviour is influenced by aims and aspirations, not just sex and aggression, as Freud proposed.
- He developed analytical psychology, which emphasises that personality involves balancing competing internal forces and structures.
- Jung introduced the concept of a **collective unconscious**[7], which includes archetypes or universal symbols, shared across humanity.
- Archetypes, such as God or Mother Earth, represent primordial images inherited rather than learned individually. They appear in myths, dreams and arts of all mankind, reflecting shared human experiences.
- Jung emphasised that the self is an archetype that seeks unity and oneness, a goal of personal development.
- Achieving unity involves becoming aware of the wisdom within both the personal and collective unconscious.
- To achieve harmony, a person must integrate this unconscious wisdom into their conscious life, living in balance with their inner knowledge.

### Karen Horney: Optimism

- Horney, emphasised on growth-oriented perspective on human development, focusing on self-actualisation and positive psychological development.
- She notably challenged Freud's view of female inferiority, arguing both gender possesses unique qualities to be valued and that neither is superior.
- Horney argued that social and cultural influences, rather than biological determinants, play a more significant role in shaping personality, especially in women.
- According to Horney, psychological issues stem from disturbed interpersonal relationships during childhood, especially due to negative parental behaviour.
- She introduced the concept of basic anxiety, arising when a child feels insecure due to indifferent, inconsistent, or discouraging parenting, leading to basic hostility or resentment towards parents.
- Excessive parental dominance inconsistent approval can lead to feelings of isolation and helplessness in children, which may hinder healthy psychological growth.

7 **Collective Unconscious** A concept introduced by Carl Jung, referring to the shared memories and experiences of humanity that influence behaviour and personality.

## Alfred Adler: Lifestyle and Social Interest

- Adler's theory is known as Individual psychology, assumes that human behaviour is purposeful and goal-directed. Each individual possesses the capacity to choose and create their own path.
- Personal goals serve as the primary sources of motivation for individuals.
- Goals that provide a sense of security are key to overcome feelings of inadequacy.
- Adler believed that everyone experiences feelings of inadequacy and guilt, which he termed the **inferiority complex**[8], stemming from childhood experiences.
- Addressing and overcoming this inferiority complex is essential for achieving optimal personality development.

## Erich Fromm: The Human Concerns

- In contrast to Freud's biological orientation, Fromm developed his theory from a social perspective, viewing humans as fundamentally social beings.
- Fromm argued that psychological qualities, such as personal growth and the realisation of potential, arise from a desire for freedom and a striving for justice and truth.
- He believed that character traits or personality, develop based on experiences with others.
- According to Fromm, culture is influenced by the mode of existence within a given society.
- The dominant character traits of individuals in a society act as forces that shape both social processes and the culture itself.
- His work highlights the importance of positive qualities, such as tenderness and love, in the development of personality.

## Erik Erikson: Search for Identity

- Erikson's theory emphasises rational, conscious ego processes in personality development.
- In his view, development is a lifelong process, with ego identity occupying a central role.
- Erikson's concept of the identity crisis during adolescence has garnered considerable attention.
- He argues that young people must create a central perspective and a direction that provides a meaningful sense of unity and purpose.
- Psychodynamic theories face several major criticisms are as follows
  - (i) The theories are primarily based on case studies, lacking a rigorous scientific basis.
  - (ii) They utilise small and atypical individuals samples for making generalisations.
  - (iii) The concepts are poorly defined, making it challenging to subject them to scientific testing.
  - (iv) Freud used males as the prototype for all human personality development, neglecting female experiences and perspectives.

### Quick Test 3

1. What are the three levels of consciousness as proposed by Freud?
2. What are the three components of personality in Freud's theory?
3. Define defence mechanisms according to Freud.
4. List three types of ego defence mechanisms with examples.
5. What are Carl Jung's two key concepts in his theory of personality?
6. How did Karen Horney view the impact of basic anxiety on personality development?
7. What did Alfred Adler mean by striving for superiority in his theory?

---

8 **Inferiority Complex** A psychological condition stemming from feelings of inadequacy, which can affect behaviour and self-worth.

## Behavioural Approach

- This approach does not prioritise the internal dynamics of behaviour.
- The behaviourists emphasise data that are definable, observable and measurable focusing on learning stimulus-response connections and their reinforcement.
- They view personality as the response of an individual to the environment.
- They see development as a change in response characteristics, where a person learns new behaviours in response to new environments and stimuli.
- For most behaviourists, the structural unit of personality is the response. Each response is a behaviour emitted to satisfy a specific need.
- For example, all of us eat due to hunger, but we can be choosy about food.
- Children often dislike certain vegetables (e.g., spinach, pumpkin, gourds), but they gradually learn to eat them often in anticipation of reinforcement from parents.
- Over time, they may continue to eat vegetables not only because their parents approve but also because they acquire a taste for them.
- Thus, the core tendency that organises behaviour is the reduction of biological or social needs that energise behaviour.
- The theories of classical conditioning (Pavlov), instrumental conditioning (Skinner) and observational learning (Bandura) are well-known in this context, each offering different perspective on learning and behaviour maintenance.
- The principles of these theories have been widely applied in developing personality theories. For example, observational learning theory considers thought processes crucial in learning, a concept that is largely absent in classical or instrumental conditioning theories.
- Observational learning theory also emphasises social learning (based on observation and imitation of others) and self-regulation, aspects that are often overlooked in other theories.

## Cultural Approach

- This approach attempts to understand personality in relation to the features of the ecological and cultural environment.
- It proposes that a group's economic maintenance system plays a vital role in the origin of cultural and behavioural variations.
- The climatic conditions, the terrain and food availability (flora and fauna) determine not only people's economic activities but also their settlement patterns, social structures, division of labour and other features such as childrearing practices. Taken together, these elements constitute a child's overall learning environment.
- People's skills, abilities, behavioural styles and value priorities are closely linked to these features.
- Rituals, ceremonies, religious practices, arts, recreational activities, games and play are ways in which personality is projected in a culture.
- People develop various personality (behavioural) qualities to adapt to the ecological and cultural features of a group's life.
- Thus, the cultural approach considers personality as an adaptation of individuals or groups to the demands of their ecology and culture.
- To illustrate these aspects, consider the example of the Birhor, a tribal group from Jharkhand.
- The Birhor people mostly lead a nomadic life, requiring constant movement in small bands from one forest to another in search of games and other forest products.
- In the Birhor society, children have great freedom to move into forests from an early age learning hunting and gathering skills.

- Their child socialisation practices aim to make children independent (able to do many things without help from elders), autonomous (capable of making decisions for themselves) and achievement-oriented (willing to accept risks and challenges involved in hunting) from an early age.
- In contrast, in agricultural societies, children are socialized to be obedient to elders, nurturant to youngsters and responsible for their duties.
- These behavioural qualities enhance functionality in agricultural societies and become dominant features of personality.
- In these societies, independence, autonomy, and achievement are less emphasised compared to the values observed in hunting-gathering societies.
- Due to the different economic pursuits and cultural demands, children in hunting-gathering and agricultural societies develop and display different personality patterns.

## Humanistic Approach

- The humanistic theories emerged mainly in response to Freud's theory.
- Notable contributors to the development of the humanistic perspective on personality include Carl Rogers and Abraham Maslow.
- This approach emphasises the positive aspects of human nature and the potential for personal growth.

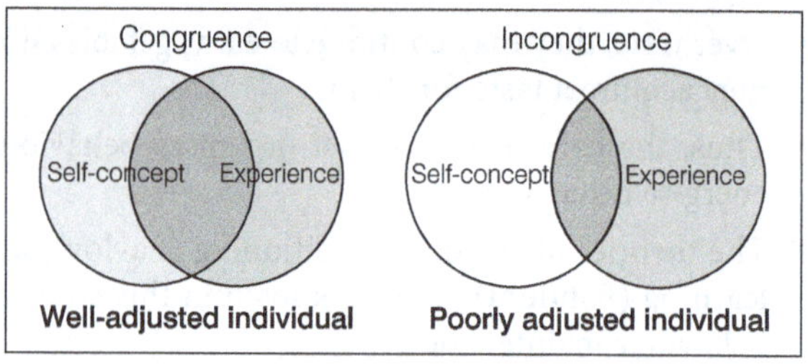


▲ *Pattern of Adjustment and Self-concept*

### Carl Rogers' Theory

- Rogers' key idea is the concept of a fully functioning person.
- He believes that fulfilment is the motivating force for personality development.
- People strive to express their capabilities, potentials and talents to the fullest.
- There is an inborn tendency among individuals that directs them to actualise their inherited nature.
- Rogers made two basic assumptions about human behaviour
  - (i) Behaviour is goal-directed and worthwhile.
  - (ii) People, who are innately good, will almost always choose adaptive, self-actualising behaviour.
- Rogers' theory developed from his experiences listening to patients in his clinic.
- He noted that the self is a crucial element in their experiences.
- Therefore, his theory is structured around the concept of self assuming individuals are constantly engaged in of actualising their true self.
- Each person has an **ideal self**[9], which is the self that they aspire to be.
- When there is a correspondence between the real self and ideal self, a person is generally happy.
- Discrepancy between the real self and ideal self often leads to unhappiness and dissatisfaction.
- Rogers' basic principle posits that individuals have a tendency to maximise their self-concept through self-actualisation.
- This process allows the self to grow, expand and become more social.
- Rogers views personality development as a continuous process of evaluating oneself and mastering self-actualisation.
- He recognises the role of social influences in developing the self-concept.

9 **Ideal Self** The concept of the person one aspires to become, often influencing self-esteem and personal development.

- When social conditions are positive, both self-concept and self-esteem are high.
- Conversely, when conditions are negative, they are low.
- People with high self-concept and self-esteem are generally flexible and open to new experiences, enabling them to continue growing and self-actualising.
- This requires creating an atmosphere of unconditional positive regard to enhance people's self-concept.
- The **client-centred therapy**[10] that Rogers developed primarily aims to create this condition.

### Abraham Maslow's Theory

- Maslow provided a detailed account of psychologically healthy people in terms of their attainment of self-actualisation, a state where individuals reach their fullest potential.
- He had an optimistic and positive view of humanity, believing in their potential for love, joy and creativity.
- According to Maslow, human beings are considered free to shape their lives and to self-actualise.
- This is achieved by analysing the motivations that govern human life.
- Biological, security and belongingness needs (often referred to as survival needs) are commonly found among both animals and humans.
- An individual focused solely on satisfying these needs is reduced to the level of animals.
- The real journey of human life commences with the pursuit of self-esteem and self-actualisation.
- The humanistic approach underscores the significance of the positive aspects of life, emphasising personal growth and fulfillment.

### Quick Test 4

1. What is the primary focus of the behavioural approach to personality?
2. How does classical conditioning differ from observational learning in shaping behaviour?
3. What does the cultural approach emphasise regarding personality development?
4. Who are the Birhor, and how is their lifestyle an example of the cultural approach?
5. What is Carl Rogers' concept of the 'fully functioning person'?
6. How does Carl Rogers' theory describe the relationship between the real self and the ideal self?

## 2.5 Assessment of Personality

- A formal effort aimed at understanding an individual's personality is termed personality assessment.
- Assessment refers to the procedures used to evaluate or differentiate people based on specific characteristics.
- The primary goal of assessment is to understand and predict behaviour accurately, it focuses on what a person generally does or how they behave, in a specific situation.
- Assessment also serves purposes like diagnosis, training, placement, counselling and various other applications.
- Common methods for assessing personality include

  (i) Psychometric Tests
  (ii) Self-Report Measures
  (iii) **Projective Techniques**[11]
  (iv) Behavioural Analysis

10 **Client-centred Therapy** A therapeutic approach developed by Carl Rogers, emphasising the importance of a supportive environment for client self-discovery.

11 **Projective Techniques** Assessment methods that reveal underlying thoughts and feelings by analysing responses to ambiguous stimuli.

## Self-Report Measures

- The concept of self-report measures was introduced by Allport. This method focuses on individuals providing their own perspectives and insights.
- These measures are generally structured and often based on established theories.
- They require subjects to respond verbally, utilising a rating scale to quantify their feelings and thoughts.
- The responses are accepted at their face value and are scored in quantitative terms, which facilitates a numerical evaluation of personality traits.
- This scoring allows for a standardised way to compare results against established norms for the specific test.
- The interpretation of the scored responses is based on the norms developed for each specific self-report measure helping to understand personality traits systematically.
- There are several well-known self-report measures commonly used in psychological assessments.
- These measures are instrumental in providing insights into personality characteristics and help in various applications within psychology.

### The Minnesota Multiphasic Personality Inventory (MMPI)

- The Minnesota Multiphasic Personality Inventory (MMPI) is a widely used psychological test for assessing personality.
- This test was developed by Hathaway and McKinley primarily as a diagnostic tool for psychiatric evaluation.
- Over time, it has proven effective in identifying various forms of psychopathology.
- The revised version of the MMPI is known as MMPI-2, which includes updates to enhance its reliability and validity.
- The MMPI consists of 567 statements that respondents must evaluate judging each statement as either 'true' or 'false' for themselves.
- The MMPI is organised into 10 subscales, to assess specific psychological conditions

  (i) Hypochondriasis (ii) Depression
  (iii) Hysteria (iv) Psychopathic Deviate
  (v) Masculinity-Femininity (vi) Paranoia
  (vii) Psychasthenia (viii) Schizophrenia
  (ix) Mania (x) Social Introversion
- In India, the Jodhpur Multiphasic Personality Inventory (JMPI) has been developed by Mallick and Joshi.
- The JMPI was created based on the MMPI framework to address the specific needs of the Indian population.

### Eysenck Personality Questionnaire (EPQ)

- The Eysenck Personality Questionnaire (EPQ) was developed by Hans Eysenck.
- Initially, the test assessed two dimensions of personality, which are

  (i) **Introverted-Extraverted** This dimension evaluates where an individual falls on the introversion-extraversion spectrum.

  (ii) **Emotionally Stable** This dimension assesses a person's emotional stability.
- These two dimensions are characterised by 32 distinct personality traits that help to describe an individual's personality profile.

- Later on, Eysenck added a third dimension known as psychoticism. This dimension is linked to psychopathology and indicates specific personality characteristics.
- Psychoticism represents a lack of feeling for others, a tough manner of interacting with people, and a tendency to defy social conventions. Individuals scoring high in this dimension are often seen as hostile, egocentric and anti-social.
- The EPQ is widely used in various psychological assessments and research settings to evaluate personality traits and psychological characteristics.

## Sixteen Personality Factor Questionnaire (16 PF)

- The Sixteen Personality Factor Questionnaire (16 PF) was developed by Cattell, a prominent psychologist.
- Based on extensive research, Cattell identified a large set of personality descriptors. These descriptors underwent factor analysis, a statistical technique, to uncover the basic personality structure.
- The test presents subjects with declarative statements. Participants respond to specific situations by selecting from a set of given alternatives that best represent their feelings or behaviours.
- The 16 PF is designed for use with both high school level students and adults, making it versatile in its application across different age groups.
- The 16 PF has proven to be extremely beneficial in carrer guidance, vocational exploration and occupational testing.
- In addition to the 16 PF, there are several other self-report measures that assess specific dimensions of personality. Examples of these dimensions include authoritarianism, locus of control and optimism. As you progress in your studies of psychology, you will encounter more assessments that evaluate these traits.
- Self-report measures, including the 16 PF, have several limitations that may affect their accuracy, such as
    (i) **Social Desirability** This is the tendency of respondents to answer in a manner that is viewed favourably by others, leading to biased results.
    (ii) **Acquiescence** This refers to the tendency to agree with questions, often by responding 'yes', regardless of the content. Such tendencies can compromise the reliability of personality assessments.
- It is crucial to approach psychological testing with caution. Understanding personality and conducting assessments necessitate great skill and training.
- Unless you have developed these skills to an optimal level and are supervised by an expert, you should refrain from testing and interpreting the personalities of friends or individuals who are not studying psychology.

# Projective Techniques

- The personality assessment techniques described earlier are known as direct techniques. These techniques rely on information that is directly obtained from individuals who are aware that their personality is being assessed.
- In situations involving direct assessment, individuals often become self-conscious and hesitate in sharing their private feelings, thoughts and motivations.
- When individuals do share their feelings, they often do so in a socially desirable manner.
- According to psychoanalytic theory, much of human behaviour is driven by unconscious motives. Direct methods of personality assessment cannot uncover these unconscious aspects, leading to an incomplete understanding of an individual's personality.
- To address the limitations of direct methods, indirect methods of assessment are used. Projective techniques are developed to assess unconscious motives and feelings.

- Projective techniques are based on less structured or unstructured stimuli will enable individuals to express their inner thoughts and feelings more freely.
- A range of projective techniques has been developed, employing different kinds of stimulus materials and situations. These techniques include
    - Association tasks (for example, word associations, inkblots).
    - Story Writing prompts based on pictures.
    - Sentence Completion exercises.
    - Drawing tasks to express feelings.
    - Choice of stimuli from a larger set of options.
- While the nature of stimuli and responses can vary greatly among projective techniques, they generally share several common features
    (i) **Unstructured Stimuli** The stimuli are unstructured and poorly defined.
    (ii) **Lack of Awareness** The person being assessed is typically not informed about the purpose of the assessment or the methods of scoring and interpretation.
    (iii) **No Correct Responses** Individuals are told that there are no correct or incorrect responses, promoting honest expression.
    (iv) **Significant Insights** Each response is considered to reveal a significant aspect of the individual's personality.
    (v) **Subjective Interpretation** Scoring and interpretation are often subjective, depending on the expert's analysis.
- Projective techniques differ from psychometric tests in several ways. They cannot be scored in an objective manner, requiring instead qualitative analyses that necessitate rigorous training.
- The following pages will provide brief descriptions of some well-known projective techniques, expanding on their use and application in personality assessment.

## The Rorschach Inkblot Test

- The Rorschach Inkblot Test was developed by Hermann Rorschach, consists of 10 inkblots
    - Five inkblots are in black and white.
    - Two inkblots feature some red ink.
    - The remaining three are in pastel colours.
- The blots are symmetrical and printed on a white cardboard that measures approximately '7 × 10' inches.
- They were originally created by dropping ink onto a piece of paper and then folding the paper in half, which is why it is called the Inkblot test.
- The test is administered individually and consists of two phases
    (i) **Performance Proper** In this phase, subjects are shown the inkblot cards and are asked to describe what they see in each one.
    (ii) **Inquiry** In this phase, a detailed report of the responses is prepared by asking the subject to explain where, how and on what basis a particular response was made.
- Fine judgement is essential to place the subject's responses in a meaningful context, allowing for more accurate interpretation.
- The use and interpretation of the Rorschach Test require extensive training to ensure valid assessments.
- Additionally, computer techniques have been developed for the analysis of data obtained from the test, enhancing the assessment process.

## The Thematic Apperception Test (TAT)

- The Thematic Apperception Test was developed by Morgan and Murray.
- This test is more structured than the Inkblot test.
- The test consists of 30 black and white picture cards and one blank card. Each picture card depicts one or more people in a variety of situations. Each picture is printed on a separate card.
- Some cards are specifically designed for adult males or females, while others are intended for boys or girls. Additionally, certain cards can be used in various combinations.
- While twenty cards are typically appropriate for a subject, a lesser number of cards (even as few as five) have also been successfully used.
- The cards are presented one at a time to the subject.
- The subject is asked to tell a story describing the situation presented in the picture. The narrative should include what led up to the situation, what is happening at the moment, what will happen in the future, and what the characters are feeling and thinking.
- A standard procedure is available for scoring TAT responses, ensuring consistency in assessment.
- The test has been modified for use with both children and the aged. Additionally, Uma Chaudhury's Indian adaptation of TAT is also available for cultural relevance.

## Rosenzweig's Picture-Frustration Study (P-F Study)

- Rosenzweig's Picture-Frustration Study (P-F Study) was developed by Rosenzweig to assess how people express aggression in frustrating situations.
- The test uses cartoon-like pictures to depict situations where one person frustrates another or highlights a frustrating condition.
- The subject is asked to describe what the frustrated person will respond to the situation.
- Analysis of the responses focuses on the type and direction of aggression expressed by the subject.
- The test examines whether the subject's focus is on
  - (i) The frustrating object
  - (ii) The protection of the frustrated person
  - (iii) A constructive solution to the problem
- The direction of aggression may be directed towards the environment, directed inward towards oneself or may be suppressed to avoid the situation.
- The test has been adapted by Pareek for use with the Indian population, ensuring cultural relevance in its application.

## Sentence Completion Test

- The Sentence Completion Test utilises a series of incomplete sentences.
- The beginning part of each sentence is presented and the subject is required to provide an ending for the sentence.
- It is believed that the types of endings chosen by subjects reflect their attitudes, motivations and conflicts, providing insight to un-conscious motivations.
- Sample items from a Sentence Completion Test may include
  - (i) My father ..................... .
  - (ii) My greatest fear is ..................... .
  - (iii) The best thing about my mother is ..................... .
  - (iv) I am proud of ..................... .

### Draw-a-Person Test

- The Draw-a-Person Test is a simple assessment in which the subject is asked to draw a person on a sheet of paper, using pencil and eraser to facilitate the drawing process.
- Upon completing the drawing, the subject is generally asked to draw the figure of a person of the opposite sex and to create a story about the drawn person, imagining them as a character in a novel or play.
- Interpretations of the drawing may include various observations
  - (i) Omission of facial features may suggest that the person tries to evade a highly conflict-ridden inter-personal relationship.
  - (ii) Graphic emphasis on the neck could indicate a lack of control over impulses.
  - (iii) A disproportionately large head may suggest organic brain disease or a preoccupation with headaches.
- The analysis of personality through projective techniques helps to understand unconscious motives, deep-rooted conflicts and emotional complexes of an individual.
- However, interpreting responses requires sophisticated skills and specialised training.
- There are also issues related to the reliability of scoring and the validity of interpretations.
- Despite these challenges, practitioners find these techniques to be quite useful.

#### Quick Test 5

1. What is the main aim of personality assessment?
2. Who introduced the self-report measures in personality assessment?
3. What is the MMPI used for in psychology?
4. How many primary factors does the 16 PF (Sixteen Personality Factor) Questionnaire assess?
5. What are projective techniques primarily designed to explore?
6. Who developed the Rorschach Inkblot Test?
7. What is the main purpose of the Thematic Apperception Test (TAT)?

## Behavioural Analysis

- Behavioural analysis focuses on a person's behaviour across various situations, to gain insights into their personality.
- The observation of behaviour serves as the foundation for this analysis.
- An observer's report may include data obtained from multiple sources, such as, interviews, observation, ratings, nominations, situational tests.
- Each procedure will be examined in detail to understand its contribution to behavioural analysis.

### Interview

- Interview is a commonly used method for assessing personality, involving direct conversation with the individual being evaluated.
- Specific questions are asked to gather information about the person's personality traits and characteristics.
- Interviews can be categorised as structured or unstructured based on the assessment's purpose or goals.
- In unstructured interviews, the interviewer aims to develop an impression of the person by asking a variety of questions.
- The way a person presents themselves and responds to questions has the potential to reveal significant aspects of their personality.
- On the other hand, structured interviews focus on very specific questions and adhere to a set procedure.
- This structured approach is often employed to facilitate objective comparisons among individuals being interviewed.
- The use of rating scales can further enhance the objectivity of evaluations conducted during interviews.

## Observation

- Behavioural observation is a widely used method for assessing personality that relies on the systematic observation of individuals' behaviours.
- While everyone forms impressions of others personalities, using observation for personality assessment requires specialised training.
- This method cannot be effectively executed by untrained individuals; it demands careful training of the observer to ensure accurate assessments.
- A detailed guideline for the analysis of behaviours is essential for accurately evaluating a person's personality.
- For instance, a clinical psychologist might observe a client's interactions with family members and home visitors to gather insights about the client's personality.
- Through meticulously designed observations, the psychologist can obtain valuable information regarding the client's personality traits and interpersonal dynamics.

### Limitations of Interview and Observation Methods

- The professional training required for accurate date collection is often demanding and time-consuming.
- The maturity of the psychologist is crucial for obtaining valid data.
- The mere presence of the observer can potentially skew the results, as the observer's status as a stranger may influence the behaviour of the person being observed, leading to less reliable data.

## Behavioural Ratings

- Behavioural ratings are commonly used for the assessment of personality in both educational and industrial settings.
- These ratings are typically gathered from individuals who know the assessee well and have interacted with them over time.
- Raters aim to categorise individuals based on their behavioural qualities.
- These ratings may consist of different numerical values or descriptive terms.
- However, it has been observed that using numbers or general descriptive adjectives in rating scales often creates confusion for the rater.
- To utilise ratings effectively, it is essential to clearly define the traits in terms of well-stated behavioural anchors.

### Limitations of Rating Method

- Despite their utility, the method of rating has several significant limitations
  - (i) Raters frequently exhibit certain biases that can skew their judgements of various traits. For example, many raters are significantly influenced by a single positive or negative trait, which can unduly affect their overall evaluation of a person; this tendency is referred to as the halo effect.
  - (ii) Additionally, raters may show a tendency to position individuals either in the middle of the scale, a phenomenon known as Middle category bias or in extreme positions, called Extreme response bias, by avoiding middle categories.
- These biases can be mitigated by providing raters with appropriate training or by developing rating scales that minimise the likelihood of response bias.

## Nomination

- Nomination is a common method for obtaining peer assessment.
- This technique is particularly effective when used with individuals who have had long-term interactions and understand each other well.
- In the nomination process, participants select one or more individuals from the group they prefer to work, study, play or engage in other activities.
- Participants may also be prompted to specify the reasons behind their selections.
- The nominations received can be analysed to gain insights into the personality and behavioural qualities of the individuals involved, while this technique is highly dependable, it may be influenced by personal biases.

## Situational Tests

- A variety of situational tests have been developed for assessing personality.
- The most commonly utilised test of this type is the situational stress test, which provides insight how a person behaves in stressful situations.
- During the test, the individual is required to perform a specific task alongside others instructed to be non-cooperative and interfering.
- The assessment involves a form of role playing, where the person is assigned a role for observation.
- A verbal report is also gathered about what the individual was instructed to do during the test.
- The situational context may either be a realistic scenario or one created through a video presentation.

### Quick Test 6

1. What is the primary focus of behavioural analysis in personality assessment?
2. How are interviews categorised in personality assessment?
3. Why is behavioural observation considered a sophisticated procedure?
4. What are behavioural ratings typically used for?
5. What is the halo effect in behavioural ratings?
6. What is the nomination method used for in personality assessment?
7. What is the purpose of situational stress tests?

# NCERT Folder

**1. What is self? How does the Indian notion of self differ from the Western notion?**

**Ans.** Self refers to the totality of an individual's conscious experiences, ideas, thoughts and feelings with regard to herself or himself.

Difference between Indian notion and Western notion of self are

| Indian Notion of Self | Western Notion of Self |
|---|---|
| The Indian view of self is characterised by the shifting nature of the boundary between self and the other. | In the Western view, the boundary between self and the other appears to be relatively fixed. |
| The Indian view does not make clear dichotomies. | The Western view seems to hold clear dichotomies between self and other, man and nature, subjective and objective. |
| In the Indian culture, the self is generally not separated from one's own group; rather both remain in a state of harmonious co-existence. | In the Western culture, the self and the group exist as two different entities with clearly defined boundaries i.e. individual members of the group maintain their individuality. |
| In India, culture is characterised as collectivistic. | Many Western cultures are characterised as individualistic. |

**2. What is meant by delay of gratification? Why is it considered important for adult development?**

**Ans.** Learning to delay or defer, the gratification of needs is called Self-control. As human beings, we can control our behaviour the way we want. We often decide to delay or defer the satisfaction of certain needs. Delay of gratification also known as self-control refers to postponing immediate pleasures or desires in favour of long-term rewards.

It is considered important for adult development because any situations of life require resistance to situational pressures and control over ourselves. Human beings can control their behaviour the way they want which is possible through what is commonly known as 'Will power'.

Delay or defer the satisfaction of certain needs or practicing self-control play a key role in the fulfillment of long-term goals.

Indian cultural tradition provides effective mechanisms (for example, fasting in vrata or roza and non-attachment with worldly things) for developing self-control.

A number of psychological techniques of self-control have been suggested which are

- **Observation of own behaviour** This provides us with necessary information that may be used to change, modify or strengthen certain aspects of self.
- **Self-instruction** It is another important technique. We often instruct ourselves to do something and behave in the way we want to. Such instructions are quite effective in self-regulation.
- **Self-reinforcement** It involves rewarding behaviours that have pleasant outcomes. For example, you may go to see a movie with friends, if you have done well in an examination. These techniques have been tried out and found quite effective with respect to self-regulation and self-control.

**3. How do you define personality? What are the main approaches to the study of personality?**

**Ans.** Personality generally refers to the physical or external appearance of an individual. In psychological terms, personality refers to our characteristic ways of responding to individuals and situations.

Personality refers to psycho-physical characteristics of a person that are relatively stable across situations and over time and make her or him unique. It also defines our existence and the ways in which our experiences are organised and show up in our behaviour. Several theories have been developed to study personality.

Main approaches to the study of personality are

- The type approach
- The trait approach
- The interactional approach
- Psychodynamic approach
- Post Freudian approach
- Behavioural approach
- Cultural approach
- Humanistic approach

**4. What is trait approach to personality? How does it differ from type approach?**

**Ans.** **Trait Approach** It focuses on the specific psychological attributes along which individuals tend to differ in consistent and stable ways.

These theories are mainly concerned with the description or characterisation of basic components of personality. Trait approach is very similar to our common experience in everyday life. It attempts to identify primary characteristics of people. A trait is considered as a relatively enduring attribute or quality on which one individual differs from another.

They include a range of possible behaviours that are activated according to the demands of the situation such as

- Traits are relatively stable over time.
- They are generally consistent across situations.

- Their strengths and combinations vary across individuals leading to individual differences in personality.

**Difference between Type and Trait Approach**

- The type approach attempts to comprehend human personality by examining certain broad patterns in the observed behavioural characteristics of individuals, while the trait approach focuses on the specific psychological attributes along which individuals tend to differ in consistent and stable ways.
- Each behavioural pattern of type approach refers to one type in which individuals are placed in terms of the similarity of their behavioural characteristics with that pattern, while in trait approach it refers to the degree of presence or absence of the concerned behavioural.

**5. How does Freud explain the structure of personality?**

**Ans.** According to Freud's theory, personality consists of three primary structural elements i.e. id, ego and superego.

(i) **Id** It is the source of a person's instinctual energy. It is energised by two instinctual forces called Life instinct and Death instinct. The instinctual life force that energises the id is called Libido. It deals with immediate gratification of primitive needs, sexual desires and aggressive impulses. It works on the pleasure principle, which assumes that people seek pleasure and try to avoid pain.

Freud considered much of a person's instinctual energy to be sexual and the rest as aggressive. Id does not care for moral values, society or other individuals.

(ii) **Ego** It grows out of id and seeks to satisfy an individual's instinctual needs in accordance with reality. It works by the reality principle and often directs the id towards more appropriate ways of behaving. The id is demanding, unrealistic and works according to pleasure principle while the ego is patient, reasonable and works by the reality principle.

(iii) **Superego** The supergo internalises moral standards and societal values, guiding and ego and id toward ethical behaviour. It serves as the conscience, enforcing moral behaviour and helping the individual conform to social norms.

**6. How would Horney's explanation of depression be different from that of Alfred Adler?**

**Ans.** Karen Horney and Alfred Adler both gave their theories for psychological disorders.

- Horney adopted a more optimistic view of human life with emphasis on human growth and self-actualisation. Whereas Adler's theory known as Individual psychology give more emphasis on human behaviour.
- According to Horney, psychological disorders were caused by disturbed interpersonal relationship during childhood. When parents' behaviour toward a child is indifferent, discouraging and erratic, the child feels insecure and a feeling called Basic anxiety results.
- Deep resentment towards parents or basic hostility occurs due to this anxiety. By showing excessive dominance or indifference or by providing too much or too little approval, parents can generate among children feelings of isolation and helplessness which interfere with their healthy development.
- According to Adler, our personal goals are the sources of our motivation. The goals that provide us with security and help us in overcoming the feelings of inadequacy are important in our personality development. In Adler's view, every individual suffers from the feelings of inadequacy and guilt i.e. inferiority complex, which arise from childhood. Overcoming this complex is essential for optimal personality development.

**7. What is the main proposition of humanistic approach to personality? What did Maslow mean by self-actualisation?**

**Ans.** **Humanistic Approach** It emphasises the significance of positive aspects of life. Carl Rogers and Abraham Maslow have particularly contributed to the development of humanistic perspective on personality.

Humanistic theories emphasise personal responsibility and innovate tendencies toward personal growth. In this theory, Roger proposed the idea of a fully functioning person. He believes that fulfillment is the motivating force for personality development.

People try to express their capabilities, potentials and talents to the fullest extent possible. There is an inborn tendency among persons that directs them to actualise their inherited nature.

**Maslow's Views about Self-actualisation** Maslow (Hierarchy of need) has given a detailed account of psychologically healthy people in terms of their attainment of self-actualisation, a state in which people have reached their own fullest potential.

Maslow had an optimistic and positive view of man who has the potentialities for love, joy and to do creative work. Human beings are considered free to shape their lives and to self-actualise. Self-actualisation becomes possible by analysing the motivations that govern our life.

We know that biological, security and belongingness needs (called survival needs) are commonly found among animals and human beings. Thus, an individual's sole concern with the satisfaction of these needs reduces her/him to the level of animals. The real journey of human life begins with the pursuit of self-esteem and self-actualisation needs.

**8. Discuss the main observational methods used in personality assessment. What problems do we face in using these methods?**

**Ans.** Observation is a method which is very commonly used for the assessment of personality. It requires careful training of the observer and a fairly detailed guideline about analysis of behaviours in order to assess the personality of a given person.

The main observational methods used in personality assessment are

(i) **Behaviourial Ratings** Behaviourial ratings are frequently used for assessment of personality in educational and industrial settings. Behavioural ratings are generally taken from people who know the assessee intimately and have interacted with her/him over a period of time or have had a chance to observe her/him.

They attempt to put individuals into certain categories in terms of their behavioural qualities. The categories may involve different numbers or descriptive terms. Use of numbers or general descriptive adjectives in rating scales always create confusion for the rater.

In order to use ratings effectively, the traits should be clearly defined in terms of carefully stated behavioural anchors.

The method of rating suffers from the following major limitations

Raters often show biases when evaluating traits. For example, most of us are greatly influenced by a single favourable or unfavourable trait. This often forms the basis of a rater's overall judgement of a person. This tendency is known as the Halo effect.

Raters have a tendency to place individuals either in the middle of the scale (called middle category bias) by avoiding extreme positions or in the extreme positions (called extreme response bias) by avoiding middle categories on the scale.

(ii) **Nomination** This method is often used in obtaining peer assessment. It can be used with persons who have been in long-term interaction and who know each other very well.

In using nomination, each person is asked to choose one or more persons of the group with whom he/she would like to work, study, play or participate in any other activity. The person may also be asked to specify the reason for his/her choices.

The choices or nominations received then may be analysed to understand the personality and behavioural qualities of the person. This technique has been found to be highly dependable, although it may also be affected by personal biases.

(iii) **Situational Tests** A variety of situational tests have been devised for the assessment of personality. The most commonly used test of this kind is the situational stress test. It provides us information about how a person behaves under stressful situations.

The test requires a person to perform a given task with other persons who are instructed to be non-cooperative and interfering. The test involves a kind of role playing. The person is instructed to play a role for which he/she is observed. A verbal report is also obtained on what he/she was asked to do. The situation may be realistic one or it may be created through a video play.

**9. What is meant by structured personality tests? Which are the two most widely used structured personality tests?**

**Ans.** Self-report measures are fairly structured personality test. This was used by Allport who suggested that the best method to assess a person is by asking him/her about himself/herself. This led to the use of self-report measures.

These tests are typically based on theory, that require subjects to give verbal responses using some kind of rating scale. The method requires the subject to objectively report his/her own feelings with respect to various items. The responses are accepted at their face value. They are scored in quantitative terms and interpreted on the basis of norms developed for the test.

**Types of Structured Personality Test**

(i) **The Minnesota Multi-phasic Personality Inventory** (MMPI) Hathaway and McKinley developed this test as a helping tool for psychiatric diagnosis, but the test has been found very effective in identifying varieties of psychopathology. It was later revised as MMPI-2 and consists of 567 statements.

The test is divided into 10 subscales, which seek to diagnose hypochondriasis, depression, hysteria, psychopathic deviate, masculinity-femininity, paranoia, psychasthenia, schizophrenia, mania and social introversion. In India, Mallick and Joshi have developed the Jodhpur Multi-phasic Personality Inventory (JMPI) along the lines of MMPI.

(ii) **Eysenck Personality Questionnaire** (EPQ) This test developed by Eysenck, initially assessed two personality, dimension called Introverted-extroverted and emotionally stable unstable. These dimensions are characterised by 32 personality traits.

Later on, Eysenck added a third dimension, called Psychoticism. It is linked to psychopathology that represents a lack of feeling for others, a tough manner of interacting with people and a tendency to defy social conventions.

**10. Explain how projective techniques assess personality. Which projective tests of personality are widely used by psychologists?** CBSE 2020

**Ans.** Projective techniques were developed to assess unconscious motives and feelings. These techniques one based on the assumption that a less stuctured or unstructured stimulus or situation will allow the individual to project his/her feelings, desires and needs onto situation. The main projective tests of personality are

(i) The Thematic Apperception Test (TAT).

(ii) Rosenzweig's Picture-Frustration Study (P-F Study).

(iii) Sentence Completion Test

(iv) Draw a Person Test

**11. Arihant wants to become a singer even though he belongs to a family of doctors. Though his family members claim to love him but strongly dis-approve his choice of career. Using Carl Rogers' terminology, describe the attitudes shown by Arihant's family.**

**Ans.** This story is related to the Rogers' idea of fully functioning person. According to him, fulfillment is the motivating force for personality development.

People try to express their capabilities, potentials and talents to the fullest extent possible. There is an inborn tendency among persons that directs them to actualise their inherited nature.

Rogers makes two basic assumptions about human behaviour

(i) Behaviour is goal-directed and worthwhile.

(ii) People (who are innately good) will almost always choose adaptive and self-actualising behaviour.

Rogers' basic principle is that people have a tendency to maximise self-concept through self-actualisation. In this process, the self grows, expands and becomes more social.

Rogers views personality development as a continuous process. It involves learning to evaluate oneself and mastering the process of self-actualisation. He recognises the role of social influences in the development of self-concept. When social conditions are positive, the self-concept and self-esteem are high.

In contrast, when the conditions are negative, the self-concept and self-esteem are low.

People with high self-concept and self-esteem are generally flexible and open to new experiences, so that they can continue to grow and self-actualise. This situation warrants that an atmosphere of unconditional positive regard must be created in order to ensure enhancement of people's self-concept.

The client-centred therapy that Rogers developed basically attempts to create this condition.

Thus, Arihant's family will disapprove his choice of career, as they want him to be a doctor to satisfy the self-concept. Arihant's family will want him to pursue the career of their inherited nature and will become stubborn about it, even though they love him. They will try their best to stop him from choosing the career of singer which is not in their inheritance.

# Exam Pattern Questions

## Objective Type Questions

### Multiple Choice Questions (MCQs)

**1.** **The ........... self emerges in relation with others and emphasises such aspects of life as co-operation, unity, affiliation, sacrifice, support or sharing.**

(a) personal (b) individual (c) social (d) positive

**2.** **.......... seeks to satisfy an individual's instinctual needs in accordance with reality.**

(a) Id (b) Ego (c) Superego (d) Libido

**3.** **Enhancement of people's self-concept is possible by creating an atmosphere of ......... .** CBSE Term I 2021

(a) conditional positive regard
(b) unconditional positive regard
(c) unconditional and biased regard
(d) identity crisis

**4.** **......... personality seem to possess low motivation, are patient and feel they have a lot of time and little work.**

(a) Type–A (b) Type–B (c) Type–C (d) Type–D

**5.** **In .........., a person defends against anxiety by adopting behaviours opposite to his/her true feelings.** CBSE Term I 2021

(a) reaction formation (b) rationalisation
(c) repression (d) regression

**6.** **The self that values family and social relationships is referred to as ......... .** CBSE 2023

I. Personal II. Social
III. Familial IV. Relational

Codes

(a) I and III (b) II and III (c) III and IV (d) I and IV

**7.** **A ...... is considered as a relatively enduring attribute or quality on which one individual differs from another.**

(a) typology (b) personality (c) trait (d) persona

**8.** **Hippocrates proposed a typology of personality based on ......... .** CBSE SQP Term I 2021

(a) trigunas
(b) humour
(c) tridosha
(d) body build and temperament

**9.** **Which of the following lists presents Freud's psychosexual stages in the order in which they occur?** CBSE SQP Term I 2021

(a) Anal, oral, genital, phallic and latency
(b) Genital, latency, anal, oral and phallic
(c) Oral, anal, phallic, latency and genital
(d) Oral, anal, latency, phallic and genital

**10.** **Dismissing anxiety provoking behaviours or thoughts from un-conscious is known as**

(a) projection (b) rationalisation
(c) repression (d) denial

**11.** **Carl Jung developed theory of**

(a) individual psychology (b) analytical psychology
(c) social psychology (d) psycho-analytic psychology

**12.** **A researcher is conducting a survey to assess the personality traits of participants. One of the items in the survey asks, "I always help others when they are in need." Which of following biases is most likely to affect the response to this item?** CBSE 2025

(a) Non-rsponse bias (b) Acquiescence
(c) Random responding (d) Social desirability

**13.** **Christopher's personality is being assessed by a psychologist. Which of the following is/are True about assessment of personality?** CBSE Term I 2021

I. It is an informal effort aimed at understanding his personality.
II. The goal of assessment is to understand and predict his behaviour with minimum error and maximum accuracy.
III. While assessing Christopher, the psychologist tries to study what he generally does or how he behaves, in a given situation.
IV. His assessment can also be useful for diagnosis, training, placement, counselling and other purposes.

Codes

(a) I, II and IV (b) Only II
(c) II, III and IV (d) I, II and III

**14.** **Which of the following is not a major criticism of Psychodynamic theories?** CBSE 2025

(a) They are largely based on case studies and lack a rigorous scientific basis.
(b) They use small and atypical individuals as samples for advancing generalisations.
(c) The concepts are well defined and easily submitted to scientific testing.
(d) They face criticism for using non-representative samples.

**15.** **Tanmay wants to assess how Geetika expresses aggression in the face of a frustrating situation with the help of cartoon-like pictures. He presents a series of situations in which one person frustrates another or**

calls attention to a frustrating condition. Tanmay is likely to be using the ....... **CBSE Term I 2021**
(a) Thematic Apperception Test
(b) Rosenzweig's Picture-Frustration Study (P-F Study)
(c) Sixteen Personality Factor Test (16 PF)
(d) Behavioural Analysis

**16.** Ivaan reached the genital stage of psychosexual development. Which of the following is/are not true about this stage?
I. Ivaan has attained maturity in psychosexual development.
II. This stage lasts from about seven years until puberty.
III. Physical growth continues and much of Ivaan's energy is channeled into social or achievement-related activities.
IV. Ivaan's sexuality, fears and repressed feelings of earlier stages are once again exhibited in this stage.

Codes
(a) I, II and IV (b) Only II
(c) II and III (d) I and III

**17.** Choose the correct options. **CBSE Term I 2021**
Ankita scores high on the dimension of psychoticism. This can be linked to psychopathology that represents ....
I. a feeling of gratitude for others
II. a tough manner of interacting with people
III. a tendency to defy social conventions
IV. socially conducive behaviour
V. hostility, egocentricity

Codes
(a) I, II, IV and V (b) I, III, IV and V
(c) II, III and V (d) II, IV and V

**18.** Sanjana loves to have burgers every day. Being aware of its ill effects on her body, she promised herself that she would buy a book of her choice if she managed to restrain herself from eating burgers for a month. This is an example of .........
(a) observation of own behaviour
(b) self-instruction
(c) self-reinforcement
(d) self-esteem

**19.** The school counsellor told Simran that people are happiest and perform their best when their personal traits and characteristics match their occupation. To assess this, she has to go through a psychological test. Her counsellor is most likely to use the ........ test.
(a) Minnesota Multiphasic Personality Inventory
(b) Eysenck Personality Questionnaire
(c) Sixteen Personality Factor Questionnaire
(d) Draw a person test

**20.** Ryan believes that he is very good at football. Therefore, he has a high ............. as far as sports is concerned. **CBSE SQP 2022-23**
(a) self-esteem (b) self-efficacy
(c) self-motivation (d) self-control

**21.** Surendra's newborn son has no idea of his own self. This refers to which of the following? **CBSE SQP 2024**
I. He is unaware of various objects in his environment, such as a chair or a table in his room.
II. He is able to cry when he is hungry.
III. Sometimes he smiles when he sleeps.
IV. People around him are part of his experiences. However, he cannot gather any meaning from it.

Codes
(a) I and II (b) I and IV
(c) III and IV (d) II and III

**22.** When we are interested in why people behave in the ways they do, we also assign causes to the behaviour shown in specific social situations. This process is called ............ . **CBSE 2024 C**
(a) impression formation
(b) attribution
(c) social cognition
(d) social inhibition

**23.** Vikas has a somewhat positive attitude towards empowerment of women. When he read about Kalpana Chawla's achievements, his attitude became more positive. This would be a/an ........ change. **CBSE 2024 C**
(a) extreme (b) simple
(c) congruent (d) incongruent

**24.** According to Sheldon's typology, which of the following combinations correctly matches the body build with the associated temperament? **CBSE 2025**
(a) Endomorphs - Thin, long, fragile, brainy, artistic, introvert
(b) Mesomorphs - Strong musculature, strong body build, rectangular, energetic, courageous
(c) Ectomorphs - Fat, soft, round, relaxed, sociable
(d) Endomorphs - Strong musculature, rectangular, energetic, courageous

## Assertion-Reason Questions

**Directions** (Q. Nos. 25-30) In the question given below, there are two statements marked as Assertion (A) and Reason (R). Read the statements and choose the correct option.
(a) Both A and R are true and R is the correct explanation of A.
(b) Both A and R are true, but R is not the correct explanation of A.
(c) A is true, but R is false.
(d) A is false, but R is true.

**25. Assertion** (A) PASS model explains that a state of arousal is basic to any behaviour as it helps in attending to stimuli. Arousal and attention enable a person to process information. **CBSE Term I 2021**

**Reason** (R) An optimal level of arousal focuses our attention to the relevant aspects of a problem. Too much or too little arousal would interfere with attention.

**26. Assertion** (A) In psychological terms, personality refers to the physical or external appearance of an individual. For example, when we find someone 'good-looking', we often assume that the person also has a charming personality. **CBSE Term I 2021**

**Reason** (R) Personality refers to our characteristic ways of responding to individuals and situations.

**27. Assertion** (A) A strong sense of self efficacy allows people to select, influence and construct the circumstances of their own life. **CBSE SQP Term I 2021**

**Reason** (R) People's expectations of mastery or achievement and their convictions about their own effectiveness determine the types of behaviours they engage in.

**28. Assertion** (A) A person who has strong aggressive tendencies may see other people as being excessively aggressive towards him/her. **CBSE SQP Term I 2021**

**Reason** (R) People adopt an ego defense mechanism called projection in which they attribute their own traits to others.

**29. Assertion** (A) Behavioural ratings suffer from major limitations like acquiescence.

**Reason** (R) Raters have a tendency to place individuals in the middle of a scale by avoiding extreme positions.

**30. Assertion** (A) Personality is solely determined by genetic factors. **Competency Based Que.**

**Reason** (R) While genetic factors contribute to the development of personality traits, the ecological and cultural environment also plays a crucial role.

# Answers

1. (c) social
2. (b) Ego
3. (b) unconditional positive regard
4. (b) Type-B
5. (a) reaction formation
6. (c) III and IV
7. (b) personality
8. (b) humour
9. (c) Oral, anal, phallic, latency and genital
10. (c) repression
11. (b) analytical psychology
12. (d) Social desirability
13. (c) II, III and IV
14. (c) The concepts are well defined and easily submitted to scientific testing.
15. (b) Rosenzweig's Picture-Frustration Study (P-F Study)
16. (c) II and III
17. (c) II, III and V
18. (c) self-reinforcement
19. (c) Sixteen Personality Factor Questionnaire
20. (a) self-esteem
21. (b) I and IV
22. (b) attribution
23. (b) simple
24. (b) Mesomorphs–Strong musculature, strong body build, rectangular, energetic, courageous
25. (a) Both A and R are true and R is the correct explanation of A.
26. (d) A is false, but R is true.
27. (a) Both A and R are true and R is the correct explanation of A.
28. (a) Both A and R are true and R is the correct explanation of A.
29. (d) A is false, but R is true.
30. (d) A is false, but R is true.

# Subjective Questions

## Very Short Answer Type Questions

**1. What do you understand by the term 'self'?**

**Ans.** Self refers to the totality of an individual's conscious experiences, ideas, thoughts and feelings with regard to themselves.

**2. What is personal identity?**

**Ans.** It refers to those attributes of a person that make him/her different from others. When a person describes himself/herself by telling his/her name, qualities, characteristics, potentialities, capabilities or beliefs, he/she discloses her/his personal identity.

**3. Explain the term social identity.**

**Ans.** It refers to those aspects of a person that link him/her to a social or cultural group or are derived from it.

**4. What is naturalistic observation?**

**Ans.** Naturalistic observation is an observation in a natural setting. For example, observing how people behave in response to a heavy discount provided by a shop.

**5. What is self-control or delay of gratification?**

**Ans.** It is the ability of an individual to control himself from satisfying his needs. Self-control plays a key role in the fulfilment of long-term goals.

**6. Which kind of people are high on 'self-monitoring'?**

**Ans.** People who are able to change their behaviour according to the demands of the external environment are high on self-monitoring.

**7. Define the term 'reaction formation'.**

**Ans.** In this mechanism, person defends against anxiety by adopting behaviours opposite to his/her true feelings.

**8. What is the major developmental achievement of phallic stage?**

**Ans.** At this stage, male child experiences the Oedipus complex. It involes love for the mother, hostility towards the father and the fear of punishment by the father.

For girls, the Oedipus complex (called the Electra Complex) follows a slightly different course as it involves love for the father.

**9. What is Oedipus Complex?**

**Ans.** During phallic stage, male child experience Oedipus Complex. It involves love for the mother, hostility towards the father and consequent fear of punishment by the father.

**10. How psychological qualities developed?**

**Ans.** According to psychologists, psychological qualities such as growth and realisation of potentials resulted from a desire for freedom and striving for justice and truth.

**11. What is Libido?**

**Ans.** The instinctual life force that energises the id is called Libido. It deals with immediate gratification of primitive needs, sexual desires and aggressive impulses.

**12. What is situational test?**

**Ans.** A variety of situational tests have been devised for the assessment of personality. The most commonly used test of this kind is the situational stress test. It provides us information about how a person behaves under stressful situations.

**13. What do you understand by the term structured personality tests?**

**Ans.** Structured personality test requires subjects to give responses using some kind of rating scale. The subject report his/her feeling objectively with respect to various items. For example, Self-report measures.

**14. Define unstructured interview.**

**Ans.** In unstructured interviews, the interviewer seeks to develop an impression about a person by asking a number of questions.

**15. Define nomination as a method of assessment.**

**Ans.** In using nomination, each person is asked to choose one or more persons of the group with whom he/she would like to work, study, play or participate in any other activity. The person may also be asked to specify the reason for his/her choices.

**16. Explain the interactional approach to personality.**

**Ans.** The interactional approach holds that situational characteristics play an important role in determining our behaviour. People may act dependent or independent not because of their internal personality trait, but because of external rewards or threats available in a particular situation.

**17. Differentiate between self as a subject and self as an object.**

**Ans.** Self is described as a subject who does something (for example, I am a lawyer) and as an object on which something is done (for example, I am the one who easily gets hurt).

**18. Why social self is called familial or relational self?**

**Ans.** Social self values family and social relationships. Hence, it is called Familial or Relational self.

**19. A child wants ice cream cone. How do you explain it by using his structural elements of personality, i.e. Id, Ego and Superego?**

**Ans.** A child wants an ice cream. The Id of the boy tells him to grab the cone and eat it. His ego tells him that if he grabs the cone without asking his mother, he may be punished. The boy knows that the best way to achieve gratification is to ask for permission to eat the cone. Then he asks his mother for it, his superego indicates that his behaviour is morally correct.

**20. What do you understand by Type-C personality?** CBSE 2018

**Ans.** Individual characterised by Type-C personality are cooperative, unassertive and patient. They suppress their negative emotions like anger and show compliance to authority. Morris has suggested that a Type-C personality is prone to cancer.

**21. How is Karen Horney's viewpoint regarding women different from that of Freud's?** CBSE 2019

**Ans.** Karen Horney developed a theory that deviated from basic Freudian principles. She challenged Freud's treatment of women as inferior. According to her, each sex has attributes to be admired by the other and neither sex can be viewed as superior or inferior.

**22. Mir had no recollection of the bicycle he received as a gift on his tenth birthday. But when Nita reminded him about the same, he was able to recall it. What do you think, why Mir had no recollection of the bicycle?**

**Ans.** Mir had no recollection of the bicycle he received as a gift on his tenth birthday. However, when reminded he was able to recall it. This happened because memories of his birthday were lying in the pre-conscious level. The pre-conscious level of consciousness includes those mental activities of that can become aware only if they attend to it closely.

**23. In India, Mallick and Joshi have developed the Jodhpur Multiphasic Personality Inventory (JMPI). Which test has it been adapted from? Explain its most important use.** CBSE SQP 2024

**Ans.** JMPI has adopted the Minnesota Multiphasic Personality Inventory (MMPI). The test is very effective in identifying varieties of psychopathology.

**24. Tripti is a psychologist. She administers a test that requires the subject to manipulate objects and other materials to perform a task. Name the type of intelligence test and state its importance.** CBSE 2024 C

**Ans.** The type of intelligence test is the Performance-based test, specifically referring to tests like the Wechsler Adult Intelligence Scale (WAIS) or Raven's Progressive Matrices. These tests require individuals to manipulate objects or solve problems that require non-verbal reasoning. The importance of these tests is that they assess practical intelligence and cognitive abilities that are independent of verbal skills, providing a more holistic measure of intelligence.

**25. Daniel often feels torn between seeking immediate pleasure and adhering to societal rules. How does the psychodynamic theory explain his conflict? Explain.** CBSE 2024 C

**Ans.** According to the psychodynamic theory (Freud's theory), Daniel's conflict can be explained by the struggle between his id, which seeks immediate pleasure and gratification (impulsive desires), and his superego, which internalizes societal rules and moral standards (the conscience). The ego acts as a mediator between the two, trying to balance the desires of the id with the constraints of the superego, leading to internal conflict when these forces are at odds.

**26. Zikra has a distorted body image that leads her to see herself as overweight. What can be the negative after-effect of this thought?**

**Ans.** The negative after-effect of Zikra's distorted body image could be the development of eating disorders such as anorexia nervosa or bulimia nervosa. These conditions are often fueled by distorted perceptions of body size and shape, leading to unhealthy behaviours like restrictive eating or purging. Additionally, it can result in low self-esteem, depression and anxiety, further affecting her mental and physical well-being.

## Short Answer Type Questions

**1. Differentiate between personal-self and social-self.**

**Ans.** **Personal-self** refers to the individual's sense of self, focusing primarily on their own feelings, needs and desires. Psychological and social needs in the context of environment lead other components of personal-self to emerge. Emphasis is given on those aspects of life that relate only to a concerned person, such as personal freedom, responsibility, achievement or comforts.

**Social-self** emerges in relation with others and emphasises aspects of life such as co-operation, unity, affiliation, sacrifice, support or sharing. This self values family and social relationships. It is also referred to as familial or relational self.

**2. Discuss briefly about the concept of self-esteem.**

**Ans.** Self-esteem is an important aspect of our self. As we always make some judgement about our own value or worth, this value judgement about ourselves is known as self-esteem.

The main features of it are

- Some people have high self-esteem, some have low self-esteem.
- By the age of 6 to 7 years children seem to have formed self-esteem in academic competence, social competence, physical/athletic competence and physical appearance, which gradually become more refined with age.
- Self-esteem shows a strong relationship with our everyday behaviour. For example, children with high academic self-esteem perform better in schools than those with low academic self-esteem.

**3. Briefly explain the concept of self-efficacy.**

**Ans.** Self-efficacy is an important aspect of our self. A strong sense of self-efficacy allows people to select, influence and construct the circumstances of their own life. This can be explained in the following ways

- The notion of self-efficacy in based on social learning theory. Bandura's social learning theory shows that children and adult learn behaviour by observing and imitating others.
- Self-efficacy can be developed. People with high self-efficacy can stop smoking the moment he decides to do so.
- Our society, parent and our own positive experience can help in the development of self-efficacy by presenting positive models during formative years of children.

**4. State the techniques of self-control.**

**Ans.** A number of psychological techniques of self-control have been suggested. Some of these are

- **Observation** It provides us with necessary information that may be used to change, modify or strengthen certain aspects of self.
- **Self-instruction** It is another important technique. We often instruct ourselves to do something and behave in the way we want to. Such instructions are quite effective in self-regulation.
- **Self-reinforcement** It is the third technique. This involves rewarding behaviours that have pleasant outcomes. For example, you may go to see a movie with friends, if you have done well in an examination.

**5. Describe any three features of personality.**

**Ans.** Personality is characterised by the following features

(i) It has both physical and psychological components.

(ii) Its expression in terms of behaviour is fairly unique in a given individual.

(iii) Its main features do not easily change with time.

(iv) It is dynamic in the sense that some of its features may change due to internal or external situational demands.

**6. State the characteristics of individual with Type-A personality.**

***Or* Describe Type-A personality.**

**Ans.** People characterised by this personality seem to possess high motivation, lack patience, feel short of time, be in a great hurry and feel like being always burdened with work. Such people find it difficult to slow down and relax. People with this personality are more susceptible to problems like hypertension and Coronary Heart Disease (CHD). The risk of developing CHD with Type A personality is sometimes even greater than the risks caused by high blood pressure, high cholesterol levels, or smoking.

**7. What are the three levels of consciousness as defined by Freud?**

**Ans.** Freud visualises the human mind in terms of three levels of consciousness.

(i) Conscious, which includes the thoughts, feelings and actions of which people are aware.

(ii) Pre-conscious, which includes mental activity of which people may become aware only if they attend to it closely.

(iii) Unconscious, which includes mental activity of which people are unaware of.

**8. Describe the theory of Karen Horney.**

**Ans.** Horney adopted a more optimistic view of human life with emphasis on human growth and self-actualisation. Horney challenge Freud's treatment of women as inferior. According to her, each sex has attributes to be admired by the other and neither sex can be viewed as superior or inferior. She countered that women were more likely to be affected by social and cultural factors than by biological factors.

She argued that psychological disorders were caused by disturbed interpersonal relationship during childhood. When parents' behaviour toward a child is indifferent, discouraging and erratic, the child feels insecure and a feeling called basic anxiety results.

**9. Describe the theory of Alfred Adler.**

**Ans.** Adler's theory is known as Individual psychology. His basic assumption is that human behaviour is purposeful and goal directed. Each one of us has the capacity to choose and create and our personal goals are the sources of our motivation.

The goals that provide us with security and help us in overcoming the feelings of inadequacy are important in our personality development. In Adler's view, every individual suffers from the feelings of inadequacy and guilt i.e. inferiority complex, which arise from childhood. Overcoming this complex is essential for optimal personality development.

**10. Discuss Erikson's concept of identity crisis.**

**Ans.** Erikson's theory emphasises on rational, conscious ego processes in personality development. He viewed development as a lifelong process and ego identity is granted a central place in this process.

Erikson used the term 'crisis' to describe a series of interest conflicts that are linked to developmental stages. According to Erikson's theory, the way a person resolves the crisis will determine their personal identity and future development. His concept of 'identity crisis' of adolescent age has drawn considerable attention. Erikson argues that young people must generate a central perspective and a direction for themselves that can give them a meaningful sense of unity and purpose.

Erikson believed that when youth successfully navigate this crisis, they develop the ability to form honest, reciprocal relationships with others and have the capacity to bond with others to achieve common goals. If youth do not resolve this crisis, their emotional development becomes stalled and as a result they will remain isolated and lonely without social supports.

**11. Explain the views of self in different culture.**

*Or* **Describe the relationship between culture and self.**

**Ans.** The characteristic features of the culture is linked with several aspects of self. Analysis of self carried out in the Indian cultural context reveals a number of important features that are distinct from those found in the Western cultural context.

The most important distinction between the Indian and the Western views is the way the boundary is drawn between the self and the other. In the Western view, this boundary appears to be relatively fixed. On the other hand, the Indian view of self is characterised by the shifting nature of this boundary.

Thus, ourself at one moment of time expands to fuse with the cosmos or include the others. But at the next moment, it seems to be completely withdrawn from it and focused fully on individual self (for example, our personal needs or goals).

The Western view seems to hold clear dichotomies between self and other, man and nature, subjective and objective. The Indian view does not make such clear dichotomies.

In the Indian culture the self is not generally separated from one's own group and both remain in a state of harmonious coexistence.

In the Western culture they often remain at a distance. Therefore, many Western cultures are characterised as individualistic where as many Asian cultures are characterised as collectivistic.

**12. Distinguish between source traits and surface traits. Give suitable examples.**

**Ans.** Raymond Cattell used factor analysis to identify underlying personality structures. Differences between source traits and surface traits are as follows

**Source Traits** Cattell found 16 primary or source traits. The source traits are stable and are considered as the building blocks of personality. Cattell described the source traits in terms of opposing tendencies. He developed a test called Sixteen Personality Factor Questionnaire (16PF), for the assessment of personality.

**Surface Traits** There are a number of surface traits that result out of the interaction of source traits. These are unstable and observable.

**13. At the age of four Sonia wants to marry her father. How can you explain it from the point of view of Freud?**

**Ans.** According to Freud at phallic stage (4-5 years) children become aware of sexuality. In this age girl loves her father very much and tries to symbolically marry him and raise a family. This is known as Electra Complex. For, this complex Sonia wants to marry her father. Gradually Sonia realises that this is unlikely, then she begins to identify with her mother and copy her behaviour as a means of getting her father's affection.

**14. "An understanding of personality allows us to deal with people in realistic and acceptable ways". Discuss.**

**Ans.** Once we are able to characterise someone's personality, we can predict how that person will probably behave in a variety of circumstances. An understanding of personality allows us to deal with people in realistic and acceptable ways. For example, if you find a child who does not like orders, the most effective way to deal with that child will be not to give orders, but to present a set of acceptable alternatives from which the child may choose. Similarly, a child who has feelings of inferiority needs to be treated differently from a child who is self-confident.

**15. "Healthy personality lies in not mere adjustment to society. It involves a quest to know oneself deeply." In the light of humanistic approach, elaborate this statement.**

**Competency Based Que.**

**Ans.** The humanistic theorists have indicated that healthy personality lies in not mere adjustment to society. It involves a quest to know oneself deeply and to be true to one's own feelings without disguise and to be oneself in the here and now. According to them, the healthy people share the following characteristics

- They become aware of themselves, their feelings and their limits.
- They do not live in the past or dwell in the future through anxious expectations and distorted defences.

**16. Is personality a dynamic organisation? Explain.**

**Ans.** Dynamic means change due to internal or external demands. All port proposed that individuals possess a number of traits which are dynamic in nature. They determine behaviour in such a manner that an individual approaches different situations with similar plans.

He acknowledged that people with same traits might express them in different ways and any variation in traits would elicit a different response in the same situation. Therefore, we can say that personality is a dynamic organisation.

**17. What did Carl Jung mean by collective unconscious?**

**Ans.** According to Swiss psychologist Carl Jung, the collective unconscious is a part of the human psyche that is inherited from ancestors and shared by all humans.

The collective unconscious is a part of the unconscious mind that contains information and ideas that are common to all humans. It is distinct from the personal unconscious, which is shaped by an individual's experiences.

**18. Explain the concept of self.**

**Ans.** The idea of self emerges and its formation begins as a child grows older. Parents, friends, teachers and other significant persons play a vital role in shaping a child's ideas about self. Our interaction with other people, our experiences and the meaning we gives to them, serve as the basis of our self. On the basis of our own experiences and the experiences we have of other people the structure of self can be changed. There are various kinds of self. They get formed as a result of our interactions with our physical and socio-cultural environments.

Concept of self can be explained by two identities of an individual i.e. are as follows

**Personal Self** The personal self leads to an orientation in which one feels primarily concerned with oneself. Psychological and social needs in the context of environment lead other components of personal self to emerge. Emphasis is given on those aspects of life that relate only to the concerned person, such as personal freedom, personal responsibility, personal achievement or personal comforts.

**Social Self** The social self emerges in relation with others and emphasises aspects of life such as co-operation, unity, affiliation, sacrifice, support or sharing. This self values family and social relationships. Hence, it is also referred to as familial or relational self.

**19. Distinguish between cardinal, central and secondary traits proposed by Allport using suitable examples.**

**Ans.** Gordon Allport is the pioneer of trait approach. He proposed that individuals possess a number of traits, which are dynamic in nature. They determine behaviour in such a manner that an individual approaches different situations with similar plans. Allport argued that the words people use to describe themselves and others provide a basis for understanding human personality. He categorised traits into cardinal, central and secondary.

**Cardinal Traits** These are highly generalised dispositions. They indicate the goal around which a person's entire life seems to revolve. Mahatma Gandhi's non-violence and Hitler's Nazism are examples of cardinal traits.

Such traits often get associated with the name of the person so strongly that they derive such identities as the 'Gandhian' or 'Hitlerian' trait.

**Central Traits** These are less pervasive in effect, but still quite generalised dispositions. These traits (for example warm, sincere, diligent, etc) are often used in writing a testimonial or job recommendation for a person.

**Secondary Traits** These are the least generalised characteristics of a person. Traits such as 'likes mangoes' or 'prefers ethnic clothes' are examples of secondary traits.

**20. A study found that one-third of British children at age six are afraid of snakes even though it is rare to encounter snakes in British Isles. The children had never come in contact with snakes in a traumatic situation, but snakes still generated anxious response. How would Carl Jung's theory of personality explain the same? Throw some light on his theory.** CBSE 2023

**Ans.** Carl Jung developed his own theory of personality, called analytical psychology. The basic assumption of his theory is that personality consists of competing forces and structures within the individual (that must be balanced) rather than between the individual and the demands of society or between the individual and reality.

Jung claimed that there was a collective unconscious consisting of archetypes or primordial images. These are not individually acquired, but are inherited. The God or the Mother Earth is a good example of archetypes. They are found in myths, dreams and arts of all mankind.

Jung held that the self strives for unity and oneness. It is an archetype that is expressed in many ways. He devoted much of his efforts to the study of such expressions in various traditions. According to him, for achieving unity and wholeness, a person must become increasingly aware of the wisdom available in one's personal and collective un-conscious and must learn to live in harmony with it.

**21. Define five factors model of personality.**

**Ans.** Paul Costa and Robert McCrae have examined all possible personality traits. The findings indicate a set of five factors. They are often called Big Five Factors. These factors include

(i) **Openness to Experience** Those who score high on this factor are imaginative, curious, open to new ideas, and interested in cultural pursuits. In contrast, those who score low are rigid.

(ii) **Extraversion** It characterises people who are socially active, assertive, outgoing, talkative and fun loving. On its opposite are people who are shy.

(iii) **Agreeableness** This factor characterises people who are helpful, co-operative, friendly, caring and nurturing. On the opposite are people who are hostile and self-centered.

(iv) **Neuroticism** People who score high on this factor are emotionally unstable, anxious, worried, fearful, distressed, irritable and hypertensive. On the opposite side are people who are well adjusted.

(v) **Conscientiousness** Those who score high on this factor are achievement-oriented, dependable, responsible, prudent, hardworking and self-controlled.

**22. Define the characteristics of Type A, Type B, Type C and Type D personality.**

**Ans.** Friedman and Rosenman have classified individuals into Type-A and Type-B personalities.

People characterised by Type-A personality seem to possess high motivation, lack of patience, feel short of time, be in a great hurry and feel like being always burdened with work. People with this personality are more susceptible to problems like Hypertension and Coronary Heart Disease (CHD). The risk of developing CHD with Type-A personality is sometimes even greater than the risks caused by high blood pressure, high cholesterol levels or smoking.

Type-B personality can be understood as the absence of Type-A traits. Morris has suggested a Type-C personality, which is prone to cancer. Individuals characterised by this personality are co-operative, unassertive and patient. They suppress their negative emotions (for example, anger) and show compliance to authority. Recently, a Type-D personality has been suggested, which is characterised by proneness to depression.

**23. Describe the word unconscious as described by Sigmund Freud.**

**Ans.** Unconscious includes mental activity that people are unaware of. Analysis of forgetting, mispronunciation, jokes and dreams provide us with a means to approach the unconscious.

According to Freud, the unconscious is a reservoir of instinctive or animal drives. It also stores all ideas and wishes that are concealed from conscious awareness, because they lead to psychological conflicts. Most of these arise from sexual desires which cannot be expressed openly and therefore are repressed.

People constantly struggle to find either some socially acceptable ways to express unconscious impulses or to keep those impulses away from being expressed. Unsuccessful resolution of conflicts results in abnormal behaviour.

The basic goal of psychoanalytic therapy is to bring the repressed unconscious materials to consciousness, thereby helping people to live in a more self-aware and integrated manner.

**24. What are behaviour rating? Give two limitations of behaviour rating.**

*Or* **Explain behaviour rating used in assessment of personality.**

**Ans.** Behaviourial ratings are frequently used for assessment of personality in educational and industrial settings. Behavioural ratings are generally taken from people who know the assessee intimately and have interacted with him/her over a period of time or have had a chance to observe him/her.

The method of rating suffers from the following major limitations

(i) Raters often display certain biases that represent their judgements of different traits. For example, most of us are greatly influenced by a single favourable or unfavourable trait. This often forms the basis of a rater's overall judgement of a person. This tendency is known as the halo effect.

(ii) Raters have a tendency to place individuals either in the middle of the scale (called middle category bias) by avoiding extreme positions or in the extreme positions (called extreme response bias) by avoiding middle categories on the scale.

**25. Explain the concept of defence mechanism.**

**Ans.** Defence mechanism is a way of reducing anxiety by distorting reality. Freud has described many different kinds of defence mechanisms such as

**Repression** It is the most important in which anxiety provoking behaviours or thoughts are totally dismissed by the unconscious.

**Projection** In this mechanism, people attribute their own traits to others. Thus, a person who has strong aggressive tendencies may see other people as acting in an excessively aggressive way towards him/her.

**Denial** In denial, a person totally refuses to accept reality. Thus, someone suffering from HIV/AIDS may altogether deny his/her illness.

**Reaction Formation** In this mechanism person defends against anxiety by adopting behaviours opposite to his/her true feelings. For example, a person with strong sexual urges, channels his energy into religious fervour.

**Rationalisation** In this, a person tries to make unreasonable feelings or behaviour seem reasonable and acceptable. For example, when a student buys new pens after performing poor in examination, he may rationalise his behaviour by asserting that "I will do much better with these pens".

**26. Differentiate between type and trait approaches to personality. Give suitable examples.**

**Ans.** The difference between type and trait approaches to personality are

(i) The type approaches attempts to comprehend human personality by examining certain broad patterns in the observed behavioural characteristics of individuals. Each behavioural pattern refers to one type in which individuals are placed in terms of the similarity of their behavioural characteristics with that pattern. It can be explained by any type theory as given by Sheldon Endomorphic, Mesomorphic Ectomorphic typology or by Jung's introverts and extroverts typology.

The trait approach focuses on the specific psychological attributes along which individuals tend to differ in consistent and stable ways. For example, one person may be less shy, whereas another may be more; or one person may be less friendly, whereas another may be more.

These theories are mainly concerned with the description or characterisation of basic components of personality. They try to discover the 'building blocks' of personality.

(ii) Personality types are used to represent and communicate a set of expected behaviours bored on similarities. Efforts to categorise people into personality types have been made since ancient times. On the other hand, Trait approach is very similar to our common experience in everyday life. It attempts to identify primary characteristics of people.

A trait is considered as a relatively enduring attribute or quality on which one individual differs from another.

**27. The tribal Birhor society of Jharkhand allow their children to move freely into forests and learn hunting and gathering skills. How it can be explained from the point of view of cultural approach of psychology?** **Competency Based Que.**

**Ans.** Cultural approach explains personality through ecological and cultural factors. It proposes that a group's 'economic maintenance system' plays a vital role in the origin of cultural and behavioural variations. The climatic conditions, the nature of terrain of the habitat and the availability of food in it determine not only people's economic activities but also their settlement pattern, social structures, division of labour and other features like child rearing practices.

The Birhor tribal group of Jharkhand is a nomadic tribe who requires constant movements in small bands from one forest to another in search of food and other products (fruits, roots, mushrooms, honey etc.) Thus in Birhor society, children from an early age are allowed enormous freedom to move into forests and learn hunting and gathering skills.

This child socialisation practices are aims to

- Making children independent i.e. do many things without the help of others.
- Making them autonomous (take several decisions for themselves) and achievement-oriented (accept risk and challenges such as those involved in hunting) from an early age of life. Because of different economic pursuit and cultural demands the Birhor tribes allowed their children to move freely in the forests.

**28. "Direct methods of personality assessment fail to provide us with a real picture of an individual's personality. This limitation be overcome by using indirect methods of assessment like projective techniques." Discuss the significance of projective techniques.** **Competency Based Que.**

**Ans.** Direct methods of personality assessment cannot uncover the unconscious part of our behaviour. Hence, they fail to provide us with a real picture of an individual's personality. These problems can be overcome by using indirect methods of assessment.

Projective techniques is an indirect method of assessment. These were developed to assess unconscious motives and feelings. The analysis of personality with the help of projective techniques appears fairly interesting.

It helps us to understand unconscious motives, deep-rooted conflicts and emotional complexes of an individual. However, the interpretation of the responses requires sophisticated skills and specialised training.

There are problems associated with the reliability of scoring and validity of interpretations. But, the practitioners have found these techniques quite useful.

**29. Discuss the main proposition of the humanistic approach to personality.** CBSE 2018

**Ans.** Humanistic approach emphasises the significance of positive aspects of life. Carl Rogers and Abraham Maslow have particularly contributed to the development of humanistic perspective on personality. Humanistic theories emphasise personal responsibility and innovate tendencies toward personal growth. In this theory, Roger proposed the idea of a fully functioning person.

He believes that fulfilment is the motivating force for personality development. People try to express their capabilities, potentials and talents to the fullest extent possible. There is an inborn tendency among persons that directs them to actualise their inherited nature.

**30. Describe any two procedures of behavioural analysis.** CBSE 2018

**Ans.** The two procedures of behavioural analysis are

(i) Interview is a commonly used method for assessing personality. This involves talking to the person being assessed and asking specific questions. Diagnostic interviewing generally involves in-depth interviewing which seeks to go beyond the replies given by the person. Interviews may be structured or unstructured depending on the purpose or goals of assessment.

(ii) Observation is another method which is very commonly used for the assessment of personality. It requires careful training of the observer and a fairly detailed guideline about analysis of behaviours in order to assess the personality of a given person.

**31. Explain the role of assessment in understanding psychological attributes. Describe the key features of any two methods used for psychological assessment.** CBSE SQP 2022

**Ans.** Assessment is the measurement of psychological attributes of an individual which often uses methods in terms of certain comparisons. An attribute of an individual will be said to exist if it can be measured by using scientific procedures. Assessment is the first step in understanding a psychological attribute. Assessment may be formal and informal.

There are various methods of assessment in which two methods are as follows

(i) **Psychological Test** It is an objective and standardised measure of an individual's mental and behavioural characteristics. Objective tests have been developed to measure all the dimensions of psychological attributes. It is commonly used for the purposes of clinical diagnosis, guidance, personnel selection, placement and training.

(ii) **Self-report** It is a method in which a person provides factual information about themselves. Such information may be obtained by using an interview schedule or a questionnaire, a psychological test or a personal diary.

## Long Answer Type Questions

**1. Explain ego defence mechanism. Illustrate with examples, the projection as a defence mechanism.**

*Or* **What are defence mechanisms? Explain different types of defence mechanisms with examples.**

**Ans.** Freud suggests human behaviour reflects an attempt to deal with or escape from anxiety. He believed that people avoid anxiety mainly by developing defence mechanisms. Defence mechanism try to defend the ego against the awareness of the instinctual needs. Defence mechanism is a way of reducing anxiety by distorting reality. Freud has described many different kinds of defence mechanisms such as

(i) **Repression** It is the most important defence mechanism in which anxiety provoking behaviours or thoughts are totally dismissed by the unconscious. When people repress a feeling or desire, they become totally unaware of that wish or desire.

(ii) **Projection** In this mechanism people attribute their own traits to others. Thus, a person who has strong aggressive tendencies may see other people as acting in an excessively aggressive way towards him/her.

(iii) **Denial** In denial, a person totally refuses to accept reality. Thus, someone suffering from HIV/AIDS may altogether deny his/her illness.

(iv) **Reaction Formation** In this mechanism, person defends against anxiety by adopting behaviours opposite to his/her true feelings. A person with strong sexual urges, who channels his/her energy into religious fervour, is an example of reaction formation.

(v) **Rationalisation** In this, a person tries to make unreasonable feelings or behaviour reasonable and acceptable. For example, when a student buys a set of new pens after doing poorly in examination, i.e. he may try to rationalise his behaviour, by asserting "I will do much better with these pens".

**2. Discuss type approaches to the study of personality.**

**Ans.** The type approaches attempt to understand human personality by examining certain broad patterns in the observed behavioural characteristics of individuals. Each behavioural pattern refers to one type in which individuals are placed in terms of the similarity of their behavioural characteristics with that pattern. Efforts to categorise people into personality types have been made since ancient times.

**As per Charak Samhita**, a famous treatise on Ayurveda in India classifies people into the categories of vata, pitta and kapha on the basis of three humoural elements called tridosha. Each refers to a type of temperament, called prakriti (basic nature) of a person. Apart from this, there is also a typology of personality based on the trigunas, i.e., sattva, rajas and tamas.

As per Sheldon proposed Endomorphic, Mesomorphic and Ectomorphic Typology on the basis of body build and temperament.

(i) The endomorphs are fat, soft and round. They are relaxed and sociable in nature.

(ii) The mesomorphs have strong muscular body. They are rectangular with a strong body build. They are energetic and courageous.

(iii) The ectomorphs are thin, long and have fragile body build. They are brainy, artistic and introvert.

As per Jung has proposed widely recognised typology by grouping people into introverts and extroverts.. Introverts are people who prefer to be alone, tend to avoid others and are shy. Extroverts are sociable, outgoing, drawn to occupations that allow dealing directly with people.

As per Friedman and Rosenman have classified individuals into Type-A and Type-B personalities. Type-A personality seem to possess high motivation, lack of patience, feel short of time, be in a great hurry, and feel like being always burdened with work. Type-B personality, can be understood as the absence of Type-A traits. This typology has been further extended.

**3. How does Freud explain the stability and potential changes in personality over a person's lifetime? Provide an overview of each stage and discuss the impact of encountering problems at any stage on personality development.** CBSE 2025

*OR*

**Describe Freud's psychosexual stages of personality development.** CBSE SQP 2022

**Ans.** Sigmund Freud explained personality development through his psychosexual stages theory, where personality is shaped by managing conflicts between biological drives and societal expectations. He described five stages which are.

(i) **Oral Stage (0-1 year)** Focus is on the mouth, like sucking and biting. If needs aren't met, it may lead to dependency or oral habits.

(ii) **Anal Stage (1-3 years)** Focus shifts to bowel control. Problems here can result in traits like being overly tidy or messy.

(iii) **Phallic Stage (3-6 years)** Attention centers on genital awareness. Issues with the Oedipus or Electra complex could affect confidence and relationships.

(iv) **Latency Stage (6-12 years)** Sexual energies are dormant and focus moves to social and intellectual skills. Trouble here may hinder social abilities.

(v) **Genital Stage (12 years onwards)** Sexual energies return, focusing on relationships. Unresolved earlier conflicts can cause difficulties in intimacy.

Problems at any stage can lead to fixation where personality traits remain tied to that stage. According to Freud, resolving these challenges is crucial for healthy personality development.

**4. How do ecological and cultural environments influence personality development? Provide concrete examples from hunting-gathering and agricultural societies to illustrate your answer.** CBSE 2025

**Ans.** Ecological and cultural environments play a vital role in shaping personality development. They influence behaviours, values and social norms by determining daily survival needs and societal structures.

- In hunting-gathering societies, individuals live close to nature and rely on teamwork for survival. Traits like cooperation, adaptability and sharing become essential because people hunt in groups and share food. For example, in such societies, children learn to work collaboratively and develop trust within their community.
- In agricultural societies, dependence on stable land and long-term planning fosters traits like diligence, patience and responsibility. Children often assist in farming tasks, learning values like hard work and discipline. In these societies people develop a sense

of belonging to a larger community with roles and responsibilities defined by their place in agriculture.

**5. How do you define personality? Explain any one approach to the study of personality.** **CBSE 2020**

*Or* **Explain the concept of personality. Describe the cultural approach to study personality.**

**Ans.** Personality generally refers to the physical or external appearance of an individual. In psychological terms, personality refers to our characteristic ways of responding to individuals and situations.

Personality refers to psychophysical characteristics of a person that are relatively stable across situations and over time and make her or him unique. It also define our existence and the ways in which our experiences are organised and show up in our behaviour. A number of approaches and theories have been developed to understand and explain personality.

Cultural approach to study personality can be explained in the following way

This approach attempts to understand personality in relation to the features of ecological and cultural environment.

It proposes that a group's 'economic maintenance system' plays a vital role in the origin of cultural and behavioural variations. The climatic conditions, the nature of terrain of the habitat and the availability of food (flora and fauna) determine not only people's economic activities but also their settlement patterns, social structures, division of labour and other features such as child-rearing practices.

Rituals, ceremonies, religious practices, arts, recreational activities, games and play are the means through which people's personality gets projected in a culture. People develop various personality (behavioural) qualities in an attempt to adapt to the ecological and cultural features of a group's life. Thus, the cultural approach considers personality as an adaptation of individuals or groups to the demands of their ecology and culture.

This can be explained with the help of Birhor Tribal Group. The Birhor tribal group of Jharkhand lives in forests and mountainous regions with hunting and gathering as their primary means of livelihood. They lead a nomadic life and move in small bands from one forest to another in search of food and forest products (for example, fruits, roots, mushrooms, honey, etc). In their society, children from an early age are allowed enormous freedom to move into forests and learn hunting and gathering skills which make the children independent, autonomous and achievement oriented from an early age of life.

**6. Discuss the cognitive aspects of self. Explain how they are assessed?** **CBSE 2019**

**Ans.** Psychologists from all parts of the world have shown interest in the study of self. These studies have brought out many cognitive aspects of self. These aspects one discussed below

**Self-concept** The way we perceive ourselves and the ideas we hold about our competencies and attributes is called self-concept. This view of oneself is positive or negative or both at the same time. The most frequently used method to find out an individual's self-concept involves asking the person about himself/herself.

**Self-esteem** The value judgment of a person about him/self/herself is called Self-esteem. Some people have high self-esteem, whereas others may have low self-esteem. Studies indicate that by the age of 6 to 7 years, children seem to have formed self-esteem at least in four areas i.e. academic competence, social competence, physical/athletic competence and physical appearance.

This self-esteem becomes more refined with age. It is known as an overall sense of self-esteem. Self-esteem shows a strong relationship with our everyday behaviour. For example, children with high academic self-esteem perform better in schools than those with low academic self-esteem and children with high social self-esteem are more liked by their peers.

On the other hand, children with low self-esteem often found to display anxiety, depression and increasing anti-social behaviour. Studies have shown that warm and positive parenting helps in the development of high self-esteem among children whereas children, whose parents help or make decisions for them even when they do not need assistance, often suffer from low self-esteem.

**Self-efficacy** It is the extent to which a person believe that he/she himself/herself control his/her life outcomes or the outcomes are controlled by luck other than situational factors. For example, passing an examination. A person who believes that he/she has the ability or behaviours required by a particular situation demonstrates high self-efficacy.

The concept of self-efficacy is based on Bandura's Social Learning Theory. He showed that children and adults learned behaviour by observing and copying others. People's expectation of mastery or achievement and their convictions about their own effectiveness also determines their behaviour.

A strong sense of self-efficacy allows us to select, influence and even construct the circumstances of their own. Self-efficacy can be developed. People with high self-efficacy can stop smoking, the moment he decides to do so.

Our society, our parents and our own positive experiences can help in the development of a strong sense of self-efficacy by presenting positive models during the developing years of children.

**7. A number of theories have been used to understand 'personality'. Discuss how efforts have been made to categories people into personality types since ancient times.** CBSE 2023

**Ans.** Personality refers to unique and relatively stable qualities that characterised an individual's behaviour across different situation over a time. The efforts that have been made to categorise the people into personality types are discussed below

- The Greek physician Hippocrates had proposed a typology of personality based on fluid or humour. He classified people into four types (i.e., sanguine, phlegmatic, melancholic and choleric).
- There is a typology of personality based on the trigunas, i.e. sattva, rajas, and tamas, as per Charak Samhita. Sattva guna includes attributes like cleanliness, truthfulness, dutifulness, detachment, discipline, etc. Rajas guna includes intensive activity, desire for sense gratification, dissatisfaction, envy for others and a materialistic mentality, etc. Tamas guna characterises anger, arrogance, depression, laziness, feeling of helplessness, etc.
- Using body build and temperament as the main basis, Sheldon proposed the Endomorphic, Mesomorphic and Ectomorphic typology. The endomorphs are fat, soft and round. By temperament they are relaxed and sociable. The mesomorphs have strong muscular body. They are rectangular with a strong body build. They are energetic and courageous. The ectomorphs are thin, long and have fragile body build. They are brainy, artistic and introvert. These body typologies are simple and have limited use in predicting behaviour of individuals.
- Jung has proposed widely recognised typology by grouping people into introverts and extroverts. Introverts are people who prefer to be alone, tend to avoid others, withdraw themselves in the face of emotional conflicts and are shy. Extroverts are sociable, outgoing, drawn to occupations that allow dealing directly with people and react to stress by trying to lose themselves among people and social activity.

**8. A psychologist used projective techniques to assess Rupa's personality. What are the chief features and benefits of using these tests for her, when compared to the direct methods.** CBSE SQP 2024

**Ans.** Projective techniques assess Rupa's personality indirectly.

Key features and benefits of using projective techniques are

- Projective techniques were developed to assess unconscious motives and feelings. These techniques are based on the assumption that a less structured or unstructured stimulus or situation will allow the individual to project his/her feelings, desires and needs on to that situation.
- Projective techniques use various kinds of stimulus materials and situations for assessing personality like
  — Some of them require reporting associations with stimuli (for example, words, inkblots).
  — Some involve story writing around pictures.
  — Some require sentence completions.
  — Some require expression through drawings.
  — Some require choice of stimuli from a large set of stimuli.
- The nature of stimuli and responses in these techniques vary to large extent. The stimuli are relatively or fully unstructured and poorly defined.
- The analysis of personality with the help of projective techniques assist us to understand unconscious motives, deep-rooted conflicts and emotional complexes of an individual.

**9. Discuss the interview and observation methods used in behavioural analysis. Describe the problems we face in using these methods.** CBSE SQP 2024

**Ans.** The interview method in behavioural analysis involves direct communication between the analyst and the subject, often using structured or semi-structured formats. This allows analysts to gather qualitative data about the subject's experiences, perceptions and motivations, offering a deep understanding of specific behaviours and their underlying causes.

The observation method entails systematically watching and recording behaviours in either naturalistic or controlled environments. This provides objective data about the frequency, duration and context of behaviours, enabling the identification of patterns and triggers.

Despite their utility, both methods present challenges

**Interview Method Challenges**

**Biases** Respondents may give socially desirable answers or withhold information, affecting the validity of the data.

**Rapport and Interpretation** Establishing rapport is crucial, and analysts must interpret both verbal and non-verbal cues accurately to avoid miscommunication.

**Observation Method Challenges**

**Observer Effect** The presence of an observer may influence the subject's behaviour, leading to the Hawthorne effect.

**Contextual Interpretation** Behaviours observed in isolation can be misinterpreted without considering the context or alternative explanations.

**10. Enumerate the structure of personality with respect of Freud's Theory of Personality.** CBSE SQP 2024

*Or* **Elaborate psychoanalytical theory of personality given by Freud.**

Ans. Sigmund Freud's Theory of Personality, known as Psychoanalytic theory, proposed that personality is structured into three components as follows

(i) **Id** The id is the most primitive and instinctual part of the personality. It operates on the pleasure principle, seeking immediate gratification of basic needs and desires, regardless of social norms or consequences. The id is driven by unconscious impulses and urges, such as hunger, thirst and sexual desires. It operates without regard for reality or morality and is present from birth.

(ii) **Ego** The ego is the rational and realistic part of the personality. It develops in early childhood to mediate between the demands of the id, the constraints of reality and the standards of the superego. The ego operates on the reality principle, seeking to satisfy the id's desires in socially acceptable ways that minimise negative consequences. It employs defence mechanisms, such as repression and rationalisation, to cope with conflicts and reduce anxiety.

(iii) **Superego** The superego represents the internalised moral standards and values of society, as well as the individual's conscience. It develops during childhood through identification with parental and societal figures and internalisation of their moral teachings. The superego strives for perfection and upholds moral ideals, often leading to feelings of guilt or shame when one's actions fall short of these standards. It serves as a counterbalance to the id's impulses and guides moral decisin-making.

## Case Based Questions

**1. Read the case and answer the questions that follow.**

Samar is a school going child. Due to lockdown, he is at home. One day he happens to have an instinct to eat ice-cream cone. However, there is only one ice-cream cone in refrigerator. He wants to grab the cone and eat it. He also realises that if he grabs the cone without asking, he may be punished.

The best way for Samar to achieve gratification is to ask for permission to eat the cone. In this way, he knows that if his behaviour is morally correct and this approach towards obtaining the ice-cream will not create guilt, fear or anxiety in him.

**(i) Which element of personality describes the realisation experienced by Samar that if he grabs the cone without asking, he may be punished? Discuss it.**

**(ii) Which element of personality determined that the behaviour of Samar is morally correct and guilt free? Discuss it.**

Ans. (i) The realisation experienced by Samar that if he grabs the cone without asking, he may be punished, cones from ego.

Ego grows out of id and seeks to satisfy an individual's instinctual needs in accordance with reality. It works by the reality principle and often directs the id towards more appropriate ways of behaving.

(ii) Superego determined that the behaviour of Samar is morally correct and guilt free.

The superego tells the id and the ego whether gratification in a particular instance is ethical. It helps control the id by internalising the parental authority through the process of socialisation.

**2. Read the case and answer the questions that follow.**

There is a tribe in Jharkhand namely Birhor. The Birhor tribe lives a nomadic life, which requires constant movement in small bands from one forest to another in search of games and other forest products (for example, fruits, roots, mushrooms, honey, etc.). In the Birhor society, children from an early age are allowed enormous freedom to move into forests and learn hunting and gathering skills. Their child socialisation practices are also aimed at making children do things without the help from elders, take decisions for themselves, and accept risks and challenges such as those involved in hunting from an early age of life.

**(i) Describe the Birhor tribe's way of life and how it influences their children.**

**(ii) In what ways do the Birhor's child-rearing practices support the tribe's nomadic lifestyle?**

Ans. (i) The Birhor tribe leads a nomadic life, constantly moving through forests to gather food and hunt. This lifestyle promotes independence in their children, as they learn skills like hunting and gathering at a young age. Children are encouraged to make decisions on their own and face risks without relying on elders.

(ii) The Birhor tribe's child-rearing practices encourage self-reliance, as children learn to navigate forests, hunt and gather on their own. By fostering independence and resilience early on, these practices equip children with the skills needed for their tribe's nomadic way of life.

# SELF ASSESSMENT TEST

## Objective Type Questions

1. The social self emerges in relation with others and emphasises such aspects of life as
   (a) co-operation (b) unity
   (c) affiliation and Sacrifice (d) All of these
2. Who developed 16 PF?
   (a) Allport (b) Cattell
   (c) Rogers (d) Erickson
3. Which of the following stage focuses on the genitals?
   (a) Phallic stage (b) Oral stage
   (c) Anal stage (d) Genital stage
4. Which of the following best describes 'Self' in psychology?
   (a) A person's physical appearance.
   (b) A person's financial status.
   (c) A person's organised experiences and reflections in behaviour.
   (d) A person's external social identity.
5. What is 'Personal Identity' most closely associated with?
   (a) An individual's relationship with their family.
   (b) Characteristics that connect an individual to their social group.
   (c) Unique attributes that differentiate an individual from others.
   (d) How others perceive an individual in society.
6. **Assertion** (A) The self can be understood both as a subject and as an object.
   **Reason** (R) When we reflect on our actions, we are observing ourselves, which illustrates the self as an object.
   (a) Both A and R are true and R is the correct explanation of A.
   (b) Both A and R are true, but R is not the correct explanation of A.
   (c) A is true, but R is false.
   (d) A is false, but R is true.

## Very Short Answer Type Questions

1. Define the meaning of self.
2. Define cultural approach to study personality.
3. What is self-concept?
4. Define self-efficacy.
5. Explain the term self-regulation.

## Short Answer Type Questions

1. Elaborate the existential theory of personality.
2. Differentiate between self as a subject and self as an object.
3. What do you mean by behavioural observation?
4. Ankit is unable to live in long-term relationship. He always finds a reason to break off his relationships. Identify and explain the level of consciousness that Ankit is exhibiting.

## Long Answer Type Questions

1. Elaborate the ego defence mechanisms.
2. Write a short note on behavioural approach.
3. Jamie is a 25 years old male. He is only child of his parents. Many a times, he feels hostile towards his father. He is also of the view that men are generally hostile. How do you explain Jamie's condition? Why does he feel hostile towards his father? What is the root cause of the problem?

## Case Based Questions

**Read the case and answer the questions that follow.**

A boy was brought to a psychology clinic by his parents for treatment because he was suffering from high levels of anxiety and frequently fought with his father. The anxiety he suffered from was causing him significant distress and negatively impacting his relationship with his peers and school teachers. In order to conduct a comprehensive assessment and to understand the family dynamics, the psychologist interviewed his parents. The psychologist finally observed that the boy was very clingy and too dependent on his mother. He often became uncomfortable when he observed intimacy between his parents. He tried to get in between his parents when they kissed or hugged. Further, he often argued with his father and challenged his authority. He was hostile towards the father and was in constant fear of punishment.

(i) What behavioural issues were observed in the boy and how did these affect his daily life?

(ii) How did the boy react to his parent's interactions and what might this indicate about his relationship with them?

# 03

CHAPTER

Stress is a physical, mental or emotional factor that causes bodily of mental tension. Stress is a form or response towards an event or stimuli.

# Meeting Life Challenges

▼ **YOUR STUDY GOALS**

3.1 Meaning of Stress
3.2 Nature, Type and Sources of Stress
3.3 Coping with Stress
3.4 Promoting Positive Health and Well-Being

▼ **YOUR PRACTICE GOAL**

– Objective Type Questions (29 Qs ; MCQs, A-R)
– Subjective Questions (22 VSAs, 16 SAs, 5 LAs, 3 Case Based)

## 3.1 Meaning of Stress

- The term stress originates from the Latin words 'strictus' (meaning tight or narrow) and 'stringere' (to tighten), reflecting the internal feelings of tightness and constriction reported by many under stress.
- Stress is often described environmental factors known as Stressors, which can include noise, crowding, bad relationships or daily commuting.
- The reaction to external stressors is called strain. Stress includes both causes and effects, which can cause confusion.
- Not all stress is harmful. Eustress refers to a level of stress that is beneficial, serving as one of a person's best assets for achieving peak performance and managing minor crises.
- It is important to note that eustress has the potential to turn into distress, leading to physical wear and tear.
- Overall, stress can be described as the pattern of responses an organism makes to a stimulus event that disturbs equilibrium and exceeds a person's ability to cope.

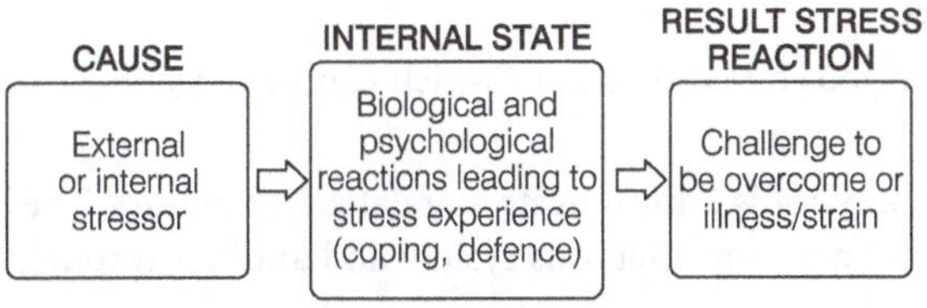


▲ *Psychological Meaning of Stress*

## 3.2 Nature, Type and Sources of Stress

- **Hans Selye**, the father of modern stress research, defined stress as 'the nonspecific response of the body to any demand', suggesting a uniform physiological reaction to all threat.
- However, many researchers argue against that different **stressors**[1] may elicit distinct patterns of stress reactions and individual responses may vary.
- Stress is shaped by a person's perception of demands and their ability to meet them that determines their feeling of being stressed.
- Stress is not merely an individual factor or an environmental characteristic; it is an ongoing process involving individuals interaction with social and cultural environments.
- Stress represents a dynamic mental/cognitive state, characterised as a disruption in **homeostasis**[2], creating a need for resolution or restoration of balance.
- The perception of stress depends on an individual's cognitive **appraisal**[3] of events and the resources available to address them, based on the cognitive theory of stress proposed by Lazarus.
- Lazarus identifies two types of appraisals–primary and secondary.

    (i) **Primary Appraisal** Primary appraisal involves perceiving a new or changing environment as positive, neutral or negative. Negative events are assessed for their possible harm, threat or challenge. Harm is t he damage already done, while threat refers to potential future damage.

- Challenge appraisals are linked with confidence in coping abilities, suggesting the potential to overcome and profit from the situation.
- When we perceive an event as stressful, secondary appraisal occurs, assessing their coping abilities and resources (mental, physical, personal) or social to handle the event's harm, threat or challenge.
- A positive attitude, good health and social support can reduce perceived stress.

    (ii) **Secondary Appraisal** This two-level appraisal process influences cognitive, behavioural, emotional and physiological responses to external events, shaping individual experiences of stress.

- Appraisals are subjective and influenced by factors like past experiences and perceived control over stressful situations. Successfully managing similar situations in the past may lessen their threat.
- Individuals who believe they can control adverse situations experience less stress than those without such a sense of control.
- Factors such as self-confidence or self-efficacy play a crucial role in determining whether an individual perceives a situation as a threat or a challenge.
- Stress includes both external (environmental, social) or internal (psychological) stressors that challenge or threaten an individual's well-being.

---

1 **Stressors** Events, circumstances or stimuli that are perceived as threats or challenges, triggering the body's stress response.
2 **Homeostasis** The body's tendency to maintain a stable internal environment, balancing physical and mental states.
3 **Appraisal** The evaluation or interpretation of a situation or event that determines if it is perceived as a threat, challenge or harm, influencing the stress response.

## Reactions to Stress

- Stressors often result in various stress reactions, which can be physiological, behavioural, emotional or cognitive.
- At the physiological level, arousal is critical in stress-related behaviours. The hypothalamus initiates two pathways–one through the autonomic nervous system and another through the pituitary gland.
  - (i) The autonomic pathway results in the adrenal gland releasing catecholamines (epinephrine and norepinephrine), causing to physiological changes related to fight-or-flight response.
  - (ii) The pituitary pathway secretes cortisol, a corticosteroid that provides energy during stress.
- Emotional reactions to stress include negative feelings such as fear, anxiety, anger or depression. Behavioural responses may include confrontational actions (fight) or withdrawal (flight).
- Cognitive responses encompass beliefs about the harm or threat posed by an event and its causes or controllability, leading to reactions like inability to concentrate or intrusive thoughts.

### Changes in Stress

- Stressors vary in terms of intensity (low vs. high), duration (short-term vs. long-term), complexity (less complex vs. more complex), and predictability (unexpected vs. predictable).
- Typically, more intense, prolonged, complex and unanticipated stresses yield more negative consequences than their less intense, short-term and predictable counterparts.
- An individual's experience of stress is influenced by their physiological strength; those with poor health are generally more vulnerable than those in good health.
- Psychological characteristics, including mental health, temperament and self-concept, significantly affect stress experience.
- The cultural context influences the meaning of events and the expected responses in various situations.
- Finally, an individual's experience of stress depends on resources, such as money, social skills, coping styles and support networks, all of which impact the appraisal of stressful situations.

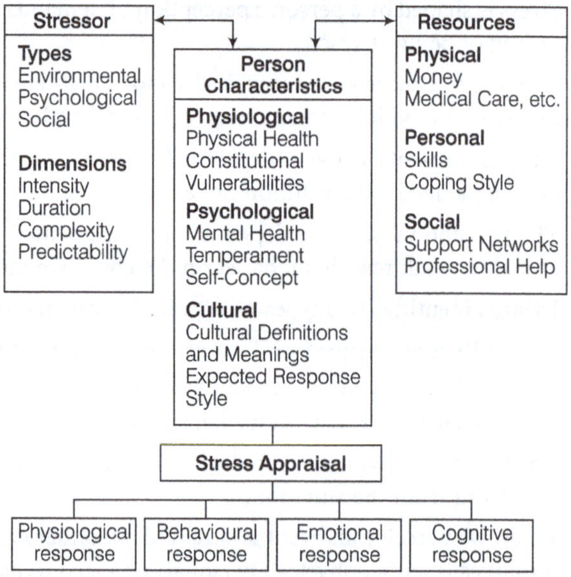


▲ *A General Model of the Stress Process*

## Signs and Symptoms of Stress

- Responses to stress differ based on personality, early upbringing, and life experiences. Each person has a unique pattern of stress response.
- The warning signs of stress may vary among individuals, as well as in their intensity.
- Some individuals can recognise their stress response patterns, allowing them to assess the severity and behavioural changes.
- Symptoms of stress can manifest in three primary ways
  - (i) **Physical Symptoms** These may include headaches, fatigue, muscle tension, gastrointestinal issues and changes in sleep patterns.
  - (ii) **Emotional Symptoms** Common emotional symptoms are feelings of anxiety, irritability, sadness or overwhelm.

(iii) **Behavioural Symptoms** Changes in behaviour may manifest as withdrawal from social activities, changes in appetite, increased substance use or difficulty concentrating.

- Any of these symptoms can indicate a certain level of stress, which, if unresolved, may lead to more serious implications.

## Types of Stress

- The three major types of stress, *viz.* physical and environmental, psychological and social

### Physical and Environmental Stress

- Physical stressors impact the body, while environmental stressors stem from our surroundings.
- Overexertion during physical activities can lead to feelings of strain.
- A lack of a nutritious diet negatively impacts our physical health. Sustaining injuries from accidents adds to physical stress.
- Insufficient sleep or rest results in fatigue and decreased performance.
- Unavoidable aspects of the environment include
    - Air pollution, which can affect respiratory health.
    - Crowding in urban areas, leading to feelings of confinement.
    - Noise from traffic or construction, causing distractions and irritation.
    - Extreme temperatures (summer heat or winter cold) can affect comfort and well-being.
- Catastrophic events such as, natural disasters like fires, earthquakes and floods create significant stress and uncertainty.

### Psychological Stress

- Psychological stress originates from internal thought processes, creating stress unique to the individual.
- Worrying about personal problems, feeling anxious or becoming depressed are symptoms of stress.
- Key sources of psychological stress are frustration, conflicts, internal and social pressures etc.

(i) **Frustration** occurs when needs and motives are blocked, preventing goal achievement. Causes can include

(a) Social discrimination

(b) Interpersonal hurt

(c) Low academic performance

(ii) **Conflicts** arise from incompatible needs or motives, such as deciding between studying dance or psychology or choosing between continuing education and starting a job.

(iii) **Internal Pressures** stem from self-imposed expectations, like striving for perfection, leading to disappointment and stress.

(iv) **Social Pressures** are external demands from others that can increase stress levels, particularly when working with difficult individuals or facing interpersonal conflicts with friends or family.

### Social Stress

- Social stress is induced by external interactions and relationships with others.
- Social events like illness or death in the family, strained relationships or conflicts with neighbours are examples of social stresses.
- Responses to social stress vary among individuals. For instance
    - A person who enjoys solitude may find attending parties stressful.
    - Conversely, an outgoing individual may feel stressed by spending too much time alone, illustrating the personal nature of social stress.

## Sources of Stress

Stress can be generated by events and conditions. Among the most important of these are major stressful life events, such as death of loved ones or personal injury, problems of everyday life, traumatic events that affect our life.

### Life Events

- Changes, whether big or small, sudden or gradual, influence our lives from the moment we are born.
- While we generally learn to cope with small, everyday changes, major life events can disrupt routine and create significant upheaval.
- When several of these life events occur within a short time frame, coping with them becomes increasingly challenging.
- These life events can be classified as either planned (e.g. moving into a new house) or unpredicted (e.g. the break-up of a long-term relationship).
- Experiencing several changes in quick succession can significantly heighten the difficulty of managing stress making individuals more susceptible to the symptoms.

#### A Measure of Stressful Life Events

- Holmes and Rahe developed a life event measure of stress, which has been adapted for different populations. The Presumptive Stressful Life Events Scale was specifically created for the Indian population by Singh, Kaur and Kaur. This scale is a self-rating questionnaire including 51 life changes that individuals may have experienced each assigned a numerical value based on its severity. For instance, the death of one's spouse is assigned a value of 95, while personal illness or injury is valued at 56. Other examples include failure in examination (43), appearing for examination or interview (43) and change in sleeping habits (33). The scale considers both positive and negative events, emphasising that both types can induce stress. The respondent's stress score is calculated as the weighted sum of all the life events they checked within the past year.
- Some sample items of the measure are

| Life Events | Mean Stress Score |
|---|---|
| Death of a close family members | 66 |
| Unexpected accident or trauma | 53 |
| Illness of a family member | 52 |
| Break-up with friend | 47 |
| Appearing for examinations | 43 |
| Change in eating habits | 27 |

- The mean number of stressful life events experienced over a year, without resulting in overt physical or mental illness is approximately two. However, the correlations between life events and the susceptibility to any specific illness are low, indicating a weak association between life events and stress. There is ongoing debate on whether life events have caused certain stress-related illnesses or if stress itself lead to these life events and illnesses. The impact of most life events varies significantly from person to person. Key factors to consider when evaluating the relationship between stressful life events and subsequent illness include, age at which the event occured, frequency of occurrence of the stressful events, duration of the stressful event, availability of social support during the stressful times.

## Hassles

- Hassles are the personal stresses individuals endure due to the occurrences in their daily lives.
- Common examples of hassles include noisy surroundings, commuting, quarrelsome neighbours, electricity and water shortages and traffic snarls.
- Daily emergencies often represent the hassles experienced by a housewife.
- Certain jobs involve frequent daily hassles, that become overwhelming.
- These daily hassles can have devastating consequences for individuals, as they often cope with them alone, while others may be unaware of these stresses. Research indicates that the more stress people report due to daily hassles, the poorer their psychological well-being.

## Traumatic Events

- Traumatic events encompass extreme incidents such as fires, accidents, robberies, earthquakes and tsunamis.
- The effects may not be immediate; they can occur after some time and may lead to persistent symptoms such as anxiety, flashbacks, dreams and intrusive thoughts.
- Severe trauma can strain relationships, complicating recovery.
- Individuals may require professional help, particularly if symptoms persist for several months after the event has concluded.

## Effects of Stress on Psychological Functioning and Health

- Stress can have both physiological and psychological effects, resulting in various changes in individuals.
- The four major effects of stress are–emotional, physiological, cognitive and behavioural.

| Effects of Stress | Description |
|---|---|
| Emotional Effects | ▪ Individuals may experience mood swings and erratic behaviour, leading to alienation from family and friends.<br>▪ Creates a vicious circle of declining confidence.<br>▪ Common emotional effects include<br>• feelings of anxiety and depression • increased physical tension<br>• increased psychological tension • mood swings<br>▪ For example, examination anxiety. |
| Psychological Effects | ▪ Stress triggers increased production of hormones such as adrenalne and cortisol<br>▪ Induces significant changes in<br>• heart rate • blood pressure levels<br>• metabolism • physical activity<br>▪ While beneficial in the short term, long-term effects can be damaging.<br>▪ Example include ▪ Release of epinephrine and nor-epinephrine<br>▪ Slowing down of the digestive system ▪ Expansion of air passages in the lungs<br>▪ Increased heart rate ▪ Constriction of blood vissels |
| Cognitive Effects | ▪ Prolonged stress can lead to mental overload, impairing decision-making.<br>▪ Faulty decisions may result in<br>• arguments • failure<br>• financial loss • loss of job<br>▪ Cognitive effects include<br>• poor concentration • reduced short-term memory capacity |

| | |
|---|---|
| Behavioural Effects | ▪ Influences behaviour, leading to unhealthy habits such as<br>▪ eating less nutritional food<br>▪ Increased intake of stimulants (e.g. caffeine)<br>▪ excessive consumption of cigarettes, alcohol and tranquilisers<br>▪ tranquilisers can be addictive with side effects like, loss of concentration, poor coordination, dizziness<br>▪ Typical behavioural effects include<br>• disrupted sleep patterns<br>• increased absenteeism • reduced work performance |

## Stress and Health

- Many individuals often fall sick during examination time due to increased stress levels.
- Common ailments include stomach upsets, body aches, nausea, diarrhea, fever.
- It is often observed that people who are unhappy in their personal lives tend to fall sick more frequently than those who are happy and enjoy life.
- Chronic daily stress can divert an individual's attention from self-care, leading to various health issues.
- When stress is prolonged, it affects both physical and psychological health.
- Individuals often experience exhaustion and attitudinal problems when the stress caused by environmental demands and constraints is too high and there is little support available from family and friends.
- Physical exhaustion is reflected in symptoms such as, chronic fatigue, weakness, low energy.
- Mental exhaustion may cause irritability, anxiety, feelings of helplessness and feelings of hopelessness.
- This combination of physical, emotional and psychological exhaustion is called Burnout.
- Research shows stress can alter the immune system, thereby increasing the risk of illness.
- Stress is linked to various health issues, including, cardiovascular disorders, high blood pressure as well as, psychosomatic disorders, such as ulcers, asthma, allergies and headaches.
- Researchers estimate that stress contributes to 50% to 70% of all physical illnesses.
- Studies also reveal that approximately 60% of medical visits are due to stress-related symptoms.

## General Adaptation Syndrome (GAS)

- GAS describes body's response to prolonged test. It was studied by Hans Selye, who observed the physiological responses to various stressors in animals and patients.
- Selye subjected animals to a variety of stressors such as, high temperature, X-rays and insulin injections also observing patients with various injuries and illnesses.
- He noticed a similar pattern of bodily response across different stressors, leading to the identification of GAS.

### Stages of GAS

(i) **Alarm Reaction Stage**

- Triggered by the stressor this stage activates the adrenal-pituitary-cortex system, releasing hormones that produce the stress response.
- The initial phase of the body's response to stress, involving physiological changes like increased heart rate and adrenaline release, preparing the body for a 'fight-or-flight' response.

(ii) **Resistance Stage**

- Occurs if the stress is prolonged.
- The parasympathetic nervous system signals for more cautious use of the body's resources while the body attempts to cope with the threat, often through confrontation.

(iii) **Exhaustion Stage**

- Results from continued exposure to the same or additional stressors.
- Drains the body of its resources.
- The physiological systems involved in the alarm reaction and resistance stages become ineffective.
- Increases susceptibility to stress-related diseases such as high blood pressure.

### Criticism of Selye's Model

- The model has been criticised for assigning a limited role to psychological factors in stress.
- Researchers emphasise that the psychological appraisal of events is crucial in determining stress levels.
- How individuals respond to stress is influenced by their perceptions, personalities and biological constitutions.

## Stress and the Immune System

- Stress can cause illness by impairing the functioning of the immune system, which protects the body against attackers from both within and outside.
- **Psychoneuroimmunology**[4] focuses on the links between the mind, brain and immune system, studying the effects of stress on immune responses.
- The immune system comprises white blood cells (leucocytes), which identify and destroy foreign bodies (antigens) such as viruses and produce of antibodies.
- T cells destroy invaders and include T-helper cells that enhance immunological activity. T-helper cells are specifically targeted by the Human Immunodeficiency Virus (HIV), the virus responsible for Acquired Immunodeficiency Syndrome (AIDS).
- B cells produce antibodies, while natural killer cells play a vital role in fighting against viruses and tumours.
- Stress can reduce natural killer cell cytotoxicity, which is crucial for defence against infections and cancer. Individuals experiencing high stress, such as students during exams, bereaved individuals and those severely depressed, show decreased levels of these cells.
- Studies indicate that social support improves inmmune function and changes in the immune system significantly affect health, particularly in those with already weakened immune systems.
- Stress is often accompanied by negative emotions and behaviours, including depression, hostility, anger and aggression, which are particularly concerning in the study of stress and health.
- Long-term stress increases the risk of psychological disorders, such as panic attacks and obsessive behaviour, with worries manifesting as physical sensations sometimes mistaken for a heart attack.
- Individuals under prolonged stress are more susceptible to irrational fears, mood swings and phobias, experiencing fits of depression, anger and irritability.
- Negative emotions are correlated with immune system function and our ability to interpret the world and invest that interpretation with personal meaning and emotion has a direct effect on the body.
- Negative moods are associated with poorer health outcomes and feelings of hopelessness can worsen disease, increasing the risk of injury and death from various causes.

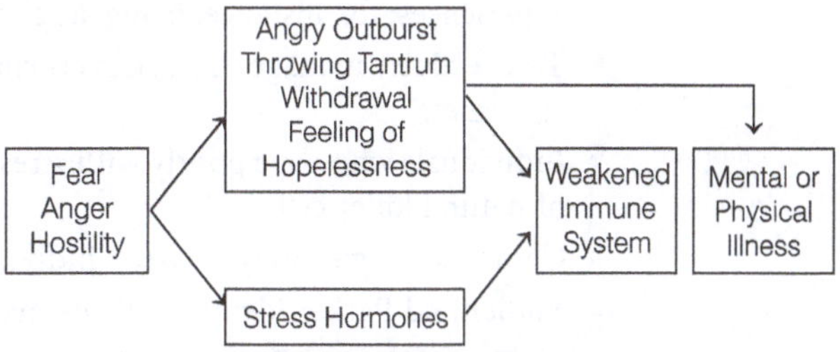


▲ *Relation of Stress with Illness*

4 **Psychoneuroimmunology** The study of the interaction between psychological processes, the nervous system and the immune system, exploring how stress impacts immune functioning.

## Lifestyle

- Stress can lead to an unhealthy lifestyle or health-damaging behaviour, affecting overall well-being.
- Lifestyle refers to the overall pattern of decisions and behaviours that determine a person's health and quality of life.
- Individuals experiencing stress may be more likely to expose themselves to pathogens, which cause physical illness.
- They often develop poor nutritional habits, tend to sleep less and are likely to engage in other health-risking behaviours, such as smoking and alcohol abuse.
- These health-impairing behaviours typically develop gradually, offering temporary pleasure, leading individuals to ignore their long-term damaging effects.
- Many people underestimate the risks of unhealthy behaviours, which can have significant consequences on their health.
- Studies indicate that health-promoting behaviours such as a balanced diet, regular exercise and family support play an important role in maintaining good health.
- Adhering to a lifestyle that includes a balanced low-fat diet, regular exercise and continued activity, along with positive thinking, can enhance health and longevity.
- The modern lifestyle, characterised by excesses in eating and drinking, along with the fast-paced notion of a good life, has led some individuals to violate basic principles of health regarding their diet, thoughts and action.

### Quick Test 1

1. What are the two types of stress based on nature?
2. What is the term for stress that arises from positive events or situations?
3. What type of stress is linked to immediate threats or challenges?
4. What is the name of the physiological response triggered by stress?
5. What are the primary sources of stress as categorized by psychologists?
6. How does role conflict contribute to stress in workplaces?

## 3.3 Coping with Stress

- Coping is defined as a dynamic, situation-specific reaction to stress involving concrete responses aimed at resolving the problem and reducing stress.
- The effectiveness of coping strategies often depends on rigid deep-seated beliefs formed through past experiences; for instance, being stuck in traffic due to the belief that traffic 'should' move faster.
- To effectively manage stress, it is crucial to reassess one's thought processes and learn appropriate coping strategies.
- Individuals who cope poorly with stress may exhibit an impaired immune response and reduced activity of natural killer cells.
- Coping strategies vary between individuals and can include both overt and covert activities.
- Endler and Parker identified three main coping strategies

  (i) **Task-oriented Strategy** This strategy involves obtaining information about the stressful situation, considering alternative courses of action, and deciding priorities to deal directly with the stress. An example would be to schedule time better or reflect on past problem-solving experiences.

  (ii) **Emotion-oriented Strategy** This strategy focuses on maintaining hope and controlling emotions. It may involve venting feelings of anger and frustration or accepting that nothing can be changed. Examples include telling oneself that the situation is not really happening or worrying about future actions.

(iii) **Avoidance-oriented Strategy** This strategy entails denying or minimising the seriousness of the situation and suppressing stressful thoughts in favour of self-protective thoughts. Activities may include watching TV, calling a friend or seeking social interaction.

## Strategies Given by Lazarus and Folkman

- Lazarus and Folkman conceptualised coping as a dynamic process rather than a fixed trait, involving constantly changing cognitive and behavioural efforts to manage, reduce or tolerate the demands created by stress.
- Coping allows individuals to manage or alter a problem while regulating their emotional response to it.
- Coping responses can be categorised into two types–problem-focused and emotion-focused responses.
  (i) **Problem-focused Strategies** address the problem directly through behaviours aimed at gaining information, altering the event or changing beliefs and commitments. These strategies enhance awareness and knowledge and expand coping options, ultimately reducing the perceived threat of the event. An example is making and following a plan of action.
  (ii) **Emotion-focused Strategies** focus on minimising emotional disruption caused by an event, with less emphasis on changing the event itself. An example is engaging in activities to release pent-up emotions.
- While both strategies are essential in dealing with stress, research indicates that people generally use problem-focused strategies more frequently than emotion-focused ones.

## Stress Management Techniques

- Stress is often considered a 'silent killer' and is significantly linked to illnesses such as hypertension, heart disease, ulcers, diabetes and even cancer.
- Due to lifestyle changes, stress levels have increased, prompting schools, offices and communities to prioritise stress management techniques.

### Relaxation Techniques

- These are active skills that reduce stress symptoms and lower risks of illnesses like high blood pressure and heart disease.
- Relaxation starts from the lower body and moves up, incorporating deep breathing with muscle relaxation to fully calm the body and mind.

### Meditation Procedures

- Meditation involves techniques to refocus attention, bringing an altered state of consciousness and complete mental focus.
- In deep meditation, the person becomes unaware of external stimuli, reaching a peaceful state of consciousness.

### Biofeedback

- This method monitors physiological responses (like heart rate) and provides feedback to help control them, usually paired with relaxation training.
- It involves three stages–awareness of physiological responses, control in calm settings and applying control in daily life.

### Creative Visualisation

- This technique uses imagery and imagination to create realistic goals and reduce stress, building confidence and inner calm.
- It is most effective when the body is relaxed, mind is clear and eyes are closed.

### Cognitive Behavioural Techniques

- These aim to prepare individuals for stress by replacing negative and irrational thoughts with positive and rational thinking.
- The three main phases are assessment (understanding the problem), stress reduction (learning to manage stress) and application (practicing strategies in real life).

### Exercise

- Physical activities like swimming, walking, running, cycling and skipping help manage stress by providing an outlet for physical arousal and improving overall health.
- Regular exercise (four times a week for at least 30 minutes per session) includes warm-up, exercise and cool-down phases, enhancing heart function, lung health, circulation and immune system strength.

#### Quick Test 2

1. What is the term for strategies aimed at resolving and reducing stress?
2. What are the two main types of coping strategies identified by Lazarus and Folkman?
3. What type of coping strategy focuses on obtaining information to deal directly with a stressful situation?
4. Which relaxation technique focuses on calming the body using deep breathing and muscle relaxation?
5. What is biofeedback primarily used for in stress management?
6. What is the recommended duration for regular physical exercise to manage stress effectively?

## 3.4 Promoting Positive Health and Well-Being

- It is unlikely to go through life without experiencing personal crises that bring acute pressure for a time.
- Many people manage to navigate these crises well, rebuilding their lives positively with constructive attitudes and emotional and social support from different sources.
- When we manage these pressures and channel our energy to create positive outcomes from challenging situations, we learn to survive in a healthy way, which builds **resilience**[5] for future crises, like an immunisation against unhealthy stress.

### Stress-Resistant Personality

- Recent studies by Kobasa reveal that individuals with high stress but low illness levels share three characteristics known as the Personality Traits of Hardiness.
- **Hardiness**[6] is defined by the 'three Cs'–Commitment, Control and Challenge.
- Commitment is having a sense of purpose in tasks and responsibilities, including work, family, hobbies and social life.
- Control refers to a sense of direction and feeling in control over life circumstances.
- Challenge is viewing life changes as normal and positive experiences rather than threats.
- Not everyone possesses these characteristics inherently; many of us need to relearn life skills in areas like rational thinking and assertiveness to improve our ability to handle everyday demands effectively.

5 **Resilience** The capacity to recover quickly from difficulties, maintaining mental health and functioning in the face of adversity.
6 **Hardiness** A personality trait associated with resilience and effective stress management, characterised by commitment, control and a sense of challenge rather than threat.

## Life Skills

- Life skills are abilities for adaptive and positive behaviour that enable individuals to deal effectively with the demands and challenges of everyday life.
- Our ability to cope depends on how well we are prepared to manage everyday demands and maintain equilibrium in our lives.
- Life skills can be learned and improved upon, helping individuals meet life's challenges.

### Assertiveness

- Assertiveness is a behaviour or skill that helps individuals communicate clearly and confidently about their feelings, needs, wants and thoughts.
- It involves the ability to say no to requests, state opinions without self-consciousness and express emotions openly (e.g., love, anger).
- Being assertive boosts self-confidence, enhances self-esteem and fosters a solid sense of identity.

### Time Management

- The way one spends time affects life quality; therefore, planning and delegating effectively can help relieve pressure.
- The central principle of time management is aligning time with personal values and achieving goals.
- Effective time management requires realism about responsibilities and organising life to balance tasks and goals.

### Rational Thinking

- Many stress-related problems arise from distorted thinking.
- Thoughts and feelings are closely connected and stress often leads to a bias toward negative thoughts.
- Principles of rational thinking include challenging irrational beliefs, eliminating anxiety-provoking thoughts and making positive statements.

### Improving Relationships

- Effective relationships rely on communication, which includes listening, expressing feelings and accepting others' opinions.
- Building healthy relationships requires avoiding behaviours like misplaced jealousy and sulking.

### Self-care

- Self-care promotes physical and emotional readiness to handle daily stressors.
- Stress impacts breathing patterns, so relaxed, diaphragmatic breathing can enhance calmness.
- Environmental stressors (e.g., noise, light, colour) affect mood and coping ability.

### Overcoming Unhelpful Habits

- Habits like perfectionism, procrastination and avoidance may offer short-term relief but increase vulnerability to stress.
- Perfectionists struggle with adjusting standards and may become self-critical.
- Procrastinators often avoid tasks out of fear of failure or rejection.

## Factors Promoting Positive Health

- Positive health encompasses physical, mental, social and spiritual well-being, not merely the absence of disease.
- Constructs of positive health include a healthy body, high-quality relationships, purpose in life, self-regard, life mastery and resilience.
- Factors that act as stress buffers and facilitate positive health include

## Diet

- A balanced diet enhances mood, energy, muscle function, circulation and overall resilience.
- Eating three main balanced meals daily promotes well-being.
- During stress, people may crave comfort foods high in fats, salt and sugar, which can impact health.

## Exercise

- Studies show a positive correlation between physical fitness and health.
- Regular exercise manages weight, reduces tension, anxiety and depression and serves as a stress buffer.
- Stretching exercises (e.g., yogic asanas) promote calm, while aerobic exercises (e.g., jogging, swimming) increase energy.

## Positive Attitude

- Positive health is reinforced by a realistic view of life, responsibility, acceptance of different views and crediting oneself for success.
- A sense of humour and the ability to laugh at oneself help maintain balance.

## Positive Thinking

- Optimism a positive outlook on life, where individuals expect favourable outcomes enhancing both psychological and physical well-being.
- Optimists tend to use problem-focused coping and seek advice, while pessimists may ignore stressors or abandon goals.

## Social Support

- Social support means having people who care, value and love you, creating a network of mutual obligation.
- Studies show that high-quality social support correlates with improved health and well-being.
- Social support can be tangible (e.g., providing goods) or informational (e.g., sharing coping strategies).
- Emotional support, especially during times of stress, boosts mental health for both the giver and receiver.

### Quick Test 3

1. What are the three components of the personality trait 'Hardiness'?
2. What is the primary focus of life skills in managing daily challenges?
3. How does assertiveness enhance personal identity?
4. What is the central principle of effective time management?
5. What type of thinking is emphasised in rational thinking to address stress-related problems?
6. How can positive thinking influence stress management?
7. What role does social support play in promoting positive health?

# NCERT Folder

**1. Explain the concept of stress. Give examples from daily life.**

**Ans.** Stress can be described as the pattern of responses an organism makes to an event that disturbs the stability and reduces a person's ability to cope. Challenges cause stress. Stress is like electricity as it gives energy, increases human arousal and affects performance.

However, high stress can produce unpleasant effects and cause our performance to deteriorate and too little stress may cause one to feel somewhat listless and low on motivation which may lead us to perform slowly and less efficiently.

Examples from daily life

- Attending parties may be stressful for a person who likes to spend quiet evenings at home.
- If a person gets low marks than his/her expectations, then it may be stressful and a sign of frustration for them.
- When someone is forced to choose the job due to family pressure, then it may be stressful for him afterwards.

**2. State the symptoms and sources of stress.**

**Ans.** Everyone has their own pattern of stress response.

- Our response to stress varies depending upon our personality, early upbringing and life experiences.
- The symptoms of stress can be physical, emotional and behavioural.
- Any symptom can indicate a degree of stress which, if left unresolved, might have serious implications.

**Sources of Stress**

There are three major sources of stress

(i) **Life Events** Major life events can be stressful, because they disturb our routine and cause upheaval. If several of these life events that are planned (e.g. moving into a new house) or unpredicted (e.g. break-up of a long-term relationship) occur within a short period of time, we find it difficult to cope with them and will be more prone to the symptoms of stress.

(ii) **Hassles** These are the personal stresses we experience as individuals, due to the happenings in our daily life, such as noisy surroundings, commuting, quarrelsome neighbours, electricity and water shortage, traffic snarls. There are some jobs in which daily hassles are very frequent.

These daily hassles may sometimes have devastating consequences for the individual. The more stress people face daily, the poorer is their psychological well-being.

(iii) **Traumatic Events** These events include extreme events such as a fire, train or road accident, robbery, earthquake, tsunami, etc. The effects of these events may occur after some lapse of time and sometimes persist as symptoms of anxiety, flashbacks, dreams and intrusive thoughts, etc.

Severe trauma can also strain relationships. Professional help will be needed to cope with them if they persist for many months after the event is over.

**3. Describe the GAS model and illustrate the relevance of this model with the help of an example.**

*Or* **What is GAS? How does Selye's model relate prolong stress to bodily response. Explain.**

*Or* **Explain the reaction of stress according to General Adaptation Syndrome.**

**Ans.** **General Adaptation Syndrome** (GAS) Selye studied the issue of stress by subjecting animals to a variety of stressors such as high temperature, X-rays and insulin injections, in the laboratory.

He also observed patients with various injuries and illnesses in hospitals in which he noticed a similar pattern of bodily response in all of them. He called this pattern the General Adaptation Syndrome (GAS).

**Stages of GAS**

(i) **Alarm Reaction Stage** The presence of a noxious stimulus or stressor activates the adrenal-pituitary-cortex system. This triggers the release of hormones producing the stress response. In this stage individual is ready for fight.

(ii) **Resistance Stage** If stress is prolonged, the resistance stage begins. The parasympathetic nervous system calls for more cautious use of the body's resources. The organism makes efforts to cope with the threat, as through confrontation.

(iii) **Exhaustion Stage** Continued exposure to the same stressor or additional stressors drains the body of its resources and leads to the third stage of exhaustion.

The physiological systems involved in alarm reaction and resistance become ineffective and susceptibility to stress-related diseases such as high blood-pressure becomes more possible.

**4. Enumerate the different ways of coping with stress.**

**Ans.** Coping is a dynamic situation-specific reaction to stress. It is a set of concrete responses to stressful situations or events aimed to resolve the problem and reduce stress.

The way we cope with stress often depends on deep-seated beliefs, based on experience. Coping strategies include both overt and covert activities. The three coping strategies given by Endler and Parker are as follows

(i) **Task-oriented Strategy** This involves obtaining information about the stressful situation and about alternative courses of action and their probable outcome. It also involves deciding priorities and acting, so as to deal directly with the stressful situation.

(ii) **Emotion-oriented Strategy** This can involve efforts to maintain hope and control one's emotions. It can also involve venting feelings of anger and frustration or deciding that nothing can be done to change things.

(iii) **Avoidance-oriented Strategy** This involves denying or minimising the seriousness of the situation. It also involves conscious suppression of stressful thoughts and their replacement by self-protective thoughts.

**Strategies given by Lazarus and Folkman** Lazarus and Folkman has conceptualised coping as a dynamic process rather than an individual trait. According to them, coping responses can be divided into two types of responses

(i) **Problem-focused Strategies** It attacks the problem itself, with behaviours designed to gain information, to alter the event and to alter belief and commitments. They increase the person's awareness, level of knowledge and range of behaviou- ral and cognitive coping options. They can act to reduce the threat value of the event.

(ii) **Emotion-focused Strategies** It call for psychological changes designed primarily to limit the degree of emotional disruption caused by an event, with minimal effort to alter the event itself.

**5. Explain the effect of stress on psychological functioning.** **CBSE 2024 C**

*Or* **Differentiate between eustress and distress. Explain the different effects of stress with example.**

**Ans.** Eustress is the term used to describe the levels of stress that is good for us. It is one of a person's best assets for achieving peak performance and managing minor crisis. In daily life it has positive connotations.

Distress in daily life has negative connotations. This stress can be described as the pattern of responses that disturbs the equilibrium and exceeds a person's ability to cope.

There are four major effects of stress associated with the stressed state. These are as follows

- **Emotional Effects** Those who suffer from stress are likely to experience mood swings and show erratic behaviour that may alienate them from family and friends. For example, feeling of anxiety and depression, increased physical tension, increased psychological tension and mood swings.
- **Physiological Effects** When the human body is placed under physical or psychological stress, it increases the production of certain hormones, such as adrenaline and cortisol. These hormones produce marked changes in heart rate, blood pressure levels, metabolism and physical activity.
  Examples of physiological effects are release of epinephrine and norepinephrine, slowing down of the digestive system, etc.
- **Cognitive Effects** If pressures due to stress continue, one may suffer from mental overload. This suffering from high level of stress can rapidly cause individuals to lose their ability to make decisions. Cognitive effects of stress are poor concentration and reduced short-term memory capacity.
- **Behavioural Effects** Stress affects our behaviour in the form of eating less nutritional food, increasing intake of stimulants such as caffeine, excessive consumption of cigarettes, alcohol and other drugs such as tranquillisers, etc.

Some of the typical behavioural effects of stress seen are disrupted sleep patterns, increased absenteeism and reduced work performance.

**6. Describe how life skills can help meet life's challenges.**

**Ans.** Life skills are abilities for adaptive and positive behaviour that enable individuals to deal effectively with the demands and challenges of everyday life.

Some life skills that will help to meet the challenges of life are

(i) **Assertiveness** It is a behaviour or skill that helps to communicate clearly and confidently, our feelings, needs, wants and thoughts.

(ii) **Time Management** The central principle of time management is to spend one's time through doing the things that one value, or that help one to achieve one's goals. It depends on being realistic and do aparticular work within a certain time period.

(iii) **Rational Thinking** Many stress-related problems occur as a result of distorted thinking.

Some of the principles of rational thinking are

- Challenging distorted thinking and irrational beliefs.
- Driving out potentially intrusive negative anxiety and provoking thoughts.
- Making positive statements.

(iv) **Improving Relationships** The key to an effective relationship is communication which consists of three essential skills i.e. listening to what the other person is saying, expressing how you feel and what you think and accepting the other person's opinions and feelings, even if they are different from your own.

(v) **Self-care** The better way to prepare physically and emotionally and to tackle the stresses of everyday life is to keep ourselves healthy, fit and relaxed. Our breathing patterns reflect our state of mind and emotions.

(vi) **Overcoming Unhelpful Habits** Perfectionism, avoidance, procrastination are strategies which provides short-term gain but makes the individual vulnerable to stress.
Perfectionists want to get everything just as they want which is not always possible.

Avoidance is ignoring the issue and refusal to face it or accept it.

Procrastination means putting off what we know we need to do. We often say 'I well do it later', just to avoid confrontation due to the fear of failure.

**7. Discuss the factors that lead to positive health and well-being.**

**Ans.** Factors facilitating positive health and well-being are

(i) **Diet** A balanced diet can improve mood, boost energy, nourish muscles, improve circulation, prevent illness, strengthen the immune system and make one feel better to cope with stresses of life. The key to healthy living is to eat three main meals a day and eat a varied well-balanced diet.

(ii) **Exercise** Exercise is the lifestyle change with the widest popular approval. Regular exercise plays an important role in managing weight and stress and it has a positive effect on reducing tension, anxiety and depression.

(iii) **Positive Attitude** Positive health and well-being can be realised by having a positive attitude. Some of the factors leading to a positive attitude are

- having a fairly accurate perception of reality.
- a sense of purpose in life and responsibility.
- acceptance and tolerance for different viewpoints of others.
- taking credit for success and accepting blame for failure.
- being open to new ideas and having a sense of humour with the ability to laugh at oneself help us to remain centred and see things in a proper perspective.

(iv) **Positive Thinking** The power of positive thinking has been increasingly recognised in reducing and coping with stress. Optimism has been linked to psychological and physical well-being.

(v) **Social Support** Social support is defined as the existence and availability of people on whom we can rely upon and people who care, value and love us. Social support can help to provide protection against stress. People with high levels of social support from family and friends may experience less stress when they confront a stressful experience and they may cope with it more successfully.

**8. How does stress affect the immune system?**

***Or* Describe the effect of stress on immune system.**

**Ans.** Stress can cause illness by impairing the workings of the immune system. The immune system guards the body against attackers, both from within and outside the body.

**Psychoneuroimmunology** focuses on the links between the mind, brain and immune system. It studies the effects of stress on the immune system. The white blood cells (leucocytes) within the immune system identify and destroy foreign bodies (antigens) such as viruses. Its also leads to the production of antibodies.

Some of the white blood cells are

- **T cells** which destroy invaders, T-helper cells which increase immunological activity and these are attacked by HIV, the virus which causes AIDS.
- **B cells** which produce antibodies.
- **Natural killer cells** which involves in the fight against both viruses and tumours.

Stress can affect natural killer cell cytotoxicity which is of major importance in the defence against various infections and cancer. Reduced levels of natural killer cell cytotoxicity have been found in people who are highly stressed.

**9. Give an example of a life event which is likely to be stressful. Suggest reasons why it is likely to cause different degrees of stress to the person experiencing it.**

**Ans.** Death of a close family member is an example of life event which is likely to be very stressful. People find it difficult to cope with this unpredicted life events and suffer from stress.

The impact of most life events varies from person to person. Thus, we see the death of a family member causes different degrees of stress to other members of the family. The reasons behind this are

(i) The age at which the event is experienced by the family members. For example, the stress of an adult person who lost his father is different from the stress of a child who lost his grand father.

(ii) Frequency of occurrence causes different degrees of stress. For example, consecutive death incidents in a family devastate the family members.

(iii) Duration of stressful event causes stress. For example, sudden death or death due to long illness produce different degress of stress among the family members.

(iv) Social support can help to cope up with the stress. Social support is defined as the existence and availability of people on whom we can rely.

People with high level of social support from family and friends may experience less stress when they confront a stressful experience.

**10. Given what you know about coping strategies, what suggestions would you give to your friends to avoid stress in their everyday lives.** Competency Based Que.

**Ans.** Coping is a dynamic situation-specific reaction to stress involving concrete responses to stressful situations or events that are intended to resolve the problem and reduce stress. The way we cope with stress often depends on rigid deep-seated beliefs, based on experience.

For example, when caught in a traffic jam we feel angry, because we believe that the traffic 'should' move faster.

To manage stress, we often need to reassess the way we think and learn coping strategies. Individuals show consistent differences in the coping strategies, which they use to handle stressful situations.

I would like to give some suggestions to my friends to avoid stress in everyday lives. These are

(i) They can follow 'Task-oriented' strategy. It involves deciding priorities and acting directly with the stressful situation. For example, a person can schedule his time better and think about how he has to solve the problems according to their priorities.

(ii) Stressed person can make efforts to maintain hope and control his own emotions. This 'Emotion-oriented' strategy involves venting feelings of anger and frustration on deciding that nothing can be done to change things.

(iii) Individual can follow 'Avoidance-oriented' strategy which involves denying or minimising the seriousness of the situation. In this strategy individual consciously suppress the stressful thoughts and replace the stress by self-protective thoughts like phone up a friend, watching TV etc.

**11. Reflect on the environmental factors that have (a) a positive impact on the being and (b) a negative effect.**

**Ans.** Environmental factors that have a positive impact on the being are fair government policies on pollution, social campaign for the plantation of trees, mass awareness movements for Clean India Mission (Swachh Bharat Mission) etc.

Environmental factors that have a negative effect are the stresses of our surroundings that are often unavoidable such as air pollution, crowding, noise, heat of the summer, winter cold, etc.

Another group of environmental stresses are catastrophic events or disasters such as fire, earthquake, floods, etc.

**12. We know that certain lifestyle factors can cause stress and may lead to diseases like cancer and coronary heart disease, yet we are unable to change our behaviour. Explain why?**

**Ans.** Lifestyle is the overall pattern of decisions and behaviours that determine a person's health and quality of life. Stress can lead to unhealthy lifestyle or health damaging behaviour.

Stressed individuals may be more likely to expose themselves to pathogens, which are agents causing physical illness. People who are stressed have poor nutritional habits, sleepless and are likely to engage in other health risking behaviours like smoking and alcohol abuse. Such health impairing behaviours develop gradually and provide pleasant experiences temporarily, but have detrimental long-term consequences.

As they are addictive and pleasurable, individuals using these psychoactive substances are unable to give them up. Such type of lifestyle ultimately cause serious health hazards like cancer, diabetes and Coronary Heart Diseases (CHD).

People know such faulty lifestyle causes but still they continue, because the consequences and side effects are not likely to occur immediately. Their effects get manifested after several years. So, people ignore them because they are aware with the side effects.

They develop anxiety because of inconsistency in their attitude and behaviour because this lifestyle becomes a part of their habit pattern. So, they find it very difficult to change and continue such hazardous lifestyle and ultimately it causes a stage of burnout.

# Exam Pattern Questions

## Objective Type Questions

### Multiple Choice Questions (MCQs)

**1.** The physical, environmental and social causes of the stress state are termed as

(a) stress (b) stressors
(c) distress (d) None of these

**2.** The general adaptation syndrome consists of three stages which include

(a) the alarm reaction (b) the stage of resistance
(c) the stage of exhaustion (d) All of these

**3.** In the ...... stage, the parasympathetic nervous system calls for more cautious use of the body's resources. **CBSE Term I 2021**

(a) alarm reaction (b) resistance
(c) exhaustion (d) adaptation

**4.** ...... stresses are demands that change the state of our body. For example, we feel strained when we overexert ourselves, lack a nutritious diet or suffer an injury.

(a) Environmental (b) Bodily
(c) Physical (d) Health-related

**5.** It is the ......... that are attacked by the Human Immuno Deficiency Virus (HIV), the virus causing Acquired Immuno Deficiency Syndrome (AIDS). **CBSE Term I 2021**

(a) B cells (b) T-helper cells
(c) T cells (d) Natual Killer cells

**6.** Social support may be in the form of ......... support when assistance is provided in the form of material aid, such as money, goods, services, etc.

(a) emotional (b) tangible
(c) informational (d) material

**7.** ......... is a stress management technique involving subjective experiences using imagery and imagination. **CBSE Term I 2021**

(a) Creative visualisation (b) Relaxation
(c) Meditation (d) Biofeedback

**8.** ......... is the term used to describe the level of stress that is good for a person as it enhances performance. **CBSE SQP 2021**

(a) Distress (b) Eustress
(c) Social Stress (d) Strain

**9.** According to experts who deals with Post Traumatic Stress Disorder, one of the key attitudes to develop in the survivours is that of ......... . **CBSE 2019**

(a) self-confidence (b) self-worth
(c) self-concept (d) self-efficacy

**10.** The state of physical, emotional and psychological exhaustion is known as

(a) resistance (b) stress (c) burnout (d) coping

**11.** Negative events are appraised for their possible ......... .

(a) harm, threat or commitment
(b) harm, thought or controllability
(c) hurt, threat, damage or challenge
(d) harm, threat or challenge

**12.** ...... results from the blocking of needs and motives by something or someone that hinders us from achieving the desired goal. **CBSE Term I 2021**

(a) Conflict (b) Internal pressure
(c) Social pressure (d) Frustration

**13.** ......... stem from beliefs based upon expectations from inside us, such as, 'I must do everything perfectly'. **CBSE SQP 2021**

(a) Conflicts (b) Frustrations
(c) Social stresses (d) Internal pressures

**14.** As per the General Adaptation Syndrome, the individual is ready for fight or flight in the ......... stage.

(a) resistance (b) burnout
(c) alarm reaction (d) exhaustion

**15.** A study finds that individuals who are regularly exposed to high stress levels have a higher incidence of infections. This observation can be explained by. **CBSE 2025**

(a) Enhanced production of antibodies during stress
(b) Increased white cell count due to stress
(c) Impaired immune response due to stress
(d) Reduced need for sleep due to stress

**16.** Sheetal was provided feedback about her current physiological activity. This was also accompanied by relaxation training. This procedure to monitor and reduce the physiological aspects of stress is known as .......... . **CBSE Term I 2021**

(a) meditation (b) relaxation
(c) biofeedback (d) coping

**17.** Reebika is experiencing stress due to noisy surroundings, commuting, quarrelsome neighbours, electricity and water shortage. These sources of stress are ......... .

(a) life events (b) hassle
(c) traumatic events (d) environmental events

**18.** Randeep puts the work-related issues under the carpet and refuses to accept or face them. This explains that he is ......... the task. CBSE Term I 2021

(a) avoiding
(b) procrastinating
(c) managing
(d) approaching

**19.** Heena lost her husband in a car accident. This life event is traumatic. Which of the following is not true about the effects this stress can have on her ? CBSE Term I 2021

I. Stress can affect her behaviour in the form of eating less nutritional food, disrupted sleep patterns, increased absenteeism and reduced work performance.
II. The cognitive effects of stress will be both, enhanced concentration and increased short-term memory capacity.
III. In her case, the stress can start a vicious circle of decreasing confidence, leading to more serious emotional problems.
IV. The effects of this stress will mostly be physiological in nature.

Codes

(a) I and II
(b) II and IV
(c) II and III
(d) I, II and IV

**20.** Which of the following statements is not true about coping with stress?

I. Coping is a dynamic situation-specific reaction to stress.
II. It is a set of concrete response to stressful situations or events that are intended to resolve the problem and reduce stress.
III. People who cope poorly with stress have high level of natural killer cell cytotoxicity.
IV. Individuals show similarity in coping strategies that they use to deal with stressful situations.

Codes

(a) II, III and IV
(b) Only III
(c) II and III
(d) I and II

**21.** Which of the following are the dimensions of stress? CBSE SQP 2022

I. Intensity
II. Duration
III. Predictability
IV. Vulnerability

Codes

(a) I, II and IV
(b) I, III and IV
(c) II, III and IV
(d) I, II and III

**22.** Ritika's stress level was good for her and enhanced her performance. The term used to describe her level of stress is called ......... . CBSE SQP 2024

(a) strain
(b) distress
(c) eustress
(d) appraisal

**23.** Meena denies the seriousness of completing her work in the office by talking to her friend on the phone. Which of the following strategies is she using? CBSE 2024 C

(a) Task-oriented strategy
(b) Emotion-oriented strategy
(c) Avoidance-oriented strategy
(d) Problem-focused strategy

## Assertion-Reason Questions

**Directions** (Q. Nos. 24-30) Two statements are given in the question below as Assertion (A) and Reason (R). Read the statements and choose the appropriate option.

(a) Both A and R are true and R is the correct explanation of A.
(b) Both A and R are true, but R is not the correct explanation of A.
(c) A is true, but R is false.
(d) A is false, but R is true.

**24.** **Assertion** (A) Neurotic people have control over their feelings.

**Reason** (R) Neurotic people are anxious, moody, touchy, restless and are quick to lose control. CBSE SQP 2021

**25.** **Assertion** (A) People with high levels of stress but low levels of illness share three characteristics, which are referred to as the personality traits of hardiness.

**Reason** (R) Hardiness consists of 'the three Cs', i.e., commitment, control, and challenge.

**26.** **Assertion** (A) Overcoming unhelpful habits like procrastination is a life skill that enables individuals to deal effectively with challenges of everyday life.

**Reason** (R) Factors that act as stress buffers and facilitate positive health are diet, exercise, positive attitude and positive thinking.

**27.** **Assertion** (A) An individual's response to a stressful situation largely depends upon the perceived events and how they are interpreted.

**Reason** (R) Lazarus has distinguished between two types of appraisal, i.e. primary and secondary. CBSE Term I 2021

**28.** **Assertion** (A) High stress too can produce unpleasant effects and cause our performance to deteriorate.

**Reason** (R) Eustress always turns into distress and also produces unpleasant effects.

**29.** **Assertion** (A) Life skills are abilities for adaptive and positive behaviour that enable individuals to deal effectively with the demands and challenges of everyday life.

**Reason** (R) To meet the challenges of life, a positive attitude, positive thinking, social support, etc. are some factors that can be of help. **CBSE Term I 2021**

**30.** **Assertion** (A) Students facing important examinations can be highly stressed.

**Reason** (R) Reduced levels of natural killer cell cytotoxicity have been found in people who are highly stressed. **CBSE SQP 2024**

# Answers

1. (b) stressors
2. (d) All of these
3. (b) resistance
4. (c) Physical
5. (b) T-helper cells
6. (d) material
7. (a) Creative visualisation
8. (b) Eustress
9. (a) self-confidence
10. (c) burnout
11. (d) harm, threat or challenge
12. (d) Frustration
13. (d) Internal pressures
14. (c) alarm reaction
15. (c) Impaired immune response due to stress
16. (c) biofeedback
17. (b) hassle
18. (a) avoiding
19. (b) II and IV
20. (b) Only III
21. (d) I, II and III
22. (c) eustress
23. (c) Avoidance-oriented strategy
24. (d) A is false, but R is true
25. (a) Both A and R are true and R is the correct explanation of A.
26. (b) Both A and R are true, but R is not the correct explanation of A.
27. (b) Both A and R are true, but R is not the correct explanation of A.
28. (c) A is true, but R is false
29. (b) Both A and R are ture, but R is not the correct explanation of A.
30. (b) Both A and R are true, but R is not the correct explanation of A.

# Subjective Questions

## Very Short Answer Type Questions

**1. What do you understand by stress?**

**Ans.** Stress can be described as the pattern of responses an organism makes to an event that disturbs the stability and diminish the person's ability.

**2. What are stressors?**

**Ans.** Stressors are events that cause our body to give the stress response. Such events include noise, crowding, a bad relationship or the daily commuting to school or office.

**3. Explain the term 'frustration'.**

**Ans.** It results from the blocking of needs and motives by something or someone that hinders us from achieving a desired goal.

**4. Explain the term 'conflict'.**

**Ans.** Conflict may occur between two or more incompatible needs or motives, e.g. whether to make an academic a career or a career in performing arts.

**5. What is psychoneuroimmunology?**

**Ans.** Psychoneuroimmunology focuses on the links between the mind, the brain and the immune system. It studies the effects of stress on the immune system.

**6. Define the term coping.**

**Ans.** Coping is a dynamic situation-specific reaction to stress. It is a set of concrete responses to stressful situations or events that are intended to resolve the problem and reduce stress.

**7. Explain emotion-oriented coping strategy.**

**Ans.** Emotion-oriented coping strategy can involve efforts to maintain hope and to control one's emotions. It can also involve venting feelings of anger and frustration or deciding that nothing can be done to change things.

**8. Explain avoidance-oriented strategy of coping.**

**Ans.** Avoidance-oriented strategy involves denying or minimising the seriousness of the situation. It also involves conscious suppression of stressful thoughts and their replacement by self-protective thoughts.

**9. Explain biofeedback.**

**Ans.** Biofeedback is a procedure to monitor and reduce the physiological aspects of stress by providing feedback about current physiological activity and is often accompanied by relaxation training.

**10. What are life skills?**

**Ans.** Life skills are abilities for adaptive and positive behaviour that enable individuals to deal effectively with the demands and challenges of everyday life.

**11. Fatima communicates her feelings and views clearly with confidence. She could say 'no' to a request or state an opinion without being self-conscious. Which life skill is she using? Suggest two more life skills that can help Fatima meet the challenges of life successfully.** CBSE SQP 2022

**Ans.** Fatima communicates her feelings and views clearly with confidence. She was using assertiveness. It is a behaviour or skill that helps to communicate clearly and confidently, our feelings, needs, wants and thoughts. Other two life skills that will help Fatima to meet the challenges of life successfully are time management and meditation procedures.

**12. What are the traumatic events?**

**Ans.** Traumatic events include being involved in a variety of extreme events such as a fire, train or road accidents, robbery, earthquake, tsunami, etc. The effects of these events may occur after sometime or persist as symptoms of anxiety.

**13. Explain the role of social support in promoting positive health and well-being.**

**Ans.** Social support reduces psychological distress, depression or anxiety during times of stress. It helps in promoting positive health and well-being.

**14. Differentiate between eustress and distress.**

**Ans.** Eustress is the term used to describe the level of stress that is good for you and is one of a person's best assets for achieving peak performance and managing minor crisis. Eustress, however, has the potential of turning into 'distress'. It is this latter manifestation of stress that causes our body's wear and tear.

**15. Megha found it quite impossible to attend the online classes without any disturbance. What is the source of stress here?**

**Ans.** Megha faced the problem of irregular internet connectivity. Thus, she could not attend her online classes smoothly. This personal stress happened in her dailylife. This is known as hassles. The daily hassles may sometimes have devastating consequences for the individual. The more stress people face in daily life as a result of hassels, the poorer becomes their psychological well-being.

**16. Ranjan has faced a lot of mishaps in his life. However, he shows low levels of illness despite high levels of stress. What makes people like Ranjan resistant to stress?** CBSE 2023

**Ans.** Hardiness is a personality trait which acts as a resistance resource in stressful situations in the life of people like Ranjan. Kobasa introduced the concept of psychological hardiness and suggested that hardiness moderates the relationship between stressful life events and illness. Kobasa characterised hardiness as comprising of three components or the 3C's i.e. Commitment, Control and Challenge.

**17. What is burnout? Explain any one cause of burnout?** CBSE 2020

**Ans.** The state of physical, emotional and psychological exhaustion is known as burnout.

Chronic daily stress due to unhappiness in personal life can divert an individual's attention from caring from himself. When stress is prolonged, it affects physical health and impairs psychological functioning. People experience exhaustion and attitudinal problems when the stress is too high and little support is available from family and friends.

**18. Explain the physiological effect of stress.** CBSE 2019

**Ans.** When the human body is placed under physical or psychological stress, it increases the production of certain hormones, like adrenalin and cortisol. These hormones produce marked changes in heart rate, blood pressure levels, metabolism and physical activity. When we are under stress for a long periods of time, release of epinephrine and non-epinephrine hormones slow down our digestive system, expand air passage in the lungs, increased heart rate and constriction of blood vessels.

**19. How can assertiveness impact an individual's response to stress?** CBSE 2025

**Ans.** Assertiveness helps manage stress by enabling individuals to express feelings, set boundaries and resolve conflicts effectively, which reduces the emotional burden and fostering control over challenging situations. It promotes healthier coping mechanisms.

**20. Mukesh is preparing for an entrance examination and is anxious. He has a persistent irrational thought that he would not succeed. Explain the therapy that can help him understand and overcome his anxiety.** Competency Based Que.

**Ans.** Two therapy can help Mukesh understand and overcome his anxiety. These are cognitive behavioural therapy and exposure therapy.

**21. Can one transform the therapeutic relationship into a healing relationship by understanding the plight of others? If yes or no, explain.** Competency Based Que.

**Ans.** Yes, one can transform the therapeutic relationship into a healing relationship by empathising and understanding the patient's plight.

The therapeutic alliance, based on empathy, trust, and understanding, can facilitate healing by creating a safe and supportive environment.

**22. Mukesh encounters a snake while on a hike. Referring to the General Adaptation Syndrome (GAS), what is the pattern of his bodily response? State one criticism of Selye's theory.** Competency Based Que.

**Ans.** The pattern of Mukesh's response would follow the alarm stage of GAS, where his body enters a state of heightened alertness, releasing adrenaline to prepare for a fight-or-flight response. One criticism of Selye's theory is that it oversimplifies the stress response, ignoring individual differences and cognitive appraisal.

## Short Answer Type Questions

**1. Define the primary appraisal of cognitive theory of stress.**

**Ans.** Primary appraisal refers to the perception of a new or changing environment as positive, neutral or negative in its consequences. Negative events are appraised for their possible harm, threat or challenge.

Harm is the assessment of the damage that has already been done by an event. Threat is the assessment of possible future damage that may be brought about by the event.

Challenge appraisals are associated with more confident expectations. It has the ability to cope with the stressful event and the potential to overcome and even profit from them.

**2. Explain Post Traumatic Stress Disorder (PTSD) by giving examples.**

**Ans.** Traumatic events include being involved in a variety of extreme events such as a fire, train or road accident, robbery, earthquake, tsunami, etc. The effects of these events may occur after some lapse of time and sometimes persist as symptoms of anxiety, flashbacks, dreams and intrusive thoughts, etc. Severe trauma can also strain relationships. Professional help will be needed to cope with them especially if they persist for many months after the event is over.

The physical exhaustion is seen in the signs of chronic fatigue, weakness and low energy. The mental exhaustion appears in the form of irritability, anxiety, feelings of helplessness and hopelessness. This state of physical, emotional and psychological exhaustion is known as burnout.

**3. Explain the significance of exercise.**

**Ans.** Exercise can provide an active outlet for the physiological arousal experienced in response to stress. Regular exercise improves

- the efficiency of the heart.
- enhances the function of the lungs.
- lowers blood pressure.
- reduces fat in the blood.
- improves the body's immune system.

**4. You are working with a client who handles high stress well and remains healthy. How would you evaluate and support their ability to manage stress effectively?** CBSE 2025

**Ans.** To evaluate stress management, observe the client's coping skills, resilience, and emotional stability under pressure. Assess their use of effective strategies like relaxation techniques, problem-solving, time management, and maintaining healthy habits (e.g., exercise, sleep, nutrition). Support them by reinforcing these strategies, offering stress-reduction techniques, and encouraging continued self-care practices to ensure long-term well-being.

**5. How stress and the lifestyle are co-related?**

**Ans.** Stress can lead to unhealthy lifestyle or health damaging behaviour. Lifestyle is the overall pattern of decisions and behaviours that determine a person's health and quality of life.

Stressed individuals may be more likely to expose themselves to pathogens, which are agents causing physical illness. People who are stressed have poor nutritional habits, sleep less and are likely to engage in other health risking behaviours like smoking and alcohol abuse.

**6. Discuss how positive health and well- being can be achieved through positive attitude.**

**Ans.** Positive health and well-being can be realised by having a positive attitude. Some of the factors leading to a positive attitude are

- Having a fairly accurate perception of reality.
- A sense of purpose in life and responsibility.
- Acceptance and tolerance for different viewpoints of others.
- Taking credit for success and accepting blame for failure.
- Being open to new ideas and having a sense of humour with the ability to laugh at oneself which help us to remain centred and see things in a proper perspective.

**7. "Stressed individuals may be more likely to expose themselves to disease." Comment. Also discuss the strategy to promote good health.** Competency Based Que.

**Ans.** Stressed individuals may be more likely to expose themselves to pathogens, which are agents causing physical illness. People who are stressed have poor nutritional habits, sleep less and are likely to engage in other health risking behaviours like smoking and alcohol abuse.

The modern lifestyle of excesses in eating, drinking and the so called fast-paced good life has led to violation of basic principles of health.

Such health impairing behaviours develop gradually and are accompanied by pleasant experiences temporarily.

Studies have revealed that health promoting behaviour like balanced diet, regular exercise, family support, etc play an important role in good health. Adhering to a lifestyle that includes balanced low fat diet, regular exercise and continued activity along with positive thinking enhances health and longevity.

**8. Describe the cognitive theory of stress.**

**Ans.** This theory was propounded by Lazarus and his colleagues. According to this, the perception of stress is dependent upon the individual's cognitive appraisal of events and the resources available to deal with them.

An individual's response to a stressful situation largely depends upon the perceived events and how they are interpreted or appraised.

There are two types of appraisal

(i) **Primary Appraisal** It refers to the perception of a new or changing environment as positive, neutral or negative in its consequences. Negative events are appraised for their possible harm, threat or challenge.

Harm is the assessment of the damage that has already been done by an event. Threat is the assessment of possible future damage that may be brought about by the event.

Challenge appraisals are associated with more confident expectations. It has the ability to cope with the stressful event and the potential to overcome and even profit from them.

(ii) **Secondary Appraisal** It is the assessment of one's coping abilities and resources and assessing whether they will be sufficient to meet the harm, threat or challenge of the event.

These resources may be mental, physical, personal or social. If one thinks one has a positive attitude, health, skills and social support to deal with the crises, she/he will feel less stressed.

**9. Explain the various types of Stress.**

**Ans.** Stress can be categorised into three main types

(i) **Physical and Environmental Stress** Physical stress arises from physical exertion, poor diet, injury or lack of sleep. Environmental stress includes unavoidable factors like pollution, noise, extreme weather, and disasters such as fires or earthquakes.

(ii) **Psychological Stress** This stems from internal sources like frustration, conflicts between desires, unrealistic expectations and social pressures from personal or societal demands.

(iii) **Social Stress** Resulting from interactions with others, social stress includes issues like family illness, strained relationships or conflicts with peers, which vary from person to person.

**10. How negative emotions affect the health of the individuals?**

**Ans.** Psychological stress is accompanied by negative emotions and associated behaviours, including depression, hostility, anger and aggression. Negative emotion states are of particular concern to the study of effects of stress on health. The incidence of psychological disorders, such as panic attacks and obsessive behaviour increases with the build up of long-term stress.

People under prolonged stress are more prone to irrational fears, mood swings and phobias and may experience depression, anger and irrita- bility. These negative emotions appear to be related to the function of the immune system.

Our ability to interpret our world and to invest that interpretation with personal meaning and emotion have a powerful and direct effect on the body. Negative moods have been associated with poorer health outcomes. Feelings of hopelessness are related to worsening of disease, increased risk of injury and death due to various causes.

**11. What is coping? Explain the coping strategies defined by Endler and Parker.**

*Or* **Individuals differ in the coping strategies that they use to deal with stressful situations. Justify this statement highlighting various coping strategies.** CBSE SQP 2023

**Ans.** Coping is a dynamic situation-specific reaction to stress. It is a set of concrete responses to stressful situations or events that are intended to resolve the problem and reduce stress.

The way we cope with stress often depends on rigid deep-seated beliefs, based on experience. Coping strategies include both overt and covert activities. The three coping strategies given by **Endler** and **Parker** are

(i) **Task-oriented Strategy** This involves obtaining information about the stressful situation and about alternative courses of action and their probable outcome. It also involves deciding priorities and acting, so as to deal directly with the stressful situation. For example, think about how I have solved similar problem previously.

(ii) **Emotion-oriented Strategy** This can involve efforts to maintain hope and to control one's emotions.

It can also involve venting feelings of anger and frustration or deciding that nothing can be done to change things.

For example, tell my self that is is not really happening te me.

(iii) **Avoidance-oriented Strategy** This involves denying or minimising the seriousness of the situation. It also involves conscious suppression of stressful thoughts and their replacement by self-protective thoughts. For example, watching TV, phone up a friend etc. to avoid stress.

**12. How life skills like rational thinking and improving relationships will help to meet the challenges of life?**

**Ans.** **Rational Thinking** Many stress-related problems occur as a result of distorted thinking. Thinking and feeling are closely connected. When we are stressed, we recall attend to negative thoughts and images from the past, which affect our perception of the present and the future.

Some of the principles of rational thinking are

- Challenging distorted thinking and irrational beliefs.
- Driving out potentially intrusive negative anxiety and provoking thoughts.
- Making positive statements.

**Improving Relationships** The key to an effective relationship is communication which consists of three essential skills i.e. listening to what the other person is saying, expressing how you feel and what you think and accepting the other person's opinions and feelings, even if they are different from your own. It also requires us to avoid misplaced jealousy and sulking (bad mood) behaviour.

**13. "Stressors result in a variety of stress reactions." Elucidate.**

**Ans.** Stress, includes all those environmental and personal events, which challenge or threaten the well-being of a person. These stressors can be external, such as environmental (noise, air pollution), social (break-up with a friend, loneliness) or psychological (conflict, frustration) within the individual. Stressors result in a variety of stress reactions, which may be physiological, behavioural, emotional and cognitive.

**Physiological Reactions** At the physiological level, arousal plays a key role in stress related behaviours.

The hypothalamus initiates action along two pathways

(i) The first pathway involves the autonomic nervous system. The adrenal gland releases large amount of catecholamines (epinephrine and norepinephrine) into the blood stream. This leads to physiological changes seen in fight-or-flight response.

(ii) The second pathway involves the pituitary gland, which secretes the corticosteroid (cortisol) that provides energy.

**Emotional Reactions** The emotional reactions to experience stress include negative emotions such as fear, anxiety, embarrassment, anger, depression or even denial.

**Behavioural Reactions** The behavioural responses are virtually limitless, depending on the nature of the stressful event. Confrontative action against the stressor (fight) or withdrawal from the threatening event (flight) are two general categories of behavioural responses.

**Congnitive Reactions** Cognitive responses include beliefs about the harm or threat an event poses and beliefs about its causes or controllability. These include responses such as inability to concentrate and intrusive, repetitive or morbid thoughts.

**14. Differentiate between problem-focused strategies and emotion-focused strategies with examples.**

**Ans.** Differences between problem-focused strategies and emotion-focused strategies with examples are as follows

**Problem-focused Strategies** It attack the problem itself, with behaviours designed to gain information, to alter the event and to alter belief and commitments. They increase the person's awareness, level of knowledge and range of behavioural and cognitive coping options. They can act to reduce the threat value of the event.
For example, "I made a plan of action and followed it".

**Emotion-focused Strategies** It call for psychological changes designed primarily to limit the degree of emotional disruption caused by an event, with minimal effort to alter the event itself. For example, "I did some things to let it out of my system".

**15. Rohan had interview for a multinational company. Prior to interview, he observed that his heart rate and blood pressure levels have increased. Why did it happen? Will it help him to function more effectively?** Competency Based Que.

**Ans.** The increased level of heart rate and blood pressure prior to interview means that Rohan is under psychological stress. The psychological stress has caused the increase in the production of certain hormones, such as adrenaline and cortisol.

These hormones produce marked changes in heart rate, blood pressure levels, metabolism and physical activity. Although, this physical reaction may help him to function more effectively under pressure for short periods of time, it can be extremely damaging to the body in the long-term effects.

**16. Describe any three skills that can help a person meet life's challenges.** CBSE SQP 2024

**Ans.** The three life skills that can help a person meet life's challenges are

(i) **Problem-solving** This life skill equips you to navigate challenges by breaking them down into manageable steps. It involves analysing the situation, identifying potential solutions, evaluating their consequences and choosing the best course of action.

(ii) **Communication** Effective communication is crucial for navigating life's challenges. It involves expressing yourself clearly, both verbally and non-verbally, while actively listening to understand others.

(iii) **Stress Management** It involves techniques like relaxation exercises, mindfulness practices and time management strategies. When faced with a stressful situation, these techniques can help you stay calm, focused and cope healthily.

## Long Answer Type Questions

**1. Explain the nature of stress giving examples. Discuss avoidance-oriented strategies of coping.**

**Ans.** Hans Selye, the father of modern stress research, defined stress as the non-specific response of the body to any demand. Despite the cause of the threat, the individual will respond with the same physiological pattern of reactions.

Many researchers do not agree with this definitions. They think that the stress response is not nearly as general and non-specific as Selye suggests. Different stressors may produce somewhat different patterns stress reaction.

Different individuals may have different characteristic modes of response. Each one of us see the situation from our own perspective and it is our ability to meet them and this will determine whether we are feeling 'stressed' or not.

Stress is not a factor that resides in the individual or the environment. It is embedded (fixed) in an ongoing process that involves individuals transacting with their social and cultural environments and attempting to cope with the issues that arise. Stress is a dynamic mental/cognitive state.

**Avoidance-oriented Strategy** This involves denying or minimising the seriousness of the situation. It also involves conscious suppression of stressful thoughts and their replacement by self-protective thoughts. Examples of this are watching TV, phone up a friend or try to be with other people.

**2. Describe the various sources of stress.** CBSE 2019

**Ans.** Stress can arise from various sources, including major life events, daily hassles and traumatic experiences.

**Life Events** Major life changes, such as the death of a loved one or a personal injury, can disrupt our routine and cause significant upheaval. Stress can be amplified when several life events occur in a short period, whether planned (e.g. moving to a new home) or unexpected (e.g. a breakup). Coping becomes more difficult and individuals may experience heightened stress symptoms.

**Hassles** Daily irritations, such as noisy environments, commuting or quarrelsome neighbours, contribute to stress. These constant annoyances can undermine an individual's psychological well-being. Jobs involving frequent hassles can exacerbate this, leading to long-term stress.

**Traumatic Events** Extreme occurrences like accidents, natural disasters or violent acts can cause lasting emotional distress. The effects may include anxiety, flashbacks or intrusive thoughts. Traumatic experiences can strain relationships and may require professional support if the symptoms persist for an extended period.

Overall, stress can stem from both immediate events and ongoing challenges, and its impact can vary depending on the individual's coping mechanisms.

**3. Explain any four stress management techniques.** CBSE 2020

**Ans.** Stress is a silent killer which plays a significant role in physical illness and disease. Hypertension, heart disease, ulcers, diabetes and even cancer are linked to stress.

Stress is increasing due to changing lifestyle. Therefore schools, other institutions, offices and communities are concerned about knowing techniques to manage stress.

Four stress management techniques are

(i) **Relaxation Techniques** It is an active skill that reduces symptoms of stress and decreases the incidence of illnesses such as high blood pressure and heart disease. Relaxation starts from the lower part of the body and progresses up to the facial muscles in such a way that the whole body is relaxed. Deep breathing is used alongwith muscle relaxation to calm the mind and relax the body.

(ii) **Meditation Procedures** The yogic method of meditation consists of a sequence of learned techniques for refocusing of attention that brings about an altered state of consciousness. It involves such a thorough concentration that the meditator becomes unaware of any outside stimulation and reaches a different state of consciousness.

(iii) **Biofeedback** It is a procedure to monitor and reduce the physiological aspects of stress by providing feedback about current physiological activity and is often accompanied by relaxation training.

Biofeedback training involves three stages

- Developing an awareness of the particular physiological response, e.g. heart rate.
- Learning ways of controlling physiological response in quiet conditions.
- Transferring control into the conditions of everyday life.

(iv) **Creative Visualisation** It is an effective technique for dealing with stress. It is a subjective experience that uses imagery and imagination. Before visualising one must set oneself a realistic goal, as it helps to build confidence.

It is easier to visualise if one's mind is quiet, body relaxed and eyes are closed. This reduces the risk of interference from unbidden thoughts and provides the creative energy needed for turning an imagined scene into reality.

**4. What is positive psychology? How positive psychologists have identified virtues and strengths of human beings?**

**Ans.** Contemporary psychologists have shown increasing interest in understanding what makes life good and meaningful. This development is termed as positive psychology. Positive psychology systematically investigates the positive aspects that is the strengths and virtues of human beings.

**Martin Seligman** has provided leadership to the movement of positive psychology. On the basis of researches on around two hundred texts from various spiritual books, they were able to identify a set of human virtues shared by various traditions. These are

(i) **Wisdom and Knowledge**

**Curiosity/Interest in the World** An openness to experience i.e. flexibility about things that don't fit your preconception.

**Love of Learning** Taking pleasure in learning new thing, taking every opportunity to expend your knowledge and expertise.

**Judgment/Critical Thinking/Open- Mindedness** Thinking things thoroughly and examining them from all sides or being objective.

**Ingenuity/Originality/Practical Intelligence** Finding new and practical ways of achieving results.

**Social Intelligence/Personal Intelligence/Emotional Intelligence** Understanding your own and others' motives and feelings or acting in socially effective ways.

**Perspective** Able to adopt the 'big picture' so as to act wisely and good at problem solving and giving advice.

(ii) **Courage**

**Valour and Bravery** Willing to confront challenges and difficulty; prepared to adopt unpopular or dangerous positions.

**Perseverance/Industry/Diligence** Finishing what you start and prepared to take on difficult projects.

**Integrity/Genuineness/Honesty** Living in a genuine, authentic way and down to earth.

(iii) **Humanity and Love**

**Kindness and Generosity** Helping to higher people and putting others' interests as highly as your own.

**Loving and Allowing Oneself to be Loved** Valuing and generating close and intimate relations with others.

(iv) **Justice**

**Citizenship/Duty/Teamwork/Loyalty** Working hard for the success of the group and valuing group goals and purposes.

**Leadership** Organising activities well and seeing that they happen, maintaining good relationship in and between groups.

(v) **Transcendence**

**Appreciation of Beauty and Excellence** Appreciating excellence in all domains and able to feel awe and wonder.

**Gratitude** Not taking things for granted and expressing gratitude to other.

**Hope/Optimism/Future-Mindedness** Maintaining a positive stance towards the future and expecting the best.

**Forgiveness and Mercy** Forgiving those who hurt or offend you and able to transform how you feel.

**Zest/Passion/Enthusiasm** Throwing yourself and soul into activities and inspiring others.

**5. Selye studied this issue by subjecting animals to a variety of stressors such as high temperature, X-rays and insulin injections, in the laboratory over a long period of time. He also observed patients with various injuries and illnesses in hospitals. Selye also noticed a similar pattern of bodily response in all of them. Identify the pattern? Also, Discuss the different stages of Selye model?** **Competency Based Que.**

**Ans.** The pattern that Selye observed among patients in hospital set up was identified as General Adaptation Syndrome (GAS). According to him, GAS involves three stages—alarm reaction, resistance and exhaustion.

(i) **Alarm Reaction Stage** The presence of a noxious stimulus or stressor leads to activation of the adrenal pituitary-cortex system. This triggers the release of hormones producing the stress response. Now the individual is ready for fight or flight.

(ii) **Resistance Stage** If stress is prolonged, the resistance stage begins. The parasympathetic nervous system calls for more cautious use of the body's resources. The organism makes efforts to cope with the threat, as through confrontation.

(iii) **Exhaustion Stage** Continued exposure to the same stressor or additional stressors drains the body of its resources and leads to the third stage of exhaustion. The physiological systems involved in alarm reaction and resistance become ineffective and susceptibility to stress-related diseases such as high blood pressure becomes more likely.

## Case Based Questions

**1. Read the case and answer the questions that follow.** **CBSE 2025**

Social stress can be broadly defined as a situation which threatens one's relationships, esteem, or sense of belonging within a dyad group, or larger social context. Social stress, can emerge in a number of situations. Social stress can stem from difficult social interactions, for example, a conflictual or tumultuous marital or family relationship. Social stress can also emerge in the context of evaluated performance situations, where others could be judgemental or critical, or in contexts in which one feels rejected, ostracised, or ignored. Social stress can also be more broadly construed, representing perceptions of one's lower role or standing within a group or community. Social stress can lead to a range of observable and measurable responses related to health outcomes.

(i) **What impact can social stress have on an individual?**
(ii) **State two causes of social stress in day-to-day life.**

**Ans.** (i) Social stress negatively affects health, causing anxiety, depression, weakened immunity, high blood pressure, sleep problems and poor social relationships.
(ii) Two common causes of social stress in daily life are conflicts in personal relationships, like family disputes and fear of judgement and criticism during performance evaluations or social interactions.

**2. Read the case and answer the questions that follow.**

Helen is a 28-year-old chemistry student who sought therapy for intense anxiety. She could not attend the lectures or enter the lecture theatre (lecture theatre phobia). She could not concentrate, study for the exams or sit an exam. She avoided getting close to the University and she also avoided anything relevant to the University. She was not able to decide whether she wanted to get her degree or not.

She was in a general state of anxiety about anything. She wanted to be perfect in everything and she worried about other people's criticism. She would think about University all the time. Thus, she was not able to enjoy herself and was always sad. She avoided being with people and finally avoided crowded places. As far as her physiological complaints are concerned, it appeared that Helen suffered from–Permanent headache, Insomnia, Stomachache, Fatigue, Loss of energy, Drowsiness, Clenching of teeth while she slept that resulted in pain. The result of all the above was that she felt anxious, disappointed and melancholic.

(i) **What symptoms indicate Helen's struggle with anxiety?**
(ii) **How did Helen's anxiety impact her daily life and academic performance?**

**Ans.** (i) Helen's symptoms include intense anxiety, difficulty attending lectures, poor concentration, insomnia, headaches, stomach aches, fatigue and constant worry. She avoids people, crowded places and anything related to university. She also experiences physical issues like clenching her teeth, which causes pain and suffers from low energy and drowsiness.
(ii) Helen's anxiety prevented her from attending classes, studying or taking exams, making her doubt her academic goals. Her constant worry about criticism and perfectionism kept her from enjoying life and led her to avoid social interactions, ultimately affecting her mental and physical well-being.

**3. Read the case and answer the question that follow.** **CBSE SQP 2024**

The fire department received a call about a fire that swept through a house. The fire started with the explosion of a gas cylinder used for cooking. The injured Suman was lying on a hospital bed. She was talking to a press reporter. She expressed that her mother was in the kitchen when the incident occurred. The cylinder burst with a loud sound and the fire spread at great speed. The exit door of the house had also caught fire her mother shouted in panic as if she had lost all hope, and she fainted in the kitchen. However, Suman was determined to save her mother. She said "I don't know how I got the energy to drag my mother to the room. I broke the window there and jumped out. My back got hurt, but without wasting any time, I sought the help of my neighbour and rescued my mother. I am happy that we are both safe." Hearing her story, the press reporter was impressed with her chivalry.

(i) **Referring to the General Adaptation Syndrome (GAS) model, what immediate impact does the fire (noxious stimulus) have on Suman's mother?**
(ii) **Suman and her mother were exposed to prolonged stress as the fire spread. How does the General Adaptation Syndrome model explain Suman and her mother's conditions.**

**Ans.** (i) The fire acts as a noxious stimulus, triggering the alarm reaction stage in Suman's mother. This stage is marked by an immediate physiological response, causing her to panic, experience an increased heart rate and eventually faint as her body responds to the acute stress.
(ii) According to the GAS model, prolonged exposure to the stress of the spreading fire moves Suman and her mother into the resistance stage. During this stage, their bodies would attempt to adapt to the ongoing stress by sustaining heightened arousal, mobilising energy and engaging in coping efforts to manage the situation.

# SELF ASSESSMENT TEST

## Objective Type Questions

**1.** Which of the following may cause our body's wear and tear?

(a) Stress (b) Distress
(c) Eustress (d) All of these

**2.** The stress which people experience vary in terms of

(a) intensity (b) duration
(c) complexity (d) All of these

**3.** Rahul is stressed due to mental overload. However, he is consciously suppressing the stressful thoughts by watching the TV continuously. The kind of coping strategy employed by Rahul to deal with stress is

(a) task-oriented (b) emotion-oriented
(c) avoidance-oriented (d) None of these

**4.** Which of the following is a factor that influences how an individual perceives stress?

(a) The weather
(b) Past experience
(c) Time of day
(d) Colour of the environment

**5.** **Assertion** (A) Stress is not inherent in a situation but is the result of an individual's perception of the situation.

**Reason** (R) An individual's coping abilities and resources determine how they experience stress.

(a) Both Aand R are true and the R is the correct explanation of the A.
(b) Both A and R are true, but the R is not the correct explanation of the A.
(c) The A is true, but the R is false.
(d) The A is false, but the R is true.

## Very Short Answer Type Questions

**1.** What do you mean by eustress?

**2.** What is stress?

**3.** Give the causes of environmental stress.

## Short Answer Type Questions

**1.** Define signs and symptoms of stress.

**2.** Describe psychological stress.

**3.** Discuss the functioning of immune system.

**4.** Roma was unable to decide about the topic of the project she had to submit for the final examination. She, therefore, did not complete the work before the deadline, was unable to concentrate on the task at hand and seemed to suffer from mental overload. Identify the kind of stress, she is exhibiting? Why did it occur?

## Long Answer Type Questions

**1.** Explain in brief the stress management techniques.

**2.** Critically analyse General Adaptation Syndrome (GAS).

**3.** Norman, a 22-year-old part-time receptionist and administrative assistant, had been employed in this role for 10 months working 30 hours per week. He had been absent from work for a month on the day of the consultation and was preparing to return to work. On entering the department, his mobility difficulties and an obviously awkward gait and altered balance were noted. Identify the effect in which stress has affected Norman? Also, identify other form of manifestations of such stress.

## Case Based Questions

**Read the case and answer the questions that follow.**

Dr. Rakesh Raushan is a professor in the Psychology Department of Patna University. Besides teaching continuously without breaks at the university he also conducts counselling sessions at home for individuals who face some or the other kinds of psychological problems such as anger, panic attack, hysteria, stress, depression and trauma.

Dr. Raushan often writes and gets his papers published, he attends conferences, national as well as international, he even travels abroad to make paper presentations; creates lesson plans, tests and does lot of research study.

All these work duties make him even stay up in the night till 1 or 2 am; which shows that he does not even get much sleep. In addition to this he also has a family to look after, his wife and children. Even though, Dr. Raushan is continuously involved in extensive work duties with stress like situation, his performance is beyond par excellence.

(i) On the basis of above passage, what is the stress like situation on Dr. Raushan? Discuss it.

(ii) What do you mean by physical and environmental stress?

04

CHAPTER

# Psychological Disorders

Abnormality refers to deviation from ideal mental health. Psychological disorders are those mental disorders which result incertain behavioural pattern such as unhappiness, discomfort, anxiety etc. They also lead to failure in adaption to life challenges.

**YOUR STUDY GOALS**

4.1 Concepts of Abnormality and Psychological Disorders
4.2 Factors Underlying Abnormal Behaviour
4.3 Major Psychological Disorders

**YOUR PRACTICE GOAL**

- Objective Type Questions (22 Qs ; MCQs, A-R)
- Subjective Questions (18 VSAs, 28 SAs, 9 LAs, 5 Case Based)

## 4.1 Concepts of Abnormality and Psychological Disorders

- Many definitions of abnormality exist, but none are universally accepted. Most definitions share common features known as the 'Four Ds'.
- These four Ds are characterised as
  (i) **Deviant** Different, extreme, unusual or bizarre behaviours.
  (ii) **Distressing** Unpleasant and upsetting to the individual and others.
  (iii) **Dysfunctional** Interfering with daily activities and constructive living.
  (iv) **Dangerous** Potentially harmful to oneself or others.
- The term 'abnormal' implies deviation from defined norms or standards.
- In psychology, there is no universal 'ideal' or 'normal' model of behaviour for comparison.

There are two conflicting views on distinguishing between normal and abnormal behaviours

1. **Deviation from Social Norms**
   - Abnormal behaviour is seen as a deviation from societal expectations.

- Behaviours significantly differing from societal norms are called abnormal.
- Each society has norms that reflect its culture, including history, values, institutions, habits, skills, technology and arts.
- For example, a culture valuing competition may accept aggressive behaviour, while one emphasising cooperation may deem it unacceptable.
- Norms may change over time, affecting societal views on psychological abnormality.
- This definition assumes that socially accepted behaviour is normal and does not consider the broader implications of well-being.

2. **Maladaptive Behaviour**
   - Abnormal behaviour is viewed as maladaptive and determined by its impact on individual and group well-being.
   - Well-being encompasses growth, fulfillment and actualisation of potential, as described in Maslow's hierarchy of needs.
   - Conformity can be considered abnormal if it interferes with optimal functioning and personal growth. For example, a student who remains silent despite having questions may exhibit maladaptive behaviour.
   - This approach emphasises addressing vulnerabilities, coping abilities and stressors in an individual's environment.

- Many people hold vague and superstitious beliefs about psychological disorders, often rooted in ignorance and fear.
- There is a prevalent stigma associated with mental illness, leading individuals to feel ashamed and reluctant to seek help from professionals.
- Psychological disorders should be viewed as medical conditions indicating a failure in adaptation, similar to any other illness.

## Historical Background of Psychological Disorders

- Understanding psychological disorders necessitates a brief historical account of their evolving perceptions over time.
- The history of **abnormal psychology**[1] reveals recurring theories regarding the nature of psychological disorders.
- One ancient theory attributes abnormal behaviour to supernatural forces, such as evil spirits *(bhoot-pret)* or the devil *(shaitan)*.
- Practices like exorcism (removal of evil through countermagic and prayer) are still prevalent in various societies.
- The *shaman* or medicine man *(ojha)* is seen as a mediator between supernatural forces and humans, helping individuals identify and appease troubling spirits.

## Approaches of Abnormality

### Biological or Organic Approach

- A recurring belief in the history of abnormal psychology is that strange behaviour arises from malfunctions in the body or brain, known as the Biological or Organic approach.
- Modern evidence supports that bodily and brain processes correlate with various types of maladaptive behaviour.
- For certain disorders, rectifying biological deficiencies can improve functioning.

1 **Abnormal Psychology** The study of psychological disorders, including their symptoms, causes and treatments. It focus on behaviour that deviates from societal norms and may cause distress or impairment.

## Psychological Approach

- The psychological approach attributes psychological problems to deficiencies in an individual's thoughts, feelings or perceptions.
- These perspective emphasises the role of mental processes in understanding psychological disorders.
- The supernatural, biological and psychological perspectives have re-emerged throughout Western history.

## Organismic Approach

- In ancient Greece, philosopher-physicians like Hippocrates, Socrates and particularly Plato formulated the organismic approach, suggesting that disturbed behaviour results from conflicts between emotion and reason.
- Galen elaboratd the role of the four humours in personal character and temperament.
- According to him, the material world was made up of four elements *viz* earth, air, fire and water which combined to form four essential body fluids, *viz* blood, black bile yellow bile, and phlegm.
- Each of these fluids was seen to be responsible for a different temperament. Imbalances among the humours were believed to cause various disorders.
- This concept is similar to the Indian notion of the three doshas (*vata, pitta, kapha*) mentioned in the *Atharva Veda* and *Ayurvedic* texts.

## Demonology and Superstition

- During the Middle Ages, demonology and superstition were prevalent in explaining abnormal behaviour.
- Many individuals with mental issues were deemed evil, leading to numerous witch-hunts.
- The early Middle Ages saw the influence of Christian charity, with thinkers like St. Augustine exploring feelings and mental conflict, paving the way for modern psychodynamic theories.

### Renaissance Period

- The Renaissance fostered humanism and curiosity about human behaviour.
- Johann Weyer highlighted psychological conflict and disturbed relationships as contributors to psychological disorders, advocating for medical treatment over theological intervention for those labelled as witches.

### Age of Reason and Enlightenment

- The seventeenth and eighteenth centuries marked the Age of Reason, where the scientific method began to replace faith and dogma in understanding abnormal behaviour.
- This scientific shift contributed to the Reform Movement, promoting compassion for individuals with psychological disorders and initiating asylum reforms in Europe and America.
- The reform movement also encouraged **deinstitutionalisation**[2], emphasising community care for recovered individuals.

## Biopsychosocial Approach

- Recent years have witnessed a convergence of these historical perspectives, culminating in the biopsychosocial approach.
- This approach recognises the interplay of biological, psychological and social factors in influencing the psychological disorders.

2 **Deinstitutionalisation** The process of reducing or eliminating the use of psychiatric hospitals for the treatment of mental illness, often leading of community-based care alternatives.

## Classification of Psychological Disorders

- A classification system consists of a list of categories of specific psychological disorders grouped into various classes based on shared characteristics.
- Classifications help facilitate communication among professionals such as psychologists, psychiatrists and social workers.
- They help in understanding the causes of psychological disorders as well as the processes involved in their development and maintenance.
- The American Psychiatric Association (APA) has published an official manual that describes and classifies various psychological disorders.
- The current version is the Diagnostic and Statistical Manual of Mental Disorders, 5th Edition (DSM-5), which presents discrete clinical criteria indicating the presence or absence of disorders.
- The classification scheme officially used in India and other countries is the tenth revision of the International Classification of Diseases (ICD-10).
- The ICD-10 includes the ICD-10 Classification of Behavioural and Mental Disorders, prepared by the World Health Organisation (WHO) which outlines the clinical features symptoms and diagnostic guidelines for each disorder.

### Quick Test 1

1. What are the 'Four Ds' that characterise psychological abnormality?
2. What is the focus of the biopsychosocial approach in understanding psychological disorders?
3. What historical period emphasised humanism and understanding abnormal behaviour?
4. Which classification system is currently used by the American Psychiatric Association for mental disorders?
5. What concept from ancient Greece suggested that behaviour results from conflicts between emotion and reason?
6. What does deinstitutionalisation aim to achieve in mental health care?

# 4.2 Factors Underlying Abnormal Behaviour

- Psychologists use different approaches to understand the complexity of abnormal behaviour.
- Each approach emphasises a different aspect of human behaviour and explains and treats abnormality accordingly.
- The approaches consider various factors, including biological, psychological, interpersonal and socio-cultural factors.

## Biological Factors

- Biological factors significantly influence all aspects of behaviour.
- Various biological factors can lead to abnormal behaviour, including
  - Faulty genes
  - Endocrine imbalances
  - Malnutrition
  - Injuries
  - Other conditions affecting normal development and functioning.
- The biological model suggests that abnormal behaviour has a biochemical or physiological basis.
- Research shows psychological disorders often relate to problems in neuro-transmission between neurons.
- A synapse is the tiny space separating neurons, where messages must move across.

- When an electrical impulse reaches a neuron, it stimulates the release of **neurotransmitters**[3].
- Abnormal activity of specific neurotransmitters is linked to various psychological disorders
  - **Anxiety disorders** Low activity of Gamma Aminobutyric Acid (GABA)
  - **Schizophrenia**[4] Excess activity of dopamine
  - **Depression** Low activity of serotonin

## Genetic Factors

- Genetic factors are associated with disorders like bipolar disorder, schizophrenia and **intellectual disability**[5].
- Although genetic factors are implicated in many mental disorders, no single gene has been identified as the sole cause.
- Multiple genes may interact to influence behaviour and emotional responses, both functional and dysfunctional.
- Biological explanations alone cannot account for most mental disorders.

## Psychological Models

- Several **psychological models** explain mental disorders, emphasising psychological and interpersonal factors.
- Key psychological factors include
  - **Maternal deprivation** Separation from the mother or lack of warmth and stimulation in early life.
  - **Faulty parent-child relationships** Including rejection, overprotection, over-permissiveness and inadequate discipline.
  - **Maladaptive family structures** Disturbed family environments and severe stress experienced by individuals.
  - The psychological models include psychodynamic, behavioural, cognitive and humanistic existential models.

### Psychodynamic Model

- The psychodynamic model is one of the oldest and most renowned psychological models.
- It posits that behaviour is influenced by unconscious psychological forces.
- These internal forces are dynamic and interact to shape behaviour, thoughts and emotions.
- **Freud** proposed that abnormal behaviour reflects unconscious mental conflicts rooted in early childhood.

### Behavioural Model

The behavioural model suggests that all behaviours, normal and abnormal, are learned.

- Psychological disorders arise from learning maladaptive behaviours.
- Behaviours can be learned through
  - **Classical conditioning** Association between two events occurring close in time.
  - **Operant conditioning** Behaviours followed by rewards.
  - **Social learning** Imitating others' behaviour.

---

3 **Neurotransmitters** Chemicals in the brain that transmit signals between neurons. Imbalances in neurotransmitter levels are linked to various mental disorders.

4 **Schizophrenia** A severe mental disorder characterised by disturbances in thought processes, perceptions, emotional responsiveness and social functioning. It often involves delusions and hallucinations.

5 **Intellectual disability** A developmental disorder characterised by significantly impaired intellectual functioning and adaptive behaviour, typically identified during childhood.

## Cognitive Model

The cognitive model emphasises that cognitive issues can lead to abnormal functioning.

- Individuals may hold irrational assumptions and attitudes about themselves, engage in illogical thinking and make over-generalisations, draw broad, negative conclusions on the basis of single insignificant events.

## Humanistic-Existential Model

The humanistic-existential model focuses on broader human existence aspects.

- Humanists believe people naturally tend towards friendliness, cooperation and constructiveness, striving for self-actualisation.
- Existentialists argue that individuals have the freedom to give meaning to their existence or avoid that responsibility, leading to dysfunctional lives if neglected.

# Socio-Cultural Factors

- In addition to biological and psychological factors, socio-cultural factors significantly influence abnormal behaviour.
- Some important socio-cultural factors include, war and violence, group prejudice and discrimination, economic and employment problems and rapid social change.
- According to the socio-cultural model, abnormal behaviour should be understood by social and cultural forces that influence individuals.
- Factors such as family structure and communication, social networks, societal conditions and Societal labels and roles become more important as they shaped the behaviour.
- Certain family systems may promote abnormal functioning in individual members.
- For instance, an enmeshed family structure leads to over-involvement in each other's lives, hindering children's independence.
- Social networks also impact mental health; individuals lacking social support may experience more prolonged depression.
- Socio-cultural theorists suggest that societal labels can affect behaviour.
- When individuals deviate from societal **norms**[6], they may be labelled as deviant or mentally ill, leading to a self-fulfilling prophecy of abnormal behaviour.

# Diathesis-Stress Model

- The diathesis–stress model suggesting that mental disorders develop due to a combination of genetic vulnerability (diathesis) and environmental stressors. It explains abnormal behaviour.
- It posits that psychological disorders develop when a diathesis (biological predisposition) interacts with a stressful situation.
- The model comprises three components
  (i) **Diathesis** Presence of a biological aberration, which may be inherited.
  (ii) **Vulnerability** This diathesis indicates a risk or predisposition to develop a psychological disorder.
  (iii) **Pathogenic stressors** Stressors that may lead to psychopathology.
- Individuals with a diathesis who encounter stressors may develop psychological disorders.
- This model has been applied to various disorders, including anxiety, depression and schizophrenia.

---

6 **Norms** Social standards or rules that dictate acceptable behaviour within a society or group. Abnormal psychology often examines how behaviours diverge from these norms.

### Quick Test 2

1 What role do neurotransmitters play in psychological disorders?
2 What does the psychodynamic model attribute abnormal behaviour to?
3 How does the cognitive model explain irrational attitudes and behaviour?
4 What is the focus of the humanistic-existential model in understanding abnormal behaviour?
5 What socio-cultural factors influence the development of abnormal behaviour?
6 What are the three components of the diathesis-stress model for psychological disorders?

## 4.3 Major Psychological Disorders

- The major psychological disorders are anxiety disorders, somatofarm disorders, dissociative disorders, mood disorders, schizophrenic disorders; behavioural and development disorders and substance-use disorders.
- Anxiety is defined as a diffuse, vague (unclear) and very unpleasant feeling of fear and apprehension.
- An anxious individual may exhibit various physical and psychological symptoms, including
  - Rapid heart rate
  - Shortness of breath
  - Diarrhoea
  - Loss of appetite
  - Fainting
  - Dizziness
  - Sweating
  - Sleeplessness
  - Frequent urination
  - Tremors

There are several types of anxiety disorders, including

### Generalised Anxiety Disorder (GAD)

- GAD is characterised by prolonged, vague, unexplained and intense fears that are not linked to any specific object.
- Symptoms include worry about the future, along with hypervigilance, which involves constantly scanning the environment for potential dangers.
- Individuals with GAD may experience motor tension, which makes relaxation difficult and causes restlessness, shakiness and tension.

### Panic Disorder

- Panic disorder involves recurrent anxiety attacks that are characterised by intense terror.
- A panic attack is defined as an abrupt surge of intense anxiety that peaks in the presence of specific thoughts or stimuli.
- Clinical features of panic disorder include
  - Shortness of breath
  - Dizziness
  - Trembling
  - Palpitations
  - Choking sensations
  - Nausea
  - Chest pain or discomfort
  - Fear of losing control, going crazy or dying

## Phobias

- **Phobias**[7] are irrational fears related to specific objects, people or situations.
- They often develop gradually or follow a generalised anxiety disorder.
- Phobias can be grouped into three main types
  - (i) **Specific Phobias** This type includes intense fears of certain animals, heights or enclosed spaces.
  - (ii) **Social Phobias** (Social Anxiety Disorder) These are characterised by intense fear and embarrassment when interacting with others, leading to avoidance of social situation.
  - (iii) **Agoraphobia** It refers to the fear of entering unfamiliar situations, often leading individuals to avoid leaving their homes, limiting daily activities.

## Separation Anxiety Disorder (SAD)

- Separation Anxiety Disorder is marked by excessive fear and anxiety regarding separation from attachment figures that is not developmentally appropriate.
- Symptoms in children may include difficulty being alone or going to school, fear of new situations and clinging to parents.
- To avoid separation, children with SAD may exhibit behaviours such as fussing, screaming, throwing severe tantrums and making suicidal gestures.

## Obsessive-Compulsive and Related Disorders

- **Obsessive-Compulsive Disorder (OCD)**[8] is defined by the inability to control preoccupations with specific ideas or thoughts.
- Individuals with OCD are compelled to engage in repetitive behaviours or actions that interfere with their daily activities.
- Obsessive behaviour refers to the inability to stop thinking about a specific idea or topic.
- People experiencing these obsessions often find their thoughts to be unpleasant and shameful, leading to considerable emotional distress.
- Compulsive behaviour is characterised by a compelling need to perform certain actions repeatedly, such as counting, ordering, checking, touching and washing.
- Others disorders in this category include hoarding disorder, trichotillomania (hair-pulling disorder), excoriation (skin-picking) disorder etc.

## Trauma and Stressor-Related Disorders

- Individuals who experience traumatic events, such as natural disasters (e.g., tsunami), bomb blasts, serious accidents or war situations, often develop post-traumatic stress disorder (PTSD).
- Symptoms of PTSD can vary widely and may include, recurrent dreams, flashbacks, impaired concentration, emotional numbing.
- Other trauma-related disorders include adjustment disorders and Acute Stress Disorder.

## Somatic Symptom and Related Disorders[9]

- Somatic symptom disorders involve physical symptoms with no clear biological cause.
- Individuals experience psychological difficulties and report physical symptoms that lack a clear medical explanation.

---

7 **Phobias** Intense, irrational fears of specific objects or situations that lead to avoidance behaviour and significant distress. Common phobias include fear of heights (acrophobia) and spiders (arachnophobia).

8 **Obsessive-Compulsive Disorder** Mental health conditions characterised by persistent, unwanted thoughts (obsessions) and repetitive behaviours (compulsions) aimed at reducing anxiety.

9 **Somatic Symptom and Related Disorders** Disorders characterised by physical symptoms that cause significant distress or impairment, often linked to psychological factors.

- Common conditions within this category include conversion disorders, somatic symptom disorders, and illness anxiety disorder among others.

### Somatic Symptom Disorder

- Individuals with somatic symptom disorder exhibit persistent symptoms and are often preoccupied with their health.
- They frequently visit doctors due to their concerns, leading to significant distress and disruptions in daily life.

### Illness Anxiety Disorder

- This disorder involves a persistent preoccupation with the fear of serious illness.
- Individuals may worry excessively about undiagnosed diseases or negative diagnostic results, displaying anxiety about health that is disproportionate to actual symptoms.
- They often disregard to reassurance from healthcare professionals and are easily alarmed by news of illnesses.
- Both somatic symptom disorder and illness anxiety disorder relate to medical illnesses.
- The key difference is that somatic symptom disorder involves physical complaints, while illness anxiety disorder focuses on anxiety about health.

### Conversion Disorders

- Individuals may report a loss of basic body functions, such as paralysis, blindness, deafness and difficulty walking.
- These symptoms often arise suddenly after a stressful experience.

## Dissociative Disorders

- Dissociation involves a severance of connections between thoughts, ideas and emotions.
- Symptoms may include feelings of unreality, estrangement, depersonalisation and occasionally a loss of identity.
- Dissociative disorders are defined by sudden temporary alterations in consciousness, often blocking painful experiences.
- Types of dissociative disorders include Dissociative Amnesia, Dissociative Identity Disorder, Depersonalisation/Derealisation Disorder.

### Dissociative Amnesia

- It's characterised by selective memory loss without any known organic cause (e.g. head injury).
- Some individuals may forget their past, while others may forget specific events or people, but retain memory of other experiences.
- Dissociative fugue is a subtype, marked by unexpected travel away from home, assuming a new identity and the inability to recall the previous identity.

### Dissociative Identity Disorder

- It's often referred to as multiple personality disorder, this condition involves the presence of alternate personalities that may or may not be aware of each other.
- It is frequently associated with traumatic childhood experiences.

### Depersonalisation/Derealisation Disorder

- Individuals may experience a dreamlike state, feeling separated from themselves and reality.
- This disorder involves a temporary change in selfperception and a loss of a sense of reality.

## Depressive Disorders

- Depression is common and recognised mental disorders is depression.
- It covers a variety of negative moods and behavioural changes. Depression can be refer to a symptom or a disorder.
- Major Depressive Disorder is defined by a period of depressed mood and/or a loss of interest or pleasure in most activities.
- Other symptoms may include change in body weight, sleep problems, tiredness, difficulty thinking agitation or slowed behaviour, thoughts of death or suicide and excessive guilt or feelings of worthlessness.
- Genetic make-up and heredity are significant risk factors for major depression and related disorders.
- Age is also a risk factor, with women particularly at risk during young adulthood, while men face the highest risk in early middle age.
- Women are more likely to report **depressive disorders**[10] compared to men.
- Other contributing factors include experiencing negative life events and a lack of social support.

## Bipolar and Related Disorders

- Bipolar I disorder involves the presence of both mania and depression, which can alternate with periods of normal mood.
- Manic episodes usually followed or preceded by depressive episodes.
- Historically, bipolar mood disorders were referred to as manic-depressive disorders.
- Various types of **bipolar and related disorders**[11] include
  - (i) Bipolar I Disorder
  - (ii) Bipolar II Disorder
  - (iii) Cyclothymic Disorder
- Suicide is considered a misfortune that can occur at any point in life.
- Suicide results from a complex interaction of various factors, including biological, genetic, psychological, sociological, cultural and environmental factors.
- Suicidal behaviour often reflects difficulties in problem-solving, stress management and emotional expression.
- Suicidal thoughts can lead to actions when they appear to be the only solution to one's difficulties. These thoughts are typically intensified during periods of acute emotional distress.
- The ramifications of suicide on the social circle and the broader community can be devastating and long-lasting.
- The stigma surrounding suicide prevents many individuals from seeking help.
- Enhancing identification, referral and management of suicidal behaviour is crucial for effective prevention.

10 **Depressive Disorders** A group of mood disorders that include major depressive disorder and persistent depressive disorder (dysthymia), characterised by persistent sadness and loss of interest.

11 **Bipolar and Related Disorders** Mental health conditions marked by extreme mood swings, including depressive episodes and manic episodes. Bipolar I and II are the most common types.

- There is a need to identify vulnerabilities, comprehend the circumstances leading to suicidal behaviour and plan appropriate interventions. Suicides are preventable through a comprehensive multi-sectoral approach that involves government, media and civil society as key stakeholders.
- Some measures suggested by the World Health Organisation (WHO) include
  - limiting access to the means of suicide.
  - ensuring responsible reporting of suicide by the media.
  - implementing alcohol-related policies.
  - ensuring early identification, treatment and care for individuals at risk.
  - training health workers to assess and manage suicide risk.
  - providing care for individuals who attempted suicide and ensuring community support.

## Identifying Students in Distress

Any unexpected or striking change affecting an adolescent's performance, attendance or behaviour should be taken seriously. Indicators of distress include

- a lack of interest in common activities
- decreasing effort in schoolwork.
- mysterious or repeated absences.
- declining grades
- misbehaviour in the classroom.
- engagement in smoking, drinking or drug misuse.

## Strengthening Students' Self-Esteem

- Positive self-esteem is essential for coping with distress effectively.
- To foster positive self-esteem in children, the following approaches can be beneficial
  - Accentuating positive life experiences to help develop a positive identity, which boosts self-confidence.
  - Providing opportunities to develop physical, social and vocational skills.
  - Establishing trustful communication between students and educators.
  - Setting specific, measurable, achievable and relevant goals that can be completed within a relevant time frame.

# Schizophrenia Spectrum and Other Psychotic Disorders

- Schizophrenia is the descriptive term for a group of psychotic disorders in which personal, social and occupational functioning deteriorate.
- It may causes of deterioration disturbed thought processes, strange perceptions, unusual emotional states, and Motor abnormalities.
- Schizophrenia is a debilitating disorder, with tremendous cost impacting patients, families and society.

## Symptoms of Schizophrenia

Symptoms of schizophrenia can be grouped into three categories

## 1. Positive Symptoms

Positive symptoms are 'pathological exesses' or 'bizarre addition' to a person's behaviour. Types of positive symptoms are

(i) **Delusions** A delusion is a false beliefs that are firmly held on inadequate grounds.

There are mainly three types of delusions

- **Delusions of Persecution** People with this delusion believe that they are being plotted against, spied on, slandered, threatened, attacked or deliberately victimised.
- **Delusions of Reference** People with this delusion attach special and personal meaning to the actions of others or to objects and events.

- **Delusions of Grandeur** People with this delusion believe themselves to the specially empowered persons.
- **Delusions of Control** People with this delusion believe that feelings, thoughts and actions are being controlled by external forces.

(ii) **Formal Thought Disorders**

- Individuals may think logically but speak in peculiar ways. These disorders can make communication extremely difficult.
- These include rapidly shifting from one topic to another so that normal structure of thinking inventing new words or phrases (neologisms) and persistent and inappropriate repetition of same thought (perseveration).

(iii) **Hallucinations**

- It is a perception that occurs in the absence of external stimuli. Auditory hallucinations are most common. Hallucinations includes some senses like

(i) **Auditory Hallucinations** Hearing voices or sounds that do not exist.

(ii) **Visual Hallucinations** Vague perceptions or distinct visions.

(iii) **Tactile Hallucinations** Sensations like tingling or burning.

(iv) **Somatic Hallucinations** Perceptions of internal sensations.

(v) **Gustatory Hallucinations** Strange tastes in food or drink.

(vi) **Olfactory Hallucinations** Unpleasant smells.

## 2. Negative Symptoms

- Negative symptoms are 'pathological deficits' and include poverty of speech, blunted and flat affects, loss of volition and social withdrawal.

Types of negative symptoms include

- **Alogia** Poverty of speech, characterised by a reduction in speech and content.
- **Blunted Affect** Reduced emotional expression such as showing less anger, sadness, joy and other feelings.
- **Flat Affect** Showing no emotion at all.
- **Avolition** Apathy and inability to initiate or complete tasks.
- **Social Withdrawal** Focus on one's own ideas and fantasies, leading to isolation.

## 3. Psychomotor Symptoms

- People with schizophrenia may show less spontaneous movement and make odd gestures or grimaces (ugly expression).
- These symptoms may take extreme forms known as catatonia. People in catatonic stupor remain motionless and silent for long time.
- Some show catatonic rigidity i.e. maintaining a rigid, upright postures for long time and others show catationic posturing i.e. assuming awkward, bizzare positions for long periods of time.

## Neurodevelopmental Disorders

- Neurodevelopmental disorders typically manifest during the early stages of development. Symptoms often appear before or during the initial years of schooling.
- These disorders hinder personal, social, academic and occupational functioning. They are characterised by deficits or excesses or delays in achieving age-appropriate behaviours.

### Attention-Deficit/Hyperactivity Disorder (ADHD)

- ADHD is primarily characterised by two features
  - (i) **Inattention** Children struggle to sustain mental effort during work or play. They may have difficulty focusing on tasks, following instructions and completing assignments. Common complaints include not listening, being easily distracted, forgetfulness and disorganisation and quickly losing interest in boring activities.
  - (ii) **Hyperactivity-Impulsivity** Impulsive children struggle to control immediate reactions, finding it challenging to wait their turn, resist temptations, and often experience minor mishaps, such as knocking things over. Children with ADHD are in constant motion have difficulty sitting still. They may fidget, squir and climb and run aimlessly.
- Children with ADHD are often described as 'driven by a motor', constantly on the go and talking incessantly.

### Autism Spectrum Disorder

- Autism Spectrum Disorder (ASD) is characterised by impairments in social interaction, communication skills and stereotyped patterns of behaviours, interests and activities.
- Children with ASD struggle with initiating social behaviours, responding to others' feelings and sharing experiences or emotions.
- They exhibit serious communication and language abnormalities that may persist over time. Many of them never develop speech and those who do, have repetitive or deviant speech patterns.
- Children with autism show narrow patterns of interests and repetitive behaviours such as lining up objects or stereotyped body movements.
- Due to difficulties in verbal and non-verbal communication, individuals with autism spectrum disorder often struggle to initiate and maintain relationships.

### Intellectual Disability

- Intellectual disability is characterised by below-average intellectual functioning (IQ of approximately 70 or below).
- Individual are deficits in the areas of communications, self-care, home living, social/interpersonal skills, functional academic skills, work etc.

### Specific Learning Disorder

- Specific learning disorder involves difficulty processing information efficiently and accurately.
- During early school years, students face problems in basic skills in reading, writing and mathematics.
- Affected children often perform below average for their age but may achieve acceptable performance levels with additional support and effort.
- It can significantly impair functioning and performance in activities requiring these skills.

## Disruptive, Impulse-Control and Conduct Disorders

The disorders included under this category are Oppositional Defiant Disorder (ODD), Conduct Disorder and others.

### Oppositional Defiant Disorder (ODD)

- Children with ODD display age-inappropriate amounts of stubbornness. They are irritable, defiant, disobedient and behave in a hostile manner.
- They do not see themselves as angry, oppositional or defiant.
- They often justify their behaviour as a reaction to circumstances or demands. Thus, the symptoms of ODD become entangled with problematic interactions with others.

#### Conduct Disorder

- The terms conduct disorder and **antisocial behaviour**[12] refer to age-inappropriate actions and attitudes that violate family expectations, societal norms, personal or property rights of others.
- The behaviours typical of conduct disorder include aggressive actions causing harm to people or animals, non-aggressive conduct that causes property damage, major deceitfulness or theft and serious rule violations.
- Children show many different types of aggressive behaviour, such as verbal aggression (e.g. name-calling, swearing), physical aggression (e.g. hitting, fighting), hostile aggression (e.g. directed at inflicting injury to others) and proactive aggression (e.g. dominating, and bullying others without provocation).

## Feeding and Eating Disorders[13]

- Another group of disorders that are of special interest to young people are eating disorders.
- These include anorexia nervosa, bulimia nervosa and binge eating.

### Anorexia Nervosa

- In anorexia nervosa, the individual has a distorted body image seeing themselves as overweight.
- Individuals often refuse to eat, exercise compulsively and develop unusual habits, such as refusing to eat in front of others. This can lead to extreme weight loss and can even starve themselves to death.

### Bulimia Nervosa

- In bulimia nervosa, the individual may eat excessive amounts of food and then purge their body by using medications such as laxatives or diuretics or by vomiting.
- They often feel disgusted and ashamed after bingeing and experiences relief after purging.
- In binge eating disorder, there are frequent episodes of uncontrolled eating.
- The individual eat rapidly than normal and continues eating until they feel uncomfortably full.
- In fact, large amounts of food may be consumed even when the individual is not feeling hungry.

## Substance-Related and Addictive Disorders

- Addictive behaviour can involve excessive intake of high-calorie food, resulting in extreme obesity or the abuse of substances such as alcohol or cocaine.
- This behaviour is one of the most severe problems faced by society today.

---

12 **Antisocial Behaviour** Actions that violate societal norms and may harm others, often characterised by a lack of empathy and remorse. It can be associated with antisocial personality disorder.

13 **Feeding and Eating Disorders** A range of disorders characterised by abnormal eating behaviours, including anorexia nervosa, bulimia nervosa and binge-eating disorder.

- Disorders relating to maladaptive behaviours resulting from regular and consistent use of the substance involved are included under **substance-related and addictive disorders**[14].
- These disorders include problems associated with the use and abuse of substances such as alcohol, cocaine, tobacco and opioids, among others.
- These substances alter the way people think, feel and behave.
- While there are many disorders listed under this category, a few frequently used substances are discussed below.

## Alcohol

- People who abuse alcohol drink large amounts regularly and rely on it to cope with difficult situations.
- Eventually, the drinking interferes with their social behaviour and ability to think and work.
- Their bodies build up a tolerance for alcohol, requiring them to drink even greater amounts to feel its effects.
- They also experience withdrawal responses when they stop drinking.
- Alcoholism destroys millions of families, social relationships and careers.
- Intoxicated drivers are responsible for many road accidents.
- This disorder also has serious effects on the children of persons who abuse alcohol.
- These children have higher rates of psychological problems, particularly anxiety, depression, phobias and substance-related disorders.
- Excessive drinking can seriously damage physical health.

### Effects of Alcohol : Some Facts

- All alcoholic beverages contain ethyl alcohol.
- This chemical is absorbed into the blood and carried into the central nervous system (brain and spinal cord), where it depresses or slows down functioning.
- Ethyl alcohol depresses areas in the brain that control judgement and inhibition; making people more talkative and friendly, confident and happier.
- As alcohol is absorbed, it affects other areas of the brain, leading to an inability to make sound judgements; speech becomes slurred and unclear and memory falters. Many people may become emotional, loud and aggressive.
- Motor difficulties increase; individuals may become unsteady while walking and clumsy in performing simple activities. Vision may become blurred, and they may have trouble hearing. Additionally, they face difficulty in driving or solving simple problems.

14 **Substance-Related and Addictive Disorders** A group of disorders related to the misuse of substances such as drugs or alcohol, leading to significant impairment or distress.

**Characteristics of Individuals with Different Levels of Intellectual Disability**

| Area of Functioning | Mild (IQ range = 55 to approximately 70) | Moderate (IQ range = 35-40 to approximately 50-55) | Severe (IQ range = 20-25 to approximately 35-40) and Profound (IQ = below 20-25) |
|---|---|---|---|
| **Self-help Skills** | Feeds and dresses self and cares for own toilet needs | Has difficulties and requires training but can learn adequate self-help skills | No skills to partial skills, but some can care for personal needs on limited; basis |
| **Speech and Communication** | Receptive and expressive language is adequate; understands communication | Receptive and expressive language is adequate; has speech problems | Receptive language is limited expressive language is poor |
| **Academics** | Optimal learning environment; third to sixth grade | Very few academic skills; first or second grade is maximal | No academic skills |
| **Social Skills** | Has friends; can learn to adjust quickly | Capable of making friends but has difficulty in many social situations | Not capable of having real friends; no social interactions |
| **Vocational Adjustment** | Can hold a job; competitive to semi-competitive; primarily unskilled work | Sheltered work environment; usually needs consistent supervision | Generally no employment; usually needs constant care |
| **Adult Living** | Usually marries, has children needs help during stress | Usually does not marry or have children; dependent | No marriage or children: always dependent on others |

## Heroin

- Heroin intake significantly interferes with social and occupational functioning.
- Most abusers develop a dependence on heroin, revolving their lives around the substance.
- Users build up a tolerance for heroin and experience withdrawal reactions when they stop taking it.
- The most direct danger of heroin abuse is an overdose with slows down the respiratory centres in the brain, almost paralysing breathing.
- In many cases, an overdose can cause death.

## Cocaine

- Regular use of cocaine may lead to abuse where the person is intoxicated throughout the day.
- This affect social relationships and work performance.
- Cocaine use may also cause problems in short-term memory and attention.
- Dependence on cocaine can develop, dominating the person's life.
- Increased use is needed to achieve the desired effects and stopping leads to depression, fatigue, sleep problems, irritability and anxiety. Cocaine poses serious dangers with dangerous effects on psychological functioning and physical well-being.

### Commonly Abused Substances (Following the DSM-5 Classification)

- **Alcohol**
- **Stimulants** dextroamphetamines, metaamphetamines, cocaine.
- **Caffeine** coffee, tea, caffeinated soda, analgesics, chocolate, cocoa.
- **Cannabis** marijuana or 'bhang'.
- **Hallucinogens** LSD, mescaline.
- **Inhalants** gasoline, glue, paint thinners, spray paints, typewriter correction fluid, sprays.
- **Tobacco** cigarettes, bidi.
- **Opioid** morphine, heroin, cough syrup, painkillers (analgesics, anaesthetics).
- **Sedatives**, Hypnotics or Anxiolytics: sleeping pills, anti-anxiety medication.

## Quick Test 3

1. What is the primary symptom of generalised anxiety disorder?
2. What triggers panic disorder episodes?
3. What is the focus of a phobia?
4. What repetitive behaviour is characteristic of OCD?
5. What emotion is central to major depressive disorder?
6. What mood alteration defines bipolar disorder?

# NCERT Folder

**1. Identify the symptoms associated with depression and mania.**

**Ans. Depression** It covers a variety of negative moods and behavioural changes. The symptoms include change in body weight, persistent sleep problems, fatigue, difficulty in to think clearly, agitation, greatly slowed behaviour and thoughts of death or suicide.

**Mania** People suffering from mania become euphoric (high), extremely active, excessively talkative and easily distractible. Manic episodes rarely appear by themselves, they usually alternate with depression.

**2. Describe the characteristics of hyperactive children.**

**Ans.** The characteristics of hyperactive children are as follows

- Children who are hyperactive often seen unable to control their movements.
- It is difficult for them to sit still and quiet.
- The child may fidget, squirm, climb and run around the room aimlessly.
- Boys are four times more likely to be given this diagnosis than girls.

**3. What are the consequences of alcohol substance addiction?**

**Ans. Substance Dependence** In this, there is intense need for the substance to which the person is addicted and the person shows tolerance, withdrawal symptoms and compulsive drug-taking. Tolerance occurs when the person needs to increasing amounts of a substance to get the same effect. Withdrawal refers to physical symptoms that occur when a person stops or cuts down on the use of a psychoactive substance. A psychoactive substance has the ability to change an individual's consciousness, mood and thinking processes.

**Substance Abuse** In this, there are recurrent and significant adverse consequences related to the use of substances. People who regularly ingest drugs damage their family and social relationships, perform poorly at work and create physical hazards.

**4. Can a distorted body image lead to eating disorders? Classify the various forms of it.**

**Ans.** A distorted body image lead to eating disorders. There are three types of eating disorders

(i) **Anorexia Nervosa** In this, the individual has a disfigured body image that leads her/ him to see herself/himself as overweight. By refusing to eat, exercising compulsively and developing unusual habits such as refusing to eat in front of others, the anorexic may lose large amounts of weight and even starve herself/himself to death.

(ii) **Bulimia Nervosa** In this, the individual may eat excessive amount of food, then clear her/his body of food by using medicines such as laxatives or diuretics or by vomiting. The person often feels disgusted and ashamed when she/he binges and is relieved of tension and negative emotions after purging.

(iii) **Binge Eating** In this, there are frequent episodes of out-of-control eating. The individual eats at a high speed than normal and takes a large amount of food even when he is not feeling hungry.

**5. "Physicians make diagnosis looking at a person's physical symptoms." How are psychological disorders diagnosed?**

**Ans.** Psychological disorders are caused by inadequacies in the way an individual thinks, feels or perceives the world. It is commonly believed that psychological disorder is some thing to be ashamed of. The stigma attached to it makes people hesitant to consult a doctor. But it should be treated as any other illness.

Classifications of psychological disorders are useful because they enable users like psychologists, psychiatrists and social workers to communicate with each other about the disorder. They help in understanding the causes of psychological disorders and the processes involved in their development and maintenance.

The American Psychiatric Association (APA) has published an official manual describing and classifying various kinds of psychological disorders.

The current version of it, the Diagnostic and Statistical Manual of Mental Disorders, 5th Edition (DSM-5), evaluates the patient on five dimensions rather than just one broad aspect of 'mental disorder'. These dimensions relate to biological, psychological, social and other aspects.

The classification scheme officially used in India is the tenth revision of the International Classification of Diseases, which is known as the ICD-10 Classification of Behavioural and Mental Disorders. It was prepared by the World Health Organisation (WHO).

For each disorder, a description of the main clinical features or symptoms and other associated features including diagnostic guidelines is provided in this scheme.

**6. Distinguish between obsessions and compulsions.**

*Or* **Differentiate between obsession and compulsion.**

**CBSE Term II 2022**

**Ans.** **Obsessions** is the inability to stop thinking about a particular idea or topic. The person involved, often finds these thoughts to be unpleasant and shameful.

**Compulsions** is the need to perform certain behaviours over and over again. Many compulsions deal with counting, ordering, checking, touching and washing.

People affected by obsessive-compulsive disorder are unable to control their preoccupation with specific ideas or are unable to prevent themselves from repeatedly carrying out a particular act or series of acts that affect their ability to carry out normal activities.

**7. Can a long-standing pattern of deviant behaviour be considered abnormal? Elaborate.**

**Ans.** The word 'abnormal' literally means 'away from the normal'. It implies deviation from some clearly defined norms or standards. In psychology, we have no 'ideal model' or 'normal model' of human behaviour to use as a base for comparison. Various approaches have been used in distinguishing between normal and abnormal behaviours.

From these approaches, two basic and conflicting views emerged

(i) The first approach views abnormal behaviour as a deviation from social norms. Abnormal behaviour, thoughts and emotions are different from a society's ideas of proper functioning.

Each society has norms, which are stated or unstated rules for proper conduct. Behaviours, thoughts and emotions that break societal norms are called abnormal.

A society whose culture values competition and assertiveness may accept aggressive behaviour, whereas one that emphasises cooperation and family values (such as in India) may consider aggressive behaviour as unacceptable or even abnormal.

(ii) The second approach views abnormal behaviour as maladaptive. The best criterion for determining the normality of behaviour is whether society promotes the well-being of the individual and i.e. the group to which she/he belongs.

Well-being is not simply a maintenance and survival but also includes growth and fulfilment i.e. the actualisation of potential. According to this criterion, conforming behaviour can be seen as abnormal if it is maladaptive i.e., if it interferes with optimal functioning and growth.

Describing behaviour as mal-adaptive suggests that vulnerability in the individual, inability to cope, or exceptional stress in the environment have led to problems in life.

**8. While speaking in public the patient changes topics frequently, is this a positive or a negative symptom of schizophrenia? Describe the other symptoms and sub-types of schizophrenia.**

**Ans.** It is a formal thought disorder which is a positive symptom of schizophrenia. People with schizophrenia may not be able to think logically and may speak in peculiar ways. People rapidly shift from one topic to another so that the normal structure of thinking is muddled and becomes illogical.

The symptoms of schizophrenia can be grouped into three categories

(i) **Positive symptoms** These are pathological excesses or bizarre (strange) additions to a person's behaviour. Delusions, disorganised thinking and speech, heightened perception and hallucinations and inappropriate affect are some symptoms in schizophrenia. These are discussed as follows:

(a) **Delusions** A delusion is a false belief that is firmly held on inadequate grounds. It is not affected by rational argument, and has no basis in reality.

(b) **Formal Thought Disorders** People with schizophrenia may not be able to think logically and may speak in strange ways. These formal thought disorders can make communication extremely difficult.

(c) **Hallucinations** It is a perception that occurs in the absence of external stimuli. Auditory hallucinations are most common in schizophrenia.

(ii) **Negative Symptoms** These are pathological deficits and include poverty of speech, blunted (weakened) and flat affect, loss of volition (self determination) and social withdrawal. People with schizophrenia show alogia or poverty of speech i.e., a reduction in speech and speech content.

(iii) **Psychomotor Symptoms** People with schizophrenia show psychomotor symptoms i.e. They move less spontaneously or make odd grimaces and gestures. These symptoms may take extreme forms known as catatonia. People in a catatonic stupor remain motionless and silent for long stretches of time. Some show catatonic rigidity i.e., maintaining a rigid, upright posture for hours while some others exhibit catatonic posturing i.e., assuming awkward, strange positions for long periods.

**9. What do you understand by the term 'dissociation'? Discuss its various forms.**

**Ans.** Dissociation involves feelings of unreality, estrangement, depersonalisation and sometimes a loss or shift of identity. Sudden temporary alterations of consciousness that blot out painful experiences are a defining characteristic of dissociative disorders.

Four conditions are included in this group

(i) **Dissociative Amnesia** It is characterised by extensive but selective memory loss that has no known organic cause (e.g., head injury).

(ii) **Dissociative Fugue** It is characterised the assumption of a new identity and the inability to recall the previous identity.

(iii) **Dissociative Identity Disorder** It is often referred to as multiple personality disorder and is the most dramatic of the dissociative disorders.

(iv) **Depersonalisation** It involves an imaginary state in which the person has a sense of being separated both from self and from reality.

**10. What are phobias? If someone had an intense fear of snakes, could this simple phobia be a result of faulty learning? Analyse how this phobia could have developed.**

**Ans.** Phobias are irrational fears related to specific objects, interactions with others, and unfamiliar situations. If someone had an intense fear of snakes, this simple phobia cannot be a result of faulty learning. It is a specific phobia which is most common. This group includes irrational fears such as intense fear of a certain type of animal, or of being in an enclosed space.

This phobia often develop gradually or begin with a generalised anxiety disorders. The symptoms include worry and apprehensive feelings about the future and hypervigilance, which involves constantly scanning the environment for dangers.

It is marked by motor tension, as a result of which the person is unable to relax, is restless, and visibly shaky (weak) and tense.

**11. Anxiety has been called the 'butterflies in the stomach feeling.' At what stage does anxiety become a disorder? Discuss its types.**

**Ans.** The term anxiety is usually defined as a diffuse, vague, very unpleasant feeling of fear and apprehension. Hence it is called 'butterflies in the stomach feeling.'

The anxious individual shows combinations of the following symptoms

- Rapid heart rate
- Shortness of breath
- Diarrhoea
- Loss of appetite
- Fainting
- Dizziness
- Sweating
- Sleeplessness
- Frequent urination
- Tremors

Types of anxiety disorders are as follows

**Generalised Anxiety Disorder** It consists of prolonged, vague, unexplained and intense fears that are not attached to any particular object.

The symptoms include worry and apprehensive feelings about the future; hypervigilance, which involves constantly scanning the environment for dangers.

**Panic Disorder** It consists of recurrent anxiety attacks in which the person experiences intense terror. A panic attack denotes an abrupt surge (rise) of intense anxiety rising to a peak when thoughts of a particular stimuli are present.

**Phobia** People who have phobias have irrational fears related to specific objects, people, or situations. Phobias can be grouped into three main types, i.e. specific phobias, social phobias, and agoraphobia.

(i) **Specific Phobia** This group includes irrational fears such as intense fear of a certain type of animal, or of being in an enclosed space.

(ii) **Social Phobia** Intense and incapacitating fear and embarrassment when dealing with others characterises social phobias.

(iii) **Agoraphobia** It is the term used when people develop a fear of entering unfamiliar situations.

**Obsessive-Compulsive Disorder** People affected by obsessive-compulsive disorder are unable to control their preoccupation with specific ideas or are unable to prevent themselves from repeatedly carrying out a particular act or series of acts that affect their ability to carry out normal activities. Obsessive behaviour is the inability to stop thinking about a particular idea or topic.

Compulsive behaviour is the need to perform certain behaviours over and over again. Many compulsions deal with counting, ordering, checking, touching and washing.

**Post-Traumatic Stress Disorder** (PTSD) People who have been caught in a natural disaster (such as tsunami) or have been victims of bomb blasts by terrorists, or been in a serious accident or in a war-related situation, experience Post-Traumatic Stress Disorderp (PTSD).

# Exam Pattern Questions

## Objective Type Questions

### Multiple Choice Questions (MCQs)

**1.** The latest system of clarification of psychological disorder is
(a) WHO (b) DSM-III R (c) DSM-IV (d) ICD-9

**2.** Developing a fear of entering unfamiliar situation is known as
(a) Panic disorder (b) Compulsive disorder
(c) Agoraphobia (d) Conversion disorder

**3.** An individual reporting loss of part or some bodily functions is sign of
(a) Dissociative disorder (b) Panic disorder
(c) Mood disorder (d) Conversion disorder

**4.** Children who have marked difficulties in social interaction and communication, desire for routine and restricted interests are suffering from
(a) Alogia (b) Impulsivity
(c) Hyperactivity (d) Autism

**5.** Anxiety disorder may be caused due to which neurotransmitter
(a) GABA (b) ICD-10 (c) Serotonin (d) Dopamine

**6.** Biological factors which influence our behaviour are
(a) Faulty genes (b) Endocrine imbalances
(c) Malnutrition (d) All of these

**7.** Galen elaborated on the role of four humours in personal character and temperament. According to him the material world is made up of four elements
(a) Earth, air, sky, water (b) Earth, fire, sky, water
(c) Earth, air, fire, water (d) Earth, sky, air, fire

**8.** People unable to prevent themselves from repeatedly carrying out a set of actions are affected by
(a) Manic-depressive disorder
(b) Panic disorder
(c) Somatoform disorders
(d) Obsessive-compulsive disorder

**9.** Psychological difficulties and complaints of physical symptoms having no biological cause are known as
(a) Manic-depressive disorders
(b) Panic disorders
(c) Somatic symptom disorders
(d) Obsessive-compulsive disorders

**10.** Michael a 10-year-old boy, was diagnosed with a disorder where he has difficulty in perceiving and processing information accurately and efficiently. This impacts his basic skills of reading, writing and doing mathematics. Identify this disorder. **CBSE 2023**
(a) Autism spectrum disorder
(b) Intellectual disability
(c) Specific learning disorder
(d) Attention-deficit hyperactivity disorder

**11.** For the past six months, Julie has been exhausted, hopeless and unable to enjoy her normal activities. She has no interest in spending time with friends and is having a hard time keeping up at work. The most likely diagnosis is
(a) depression
(b) schizotypal personality disorder
(c) seasonal affective disorder
(d) dissociative disorder

**12.** While paying bills, Jen was suddenly overwhelmed by anxiety. Her heart pounded, she felt like she couldn't breathe and she became dizzy. This was most likely
(a) a panic attack
(b) a dissociative episode
(c) a manic episode
(d) a generalised anxiety episode

**13.** Which of the following is/are true about psychological disorders in the middle ages? **CBSE SQP 2022**
I. Demonology and superstition were used as explanations of psychological disorders.
II. Mental anguish and conflict were considered as reasons for psychological disorders.
III. Disturbed interpersonal relationships were emphasised to explain mental disorders.
IV. There was emphasis on de-institutionalisation for people with psychological disorders.

Choose the correct option.
(a) Only I
(b) I and II
(c) Only III
(d) II and IV

**14.** **An ancient theory holds that abnormal behaviour can be explained by the ......... .** **CBSE SQP 2024**

(a) inadequacies in thinking, feeling, or perceiving the world
(b) operation of supernatural and magical forces
(c) disturbed interpersonal relationships
(d) belief that individuals behave strangely because their bodies and brains are not working properly

**15.** **Ranjeet is unable to stop thinking about locking his house. At work, he is preoccupied with this unreasonable and repetitive thought. This is predominantly a symptom of ......... .** **CBSE SQP 2024**

(a) anxiety disorder (b) panic disorder
(c) obsessive behaviour (d) compulsive behaviour

**16.** **Ravi constantly believes he is a failure because he once performed poorly on a test. Which cognitive problem is he exhibiting according to the Cognitive Model?** **CBSE 2025**

(a) Accurate self-assessment
(b) Overgeneralisation
(c) Rational thinking
(d) Logical reasoning

**17.** **Which of the following statements best describes how societal norms influence the perception of abnormal behaviour?** **CBSE 2025**

(a) Societal norms are universally consistent and do not change over time.
(b) Behaviours, thoughts and emotions that align with societal norms are always considered abnormal.
(c) Societal norms are derived from society's culture, including its history, values and institutions and these norms can change over time.
(d) Aggressive behaviour is universally accepted as normal behaviour across all cultures.

## Assertion-Reason Questions

**Direction** (Q. Nos. 18-22) Two statements are given in the question below as Assertion (A) and Reason (R). Read the statements and choose the appropriate option.

(a) Both A and R are true and R is the correct explanation of A.
(b) Both A and R are true, but R is not the correct explanation of A.
(c) A is true, but R is false.
(d) A is false, but R is true.

**18.** **Assertion** (A) Psychological disorders are characterised by deviant, distressing, dysfunctional and sometimes dangerous behaviours.

**Reason** (R) The four Ds—deviance, distress, dysfunction and danger—are common criteria used to define abnormality.

**19.** **Assertion** (A) Abnormal behaviour can be seen as a deviation from societal norms.

**Reason** (R) Societal norms are static and do not change over time.

**20.** **Assertion** (A) The biological approach suggests that abnormal behaviour results from physical dysfunctions in the body or brain.

**Reason** (R) Imbalances in neurotransmitters like dopamine and serotonin are linked to psychological disorders.

**21.** **Assertion** (A) The psychodynamic model views abnormal behaviour as resulting from unresolved internal conflicts.

**Reason** (R) According to the psychodynamic model, behaviour is influenced by unconscious psychological forces such as the id, ego and superego.

**22.** **Assertion** (A) When an electrical impulse reaches a neuron's ending, the nerve ending is stimulated to release a chemical called a neurotransmitter.

**Reason** (R) Studies indicate that abnormal activity by certain neurotransmitters can lead to adaptive behaviour.

# Answers

1. (c) DSM-IV
2. (c) Agoraphobia
3. (d) Conversion disorder
4. (d) Autism
5. (a) GABA
6. (d) All of these
7. (c) Earth, air, fire, water
8. (d) Obsessive-compulsive disorder
9. (c) Somatic symptom disorders
10. (c) Specific learning disorder
11. (a) depression
12. (a) a picnic attack
13. (b) I and II
14. (b) operation of supernatural and magical forces
15. (c) obsessive behaviour
16. (b) Overgeneralisation
17. (c) Societal norms are derived from society's culture, including its history, values and institutions and these norms can change over time.
18. (a) Both A and R are true and R is the correct explanation of A.
19. (c) A is true, but R is false.
20. (a) Both A and R are true and R is the correct explanation of A.
21. (a) Both A and R are true and R is the correct explanation of A.
22. (c) A is true, but R is false.

# Subjective Questions

## Very Short Answer Type Questions

**1. What is abnormality?**

**Ans.** The word 'abnormal' literally means 'away from the normal'. It implies deviation from some clearly defined norms or standards.

**2. Define well-being.**

**Ans.** Well-being means to have positive health. Health is a state of complete physical, mental, social and spiritual well-being.

**3. What do you know about stigma?**

**Ans.** People are hesitant to consult a doctor or psychologist because they are ashamed of their problems. This is known as stigma attached to mental illness.

**4. What are neurotransmitters?**

**Ans.** When an electrical impulse reaches a neuron's ending, the nerve ending is stimulated to release a chemical, called a neurotransmitter.

**5. What is panic disorder?**

**Ans.** Panic disorder consists of recurrent anxiety attacks in which the person experiences intense terror. A panic attack denotes an abrupt surge of intense anxiety rising to a peak when thoughts of a particular stimuli are present.

**6. Define the term avolition.**

**Ans.** Avolition means apathy and an inability to start or complete a course of action. Patients with schizophrenia experience avolition.

**7. What is specific phobia?**

**Ans.** Phobia is the most commonly occurring type of phobia. This group includes irrational fears such as intense fear of a certain type of animal, or of being in an enclosed space.

**8. Explain the term phobia.**

**Ans.** People who have phobias have irrational fears related to specific objects, people, or situations. Phobias can be grouped into three main types, i.e. specific phobias, social phobias, and agoraphobia.

**9. What is Post-Traumatic Stress Disorder?**

**Ans.** People who have been caught in a natural disaster (such as tsunami) or have been victims of bomb blasts by terrorists or been in a serious accident or in a war-related situation, experience Post-Traumatic Stress Disorder (PTSD).

PTSD symptoms may include recurrent dreams, flashbacks, impaired concentration, and emotional numbing.

**10. Define delusions.**

**Ans.** A delusion is a false belief that is firmly held on inadequate grounds. It is not affected by rational argument and has no basis in reality.

**11. Define alogia.**

**Ans.** Alogia means poverty of speech i.e. a reduction in speech and speech content. People with schizophrnia show alogia.

**12. Explain the term anorexia nervosa.**

**Ans.** In this, the individual has a distorted body image that leads her/him to see herself/himself as overweight. By refusing to eat, exercising compulsively and developing unusual habits such as refusing to eat in front of others, the anorexic may lose large amounts of weight and even starve herself/himself to death.

**13. What is interactional approach to explain psychological disorders?**

**Ans.** According to this approach, all three factors i.e. biological, psychological and social play important role in influencing the expression and outcome of psychological disorders.

**14. How does humanistic-existential model explain psychological disorder?**

**Ans.** Humanistic-existential model focuses on broader aspects of human existence. Humanists believe that human beings are born with a natural tendency to be friendly, cooperative and constructive and are driven to self-actualise i.e. to fulfil this potential for goodness and growth.

Existentialists believe that from birth we have total freedom to give meaning to our existence or to avoid that responsibility.

**15. State any two differences between somatic symptom and illness anxiety disorder.** CBSE SQP Term II 2021

**Ans.** The two differences between somatic symptom and illness anxiety disorder are as follows

| Somatic symptom disorder | Illness anxiety disorder |
|---|---|
| A person have body-related symptoms which may or may not be related to any serious medical condition. | In this a person experiences worry about developing a serious medical illness. |
| They experience distress and disturbance in their life. | It is the anxiety which is the main concern about its health. |

**16. Differentiate between externalising and internalising disorders of childhood.**

**Ans.** The externalising disorders or under controlled problems, include behaviours that are disruptive and often aggressive and aversive to others in the child's environment.

The internalising disorders or over-controlled problems are those conditions where the child experiences depression, anxiety and discomfort that may not be evident to others.

**17. What is substance dependence?** CBSE 2018

**Ans.** Sometimes disorders related to maladaptive behaviour result from regular and consistent use of substance like alcohol, cocaine, tobacco etc. These substances alter the way people think, feel and behave and person become more and more dependent on these substances to get the same effect which he likes.

**18. Explain Separation Anxiety Disorder (SAD).** CBSE 2018

**Ans.** Individuals with Separation Anxiety Disorder (SAD) are fearful and anxious about separation from attachment figures to such an extent, that it is not appropriate. For example, children with SAD may show tantrums to go school for the first time as they become afraid to enter a new place rather than his home.

## Short Answer Type Questions

**1. Explain how the Age of Reason and Enlightenment influenced the treatment and perception of psychological disorders in the seventeenth and eighteenth centuries.** CBSE 2025

**Ans.** The Age of Reason and Enlightenment shifted views on psychological disorders. People began seeing mental illness as a medical issue, not supernatural. Harsh treatments were replaced with compassionate care, and shelters were established to offer humane environments. Shelters were established to provide humane environments. This era emphasised therapy, social interaction, and recovery-focused approaches, laying the foundation for modern mental health care.

**2. Explain the approach which views abnormal behaviour as a deviation from social norms.**

**Ans.** Various approaches have been used in distinguishing between normal and abnormal behaviours. Among these, the first approach views abnormal behaviour as a deviation from social norms. Abnormal behaviour, thoughts and emotions are different from a society's ideas of proper functioning.

Each society has norms, which are stated or unstated rules for proper conduct. Behaviours, thoughts and emotions that break societal norms are called abnormal.

A society whose culture values competition and assertiveness may accept aggressive behaviour, whereas one that emphasises cooperation and family values (such as in India) may consider aggressive behaviour as unacceptable or even abnormal.

**3. Describe the role of biological factors in abnormal behaviour.**

**Ans.** Biological factors influence all aspects of our behaviour. A wide range of these factors such as faulty genes, endocrine imbalances, malnutrition, injuries and other conditions may interfere with normal development and functioning of the human body. These factors may be the potential causes of abnormal behaviour.

According to biological model, abnormal behaviour has a biochemical or physiological basis. Biological researchers have found that psychological disorders are related to problems in the transmission of messages from one neuron to another. When an electrical impulse reaches the end of a neuron, the nerve ending is stimulated to release a chemical, called a Neurotransmitter.

Studies indicate that abnormal activity by certain neurotransmitters can lead to specific psychological disorders. Anxiety disorders have been linked to low activity of the neurotransmitter Gamma Amino Butyric Acid (GABA), schizophrenia to excess activity of dopamine and depression to low activity of serotonin.

**4. Discuss briefly diathesis-stress model.**

**Ans.** This model states that psychological disorders develop when a diathesis (biological pre-disposition to the disorder) is set off by a stressful situation. This model has three components

(i) The first component is the diathesis or the presence of some biological disorder which may be inherited.

(ii) The second component is that the diathesis may carry a vulnerability to develop a psychological disorder. This means that the person is 'at risk' or 'predisposed' to develop the disorder.

(iii) The third component is the presence of pathogenic stressors i.e. factors/stressors that may lead to psychopathology.

This model has been applied to several disorders including anxiety, depression, and schizophrenia.

**5. Ashok, who suffers from obsessive compulsive disorder (OCD), is considering alternative therapies to complement his current treatment. Recommend and justify which approach might be most beneficial for Ashok.** CBSE 2025

**Ans.** Ashok can try Cognitive Behavioural Therapy, especially Exposure and Response Prevention, because this therapy helps him to face his fears and reduce compulsive behaviours gradually.

CBT and ERP therapies are effective because they teach Ashok to manage anxiety without relying on rituals and improve his daily life. Combining this with mindfulness can further enhance his emotional control and well-being.

**6. State the salient feature of dissociative amnesia.**

**Ans.** It is characterised by extensive but selective memory loss that has no known organic cause (e.g. head injury). Some people cannot remember anything about their past. Others can no longer recall specific events, people, places or objects, while their memory for other events remains intact. This disorder is often associated with an overwhelming stress.

**7. What is Bipolar mood disorder?**

**Ans.** Bipolar mood disorder is a mood disorder, in which periods of mania and depression alternately, sometimes interrupted by periods of normal mood. Bipolar mood disorders were earlier referred to as manic-depressive disorders.

Among the mood disorders, the lifetime risk of a suicide attempt is high in individuals with bipolar mood disorders. Several risk factors in addition to mental health status of a person predict the likelihood of suicide. These include age, gender, ethnicity or race and recent occurrence of serious life events.

**8. Explain autistic disorder.**

**Ans.** Autistic disorder or autism is one of the most common of these disorders. Children with autistic disorder have marked difficulties in social interaction and communication, a restricted range of interests and strong desire for routine. Children with autism experience profound difficulties in relating to other people.

These difficulties are

- They are unable to initiate social behaviour and seem unresponsive to other people's feelings.
- They are unable to share experiences or emotions with others.
- They show serious abnormalities in communication and language that persist over time.
- Many autistic children never develop speech and those who do, have repetitive and deviant speech patterns.
- Children with autism often show narrow patterns of interests and repetitive behaviours such as lining up objects or stereotyped body movements such as rocking. These motor movements may be self-stimulatory such as hand flapping or self-injurious such as banging their head against the wall.

**9. Explain any three psychological models used to understand mental disorders.** CBSE 2023

**Ans.** There are several psychological models which provide a psychological explanation of mental disorders. Three psychological models used to understand mental disorders are

(i) **Psychodynamic Model** Developed by Freud, this model suggests that abnormal behaviour results from unconscious conflicts, often stemming from early childhood experiences. The interaction between the id, ego and superego shapes behaviour.

(ii) **Behavioural Model** This model posits that both normal and abnormal behaviours are learned through conditioning. Maladaptive behaviours are viewed as learned responses, which can be unlearned through classical, operant or social learning.

(iii) **Cognitive Model** This model emphasises that abnormal behaviour results from irrational and distorted thinking. It focuses on how individuals' thoughts and assumptions can lead to psychological disorders.

**10. Differentiate between delusions and hallucinations.**

**Ans. Delusions** A delusion is a false belief that is firmly held on inadequate grounds. It is not affected by rational argument, and has no basis in reality. People with this delusion believe that they are being plotted, slandered, threatened, attacked or deliberately victimised.

**Hallucinations** It is a perception that occurs in the absence of external stimuli. Auditory hallucinations are most common in schizophrenia.

Hallucinations includes some senses like

- Tactile hallucinations (i.e. forms of tingling, burning)
- Somatic hallucinations (i.e. something happening inside the body such as a snake crawling inside one's stomach)
- Visual hallucinations (i.e. unclear perceptions of colour or distinct visions of people or objects)
- Gustatory hallucinations (i.e. food or drink taste strange).
- Olfactory hallucinations (i.e. smell of poison or smoke).

**11. Why children are predisposed to developed behavioural disorders?**

**Ans.** There are certain disorders that are specific to children and if neglected can lead to serious consequences later in life.

Among children, these disorders are prevalent because

- Children have less self-understanding.
- They have not yet developed a stable sense of identity.
- Do not have an adequate frame of reference regarding reality, possibility and value.
- They are unable to cope with stressful events, which might be reflected in behavioural and emotional problems.

**12. What are somatic symptom disorders? Explain with examples.**

**Ans.** In somatic symptom disorder a person has persistent body-related symptoms which may or may not be related to any serious medical condition. People with this disorder tend to be overly preoccupied with their symptoms.

They continually worry about their health and make frequent visits to doctors. As a result, they experience significicant distress and disturbances in their daily life.

**13. Radhika has been diagnosed with generalised anxiety disorder. Explain the development of this disorder with the help of the diathesis-stress model.** CBSE SQP Term II, 2021

**Ans.** Diathesis Stress Model states that psychological disorders develop when a diathesis (a tendency to suffer from a particular medical condition) is set off by a stressful situation.

This model has three components are as follows

- The first component is the diathesis or the presence of some biological aberration which may be inherited.
- The second component is the presence of pathological stressor that may lead to psychopathology.
- The third component is the person is 'at risk' or predisposition may actually evolve into a disorder.

This model can be applied to explain Radhika's GAD. According to the model, Radhika has genetic predisposition to develop anxiety disorders which she may have inherited. Due to external stressors, generalised anxiety disorder may get triggered.

**14. Imran is a forty-years old male who complains of difficulty in breathing and other body related symptoms. On being examined, the doctors were unable to find any medical explanation for his reported symptoms. Explain this disorder and discuss its various types.** CBSE Term II 2022

**Ans.** Imran is suffering from anxiety disorder. The term anxiety is usually defined as a diffuse, vague, very unpleasant feeling of fear and apprehension. Hence it is called "butterflies in the stomach feeling".

Some types of anxiety disorders are

- **Generalised Anxiety Disorder** It consists of prolonged, vague, unexplained and intense fears that are not attached to any particular object.
  The symptoms include worry and apprehensive feelings about the future; hypervigilance, which involves constantly scanning the environment for dangers.
- **Panic Disorder** It consists of recurrent anxiety attacks in which the person experiences intense terror. A panic attack denotes an abrupt surge (rise) of intense anxiety rising to a peak when thoughts of a particular stimuli are present.
- **Phobia** People who have phobias have irrational fears related to specific objects, people or situations. Phobias can be grouped into three main types, i.e. specific phobias, social phobias and agoraphobia.

**15. Describe socio-cultural model of abnormal behaviour.**

*Or* **Explain mental disorder from socio-cultural perspective.**

**Ans.** The socio-cultural model suggests that abnormal behaviour is best understood in the context of social and cultural forces that influence an individual. As behaviour is shaped by societal forces, factors such as family structure and communication, social networks, societal conditions and societal labels and roles become more important.

It has been found that certain family systems are likely to produce abnormal functioning in individual members. Some families have a structure in which the members are overinvolved in each other's activities, thoughts and feelings. Children from such families may struggle to become independent.

The broader social networks in which people operate include their social and professional relationships. Studies have shown that people who are isolated and lack social support i.e. strong and fulfilling interpersonal relationships in their lives, are likely to become more depressed and remain depressed longer than those who have good friendships.

**16. Briefly describe various forms of delusions.**

**Ans.** Many people with schizophrenia develop delusions. A delusion is a false belief that is firmly held on inadequate grounds. It is not affected by rational argument and has no basis in reality. There are four types of delusions

(i) **Delusions of Persecution** These are the most common in schizophrenia. People with this delusion believe that they are being plotted slandered, threatened, attacked or deliberately victimised.

(ii) **Delusions of Reference** It this these people attach special and personal meaning to the actions of others or to objects and events.

(iii) **Delusions of Grandeur** In this, people believe themselves to be specially empowered persons like a Star or God.

(iv) **Delusions of Control** In this the people believe that their feelings, thoughts and actions are controlled by others.

**17. What are the substance-use disorders? Illustrate two categories of substance-use disorders.**

**Ans.** Substance-use disorders involve excessive intake of substances like alcohol, cocaine or high-calorie food, leading to maladaptive behaviours. These include two sub-groups–Substance Dependence, characterised by tolerance, withdrawal and compulsive use and Substance Abuse, where use causes significant personal, social or occupational harm.

Two key categories are

(i) **Substance Dependence** This involves a strong need for the substance, tolerance (requiring more for the same effect) and withdrawal symptoms when stopping.

(ii) **Substance Abuse** It refers to the recurrent negative consequences of substance use, such as damaging relationships, poor work performance and physical harm. Examples include alcohol and heroin abuse, which cause significant harm to personal and social functioning.

**18. Explain the factors to prevent suicide.**

**Ans.** Suicide can be prevented by being alert to some of the symptoms which include

- Changes in eating and sleeping habits.
- Withdrawal from friends, family and regular activities.
- Violent actions and rebellious behaviour.
- Drug and alcohol abuse.
- Marked personality change.
- Persistent boredom.
- Difficulty in concentration.
- Complaints about physical symptoms.
- Loss of interest in pleasurable activities.

**19. Discuss the various effects of alcohol.**

**Ans.** Some effects of alcohol are

- Alcoholism destroys millions of families, social relationships and careers.
- All alcohol beverages contain ethyl alcohol which is absorbed into the blood and carried into the central nervous system (brain and spinal cord) where it depresses or slows down functioning.
- Ethyl alcohol depresses those areas in the brain that control judgement and inhibition, people become more talkative and friendly and they feel more confident and happy.
- As alcohol is absorbed, it affects other areas of the brain. For example, drinkers are unable to make sound judgements, speech becomes less careful and less clear and memory falters.
- Motor difficulties increase. For example, people become unsteady when they walk and clumsy in performing simple activities.
- It also has serious effects on the children of persons with this disorder. These children have higher rates of psychological problems, particularly anxiety, depression, phobias and substance-related disorders.

**20. "Abnormal behaviours are those that differ markedly from a society's ideas of proper functioning." Discuss.**

**Ans.** Abnormal behaviour, thoughts and emotions are those that differ markedly from a society's ideas of proper functioning.

Each society has norms, which are stated or unstated rules for proper conduct. Behaviours, thoughts and emotions that break societal norms are called Abnormal.

A society's norms grow from its particular culture i.e. its history, values, institutions, habits, skills, technology and arts. Thus, a society whose culture values competition and assertiveness may accept aggressive behaviour, whereas one that emphasises cooperation and family values (such as in India) may consider aggressive behaviour as unacceptable or even abnormal.

**21.** **What are dissociative disorders. Explain their various types.** CBSE 2019

*Or* **What are dissociative disorders? Describe some of the identifying symptoms of different types of dissociative disorders.** CBSE SQP Term II 2021

**Ans.** Dissociation involves feeling of unreality, estrangement, depersonalisation and sometimes a loss or shift of identity. Sudden temporary alterations of consciousness that mark out painful experiences are a defining characteristic of dissociative disorders. Four conditions are included in this disorder.

These are

(i) **Dissociative Amnesia** is characterised by extensive or selective memory loss that has no known organic cause. This order is often associated with an overwhelming stress.

(ii) **Dissociative Fugue** in characterised the assumption of a new identity and the inability to recall the previous identity. The fugue usually ends when the person suddenly 'wakes up' with no memory of the events that occurred during the fugue.

(iii) **Dissociative Identity Disorder** is referred to as multiple personality disorder and is the most dramatic of the dissociative disorders. In this disorder individual assumes alternate personalities that may or may not be aware of each other and is often associated with traumatic experiences in childhood.

(iv) **Depersonalisation** involves an imaginary state in which the person has a sense of being separated both from self and from reality.

**22.** **Explain disruptive, impulse-control and conduct disorders.** CBSE 2019

*Or* **Describe the defining symptoms of oppositional defiant disorders and conduct disorder.** CBSE SQP Term II 2021

**Ans.** The disorders included under disruptive, impulse-control and conduct disorders category are Oppositional Defiant Disorder (ODD), Conduct Disorders and Others.

**Oppositional Defiant Disorder** (ODD) Children with Oppositional Defiant Disorder (ODD) are irritable, defiant, disobedient and behave in a hostile manner. Individuals with ODD do not see themselves as angry, oppositional or defiant. They often justify their behaviour as reaction to circumstances or demands. So, the symptom of the disorder become entangled with the problematic interactions with others.

**Conduct Disorder (CD) and Anti-social Behaviour** It refers to age inappropriate actions and attitudes that violate family expectations, societal norms and the personal or property rights of others. The behaviours in conduct disorder include aggressive actions that cause or threaten harm to people or animals, non-aggressive conduct that causes property damage, major deceitfulness or theft and serious rule violations.

Some types of aggressive behaviour are

- Verbal aggression (i.e. name-calling, swearing)
- Physical aggression (i.e. hitting, fighting)
- Hostile aggression (i.e. directed at inflicting injury to others)
- Proactive aggression (i.e. dominating and bullying others without provocation).

**23.** **Describe the symptoms of any two anxiety disorders.** CBSE 2020

**Ans.** One of the major psychological disorders is anxiety disorder. The term anxiety is defined as a diffuse, vague, very unpleasant feeling of fear and apprehension. The mental disorder which arises due to anxiety is known as anxiety disorder.

Two main types of anxiety disorders are

**Generalised Anxiety Disorder** It consists of continued, vague (unclear), unexplained and intense fears that are not attached to any particular object. The symptoms include worry and apprehensive feelings about the future; hypervigilance, which involves constantly scanning the environment for dangers.

It is marked by motor tension, as a result of which the person is unable to relax, is restless and visibly shaky (weak) and tense.

**Panic Disorder** It consists of recurrent anxiety attacks in which the person experiences intense terror. A panic attack denotes an abrupt rise of intense anxiety rising to a peak when thoughts of a particular stimuli are present. Such thoughts occur in an unpredictable manner. The clinical features include shortness of breath, dizziness, trembling, palpitations , choking, nausea, chest pain or discomfort, fear of going crazy, losing control or dying.

**24.** **Classify and explain the symptoms of eating disorders.** CBSE 2020

**Ans.** There are three types of eating disorders

(i) **Anorexia Nervosa** In this, the individual has a disfigured body image that leads her/him to see herself/himself as over- weight. By refusing to eat, exercising compulsively and developing unusual habits such as refusing to eat in front of others, the anorexic may lose large amounts of weight and even starve herself/himself to death.

(ii) **Bulimia Nervosa** In this, the individual may eat excessive amount of food, then clear her/his body of food by using medicines such as laxatives or diuretics or by vomiting. The person often feels disgusted and ashamed when she/he binges and is relieved of tension and negative emotions after purging.

(iii) **Binge Eating** In this, there are frequent episodes of claborad out-of-control eating. In this case individual eats large amount of food, even he is not feeling hungry. He tends to eat at a higher speed than normal and continues eating till he feels uncomfortably full.

**25. Explain obsessive-compulsive behaviour.**

**Ans.** Obsessive-Compulsive Disorder (OCD) involves uncontrollable thoughts (obsessions) and repetitive actions (compulsions) that disrupt daily life. Obsessions are persistent, intrusive thoughts or urges, while compulsions are repetitive behaviours performed to alleviate the anxiety caused by obsessions.

Common compulsions include counting, checking, washing and touching. These behaviours may interfere with normal activities and can cause significant distress.

Other related disorders include hoarding disorder, trichotillomania (hair-pulling) and excoriation (skin-picking) disorder. OCD often requires treatment through therapy, medication or a combination of both.

**26. Explain mental disorders from a cognitive perspective.** **CBSE 2018**

**Ans.** Mental disorder is often viewed as a deviation from social norms. Each society has norms which are stated or unstated rules for proper conduct. Behaviour, thoughts and emotions that deviate from societal norms are considered abnormal.

To explain mental disorders there are several psychological models. These models maintain that psychological and interpersonal factors have a significant role to play in abnormal behaviour. These psychological models include the cognitive model. Psychological factors are emphasised by the cognitive model.

This model states that abnormal functioning can result from cognitive problems.

People may hold assumptions and attitudes about themselves that are irrational and inaccurate. They may also repeatedly think in illogical ways. Sometimes they make overgeneralisa- tions and draw broad, negative conclusions on the basis of a single insignificant event.

**27. Raman washes his hands every time, he touches something. One of his colleague also observed that he washes even things like coins. He further noticed that Raman steps only within the patterns on the floor or road while walking. Identify and describe the symptoms of this disorder.**

**Ans.** Raman is suffering from obsessive-compulsive disorder. In this disorder, people are unable to control their preoccupation with specific ideas or are unable to prevent themselves from repeatedly carrying out a particular act or series of acts that affect their ability to carry out normal activities.

Obsessive behaviour is the inability to stop thinking about a particular idea or topic. The person involved, often finds these thoughts to be unpleasant and shameful. Compulsive behaviour is the need to perform certain behaviours over and over again. Many compulsions deal with counting, ordering, checking, touching and washing. Other disorders in this category include hoarding disorder, trichotillomania (hair-pulling disorder), excoriation (skin-picking) disorder etc.

**27. Can a long-standing pattern of deviant behaviour be considered abnormal? Elaborate and state an example of the same.** **CBSE SQP 2024**

**Ans.** Yes, a long-standing pattern of deviant behaviour can be considered abnormal, particularly if it significantly deviates from societal norms, causes distress or impairment, and persists over time. For example, chronic substance abuse can be considered a long-standing pattern of deviant behaviour that is abnormal.

Substance abuse involves the excessive and recurrent use of drugs or alcohol despite negative consequences on an individual's physical health, mental well-being, relationships and functioning. While occasional experimentation with substances may not be uncommon, persistent and compulsive substance abuse that interferes with daily life and responsibilities is considered abnormal.

**28. Is separation anxiety disorder classified under neurodevelopmental disorders? Give reasons for your answer by enumerating the symptoms of separation anxiety disorder.** **CBSE SQP 2024**

**Ans.** No, separation anxiety disorder is not classified under neurodevelopmental disorders. It is classified under anxiety disorders. Neurodevelopmental disorders are conditions that arise in childhood and are characterised by atypical development in specific areas, such as communication, social interaction, or motor skills. Separation anxiety disorder, on the other hand, focuses on excessive anxiety and fear related to separation from attachment figures.

The symptoms of separation anxiety disorder are

- Excessive distress when separation from attachment figures is anticipated or occurs.
- Excessive worry about losing attachment figures or harm befalling them.

- Persistent worry about an event that might lead to separation.
- Unwillingness to leave attachment figures or go to places where they might not be present.
- Difficulty sleeping or nightmares related to separation.
- Physical symptoms like headaches, stomachaches or nausea when separation is imminent.

## Long Answer Type Questions

**1. Describe the psychological models to explain abnormal behaviour/mental disorders.** **CBSE 2019, 2014**

**Ans.** (i) **Psychological Models** There are several psychological models which provide a psychological explanation of mental disorders. The psychological and inter- personal factors have a significant role to play in abnormal behaviour.

These factors include

- Maternal deprivation (separation from the mother or lack of warmth and stimulation during early years of life).
- Faulty parent-child relationships (rejection, overprotection, over permissiveness, faulty discipline, etc.)
- Maladaptive family structures (inadequate or disturbed family) and severe stress.

The psychological models include the following

(ii) **Psychodynamic Model** It is the oldest and most famous of the modern psychological models. Psychodynamic theorists believe that behaviour, whether normal or abnormal is determined by psychological forces within the person of which she/he is not consciously aware.

(iii) **Behavioural Model** This model states that both normal and abnormal behaviours are learned and psychological disorders are the result of learning maladaptive ways of behaving.

(iv) **Cognitive Model** This model states that abnormal functioning can result from cognitive problems. People may hold assumptions and attitudes about themselves that are irrational and inaccurate.

(v) **Humanistic-Existential Model** It focuses on broader aspects of human existence. Humanists believe that human beings are born with a natural tendency to be friendly, cooperative and constructive and are driven to self-actualise i.e., to fulfil this potential for goodness and growth.

Existentialists believe that from birth we have total freedom to give meaning to our existence or to avoid that responsibility.

(vi) **Socio-Cultural Model** According to the socio-cultural model, abnormal behaviour is best understood by the social and cultural forces that influence an individual.

(vii) **Diathesis-Stress Model** This model states that psychological disorders develop when a diathesis (biological pre-disposition to the disorder) is set off by a stressful situation.

**2. Explain abnormality. Trace a brief history of how our understanding of psychological disorders has evolved to its current status.** **CBSE 2019**

**Ans.** Thinkers have given many definitions of abnormality over the years. Abnormality implies deviation from some clearly defined norms or standards. In psychology, we have no 'ideal model' or 'normal model' of human behaviour to use as a base for comparison. Various approaches have been used in distinguishing between normal and abnormal behaviours.

It is generally accepted that socially accepted behaviour is not abnormal and that normality is nothing more than conformity to social norms. Each society has different set of social norms which are stated or unstated rules for proper conduct. Behaviour, thoughts and emotions that break this societal norms are called abnormal. This abnormal behaviour is regarded as psychological disorders.

**Ancient Theory** It is about abnormality holds that abnormal behaviour can be explained by the operation of supernatural and magical forces such as evil spirits (*bhoot-pret*) or the devil (*shaitan*).

Exorcism i.e. removing the evil that resides in the individual through countermagic and prayer is still commonly used. In many societies, the *shaman* or medicine man (*ojha*) is a person who is believed to have contact with supernatural forces and is the medium through which spirits communicate with human beings.

**Ancient Western Theory** In the ancient Western world, philosopher and temperament, physicians of ancient Greece such as Hippocrates, Socrates and Plato developed the organismic approach and viewed disturbed behaviour as arising out of conflicts between emotion and reason.

**Renaissance Period** In this period Johann Weyer emphasised psychological conflict and disturbed interpersonal relationship as causes of psychological disorder. The growth of scientific attitude toward psychological disorder developed in the 18th century as a result of Reform Movement. It provided community care for mentally ill person. In recent years, it is believed that biological, psychological and social factors play important roles in influencing the expression and outcome of psychological disorders.

**3. What do you understand by the term dissociation? Explain the types of dissociative disorders.**

**Ans.** Dissociation refers to a psychological process where an individual experiences a disconnection from their thoughts, feelings, memories or sense of identity. It often involves a sense of unreality, estrangement or depersonalisation, marking a response to overwhelming stress or trauma.

There are four main types of dissociative disorders

(i) **Dissociative Amnesia** This involves selective memory loss, where a person forgets important personal information or specific events, often linked to trauma, without any organic cause like brain injury.

(ii) **Dissociative Fugue** A subtype of dissociative amnesia, it involves the person assuming a new identity and forgetting their previous one. The fugue state ends abruptly, with no memory of the events during this period.

(iii) **Dissociative Identity Disorder** Often called multiple personality disorder, it is characterised by the presence of two or more distinct personalities within one individual. These personalities may or may not be aware of each other, often stemming from childhood trauma.

(iv) **Depersonalisation** This disorder involves a feeling of detachment from one's body or mind, leading to a sense of being outside of oneself or experiencing reality in a distorted way.

**4. What are depression? Discuss the main types of mood disorders.**

**Ans.** The most common mood disorder is depression. Depression covers a variety of negative moods and behavioural changes.

We often use the term depression to refer to normal feelings after a significant loss, such as the break-up of a relationship or the failure to attain a significant goal.

Genetic make-up or heredity, age, gender, negative life events and lack of social support are some important risk factors for major depression.

**Major Depressive Disorder** It is defined as a period of depressed mood and/or loss of interest or pleasure in most activities, with other symptoms like change in body weight, constant sleep problems, tiredness, inability to think clearly, agitation, greatly slowed behaviour and thoughts of death and suicide. Other symptoms include excessive guilt or feelings of worthlessness.

**Mania** People suffering from mania become euphoric ('high'), extremely active, excessively talkative and easily distractible.

Bipolar is a mood disorder, in which both mania and depression are alternately present, is sometimes interrupted by periods of normal mood. Bipolar mood disorders were earlier referred to as manic-depressive disorders.

Some types of bipolar and related disorders include 'Bipolar I Disorder', 'Bipolar II Disorder' and 'Cyclothymic Disorder'. Among the mood disorders, the lifetime risk of a suicide attempt is high in case of bipolar mood disorders.

**Suicide** Several risk factors in addition to mental health status of a person predict the likelihood of suicide. Every suicide is a misfortune.

**5. Describe the schizophrenic disorders.**

**Ans.** Schizophrenia is the descriptive term for a group of psychotic disorders in which personal, social and occupational functioning deteriorate as a result of disturbed thought process, strange perceptions, unusal emotional states and motor abnormalities. It is a debilitating disorder.

The symptoms of schizophenia can be group into

- **Positive symptoms** Delusions, disorganised thinking and speech, heightened perception and hallucinations and inappropriate affect are some positive symptoms of schizophrenia.

  Many people with schizophrenia develop delusions which is a false belief. Delusions can be of different types like delusions of persecution, delusions of reference, delusions of grandeur and delusions of control.

  People with schizophrenia may not be able to think logically and may speak in peculiar ways and this is known as formal thought disorder people with schizophrenia may have hallucinations i.e. perceptions that occur in the absence of of external stimuli.

  Hallucination may be of different type, like tactile, somatic, visual, gustatory and olfacoryhallucinations. People with schizophrenia show inappropriate affect, i.e. emotions that are unsuited to the situation.

- **Negative symptoms** Negative symptoms are 'pathological deficits' and include poverty of speech, i.e. Alogia, Blunted affect, i.e. people with schizophrenia show less anger, sadness, joy and other feeling than other people and Flat affect, i.e. no emotions at all.

- **Psychomotorsymptoms** People with schizophrenia show psychomotor symptoms, i.e. they move less spontaneously or make odd grimaces (ugly expression with face) and gestures. These gestures may take extreme forms which is known as 'Catatonia'.

**6. What do you mean by Autism Spectrum Disorder? Explain the condition of autistic children.**

**Ans** Autism Spectrum Disorder (ASD) is a developmental condition characterised by significant challenges in social interaction, communication and behaviour. It is one of the most common neurodevelopmental disorders affecting children.

Children with ASD often face difficulty in relating to others. They may be unable to initiate social interactions and may seem unresponsive to others' feelings. These children struggle with sharing experiences or emotions and many exhibit communication and language abnormalities. Some children with autism never develop speech, while others may develop speech with repetitive or unusual patterns.

Additionally, children with autism often display restricted interests and repetitive behaviours. These behaviours can include activities such as lining up objects or engaging in stereotyped body movements like rocking or hand-flapping. Some may engage in self-stimulatory movements or self-injurious behaviours like banging their head against walls.

Overall, children with autism face profound challenges in forming and maintaining relationships, both with peers and adults, due to their unique way of interacting with the world. Their desire for routine and difficulty with changes can further impact their daily functioning.

**7. Richard is a 62-year-old single man who says that he started to drink in late teens to 'feel better' when his episodes of depression made it hard for him to interact with his peers. He also states that alcohol and cocaine are a natural part of his manic episodes. He also notes that coming off the cocaine and binge drinking contribute to low mood and past efforts have led to only temporary abstinence. Yet, Richard is now trying to forge a closer relationship to his adult children and he says he is especially motivated to get a better handle on his disorder. Identify the diseases that Richard is suffering from and also describe the symptoms. Suggest measures to overcome the issues pertaining with his disorder.** Competency Based Que.

**Ans.** Richard has substance dependence and bipolar disorder. Disorders relating to maladaptive behaviours resulting from regular and consistent use of the substance involved are included under substance related and addictive disorders. These disorders include problems associated with the use and abuse of alcohol, cocaine, tobacco and opiods among others.

In People who abuse alcohol drink, the drinking interferes with their social behaviour and ability to think and work. In case of cocaine, more of the drug is needed to get the desired effects, and stopping it results in feelings of depression, fatigue, sleep problems, irritability and anxiety.

Bipolar disorder involves both mania and depression, which are alternately present and sometimes interrupted by periods of normal mood. Manic episodes rarely appear by themselves; they usually alternate with depression. Both alcohol and cocaine, interferes with psychological functioning and harm the physical well-being.

In order to overcome his disorder, Richard must have to comply with his mood stabilising and antidepressant medication prescribed by doctors. Further, his psychiatrist should like his dual diagnoses addressed with psychotherapy.

**8. What do you understand by the term 'Dissociation'? Explain its various forms.** CBSE SQP 2024

**Ans.** Dissociation is a psychological phenomenon characterised by a disruption or detachment from one's thoughts, feelings, memories or sense of identity. It involves a disconnection between different aspects of consciousness, leading to a sense of detachment, unreality or loss of control over one's thoughts and actions. The various forms of dissociation are as follows

- **Depersonalisation** This involves feeling disconnected from one's body or self as if observing oneself from an external perspective. Individuals may feel as though they are floating or detached from reality, leading to a sense of unreality or numbness.
- **Derealisation** Derealisation involves feeling disconnected from one's surroundings, leading to a perception of the external world as unreal, distorted or unfamiliar. Objects may appear distorted, colours may seem muted and the environment may feel surreal or dreamlike.
- **Dissociative Amnesia** This involves the inability to recall important personal information, typically associated with traumatic or stressful events. Memory loss may be selective, affecting specific events or periods and may be accompanied by feelings of confusion or disorientation.
- **Dissociative Identity Disorder (DID)** It formerly known as Multiple personality disorder, DID involves the presence of two or more distinct personality states or identities within the same individual. Each identity may have its memories, behaviours and sense of self, leading to gaps in memory and disruptions in identity.

**9. What are the common features of neurodevelopmental disorders? Describe any three neurodevelopmental disorders.** CBSE SQP 2024

**Ans.** The common features of neurodevelopmental disorders are as follows

**Onset in Early Development** Neurodevelopmental disorders typically emerge during early childhood, often before the age of three. Symptoms may become apparent as developmental milestones are missed or delayed, leading to concerns about the child's functioning.

**Persistence** Neurodevelopmental disorders tend to persist over time, with symptoms continuing into adolescence and adulthood. However, the severity and presentation of symptoms may change as individuals grow and develop.

**Impact on Multiple Domains** These disorders affect multiple areas of functioning, including intellectual abilities, language skills, motor coordination, attention, social interaction and emotional regulation.

The three forms of neurodevelopmental disorders are

(i) **Autism Spectrum Disorder (ASD)** It is characterised by persistent deficits in social communication and interaction, as well as restricted, repetitive patterns of behaviour, interests or activities. Individuals with ASD may have difficulty understanding social cues, forming relationships, and communicating effectively.

(ii) **Attention-Deficit/Hyperactivity Disorder (ADHD)** It is characterised by persistent patterns of inattention, hyperactivity and impulsivity that interfere with functioning or development. Symptoms may include difficulty sustaining attention, fidgeting, excessive talking and difficulty waiting one's turn.

(iii) **Intellectual Disability (ID)** It is characterised by deficits in intellectual functioning (such as reasoning, problem-solving and adaptive skills) and deficits in adaptive functioning (such as daily living skills). Individuals with ID may have difficulty learning new information, understanding abstract concepts and performing everyday tasks independently.

## Case Based Questions

**1. Read the case study given below and answer the questions that follow.** CBSE 2025

At any one time, a diverse set of individual, family, community and structural factors may combine to protect or undermine mental health. Although most people are resilient, people who are exposed to adverse circumstances including poverty, violence, disability and inequality are at higher risk of developing a mental health condition. Protective and risk factors include individual, psychological and biological factors, such as emotional skills as well as genetics. Many of the risks and protective factors are influenced through changes in brain structure and/or function.

People with mental disorders also require social support, including support in developing and maintaining personal, family and social relationships. People with mental disorders may also need support for educational programmes, employment, housing and participation in other meaningful activities.

**(i) According to the above paragraph, what type of people are more likely to have a psychological disorder?**

**(ii) State two steps which are helpful in addressing the concerns of mentally-ill people.**

Ans. (i) People exposed to poverty, violence, disability, inequality or adverse circumstances are more likely to develop psychological disorders.

(ii) Two steps which are helpful in addressing the concerns of mentally-ill people include providing social support for maintaining relationships and offering access to educational programmes, employment opportunities, housing and other meaningful activities to improve their quality of life.

**2. Read the case and answer the questions that follow.**

Anna is a 28-years-old Caucasian woman who has struggled with alcohol use for most of her teenage and young adult life. She began drinking in high school, at age 15 and dropped out of college partway through her first year because she was missing so many classes due to alcohol use. She has attempted to go back to school twice since then but has been unsuccessful each time due to relapses.

Anna reports multiple attempts to stop drinking, but has only been able to maintain sobriety for 2-4 weeks at a time. Whenever she tries to stop drinking, she gets nauseous, shaky and disoriented. Within the last 4 months, she has withdrawn from her friends, feels sad almost every day and has frequent suicidal ideation. Her appetite has decreased, but her alcohol use has continued to increase and she is currently consuming approximately half a 'fifth' of vodka per day. She has frequent arguments with her parents, who are now threatening to cut her off financially because she spends most of her rent money on alcohol. She "can't stop thinking about my next drink," and reports feelings of guilt and worthlessness over being unable to stop drinking.

**(i) What symptoms is Anna experiencing related to her alcohol use and mental health?**

**(ii) How has Anna's alcohol use affected her life and relationships?**

Ans. (i) Anna experiences frequent relapses, physical withdrawal symptoms (nausea, shakiness, disorientation), sadness, suicidal thoughts, decreased appetite and guilt. She struggles with maintaining sobriety and feels isolated from her friends and family. Her alcohol consumption has increased and she is facing financial and relational difficulties due to her drinking.

(ii) Anna's alcohol use has led to academic setbacks, damaged relationships with her parents and financial problems. She is facing the threat of being cut off financially by her parents and her ongoing alcohol consumption is causing significant emotional distress, including feelings of worthlessness and an inability to stop drinking despite multiple attempts.

**3. Read the case and answer the questions that follow.**

Malay, a student of Class IX, was referred to a mental health clinic with complaints of stealing money, excessive lying, setting fire to household items, teasing young girls of the locality and passing lewd remarks and making obscene gestures. The onset was about three years ago and has increased over the past eight months. Of late, he has started using alcohol and spending more time outdoors with friends of similar interest. School reports suggested gradual development of inappropriate behaviours such as openly defying rules in school, playing truant, instigating fellow students to pass silly remarks in class, disrespectful attitude towards elders ultimately resulting in frequent school absenteeism, mixing with local goons and excessive aggression. Further investigation revealed that family history is disturbed, relationship with father was extremely hostile and there were frequent conflicts amongst the family members. Birth and developmental milestones are normal. **CBSE SQP 2022**

(i) **Identify the disorder Malay is exhibiting. Distinguish it from Attention–Deficit/ Hyperactivity Disorder (ADHD).**

(ii) **How would the socio-cultural model help us to understand Malay's disorder?**

**Ans.** (i) Malay is exhibiting conduct disorder.

The major difference between conduct disorder and Attention Deficit Hyperactivity Disorder (ADHD) is that conduct disorder affects the behavioural activity, whereas ADHD affects brain activity. The conduct disorder has a genetic influence, on the other hand, the ADHD is a chronic disorder. It is important to know that children with ADHD are also prone to develop a conduct disorder.

(ii) According to the socio-cultural model, abnormal behaviour is best understood in light of the social and cultural forces that influence an individual. Through this model, we can understood Malay's psychological disorder. As we learnt that Malay's abnormal activities are closely related to his social, cultural and family background. The socio-cultural model states that the behaviour is shaped by societal forces. Factors such as family structure and communication, social networks, social conditions, etc.

**4. Read the following case study and answer the questions that follow.**

Sundar, a college going 20-year-old male, has moved from his home town to live in a big city. He has continuous fear of insecurity and feels that the enemy soldiers are following him. He gets very tense when he spots anyone in a uniform and feels that they are coming to catch him. This intense anxiety is interfering with his work and relationship and his friends are extremely concerned as it does not make any sense to them. Sundar occasionally laughs abruptly and inappropriately and sometimes stops speaking mid-sentence, scanning off in the distance as though he sees or hears something. He expresses concern about television and radio in the room potentially being monitored by the enemies. His beliefs are fixed and if they are challenged, his tone becomes hostile. **CBSE Term II 2022**

(i) **Based on the symptoms being exhibited, identify the disorder. Explain the other symptoms that can be seen in this disorder.**

(ii) **Define delusion and inappropriate affect. Support it with the symptoms given in the above case study.**

**Ans.** (i) Sundar is suffering from Schizophrenia. Some symptoms of schizophrenia are delusions, disorganised thinking and speech, heightened perception, some hallucinations and inappropriate affects.

(ii) Delusional disorder is a mental illness in which a person has delusions, but with no accompanying prominent hallucinations, thought disorder, mood disorder or significant flattening of affect.

Some early symptoms of delusional disorder may include feeling exploited, being preoccupied with the loyalty or trustworthiness of friends, reading threatening meanings into benign remarks or events, etc.

Sundar occasionally laughs abruptly and inappropriately and occasionally he pauses mid –sentence, indicating emotions that are inappropriate for the circumstance.

**5. Read the case and answer the questions that follow.**

Vaishali was admitted to a hospital in the midst of a manic episode. She had been in psychotherapy for depression for several months while she was in college. She found a job in an advertising office of a local newspaper, where she had been working for a year. Vaishali's manic episode could be traced to experiences that began three or four months prior to her admission to the hospital. She had been feeling unusually good for several weeks. At first, she didn't think anything was wrong. In fact, her impression was quite the opposite. Everything seemed to be going right for her, except her job. She had lost all focus from her work as her energy level was extremely high. She felt a renewed confidence in herself and her relationships with other people. She was feeling particularly exhilarated. Vaishali initially welcomed these feelings, especially because she had been so lethargic and also tended to be reserved with people. Soon she realised that her moods shifted constantly. The enthusiasm of gleefully throwing herself into new and exciting activities, would soon be over. Now she started being quite normal in her behaviour. She resumed work sincerely and appeared calm.

(i) **Name and state a characteristic feature of the disorder that Vaishali is experiencing.**

**Ans.** Vaishali is most likely experiencing Bipolar Disorder (also known as Manic-Depressive Disorder). A characteristic feature of this disorder is mood swings that alternate between periods of mania (elevated mood, excessive energy) and depression (low mood, lack of energy). The manic episode Vaishali experienced, where she felt unusually good and had high energy, is a hallmark of this disorder.

(ii) **'She had been in psychotherapy for depression for several months while she was in college.' What are the symptoms that she may have experienced during this phase of depression?**

**Ans.** During her phase of depression, Vaishali may have experienced symptoms such as

(i) Persistent sadness or low mood
(ii) Loss of interest in activities
(iii) Fatigue and low energy
(iv) Feelings of worthlessness or excessive guilt
(v) Difficulty concentrating or making decisions
(vi) Changes in sleep patterns (insomnia or excessive sleep)
(vii) Appetite changes (either loss or overeating)

# SELF ASSESSMENT TEST

## Objective Type Questions

**1.** Alogia means

(a) Sponge taste of drink
(b) Poverty of speech
(c) Smell of poison
(d) None of these

**2.** A maniac becomes

(a) Dull
(b) Extremely active
(c) Less talkative
(d) Fatigue

**3.** Which of the following is an opioid?

(a) Morphine
(b) Heroin
(c) Cough syrup
(d) All of these

**4.** Which of the following contains nicotine?

(a) Tobacco
(b) Bhang
(c) Coffee
(d) Heroin

**5.** **Assertion** (A) Psychological disorders can be categorised based on shared characteristics.

**Reason** (R) Classification systems like the DSM-5 help professionals communicate effectively and understand the causes of disorders.

(a) Both A and R are true and R is the correct explanation of A.
(b) Both A and R are true, but R is not the correct explanation of A.
(c) A is true, but R is false.
(d) A is false, but R is true.

## Very Short Answer Type Questions

**1.** What is phobia?

**2.** Define neurotransmitter.

**3.** Write four symptoms of generalised anxiety disorder.

**4.** What is agoraphobia?

**5.** What is Separation Anxiety Disorder (SAD)?

## Short Answer Type Questions

**1.** Discuss conduct disorder.

**2.** Briefly discuss anorexia nervosa.

**3.** Describe in brief the sub-types of schizophrenia.

**4.** Explain diathesis-stress model.

**5.** Describe biological and genetic factors responsible for abnormal behaviour.

**6.** Shalini often eat excessive amounts of food, then purge her body of food by using medicines such as laxatives or diuretics or by vomiting. Identify the psychological disorder that Shalini may have. Also, give reason why she might be doing so.

## Long Answer Type Questions

1. Elaborate major anxiety disorders and their symptoms.
2. Elaborate the symptoms of schizophrenia.
3. Explain various effects of alcohol.
4. A psychologist while diagnosing is patient has concluded that the psychological disorder of patient can be attributed to biochemical or physiological basis. Identify the approach that psychologist has employed to diagnose his patient. Also, enumerate the various factors that have been included in his approach.

## Case Based Questions

**Read the case and answer the questions that follow.**

Gary is a 19-year-old who withdrew from college after experiencing a manic episode during which he was brought to the attention of the Campus Police. He had changed his major from engineering to philosophy and increasingly had reduced his sleep, spending long hours engaging his friends in conversations about the nature of reality. He had been convinced about the importance of his ideas, stating frequently that he was more learned and advanced than all his professors. He told others that he was on the verge of revolutionising his new field and he grew increasingly irritable and intolerant of any who disagreed with him. He also increased a number of high-risk behaviours – drinking and engaging in sexual relations in a way that was unlike his previous history.

At the present time, he has returned home and his been placed on a mood stabiliser (after a period of time on an antipsychotic), and his psychiatrist is requesting adjunctive psychotherapy for his disorder. The patient's parents are somewhat shocked by the diagnosis, but they acknowledge that Gary had early problems with anxiety during pre-adolescence, followed by some periods of withdrawal and depression during his adolescence. His parents are eager to be involved in treatment, if appropriate.

(i) What symptoms did Gary experience during his manic episode?

(ii) How have Gary's parents responded to his diagnosis and treatment?

# 05

CHAPTER

# Therapeutic Approaches

There are various types of psychotherapy. Some focus on acquiring self-understanding, while others are more action-oriented. All therapeutic approaches are supportive and corrective in nature, involving an interpersonal relationship between the patient and the therapist. They can be either directive or non-directive in nature.

**YOUR STUDY GOALS**

5.1 Nature and Process of Psychotherapy
5.2 Types of Therapies
5.3 Rehabilitation of The Mentally Ill

**YOUR PRACTICE GOAL**

- Objective Type Questions (22 Qs ; MCQs, A-R)
- Subjective Type Questions (15 VSAs, 22 SAs, 3 LAs, 2 Case Based)

## 5.1 Nature and Process of Psychotherapy

- **Psychotherapy**[1] is a voluntary relationship between two individuals—the client (the person seeking treatment) and the therapist (the one providing treatment).
- The purpose of this relationship is to help the client address and resolve psychological issues that they are experiencing.
- Psychotherapy aim at changing the abnormal behaviours that may be harmful or unhelpful to the client.
- It reduce personal distress and help the client manage emotions effectively.
- It also enhance the client's ability to adapt to their environment, improving their overall well-being.

1 **Psychotherapy** Psychotherapy is a broad term encompassing therapeutic techniques aimed at all eviating psychological distress and improving mental health. Various methods and modalities are employed within psychotherapy to address diverse mental health issues.

## Characteristics of Psychotherapy

- Psychotherapy involves the systematic application of principles from various psychological approaches.
- Only practitioners with extensive training and expert supervision are qualified to ethically practice psychotherapy. An untrained individual may unintentionally cause more harm than benefit to the client.
- The therapeutic process involves both a therapist and a client seeking help for emotional or psychological issues.
- The client remains the central focus throughout the therapy process.
- The interaction between therapist and client establishes a therapeutic relationship, essential for effective therapy.
- This relationship is confidential, interpersonal and dynamic, serving as the primary catalyst for change.
- The therapeutic relationship provides a strong foundation for personal growth and change.
- It is characterised by trust, confidentiality and active engagement from both the client and the therapist, enhancing the effectiveness of the therapy.

## Goals of Psychotherapy

All psychotherapies aim at a few or all the following goals

- Reinforcing the client's resolve for improvement
- Reducing emotional distress
- Unleashing potential for positive growth
- Modifying unhelpful habits
- Changing thought patterns
- Enhancing self-awareness
- Improving interpersonal relationships and communication
- Facilitating better decision-making
- Becoming more aware of life choices
- Relating to the social environment in a creative and self-aware way

## Therapeutic Relationship

- The therapeutic relationship between the client and therapist is known as the therapeutic relationship or alliance.
- This relationship is neither a casual acquaintance nor permanent, but a temporary, professional alliance aimed at resolving the client's issues. Key components of this alliance include
    (i) **Contractual Nature** The alliance is a partnership between two willing individuals, the client and therapist, both committed to addressing the client's psychological challenges.
    (ii) **Limited Duration** This relationship lasts only until the client gains the skills and confidence to handle their problems independently.

## Properties of the Therapeutic Relationship

- **Trust and Confidentiality** Built on a high level of trust, enabling the client to freely share personal issues. The therapist ensures strict confidentiality, safeguarding client privacy.
- **Acceptance, Empathy and Warmth** The therapist maintains **unconditional positive regard**[2] by accepting the client without judgment, fostering a safe space for open communication.
- **Empathy** Empathy here goes beyond sympathy or intellectual understanding. It involves a genuine ability to understand the client's perspective or 'putting oneself in their shoes', enriching the therapeutic relationship and fostering healing.
- **Professional Boundaries** The therapist strictly maintains a professional relationship, upholding ethical standards and avoiding any exploitation of the client's trust or confidence.
- This relationship remains focused on client welfare, emphasising a supportive and non-judgemental approach throughout therapy.

## Parameters of Classification of Psychotherapies

The classification of psychotherapies is based on the following parameters

### 1. Cause of the Problem

- **Psychodynamic therapy**[3] holds that problems arise from intrapsychic conflicts existing within an individual's psyche.
- **Behaviour therapy**[4] posits that psychological problems result from faulty learning of behaviours and cognitions.
- **Existential therapy** suggests that existential questions regarding life's meaning are the root of psychological problems.

### 2. Existence of the Cause

- In psychodynamic therapy, unresolved childhood fears and unfulfilled desires contribute to intrapsychic conflicts.
- According to behaviour therapy, maladaptive behaviours stem from faulty conditioning patterns, learning issues and incorrect beliefs.
- Existential therapy focuses on current feelings of loneliness, alienation and a sense of futility as contributing factors to psychological problems.

### 3. Method of Treatment

- Psychodynamic therapy employs methods like free association and dream reporting to elicit thoughts and feelings, which are then interpreted to help clients resolve their conflicts.
- Behaviour therapy identifies and modifies faulty conditioning patterns, establishing alternative behavioural contingencies to improve behaviour.
- Cognitive behavioural therapy challenges and alters the faulty thinking patterns of clients to assist them in overcoming psychological distress.
- Existential therapy creates a therapeutic environment that is positive, accepting and non-judgemental, fostering personal growth and problem discussion.

---

2 **Unconditional Positive Regard** Unconditional positive regard is a concept from client-centred therapy where the therapist offers acceptance and support regardless of the client's feelings, thoughts or behaviours. This approach fosters a safe space for growth, enabling to explore their emotions without fear of judgement.

3 **Psychodynamic Therapy** Psychodynamic therapy is rooted in psychoanalytic theory and explores unconscious processes. It investigates how past experiences influence current behaviours and relationships, helping clients gain insight into their motivations and emotional patterns.

4 **Behaviour Therapy** Behaviour therapy is a type of therapy focused on modifying observable behaviours using various techniques. It is commonly used to treat conditions such an anxiety, phobias and other behavioural issues by reinforcing desirable behaviours and reducing maladaptive ones.

## 4. Nature of the Therapeutic Relationship

- Psychodynamic therapy assumes the therapist understands the client's intrapsychic conflicts better and interpreting thoughts and feelings to enhance the client's insight.
- In behaviour therapy, the therapist identifies faulty behaviours and thought patterns, aiming to find adaptive alternatives for the client.
- Both psychodynamic and behaviour therapies view the therapist as capable of determining solutions to the client's problems.
- In contrast, existential therapies emphasise a warm, empathetic relationship, where the therapist provides a secure space for the client to explore the nature and causes of their problems independently.

## 5. Chief Benefit to the Client

- Psychodynamic therapy values emotional insight as the main benefit, which occurs when clients intellectually understand their conflicts, and adjust their emotions toward these conflicts.
- Behaviour therapy considers the primary benefit to be the changing of faulty behaviours and thought patterns into adaptive ones, which reduces distress and alleviates symptoms.
- In **humanistic therapy**[5], personal growth is viewed as the chief benefit, involving an increased understanding of oneself, including one's aspirations, emotions and motives.

## 6. Duration of Treatment

- The duration of classical psychoanalysis may extend for several years; however, many modern versions of psychodynamic therapies can be completed in 10–15 sessions.
- Behaviour and cognitive behavioural therapies, along with existential therapies, typically have shorter durations, often concluding within a few months.
- Despite their differences across various parameters, all types of psychotherapies share a common goal: to treat psychological distress through psychological means.
- The therapist, the therapeutic relationship and therapy process serve as agents of change, contributing to the alleviation of psychological distress.
- The process of psychotherapy begins by formulating the client's problem.

### Steps in the Formulation of a Client's Problem

- Clinical formulation refers to formulating the problem of the client in the therapeutic model being used for the treatment. Its advantages include
  - (i) **Understanding of the problem** The therapist is able to understand the full implications of the distress being experienced by the client.
  - (ii) **Identification of the areas to be targeted for treatment in psychotherapy** The theoretical formulation clearly identifies the problem areas to be targeted for therapy. Thus, if a client seeks help for inability to hold a job and reports inability to face superiors, the clinical formulation in behaviour therapy would state it as lack of assertiveness skills and anxiety. The target areas have thus been identified as inability to assert oneself and heightened anxiety.
  - (iii) **Choice of techniques for treatment** The choice of techniques for treatment depends on the therapeutic system in which the therapist has been trained. However, even within this broad domain, the choice of techniques, timing of the techniques, and expectations of outcome of the therapy depend upon the clinical formulation.
- The clinical formulation is an ongoing process which may require reformulations as clinical insights are gained in the process of therapy.

5 **Humanistic Therapy** Humanistic therapy is an approach that emphasises individuals potential and highlights the importance of personal growth and self-actualisation. This therapy often focuses on personal experiences and emotions, allowing clients to explore their unique paths toward fulfillment.

## Quick Test 1

1. What is the main goal of psychotherapy?
2. Who is the central focus in psychotherapy?
3. What kind of relationship is essential in psychotherapy?
4. What does behaviour therapy aim to modify?
5. What does existential therapy primarily address?
6. What is the main benefit of psychodynamic therapy?

## 5.2 Types of Therapies

The different types of therapies of psychotherapy are discussed below

### Behaviour Therapy

- Behaviour therapy claims that psychological distress arises from faulty behaviour patterns or thought patterns.
- It focuses on the present behaviours and thoughts of the client. The past is relevant only for understanding the origins of these faulty patterns; it is not activated or relived during the therapy process.
- The clinical application of learning theory principles constitutes behaviour therapy using a large set of specific techniques and interventions.
- Behaviour therapy is not a unified theory that is applied irrespective of the clinical diagnosis or symptoms present. Instead, it is tailored to address the unique issues of each client.
- The symptoms of the client and the clinical diagnosis guide the selection of specific techniques or interventions. For instance, treating phobias requires a different set of techniques compared to the treatment of anger outbursts and treatment for depression differs from that of anxiety.
- The foundation of behaviour therapy lies in formulating dysfunctional or faulty behaviours, identifying the factors that reinforce and maintain these behaviours and devising methods by which they can be changed.

#### Method of Treatment

- The client experiencing psychological distress or physical symptoms undergoes an interview to analyse their behaviour patterns.
- A behavioural analysis is conducted to find faulty behaviours, the antecedent of faulty learning and the factors that contribute to the persistence of the faulty behaviour.
- After identifying the faulty behaviours, a treatment package is chosen to replace them with adaptive behaviour patterns.
- The therapist utilises antecedent operations and consequent operations, where antecedent operations control behaviour by changing something that precedes it, while establishing operations adjust the reinforcing value of consequences.
- For instance, if a child struggles with eating dinner, the therapist might decrease the quantity of food served at tea time, which increases the child's hunger at dinner, enhancing the reinforcing value of food during that time.
- Finally, praising the child for eating properly encourages the desired behaviour, reinforcing the effectiveness of the treatment approach.

## Behavioural Techniques

A variety of techniques is available for changing behaviour, focusing on reducing the arousal level of the client and altering behaviour through classical conditioning or operant conditioning with different contingencies of reinforcements. Some techniques of behaviour modification are as follow

- **Negative Reinforcement** This major technique involves responses that help organisms avoid or escape from painful stimuli. For example, wearing woollen clothes or using heaters to avoid unpleasant cold weather is an example of negative reinforcement.
- **Aversive Conditioning** This technique involves repeated associations of an undesired response with an aversive consequence. For instance, pairing the smell of alcohol with a mild electric shock can make the smell aversive, leading an alcoholic to give up drinking.
- **Positive Reinforcement** When an adaptive behaviour occurs infrequently, positive reinforcement is utilised to increase it. For example, a mother might prepare her child's favourite dish as a reward for completing homework on time, thereby increasing the likelihood of that behaviour.
- **Token Economy** This method rewards individuals with tokens for displaying desired behaviours, which can later be exchanged for rewards, such as outings or treats, encouraging the maintenance of positive behaviours.
- **Differential Reinforcement** This approach involves simultaneously reducing unwanted behaviour and increasing desired behaviour. It can be achieved through positive reinforcement for wanted behaviours and negative reinforcement for unwanted behaviours or by positively reinforcing desired behaviours while ignoring unwanted ones.
- **Systematic Desensitisation** Introduced by Wolpe for treating phobias, this technique involves creating a hierarchy of anxiety-provoking stimuli and gradually exposing the client to these stimuli while maintaining relaxation. This process helps the client become desensitised to fear.
- **Reciprocal Inhibition** This principle states that the presence of two mutually opposing forces at the same time can inhibit the weaker force. For example, relaxation techniques can help clients tolerate greater levels of anxiety.
- **Modelling** In this procedure, clients learn to behave in specific ways by observing the behaviour of a role model or therapist. Through vicarious learning, clients gradually acquire the desired behaviours by witnessing and rewarding small changes in their behaviour.
- **Therapist's Skill** The effectiveness of behavioural therapy largely depends on the therapist's ability to conduct an accurate behavioural analysis and to build a treatment package with the appropriate techniques tailored to the client's needs.

# Cognitive Therapy

Cognitive therapies locate the cause of psychological distress in irrational thoughts and beliefs that individuals hold.

## Rational Emotive Therapy (RET)

- RET was developed by Albert Ellis, RET posits that irrational beliefs serve as a mediating factor between antecedent events and their emotional or behavioural consequences.
- The initial step in RET involves conducting an Antecedent-Belief-Consequence (ABC) analysis. Antecedent events, which caused the psychological distress are noted.
- The client is also interviewed to find the irrational beliefs which are distorting the present reality.
- These irrational beliefs are often characterised by thoughts featuring 'musts' and 'should', such as 'One should be loved by everybody all the time' or 'Human misery is caused by external events beyond one's control'. Such beliefs lack empirical support.

- Irrational beliefs are evaluated using questionnaires and interviews. The therapist using non-directive questioning to help clients identify these beliefs.
- The therapist employs a gentle questioning style, encouraging clients to explore their assumptions about life without being probing or directive.
- This helps clients reflect on their beliefs deeply.
- Through this reflective process, clients gradually begin to change their irrational beliefs by developing a new philosophy about life, ultimately replacing irrational belief system with a more rational one.
- As clients replace irrational beliefs with rational ones, they experience a reduction in psychological distress.

## Cognitive Therapy by Aaron Beck

- Another significant cognitive therapy approach is that of Aaron Beck, which emphasises how early childhood experiences shape core schemas or systems that include beliefs and action patterns.
- For instance, a client who was neglected as a child may develop a core schema of 'I am not wanted'. A subsequent critical incident, such as being publicly ridiculed, can trigger this schema, leading to negative automatic thoughts.
- These negative thoughts may include statements like 'nobody loves me', 'I am ugly', 'I am stupid' or 'I will not succeed'. They are often accompanied by cognitive distortions that create a skewed perception of reality.
- These cognitive distortions are general patterns of thinking that negatively impact one's understanding of social reality and contribute to anxiety and depression.
- The therapist utilises a gentle and non-threatening method of disputing the client's beliefs and thoughts with questions like, 'Why should everyone love you'? or 'What does it mean to you to succeed'?
- Such questioning facilitates clients in gaining insight into their dysfunctional schemas, enabling them to alter their cognitive structures.
- The primary aim of this therapy is to achieve cognitive restructuring, which leads to a reduction in anxiety and depression.
- Similar to behaviour therapy, cognitive therapy targets specific problems experienced by the client, providing a structured approach to therapy.
- Unlike psychodynamic therapy, cognitive therapy is characterised by its openness, with the therapist openly sharing methods and techniques used in the process.
- Cognitive therapy is typically brief, lasting between 10–20 sessions, making it more accessible for clients seeking effective treatment.

## Cognitive Behaviour Therapy (CBT)

- Currently, **Cognitive Behaviour Therapy (CBT)**[6] is recognised as the most popular form of therapy.
- Research has shown that CBT is a short and efficacious treatment for a wide range of psychological disorders, including anxiety, depression, panic attacks and borderline personality disorder.
- CBT adopts a bio-psychosocial approach to delineate psychopathology, integrating multiple perspectives in understanding psychological issues.
- This therapy combines cognitive therapy with behavioural techniques, allowing for a more holistic treatment method.
- The rationale behind CBT is that the client's distress originates from biological, psychological and social realms.

6 **Cognitive Behaviour Therapy (CBT)** Cognitive Behaviour Therapy (CBT) is a structured, time-limited therapeutic approach that addresses dysfunctional emotions and behaviours. It employs cognitive restructuring and behavioural interventions to help clients identify and change negative thought patterns.

- CBT addresses the biological aspects of distress through techniques such as relaxation procedures, which help reduce physiological symptoms.
- Psychological distress is managed using both behaviour and cognitive therapy techniques, to alter unhelpful thought patterns and behaviours.
- The social aspects are addressed by modifying the client's environment to support better mental health.
- CBT is a comprehensive technique that is easy to implement and applicable to a variety of disorders.
- Its effectiveness has been proven across numerous studies, making CBT a widely accepted treatment in clinical practice.

### Quick Test 2

1. Name some behavioural techniques.
2. What type of therapy focuses on modifying thought patterns?
3. Which therapy involves changing maladaptive behaviours?
4. What technique is used to desensitise phobias?
5. Which therapy addresses unconscious conflicts?
6. What is the aim of cognitive therapy in addressing mental disorders?

## Humanistic-existential Therapy

- The humanistic-existential therapies claims that psychological distress arises from feelings of loneliness, alienation and an inability to find meaning and genuine fulfillment in life.
- Human beings are motivated by a desire for personal growth and self-actualisation, which is the innate need to grow emotionally.
- When these needs are curtailed by society and family, individuals experience psychological distress.
- **Self-actualisation**[7] is defined as an innate force that propels a person to become more complex, balanced and integrated.
- Being integrated means having a sense of wholeness, being a complete person and remaining fundamentally the same despite a variety of experiences.
- Just as a lack of food or water causes distress, frustration of the self-actualisation process also leads to emotional suffering.
- Healing occurs when the client identifies and removes the obstacles to self-actualisation in their life.
- Self-actualisation requires free emotional expression, but this is often curtailed by family and society due to fears of unleashing destructive forces.
- This restriction leads to destructive behaviour and negative emotions by hindering emotional integration.
- The therapy creates a permissive, non-judgemental atmosphere where the client can freely express emotions, facilitating complexity, balance and integration.
- The fundamental assumption of this therapy is that the client has the freedom and responsibility to control their own behaviour.
- The therapist as a facilitator and guide, with the client being responsible for the therapy's success.
- The main aim is to expand the client's awareness.
- Healing occurs through a process of understanding the client's unique personal experiences by themselves.
- The client initiates the process of self-growth, which ultimately leads to healing.

7 **Self-actualisation** Self-actualisation is the realisation or fulfillment of one's talents and potential, often regarded as a key goal in humanistic therapy. It involves individuals striving to become the best versions of themselves, engaging in meaningful pursuits that reflect their true selves.

## Existential Therapy

- Victor Frankl, a psychiatrist, and neurologist, developed Logotherapy, which means treatment for the soul, derived from the Greek word 'logos' for soul.
- Frankl refers to the process of finding meaning, even in life-threatening circumstances, as the process of meaning making.
- The foundation of meaning making lies in a person's quest for discovering the spiritual truth of their existence. The spiritual unconscious included low, aesthetic awareness and values of life.
- Neurotic anxieties emerge when life problems are linked to the physical, psychological or spiritual dimensions of one's existence.
- Frankl emphasised the significance of spiritual anxieties in leading to meaninglessness, which may be termed existential anxiety, representing a neurotic anxiety of spiritual origin.
- The primary goal of logotherapy is to assist patients in discovering meaning and responsibility in their lives, regardless of their circumstances.
- The therapist highlights the unique nature of the patient's life and encourages them to seek meaning in their own existence.
- In logotherapy, the therapist is open and shares their feelings, values and existence with the client, fostering an authentic therapeutic relationship.
- The logotherapy focuses on the present moment rather than past experiences.
- Transference is actively discouraged, as the therapist reminds the client of the immediacy of the present moment.
- The ultimate goal of logotherapy is to help the client find the meaning of their being and to embrace their unique existence.

## Client-centred Therapy

- **Client-centred therapy**[8] was developed by Carl Rogers, who combined scientific rigor with the individualised practice of psychotherapy.
- Rogers introduced the concept of the self, emphasising freedom and choice as central elements of one's being. This therapy fosters a warm relationship allowing the client to reconnect with their disintegrated feelings.
- The therapist demonstrates empathy, which involves understanding the client's experience as their own, thereby creating an emotional connection.
- The therapist is characterised by unconditional positive regard, which means providing total acceptance of the client as they are, without conditions.
- Empathy establishes an emotional resonance between the therapist and the client, allowing for deeper understanding and connection.
- Unconditional positive regard ensures therapist's warmth and acceptance are not dependent on the client's actions or disclosure.
- This unique form of warmth helps the client feel secure, promoting trust in the therapeutic relationship.
- When clients feel secure, they can safely explore their feelings and experiences.
- The therapist reflects the client¡¦s feelings in a non-judgemental manner, enhancing the client's self-awareness.
- The reflection is achieved by rephrasing the client's statements, which seeks simple clarifications to deepen the meaning of what the client expresses.
- This process helps the client integrate and consolidate their feelings and experiences.

8 **Client-centred Therapy** Client-centred therapy is a humanistic approach developed by Carl Rogers. This approach emphasises the significance of the therapist's empathy, unconditional positive regard and genuineness, which are essential for facilitating client growth and self-discovery.

- As personal relationships improve, the client experiences better adjustment and emotional well-being.
- Ultimately, this therapy aims to help the client become their real self, with the therapist acting as a facilitator in the process of self-discovery and growth.

### Gestalt Therapy

- The German word gestalt means 'whole'. **Gestalt therapy**[9] was developed by Fritz Perls and his wife Laura Perls.
- The primary goal of gestalt therapy is to increase an individual's self-awareness and self-acceptance.
- Clients are taught to recognise bodily processes and emotions that they may be blocking out from their awareness. The therapist encourages the client to act out fantasies related to their feelings and conflicts.
- Gestalt therapy can be effectively used in group settings, allowing for shared experiences and insights among participants.

## Factors Contributing to Healing in Psychotherapy

Psychotherapy aims to alleviate psychological distress. Several factors contribute to the healing process in psychotherapy.

- A major factor in healing is the techniques adopted by the therapist and their implementation with the patient or client. For instance, when addressing an anxious client, if the behavioural system and Cognitive Behavioural Therapy (CBT) approach are utilised, techniques such as relaxation procedures and cognitive restructuring play a significant role in the healing process.
- The **therapeutic alliance**[10] formed between the therapist and the patient or client has intrinsic healing properties. This relationship is enhanced by the regular availability of the therapist, combined with the warmth and empathy that the therapist provides during sessions.
- At the beginning of therapy, the client discusses their problems. This process, known as **Emotional unburdening**, allows them to express their emotional challenges, which contributes to healing. This emotional release is known as **catharsis** and it has therapeutic benefits.
- Several non-specific factors are associated with psychotherapy. These factors can be attributed to either the patient/client or the therapist and they are termed **non-specific** because they occur across various psychotherapy systems, clients and therapists.
- Non-specific factors attributable to the client or patient are known as **patient variables**. These include the motivation for change and the expectation of improvement, which can significantly influence the healing process.
- Non-specific factors that can be attributed to the therapist are referred to as Therapist variables. These factors encompass a positive nature, the absence of unresolved emotional conflicts, and the presence of good mental health, all of which can enhance the therapeutic experience and promote healing.

### Ethics in Psychotherapy

Some of the ethical standards that need to be practiced by professional psychotherapists are

- Informed consent must be obtained from the client before any therapeutic intervention begins.
- The confidentiality of the client should be always maintained to build trust and protect the client's privacy.
- The primary goal of the therapist should be to alleviate personal distress and suffering.
- The integrity of the practitioner-client relationship is crucial.
- Respect for human rights and dignity is essential.
- Professional competence and skills are required.

9 **Gestalt Therapy** Gestalt therapy is a form of therapy that emphasises personal responsibility and focuses on the individual's experience in the present moment. It encourages clients to develop awareness and self-acceptance, helping them to explore their thoughts and feelings fully.

10 **Therapeutic Alliance** The therapeutic alliance is the collaborative relationship betwen the therapist and client, characterised by trust, mutual respect and shared goals. This alliance is crucial for effective therapy and contributes significantly to the therapeutic process.

## Alternative Therapies

**Alternative therapy**[11] are treatment options that serve as alternatives to conventional drug treatments or psychotherapy which includes yoga, meditation, acupuncture and herbal remedies.

### Yoga and Meditation

- In the past 25 years, yoga and meditation have gained popularity as effective treatment programmes for psychological distress.
- Yoga is an ancient Indian technique detailed in the Ashtanga Yoga of Patanjali's Yoga Sutras. It commonly refers to both asanas (body postures) and pranayama (breathing practices).
- Yoga techniques enhance overall well-being, improve mood, increase attention, boost mental focus and enhance stress tolerance.
- To maximise the benefits of yoga, individuals should engage in proper training from a skilled teacher and practice for at least 30 minutes every day.
- Insomnia can be effectively treated with yoga, which helps reduce the time it takes to fall asleep and improves sleep quality.
- Meditation involves focusing attention on the breath, an object, a thought or a mantra.
- In Vipasana meditation, also known as **mindfulness-based meditation**, practitioners do not focus on a fixed object. Instead, they passively observe various bodily sensations and thoughts that arise in their awareness.
- Mindfulness-based meditation or vipasana may aid in the prevention of repeated episodes of depression.

### Sudarshana Kriya Yoga (SKY)

- Sudarshana Kriya Yoga (SKY) uses rapid breathing techniques are utilised to induce hyperventilation.
- SKY is beneficial in treating stress, anxiety, Post-Traumatic Stress Disorder (PTSD), depression, stress-related medical illnesses, substance abuse and the **rehabilitation**[12] of criminal offenders.
- Research conducted at the National Institute of Mental Health and Neurosciences (NIMHANS) in India has shown that SKY significantly reduces depression.
- Furthermore, alcoholic patients who practice SKY have reported reduced depression and stress levels.

### Kundalini Yoga

- Kundalini Yoga, taught in the USA, is effective in treating various mental disorders.
- The Institute for Non-linear Science at the University of California, San Diego, has established that Kundalini Yoga is effective in the treatment of obsessive-compulsive disorder.
- This form of yoga combines pranayama (breathing techniques) with the chanting of mantras, enhancing its therapeutic benefits.

## 5.3 Rehabilitation of the Mentally ILL

- The treatment of psychological disorders has two main components–the reduction of symptoms and the improvement of functioning or quality of life.
- In cases of milder disorders, such as generalised anxiety, reactive depression or phobia, the reduction of symptoms is often linked to an improvement in the quality of life.

11 **Alternative therapy** Alternative therapy refers to non-conventional treatment methods that serve as alternatives to traditional psychotherapy or drug treatments. This category includes practices such as yoga and meditation, which are often employed to promote mental and emotional well-being.

12 **Rehabilitation** Rehabilitation refers to the process of assisting individuals with mental illness in improving their quality of life and functioning. This often involves skill development, social support and strategies to enhance self-sufficiency and reintegration into society.

- Conversely, in severe mental disorders, such as schizophrenia, the reduction of symptoms may not correlate with an enhancement in the quality of life.
- Many patients with severe disorders experience negative symptoms, including disinterest and a lack of motivation to engage in work or social interactions.
- Rehabilitation is essential for helping these patients become self-sufficient and regain functionality in society.
- The primary goal of rehabilitation is to empower the patient to become a productive member of society to the greatest extent possible.
- In rehabilitation, patients typically receive various forms of therapy, including occupational therapy, social skills training and vocational therapy.
- During occupational therapy, patients are taught specific skills, such as candle making, paper bag making and weaving, which help them develop a sense of work discipline.
- Social skills training is focused on helping patients develop interpersonal skills through techniques like role play, imitation and instruction enabling the patient to function effectively within a social group.
- Cognitive retraining is provided to enhance basic cognitive functions, including attention, memory and executive functions.
- Once the patient has made sufficient progress, they receive vocational training, which equips them with the skills necessary for productive employment.

## Quick Test 3

1. Who developed Gestalt therapy?
2. What are alternative therapies?
3. What is the primary focus of rehabilitation for the mentally ill?
4. Which type of therapy focuses on teaching specific skills like candle making?
5. What type of training enhances attention, memory and executive functions?
6. What is the aim of social skills training in rehabilitation?

# NCERT Folder

**1. Describe the nature and scope of psychotherapy. Highlight the importance of therapeutic relationship in psychotherapy.**

***Or* Explain the importance of therapeutic relationship in psychotherapy. State the ethical standards in psychotherapy.** **CBSE 2018**

**Ans.** Psychotherapy is a voluntary relationship between the client (patient) and the therapist. The purpose of the relationship is to help the client to solve the psychological problems being faced by her or him.

Psychotherapies aim at changing the maladaptive behaviours, reduce personal distress and helping the clients adapt more effectively to their environment. Inadequate marital, occupational and social adjustment also requires that major changes be made in an individual's personal environment.

The interactions between the therapist and the client results in the formation of therapeutic relationship. This is a confidential, interpersonal and dynamic relationship. This human relationship is central to any type of psychotherapy. The ethical standards in psychotherapy should include

- Support client for attaining betterment
- Lessening emotional pressure
- Unfolding the potential for positive growth
- Modifying habits
- Changing thinking patterns
- Increasing self-awareness
- Improving interpersonal relations and communication
- Facilitating decision-making
- Becoming aware of one's choices in life and
- Relating to one's social environment in a more creative and self-aware manner

**2. What are the different types of psychotherapy? On what basis are they classified?**

**Ans.** Different types of psychotherapy are

(i) Behaviour therapy
(ii) Humanistic-existential therapy
(iii) Biomedical therapy

Also, there are many alternative therapies such as yoga, meditation, accupuncture, herbal remedies etc.

Basis of classification of psychotherapy are

- On the basis of cause which has led to the problem.
- On the basis of existence of the cause.
- On the basis of the chief method of treatment.
- On the basis of the nature of the therapeutic relationship between the client and the therapist.
- On the basis of the chief benefit to the client.
- On the basis of the duration of treatment.

**3. Discuss the various techniques used in behaviour therapy.** **CBSE 2020**

**Ans.** Various techniques of behaviour modification are as follow

- **Negative Reinforcement** It refers to following an undesired response with an outcome that is painful or not liked.
- **Aversive Conditioning** It refers to repeated association of undesired response with an aversive consequence.
- **Positive Reinforcement** If an adaptive behaviour occurs rarely, positive reinforcement is given to increase the deficit.
- **Token Economy** Person with behavioural problems can be given a token as a reward every time when a wanted behaviour occurs. The tokens are collected and exchanged for a reward such as an outing for the patient or a treat for the child. This is known as token economy.
- **Differential Reinforcement** Unwanted behaviour can be reduced and wanted behaviour can be increased simultaneously through differential reinforcement. Positive reinforcement for the wanted behaviour and negative reinforcement for the unwanted behaviour attempted together may be one such method.
- **Systematic Desensitisation** It is a technique introduced by Wolpe for treating phobias or irrational fears. The client is interviewed to elicit fear-provoking situations. The therapist relaxes the client and asks the client to think about the least anxiety-provoking situation.
- **Principle of Reciprocal Inhibition** This principle states that the presence of two mutually opposing forces at the same time inhibits the weaker force. Thus, the relaxation response is first built up and mildly anxiety-provoking scene is imagined, through which the anxiety is overcome by the relaxation. The client is able to tolerate progressively greater levels of anxiety because of her/his relaxed state.
- **Modelling** It is the procedure wherein the client learns to behave in a certain way by observing the behaviour of a role model or the therapist who initially acts as the role model.

**4. Explain with the help of an example how cognitive distortions take place.**

***Or*** **Explain cognitive distortion with the help of an example.** CBSE 2019

***Or*** **Explain cognitive distortions. Give an example of cognitive distortion that a client might be experiencing.** CBSE 2023

**Ans.** Psychological distress develops due to negative experiences provided by family and society. Individual develops negative thoughts like 'Nobody loves me', 'I am ugly', 'I am stupid', 'I will not succeed etc'. Such negative automatic thoughts are characterised by cognitive distortions.

Cognitive distortions are ways of thinking which are general in nature but which distort the reality in a negative manner. These patterns of thought are called dysfunctional cognitive structure. They lead to errors of cognition about the social reality.

Repeated occurrence of these thoughts lead to the development of feelings of anxiety and depression. The therapist uses questioning which is gengle non-threatening disputation of the client's beliefs and thoughts. The therapist asks him 'why should everyone love you', or 'what does it mean to you to succeed'? The question make the client think in a direction opposite to that of the negative automatic thoughts. He gains insight into the nature of his dysfunctional schemas and is able to alter his cognitive structure. The aim of this therapy is to achieve this cognitive restructuring which in turn reduces anxiety and depression.

**5. Which therapy encourages the client to seek personal growth and actualise their potential? Write about the therapies which are based on this principle.**

**Ans.** Humanistic-existential therapy encourages the client to seek personal growth and actualise their potential. This therapy claims that psychological distress arises from feelings of loneliness, alienation and an inability to find meaning and genuine fulfillment in life.

Human beings are motivated by the desire for personal growth and self-actualisation and an innate need to grow emotionally. When these needs are curbed by society and family, human beings experience psychological distress.

Therapies which are based on this principles are Existential therapy, client centered therapy and Gestalt therapy.

These therapies emphasise that selfactualisation is an inborn force driving individuals to become more balanced and integrated. Psychological distress occurs when this natural drive is frustrated.

Healing occurs when clients can identify and overcome the obstacles preventing self-actualisation. The therapist facilitates this process by creating a nonjudgmental, accepting environment where emotions can be freely expressed, helping the client gain awareness. The therapist serves as a guide, while the client takes responsibility for their growth. The primary goal is to expand the client's awareness, with healing emerging from the client's own understanding of their unique experiences and their initiation of self-growth.

**6. What are the factors that contribute to healing in psychotherapy? Enumerate some of the alternative therapies.**

**Ans.** Several factors contribute to healing in psychotherapy

(i) **Therapeutic Techniques** The specific methods used by the therapist, such as Cognitive Behavioural Therapy (CBT) or behavioural techniques, play a major role in the healing process. Techniques like relaxation and cognitive restructuring can help alleviate anxiety.

(ii) **Therapeutic Alliance** The relationship between the therapist and the client is crucial. A strong alliance, characterised by empathy, trust and consistent support, promotes healing.

(iii) **Emotional Unburdening** In early therapy sessions, clients often express and release emotional burdens, a process known as Catharsis, which aids in healing.

(iv) **Non-Specific Factors** These factors, such as the client's motivation for change or the therapist's mental health, influence healing across various therapeutic approaches.

**Alternative Therapies**

Alternative therapies offer non-conventional treatment options for psychological distress. These include

- **Yoga** Yoga enhances mental focus, reduces stress, and improves sleep. Practices like pranayama and asanas have been shown to reduce anxiety and improve overall well-being.
- **Meditation** Meditation techniques, such as mindfulness-based meditation (Vipassana), help manage stress and prevent depression relapse by encouraging awareness and emotional regulation.
- **Sudarshana Kriya Yoga (SKY)** SKY uses breathing exercises to reduce stress, anxiety and PTSD symptoms, showing significant therapeutic benefits.
- **Kundalini Yoga** Kundalini Yoga, which combines breathing and chanting, has proven effective in treating obsessive-compulsive disorder and promoting emotional balance.

**7. What are the techniques used in the rehabilitation of the mentally ill?**

**Ans.** The treatment of psychological disorders involves two key components i.e. reduction of symptoms and improving the individual's level of functioning or quality of life.

Rehabilitation is required to help patients to become self-sufficient. The aim of rehabilitation is to empower the patient to become a productive member of society to the extent possible. In rehabilitation, the patients are given occupational therapy, social skills training and vocational therapy.

- In occupational therapy, the patients are taught skills such as candle making, paper bag making and weaving to help them to form a work discipline.
- Social skills training helps the patients to develop interpersonal skills through role play, imitation and instruction. The objective is to teach the patient to function in a social group.
- Cognitive retraining is given to improve the basic cognitive functions of attention, memory and executive functions. After the patient improves sufficiently, vocational training is given wherein the patient is helped to gain skills necessary to undertake productive employment.

**8. How would a social learning theorist account for a phobic fear of lizards/cockroaches? How would a psychoanalyst account for the same phobia?**

*Or* **A person has a phobia of cockroaches. Explain this phobia from the social learning perspective and psychoanalyst view point by giving examples.** CBSE 2018

*Or* **A person has a phobia of cockroaches. Explain the phobia from the social learning perspective and psychoanalyst view point by giving example.** CBSE 2018

**Ans.** Systematic is a technique introduced by Wolpe for treating phobias or irrational fears. Together with the client, the therapist prepare a hierarchy of anxiety-provoking stimuli with least anxiety-provoking stimuli at the bottom of the hierarchy.

The client is interviewed to elicit fear-provoking situations. The therapist relaxes the client and asks the client to think about the least anxiety-provoking situation. The client is asked to stop thinking of the fearful situation if the slightest tension is felt. After some sessions, the client is able to imagine more severe fear-provoking situations while maintaining the relaxation. The client gets systematically desensitised to the fear.

**9. What kind of problems is cognitive behaviour therapy best suited for?**

**Ans.** Cognitive behaviour therapy is a short and efficacious treatment for a wide range of psychological disorders such as anxiety, depression, panic attacks and borderline personality, etc. It is the most popular therapy. It adopts a biopsychosocial approach to the delineation of psychopathology. It combines cognitive therapy with behavioural techniques. It address the biological aspects through relaxation procedures.

The psychologist through behaviour and cognitive therapy techniques and the sociologist with environmental manipulations makes CBT a comprehensive technique which is easy to use and is applicable to a variety of disorders.

# Exam Pattern Questions

## Objective Type Questions

### Multiple Choice Questions (MCQs)

**1.** **Repeated association of undesired response with an aversive consequence refers to**

(a) positive reinforcement (b) aversive conditioning
(c) negative reinforcement (d) modelling

**2.** **RET has been proposed by**

(a) Abraham Maslow (b) Albert Ellis
(c) Aaron Beck (d) Carl Rogers

**3.** **Cognitive therapy for the treatment of depression is given by**

(a) Albert Ellis (b) Sigmund Freud
(c) Aaron Beck (d) None of these

**4.** **Logotheraphy is given by**

(a) Victor Frankl (b) Sigmund Freud
(c) Ivan Pavlov (d) Carl Rogers

**5.** **Systematic desensitisation begins with some form of**

(a) instrumental conditioning (b) relaxation training
(c) instrumental training (d) None of these

**6.** **Nishant feels very strongly that everyone should love him and he should be selected to represent the school for all competitions. When this does not happen, he feels miserable and is unable to concentrate. Which form of therapy would be the most suitable for him to overcome this problem?** **CBSE 2019**

(a) Cognitive therapy (b) Psychodynamic therapy
(c) Behaviour therapy (d) Biomedical therapy

**7.** **Ritik is undergoing a therapy where he is being taught to recognise bodily processes and the emotions that are being blocked out from his awareness. Which therapy is being applied here?** **CBSE 2023**

(a) Client-centred therapy
(b) Logotherapy
(c) Cognitive behaviour therapy
(d) Gestalt therapy

**8.** **Mukesh meets Mr. Kamlesh every week. Considering that Mr. Kamlesh is helping Mukesh to overcome his maladaptive behaviours for a certain period, the relation between Mukesh and Mr. Kamlesh will be called**

(a) mentor-student alliance (b) personal alliance
(c) therapeutic alliance (d) contractual alliance

**9.** **Which of the following is/are true about behaviour therapy?**

I. **Behaviour therapy consists of a large set of specific techniques and interventions.**
II. **Cognitive behavioural play therapy is commonly used as a treatment for mental health conditions in children.**
III. **Cognitive behavioural therapy integrates aspects of multiple approach such as cognitive restructuring, positive reinforcement, habituation counter conditioning and modelling.**
IV. **Aversion therapy is used to treat disorders like substance use and alcohol use disorder.**

Codes

(a) I and II (b) II and III
(c) I, II and III (d) I, II, III and IV

**10.** **What is the primary purpose of psychotherapy?**

(a) To establish a permanent friendship with the therapist
(b) To address and resolve psychological issues
(c) To explore career options
(d) To provide physical treatment for psychological symptoms

**11.** **In a therapeutic relationship, what characteristic is essential to create a safe space for the client?**

(a) Formality and strictness
(b) Confidentiality and trust
(c) Intimacy and informality
(d) Professional distance and detachment

**12.** **Which type of therapy focuses on intrapsychic conflicts as the root of psychological issues?**

(a) Behaviour therapy
(b) Psychodynamic therapy
(c) Cognitive Behavioural therapy
(d) Existential therapy

**13.** **Which approach to therapy emphasises the importance of creating a non-judgemental, positive therapeutic environment?**

(a) Psychodynamic therapy
(b) Behaviour therapy
(c) Existential therapy
(d) Cognitive Behavioural therapy

**14.** What is a chief benefit of Behaviour Therapy?

(a) Gaining emotional insight
(b) Modifying maladaptive behaviours
(c) Discovering life's meaning
(d) Exploring childhood memories

**15.** Hina's therapist at the rehabilitation centre administers ......... to improve the basic functions of her attention and memory. **CBSE SQP 2024**

(a) social skills training
(b) vocational training
(c) cognitive retraining
(d) occupational therapy

**16.** 'Systematic desensitisation is a technique introduced by Wolpe for treating phobias or irrational fears.'

Referring to the above therapy, arrange the following in the correct sequence

(i) Together with the client, the therapist prepares a hierarchy of anxiety-provoking stimuli with the least anxiety-provoking stimuli at the bottom of the hierarchy.
(ii) The client is interviewed to elicit fear-provoking situations.
(iii) Over sessions, the client is able to imagine more severe fear-provoking situations while maintaining the relaxation.
(iv) The therapist relaxes the client and asks the client to think about the least anxiety-provoking situation. **CBSE 2024 C**

(a) (i), (iv), (iii), (ii)
(b) (iii), (iv), (i), (ii)
(c) (iv), (i), (ii), (iii)
(d) (ii), (i), (iv), (iii)

**17.** Which of the following are not true about therapeutic approaches?

(i) Therapeutic approaches are corrective and helping in nature.
(ii) Therapeutic approaches do not involve an interpersonal relationship between the therapist and the client.
(iii) Some therapeutic approaches such as client-centred therapy are directive in nature.
(iv) Some therapeutic approaches are non-directive such as humanistic-existential therapy. **CBSE 2024 C**

(a) (i) and (ii)
(b) (ii) and (iii)
(c) (i) and (iii)
(d) (ii) and (iv)

## Assertion-Reason Questions

**Direction** (Q. Nos. 18-22) In the following question, a statement of Assertion (A) is followed by a statement of Reason (R). Mark the correct choice. **CBSE SQP 2022**

(a) Both A and R are true and R is the correct explanation of A.
(b) Both A and R are true, but R is not the correct explanation of A.
(c) A is true, but R is false.
(d) A is false, but R is true.

**18.** **Assertion** (A) The principle of reciprocal inhibition states that the presence of two mutually opposing forces at the same time will lead to the stronger force inhibiting the weaker one.

**Reason** (R) The principle of reciprocal inhibition is a procedure wherein the client learns to behave in a certain way by observing the behaviour of the therapist.

**19.** **Assertion** (A) Psychotherapy aims to improve the client's ability to adapt to their environment.

**Reason** (R) Enhancing self-awareness is an important goal of psychotherapy.

**20.** **Assertion** (A) Behaviour Therapy is focused on modifying faulty conditioning patterns.

**Reason** (R) Behaviour Therapy believes that psychological issues arise from existential questions.

**21.** **Assertion** (A) A therapeutic relationship must maintain professional boundaries.

**Reason** (R) Professional boundaries help the therapist avoid any form of exploitation of the client's trust.

**22.** **Assertion** (A) Existential Therapy emerged as a response to Psychodynamic Therapy and Behaviour Therapy.

**Reason** (R) Existential Therapy addresses existential questions as a source of psychological distress.

# Answers

1. (b) aversive conditioning
2. (b) Albert Ellis
3. (c) Aaron Beck
4. (a) Victor Frankl
5. (b) relaxation training
6. (a) Cognitive therapy
7. (d) Gestalt therapy
8. (c) therapeutic alliance
9. (d) I, II, III and IV
10. (b) To address and resolve psychological issues
11. (b) Confidentiality and trust
12. (b) Psychodynamic Therapy

13. (c) Existential Therapy
14. (b) Modifying maladaptive behaviours
15. (c) cognitive retraining
16. (d) (ii), (i), (iv), (iii)
17. (a) (i) and (ii)
18. (c) A is true, but R is false
19. (b) Both A and R are true, but R is not the correct explanation of A.
20. (c) A is true, but R is false.
21. (a) Both A and R are true and R is the correct explanation of A.
22. (a) Both A and R are true and R is the correct explanation of A.

# Subjective Questions

## Very Short Answer Type Questions

**1. What is meant by therapeutic contract?**

**Ans.** The therapeutic relationship is contractual in nature in which two willing individuals, the client and the therapist enter into partnership which aims at helping the client to overcome his/her problems.

**2. Explain 'positive reinforcement'.**

**Ans.** If an adaptive behaviour occurs rarely, positive reinforcement is given to encourage adaptive behaviour. For example, if a child does not do homework regularly, positive reinforcement may be used by the child's mother by preparing the child's favourite dish whenever she/he does homework at the appointed time.

**3. Explain the term empathy.**

**Ans.** Empathy means reacting to another's feelings with an emotional response that is similar to the other's feelings.

**4. What do you mean by free association method?**

**Ans.** Free association method is the main method for understanding the client's problems. The therapist helps the client to feel comfortable and encourage them to speak freely without censoring their thoughts in anyway. The client is encouraged to freely associate one thought with another.

**5. Explain vicarious learning.**

**Ans.** Vicarious learning is learning by observing others. It is the process of rewarding small changes in the behaviour in which the client gradually learns to acquire the behaviour of the model.

**6. What is cognitive behaviour therapy?**

**Ans.** Cognitive behaviour therapy is a short and efficacious treatment for a wide range of psychological disorders such as anxiety, depression, panic attacks and borderline personality, etc.

**7. What is meant by self-actualisation?**

**Ans.** Self-actualisation is a state in which people have reached their fullest potential and develop a complex, balanced and integrated personality.

**8. What is existential anxiety?**

**Ans.** Spiritual anxiety leads to meaninglessness and it may be called as existential anxiety i.e. neurotic anxiety of spiritual origin.

The goal of logo therapy is to help the patients to find meaning and responsibility in their life irrespective of their life circumstances.

**9. What is integration in humanistic-existential therapy?**

**Ans.** It is an aspect of self-actualisation which was conceptualised by Maslow. 'Integrated' means a sense of whole, being a complete person, maintaining the traits of personality despite of the variety of experience that one is subjected to.

**10. What is occupational therapy?**

**Ans.** In occupational therapy, the patients are taught skills such as candle making, paper bag making and weaving to help them to form a work discipline.

**11. Explain token economy technique for changing behaviour.**

**Ans.** Person with behavioural problems can be given a token as a reward every time when a wanted behaviour occurs.

The tokens are collected and exchanged for a reward such as an outing for the patient or a treat for the child. This is known as Token economy.

**12. How can a therapist maintain the trust of his client?**

**Ans.** The therapist encourages the client to discharge his/her emotions and feel free from the conflicts and anxiety by providing unconditional positive regard and empathy.

The therapist provides an accepting, empathic, genuine, non-judgemental and warm relationship in order to maintain the trust of his client.

**13. State the ethical standards practised by professional psychotherapist.**

*Or* **State any two ethical standards that need to be practiced by professional psychotherapists.** CBSE SQP 2022

*Or* **Vihan is treating his client. What are the ethical standards that he has to keep in mind when he is administering psychotherapy? Discuss.** CBSE 2024 C

**Ans.** Some of the ethical standards that need to be practised by professional psychotherapist are

- Informed consent need to be taken.
- Integrity of the therapist-client relationship is important.
- Respect for human rights and dignity.
- Professional competence and skills are essential.

**14. What is systematic desensitisation?**

**Ans.** Systematic desensitisation is a technique introduced by psychologist Wolpe for treating phobias on irration fears. The therapist relaxes the client and asks the client to think about the least-anxiety-provoking situation. Gradually the client is able to imagine more severe for-provoking situations while maintaining the relaxation and in this way the client gets systematically desensitised to the fear.

**15. The therapy which considers a person as a whole entity consisting of body, mind and emotions, also explains the alleviation of the client's problems. Identify the therapy and state any two key features of this therapy.** CBSE SQP 2024

**Ans.** The therapy that considers a person as a whole entity consisting of body, mind and emotions, is holistic therapy. The two key features of holistic therapy are

(i) **Mind-Body-Spirit Integration Holistic therapy** views a person as a whole interconnected system, where physical, mental and emotional well-being are all considered crucial for overall health.

(ii) **Focus on Root Causes Holistic therapy** aims to identify the underlying causes of a client's problems.

## Short Answer Type Questions

**1. Define the nature and process of psychotherapy.**

**Ans.** Psychotherapy is a voluntary relationship between the client (patient) and the therapist. The purpose of the relationship is to help the client to solve the psychological problems being faced by her or him.

Psychotherapies aim at changing the maladaptive behaviours, decreasing the sense of personal distress and helping the client to adapt better to her/his environment.

Inadequate marital, occupational and social adjustment also requires that major changes be made in an individual's personal environment.

**2. What are the major components of a therapeutic alliance?**

**Ans.** The special relationship between the client and the therapist is known as the Therapeutic elationship or Alliance. There are two major components of a therapeutic alliance

(i) The first component is the contractual nature of the relationship in which two willing individuals, the client and the therapist, enter into a partnership which aims at helping the client to overcome her/his problems.

(ii) The second component of therapeutic alliance is the limited duration of the therapy. This alliance lasts until the client becomes able to deal with her/his problems and take control of her/his life.

**3. Explain positive regards for others in the context of counselling.**

**Ans.** Unconditional positive regard indicates that the positive warmth of the therapist is not dependent on what the client reveals or does in the therapy sessions. This unique unconditional warmth ensures that the client feels secure, can trust the therapist and feels secure enough to explore her/his feelings. The therapist reflects the feelings of the client in a non-judgemental manner.

The reflection is achieved by rephrasing the statements of the client i.e. seeking simple clarifications to enhance the meaning of the client's statements. This process of reflection helps the client to become integrated. This therapy helps a client to become her/his real self with the therapist working as a facilitator.

**4. Explain the main feature of therapeutic relationship.**

**Ans.** This relationship has several unique properties. It is a trusting and confiding relationship. The high level of trust enables the client to unburden herself/himself to the therapist and confide her/his psychological and personal problems to the latter.

The therapist encourages this by being accepting, empathic, genuine and warm to the client. The therapist conveys by her/his words and behaviours that she/he is not judging the client and will continue to show the same positive feelings towards the client even if the client is rude. The therapeutic alliance also requires that the therapist must keep strict confidentiality of the experiences, events, feelings or thoughts disclosed by the client.

The therapist must not exploit the trust and the confidence of the client in anyway. It is a professional relationship between the therapist and the client.

**5. What is the meaning of logotherapy?**

**Ans.** Victor Frankl, a psychiatrist and neurologist propounded the Logotherapy. Logos is the Greek word for soul and Logotherapy means treatment for the soul. Frankl describes the process of finding meaning even in life-threatening circumstances as the meaning making. The basis of meaning making is a person's quest for finding the spiritual truth of one's existence.

The spiritual unconscious include love, aesthetic awareness, and life values. Neurotic anxieties arise when the problems of life are attached to the physical, psychological or spiritual aspects of one's existence. Frankl emphasised the role of spiritual anxieties in leading to meaninglessness.

This may be referred to as existential anxiety which is neurotic anxiety of spiritual origin. The goal of logotherapy is to help the patients to find meaning and responsibility in their life irrespective of their life circumstances. The therapist emphasises the unique nature of the patient's life and encourages them to find meaning in their life.

**6. Discuss briefly Gestalt Therapy.**

**Ans.** The German word gestalt means 'whole'. This therapy was given by Freiderick (Fritz) Perls together with his wife Laura Perls. The goal of gestalt therapy is to increase an individual's self-awareness and self acceptance. The client is taught to recognise the bodily processes and the emotions that are being blocked out from awareness. The therapist does this by encouraging the client to act out fantasies about feelings and conflicts. This therapy can also be used in group settings.

**7. How is behaviour therapy used to treat phobia?**

*Or* **A client approaches a therapist to overcome her/his phobia for heights. Describe a behavioural technique that the therapist might choose to help her/him to overcome this phobia for heights.** CBSE SQP Term II 2021

**Ans.** It is a technique introduced by Wolpe for treating phobias or irrational fears. The client is interviewed to elicit fear-provoking situations.

The therapist relaxes the client and asks the client to think about the least anxiety- provoking situation. The client is asked to stop thinking of the fearful situation if the slightest tension is felt. After some sessions, the client is able to imagine more severe fear-provoking situations while maintaining the relaxation. The client gets systematically desensitised to the fear. Wolpe introduced this systematic desensitisation technique for treating phobias.

**8. Nikhil has some psychological disorder. He is taking psychoanalytic therapy. What are the different stages and duration of his treatment?** Competency Based Que.

**Ans.** Psychoanalytic therapy of Nikhil consists of three stages. In **stage one** he becomes familiar with the routines, establishes a therapeutic relationship with the analyst. He gets some relief with the process of recollecting the superficial materials from the consciousness about the past and present troublesome events.

**Stage two** is the middle phase, which is a long process and it is characterised by transference, resistance on the part of Nikhil and confrontation and clarification, i.e. working through on the therapist's part. All these processes finally lead to insight.

The third stage is the termination phase where in the relationship with the analyst and Nikhil is dissolved and he prepares to leave the therapy.

**9. "Dreams are the symbols of the unfulfilled desires present in the unconscious." Elaborate.**

**Ans.** Psychoanalysts look upon dreams as symbols of the unfulfilled desires present in the unconscious. The images of the dreams are symbols which signify intrapsychic forces. Dreams use symbols because they are indirect expressions and hence would not alert the ego. If the unfulfilled desires are expressed directly, the ever-vigilant ego would suppress them and that would lead to anxiety. These symbols are interpreted according to an accepted convention of translation as the indicators of unfulfilled desires and conflicts.

**10. The aim of the behaviour therapy is to extinguish the faulty behaviour. Illustrate with example how antecedent operations and consequent operations are used in this therapy.**

**Ans.** The aim of the behaviour therapy is to extinguish the faulty behaviour and substitute them with adaptive behaviour pattern. The therapist does this through establishing antecedent operations and consequent operations. Antecedent operations control behaviour by changing something that precedes such a behaviour. The change can be done by increasing or decreasing the reinforcing value of a particular consequence. This is called establishing operation.

For example, if a child gives trouble in eating dinner, an establishing operation would be, to decrease the quantity of food served at tea time. This would increase the hunger at dinner and thereby increase the reinforcing value of food at dinner. Praising the child when she/he eats properly tends to encourage this behaviour. It establishes the response of eating dinner.

**11. Ankit rarely does his homework regularly. Her mother promised him to prepare his favourite dish whenever he does homework at the appointed time. Identify the reinforcement given by Ankit's mother. How does it benefit the person?**

**Ans.** In the given case, Ankit's mother is giving positive reinforcement. Positive reinforcement may be used by the child's mother by preparing the child's favourite dish whenever he does homework at the appointed time. The positive reinforcement of food will increase the behaviour of doing homework at the appointed time. Persons with behavioural problems can be given a token as a reward every time a wanted behaviour occurs. Thus, appositive reinforcement is given to increase the deficit.

**12. Shyam believes that he should be loved by everybody, all the time. Most of his beliefs have a 'must' or 'should' component. When things don't go his way, he feels distressed. Suggest a suitable therapy that will make Shyam think deeper into his irrational belief system and help him to feel better.** CBSE Term II 2022

**Ans.** Therapy suitable for Shyam is Rational Emotive that will make him think deeper into his irrational belief system and help him to feel better. This theory was formulated by Albert Ellis. The central idea of this therapy is that irrational beliefs mediate between the antecedent events and their consequences. The first step in RET is the Antecedent Belief-Consequence (ABC) analysis. Antecedent events, which caused the psychological distress, are noted.

The client is also interviewed to find the irrational beliefs, which are distorting the present reality. These beliefs are characterised by thoughts with 'musts' and 'shoulds', i.e. things 'must' and 'should' be in a particular manner. The distorted perception of the antecedent event due to the irrational belief leads to the consequence i.e. negative emotions and behaviours. Irrational beliefs are assessed through questionnaires and interviews.

In the process of RET, the irrational beliefs are opposed by the therapist through a process of non-directive questioning. The questions make the client to think deeper into her/his assumptions about life and problems. Gradually, the client is able to change the irrational beliefs by making a change in her/his philosophy about life. The rational belief system replaces the irrational belief system and there is a reduction in psychological distress.

**13. Explain negative reinforcement and aversive conditioning techniques for behaviour modification.**

**Ans.** **Negative Reinforcement** It is a major technique of behaviour modification. Responses that lead organisms to get rid of painful stimuli or avoid and escape from them provide negative reinforcement.

For example, one learns to put on woolen clothes, burn firewood or use electric heaters to avoid the unpleasant cold weather. Person learns to move away from dangerous stimuli because they provide negative reinforcement.

**Aversive Conditioning** It refers to repeated association of undesired response with an aversive consequence. For example, an alcoholic is given a mild electric shock and asked to smell the alcohol. With repeated pairings the smell of alcohol is aversive as the pain of the shock is associated with it and the person will give up alcohol.

**14. Describe the rehabilitation of the Mentally Ill.**

***Or*** **Describe the process of rehabilitation of the mentally ill in detail.** **CBSE Term II 2022**

**Ans.** Rehabilitation of the mentally ill focuses on reducing symptoms and improving quality of life. For milder disorders, symptom reduction often leads to a better quality of life. In severe disorders like schizophrenia, symptoms may improve, but quality of life may still be impacted.

The goal of rehabilitation is to help patients become self-sufficient and productive members of society. This includes occupational therapy (e.g., candle making, weaving), social skills training (role play, interaction) and cognitive retraining (improving memory and attention). Vocational therapy further equips patients with skills for employment, enhancing independence and social integration.

**15. Rajesh is an alcoholic patient with depression. How the alternative therapies can help him to overcome this difficulty?**

**Ans.** Alternative therapies are alternative treatment possibilities to the conventional drug treatment or psychotherapy. Rajesh an alcoholic patient with depression who takes regular medicine prescribed by the psychiatrist.

Besides this, his doctor advises him to practice yoga. Yoga is an ancient Indian technique given by Patanjali in his 'Yoga Sutra'. Yoga is commonly understood as asanas or body posture with specific breathing practices.

Pranayam and meditation are two important components of yoga. Yoga and meditation can help the patient to reduce his depression. It is found that alcoholic patients who practice Sudarshana Kriya Yoga (SKY) have reduced depression and stress level.

Research conducted at the National Institute of Mental Health and Neuroscience (NIMHANS) has shown that SKY definitely reduces depression.

Thus, by practising SKY Rajesh can overcome his depression due to alcoholism.

**16. Explain psychological distress according to Humanist-Existential therapy.**

***Or*** **Mention the therapy that encourages to seek personal growth and actualise their potential. Give its salient features.**

**Ans.** **Humanistic-Existential** therapies claims that psychological distress arises from feelings of loneliness, alienation and an inability to find meaning and genuine fulfillment in life. Human beings are motivated by the desire for personal growth and self-actualisation and an innate need to grow emotionally. When these needs are controlled by society and family, the individual experiences psychological distress.

Self-actualisation is defined as an inborn force that moves the person to become more complex, balanced and intergrated. As lack of food and water causes distress, frustration of self-actualisation also causes distress.

The chief aim of the Humanistic-Existential therapy is to expand the client's awareness. Healing takes place though a process of understanding the client's unique personal experience.

**17. Describe four factors which contribute to treatment of psychological distress.**

**Ans.** There are several factors which contribute to the healing process. Some of these factors are as follows

(i) A major factor in the healing is the techniques adopted by the therapist and the implementation of the same with the patient/client. If the behavioural system and the CBT school are adopted to heal an anxious client, the relaxation procedures and the cognitive restructuring largely contribute to the healing.

(ii) The therapeutic alliance, which is formed between the therapist and the patient/client, has healing properties, because of the regular availability of the therapist and the warmth and empathy provided by the therapist.

(iii) At the beginning of therapy, while the patient/client is being interviewed in the initial sessions to understand the nature of the problem, she/he unburdens the emotional problems being faced. This process of emotional unburdening is known as Catharsis and it has healing properties.

(iv) There are several non-specific factors associated with psychotherapy. Some of these factors are attributed to the patient/client and some to the therapist. Non-specific factors attributable (available) to the client/patient are motivation for change, expectation of improvement due to the treatment, etc. These are called Patient variables. Non-specific factors attributable to the therapist are positive nature, absence of unresolved emotional conflicts, presence of good mental health, etc. These are called Therapist variables.

**18. Explain psychological distress according to behaviour therapy. Describe any one behavioural techniques.**

**Ans.** Behaviour therapies postulates that psychological distress arises because of faulty behaviour patterns or thought patterns. It is focused on the behaviour and thoughts of the client in the present.

The past is relevant only to the extent of understanding the origins of the faulty behaviour and thought patterns. Only the faulty patterns are corrected in the present. Behaviour therapy consists of a large set of specific techniques and interventions. The symptoms of the client and the clinical diagnosis are the guiding factors in the selection of the specific techniques of behaviour therapy.

**Aversive Conditioning** is a major technique of behaviour modification. Aversive conditioning refers to repeated association of undesired response with an aversive consequence. For example, an alcoholic is given a mild electric shock and asked to smell the alcohol. With repeated pairings the smell of alcohol is aversive as the pain of the shock is associated with it and the person will give up alcohol.

**19. How is Rational Emotive Therapy (RET) used in treating psychological disorders?**

*Or* **How does Rational Emotive Therapy help in reducing distress? Support your answer with the help of an example.** CBSE 2019

*Or* **Discuss cognitive therapy given by Albert Ellis.**

*Or* **Explain the key features of cognitive therapies as explained by Albert Ellis and Aron Beck.** CBSE 2020

**Ans.** Cognitive therapies identify the cause of psychological disorders as rooted in irrational thoughts and beliefs.

Albert Ellis formulated the Rational Emotive Therapy (RET). The RET method helps reducing psychological disorders in the followings ways

- The first step in RET is the Antecedent Belief-Consequence (ABC) analysis. Antecedent events, which caused the psychological distress, are noted.
- The client is also interviewed to find the irrational beliefs, which are distorting the present reality. Irrational beliefs may not be supported by empirical evidence in the environment. These beliefs are characterised by thoughts with 'musts' and 'shoulds', i.e. things 'must' and 'should' be in a particular manner.
- The distorted perception of the antecedent event due to the irrational belief leads to the consequence i.e. negative emotions and behaviours. For example, 'One should be loved by everybody all the time' is an irrational belief which leads to consequence of negative emotions and behaviours. Irrational beliefs are assessed through questionnaires and interviews. In the process of RET, the irrational beliefs are refuted by the therapist through a process of non-directive questioning.
- The questions make the client to think deeper into her/his assumptions about life and problems. Gradually, the client is able to change the irrational beliefs by making a change in her/his philosophy about life. The rational belief system replaces the irrational belief system and there is a reduction in psychological distress.

**20. Explain the alternative treatment possibilities to psychotherapy. How does rehabilitation of the mentally ill improve the quality of their life?** **CBSE SQP Term II 2021**

**Ans.** Alternative treatments to psychotherapy include practices like yoga, meditation, acupuncture and herbal remedies. Yoga and meditation, particularly mindfulness-based practices like Vipasana, have gained popularity in recent years for managing stress, improving sleep and reducing the recurrence of depression. Techniques like Sudarshana Kriya Yoga and Kundalini Yoga have shown benefits in treating conditions such as PTSD, anxiety and obsessive-compulsive disorders.

Rehabilitation plays a crucial role in improving the lives of mentally ill individuals by helping them regain independence. Through occupational therapy, social skills training and vocational therapy, patients develop essential life skills and the ability to reintegrate into society, ultimately enhancing their overall quality of life.

**21. Explain the different cognitive therapies that are used to reduce distress.** **CBSE SQP Term II 2021**

**Ans.** Cognitive therapies aim to reduce psychological distress by addressing irrational thoughts and beliefs.

(i) **Rational Emotive Therapy (RET)**, by Albert Ellis, identifies irrational beliefs that mediate between events and emotional consequences. Through he ABC analysis and questioning, clients change their irrational beliefs, leading to reduced distress.

(ii) **Aaron Beck's Cognitive Therapy** targets negative cognitive distortions such as 'I am worthless', aiming to restructure these beliefs, alleviating anxiety and depression.

(iii) **Cognitive Behaviour Therapy (CBT)** combines cognitive and behavioural techniques, addressing biological, psychological and social factors to treat various disorders, including anxiety and depression.

**22. Shahid showed a reduction in symptoms after he received treatment for Schizophrenia. He was sent to the rehabilitation centre to improve his quality of life. What steps would be taken in the rehabilitation centre to help him become a productive member of the community? Explain.** **CBSE SQP 2022**

**Ans.** Shahid showed a reduction in symptoms after he received treatment for Schizophrenia. In disorders like Schizophrenia, reduction of symptoms may not be associated with an improvement in the quality of life. Rehabilitation is required to help patients to become self-sufficient. The aim of rehabilitation is to empower the patient to become a productive member of society to the extent possible. In rehabilitation, the patients are given occupational therapy, social skills training and vocational therapy.

In occupational therapy, the patients are taught skills such as candle making, paper bag making and weaving to help them to form a work discipline.

Social skills training helps the patients to develop inter-personal skills through role play, imitation and instruction. The objective is to teach the patient to function in a social group.

Cognitive retraining is given to improve the basic cognitive functions of attention, memory and executive functions. After the patient improves sufficiently, vocational training is given wherein the patient is helped to gain skills necessary to undertake productive employment.

## Long Answer Type Questions

**1. What is psychotherapy? Discuss the factors that contribute to healing in Psychotherapy.**

**Ans.** Psychotherapy is a voluntary relationship between the client (patient) and the therapist. The purpose of the relationship is to help the client to solve the psychological problems being faced by her or him. There are several factors which contribute to the healing process. Some of these factors are as follows

- A major factor in the healing is the techniques adopted by the therapist and the implementation of the same with the patient/ client. If the behavioural system and the CBT school are adopted to heal an anxious client, the relaxation procedures and the cognitive restructuring largely contribute to the healing.
- The therapeutic alliance, which is formed between the therapist and the patient/client, has healing properties, because of the regular availability of the therapist and the warmth and empathy provided by the therapist.
- At the outset of therapy while the patient/client is being interviewed in the initial sessions to understand the nature of the problem, she/he unburdens the emotional problems being faced. This process of emotional unburdening is known as Catharsis and it has healing properties.

There are several non-specific factors associated with psychotherapy. Some of these factors are attributed to the patient/client and some to the therapist. These factors are called non-specific because they occur across different systems of psychotherapy and across different clients/patients and different therapists.

Non-specific factors attributable to the client/ patient are motivation for change, expectation of improvement due to the treatment, etc. These are called Patient variables.

Non-specific factors attributable to the therapist are positive nature, absence of unresolved emotional conflicts, presence of good mental health, etc. These are called Therapist variables.

**2. Discuss six key ethical standards that professional psychotherapists must adhere to. Explain how each standard contributes to the effectiveness of psychotherapy and ensures the well-being of clients.** CBSE 2025

**Ans.** Psychotherapists follow six key ethical standards to ensure effective therapy and client well-being and these are

(i) **Confidentiality** Therapists must keep client information private, which creates trust and a safe space for sharing thoughts and feelings.

(ii) **Informed** Consent Clients must understand the therapy process, including its goals and methods. This empowers clients to make informed decisions about their treatment.

(iii) **Competence** Therapists should possess adequate knowledge and skills in their field. Competent therapists provide high-quality care and help clients achieve positive outcomes.

(iv) **Non-Maleficence** Therapists avoid causing harm to clients by practicing responsibly and ensuring their methods do not worsen the client's condition.

(v) **Beneficence** Therapists actively work for the client's well-being, designing therapy plans that address their specific needs and improve their mental health.

(vi) **Professional** Boundaries Therapists maintain clear boundaries, such as avoiding dual relationships, to ensure ethical and effective interactions.

**3. Explain any four techniques used in behaviour therapy.** CBSE SQP 2024

**Ans.** The four techniques used in behaviour therapy are as follows

(i) **Positive Reinforcement** Rewarding desired behaviours makes them more likely to happen again.

(ii) **Exposure Therapy** Gradually exposing a person to her fears in a safe environment helps his/her to manage anxiety. This could involve showing pictures of spiders (mild fear) before progressing to seeing real ones (greater fear).

(iii) **Aversion Therapy** Pairing an unwanted behaviour with something unpleasant discourages it. For example, someone trying to quit smoking might imagine the unpleasant taste of cigarettes to curb cravings.

(iv) **Token Economies** Rewarding desired behaviours with tokens that can be exchanged for privileges motivates positive change. Imagine children earning tokens for good behaviour that they can later trade for playtime.

**4. Meera has an intense irrational fear of spiders and experiences sudden episodes of intense terror with breathlessness and dizziness. Identify the two types of anxiety disorders she might be suffering from and suggest one coping strategy for each.** CBSE 2025

**Ans.** Meera appears to be suffering from two types of anxiety disorders specific phobia and panic disorder.

(i) **Specific Phobia** Meera's intense, irrational fear of spiders is characteristic of a specific phobia. Individuals with this disorder experience persistent, excessive fear of a particular object or situation, leading to avoidance behaviour. The anxiety is disproportionate to the actual danger posed by the feared object, in this case, spiders.

**Coping Strategy for Specific Phobia** One effective coping strategy for specific phobia is gradual exposure therapy. This involves Meera slowly and progressively confronting her fear in a controlled and safe environment. Starting with less anxiety-provoking aspects, like looking at pictures of spiders, and gradually moving to more direct exposures, such as being in the same room as a spider, can help reduce her fear response over time. This process helps to desensitise her to the object of fear, ultimately reducing her anxiety.

(ii) **Panic Disorder** Meera's sudden episodes of intense terror, accompanied by physical symptoms like breathlessness and dizziness, suggest she may have panic disorder. This disorder is characterised by recurrent, unexpected panic attacks, which are intense periods of fear and discomfort that may occur without warning.

**Coping Strategy for Panic Disorder** Deep breathing exercises and relaxation techniques can be effective in managing panic attacks. Meera can practice slow, deep breathing to help regulate her breathing and calm her body's fight-or-flight response during an attack. Additionally, cognitive-behavioural therapy (CBT) could help address irrational thoughts and develop coping mechanisms for managing anxiety.

## Case Based Questions

**1. Read the case and answer the questions that follow.**

The client is interviewed to elicit fear provoking situations and together with the client. The therapist relaxes the client and asks the client to think about the least anxiety-provoking situation. Over sessions, the client is able to imagine more severe fearprovoking situations while maintaining the relaxation. The client gets systematically desensitised to the fear.

**(i) What technique is being used by the therapist in this case?**

**(ii) How does the therapist help the client in this process?**

**Ans.** (i) The technique used is systematic desensitisation, a type of behavioural therapy that gradually exposes the client to fear-provoking situations while they remain relaxed. This method helps the client manage anxiety and eventually reduce their fear response.

(ii) The therapist guides the client through relaxation exercises and starts with the least fear-provoking situation. Over multiple sessions, the therapist gradually introduces more intense situations, helping the client maintain relaxation, thereby desensitising them to their fear.

**2. Read the case and answer the questions that follow.** CBSE SQP Term II 2021

Mental health professionals have attempted to understand psychological disorders using different approaches through the ages. Today, we have sophisticated facilities and hospitals dedicated to the treatment of the mentally ill. While studying the history of psychological disorders it is interesting to note that some practices from ancient times are still in use. Take the case of Lakshmi and her daughter, Maya. Maya exhibits abnormal behaviours and Lakshmi believes that this is because of evil spirits that have possessed her. She has been taking her daughter to a self-proclaimed healer, who uses counter-magic and prayer to cure her. Stigma and lack of awareness prevents Lakshmi from using the modern facilities and hospitals that provide quality mental health care.

On the other hand, when young Rita reported seeing people and hearing voices, mental health professionals at a modern facility were able to understand her hallucinations using a convergence of three approaches. Psychologists use official manuals like the Diagnostic and Statistical Manual of Mental Disorders – 5th Edition (DSM-5) and International Classification of Diseases (ICD-10) to indicate presence or absence of disorders. Today there is increased compassion for people who suffer from disorders and a lot of emphasis is placed on providing community care.

**(i) Identify the method used by the healer to cure Maya's illness. How does this theory from ancient times explain Maya's treatment?**

**(ii) Which approach do you think would best explain Rita's treatment? How do you think DSM-5 and ICD-10 help mental health professionals in indicating the presence or absence of disorders?**

**Ans** (i) Exorcism is an ancient method which is used by the healer to cure Maya's illness.

It is removing the evil that resides in the individual through counter magic and prayer.

Abnormal behaviour can be explained by the operation of supernatural and magical forces such as bhoot-pret or shaitan.

(ii) Interactional Approach, which is a bio-psycho-social approach i.e. biological, psychological and Social play an important role in Rita's treatment.

The Diagnostic and Statistical Manual of Mental disorder, 5th Edition and International Classification of Diseases, which is known as ICD-10 Classification of Behavioural and Mental Disorders. For each disorder there is a description of the main clinical features or symptoms and of other associate features including diagnostic guidelines is provided in this scheme.

# SELF ASSESSMENT TEST

## Objective Type Questions

1. Who pioneered psychodynamic therapy?
   (a) Carl Jung (b) Sigmund Freud (c) Carl Roger (d) Carl Lewis
2. Who introduced systematic desensitisation technique?
   (a) Carl Jung (b) Wolpe (c) Laura Peris (d) Fritz
3. Behaviour therapy is
   (a) open (b) close (c) indoor therapy (d) None of these
4. Who wrote Yoga Sutras?
   (a) Patanjali (b) Kautilya (c) Manu (d) Vrahmihir

## Very Short Answer Type Questions

1. Define psychotherapy.
2. What are the aims of psychotherapies?
3. What do you mean by alliance?
4. What does psychodynamic therapy states?
5. What do you meant by transference?
6. Define modelling.

## Short Answer Type Questions

1. Explain the technique of token money.
2. Elaborate the concept of Electro-convulsive Therapy.
3. Analyse the importance of working through in psychodynamic therapy.

## Long Answer Type Questions

1. Discuss methodology used in behaviour therapy.
2. Describe modality of psychoanalysis as a therapy.
3. How can we formulate a client's problems?

## Case Based Questions

**Read the case and answer the questions that follow.**

Anna is 20 year old girl pursuing the second year graduation course in the University of Delhi. She is a very good student. However, she lacks the motivation for learning. There are a lot of problems with concentration and attention retention during the classes. She is burdened with difficult family situation, namely by living with her sister and mother in the household.

She has rare contacts with her father, since her parents divorced a few years ago and he moved away from Delhi. She felt like she has been neglected by her parents as a child. Consequently, she developed a feeling that I am not wanted. During the course of college life, a critical incident occurs in her life. She was publicly ridiculed by her teacher in the college. This critical incident triggers her belief again that I am not wanted. This further led to the development of negative automatic thoughts.

(i) Identify the form of psychological disorder that Anna is exhibiting. Discuss its treatment.
(ii) What is the patterns of thought exhibited by Anna called? Discuss them.

# 06

CHAPTER

Social psychology is a branch of psychology that examines how individuals' behaviours are influenced by others and their social environment. It studies how we form attitudes, impressions of others and attributions for their behaviours. The underlying processes behind these behaviours are complex, highlighting the intricate nature of human interactions and social influence.

**YOUR STUDY GOALS**

6.1 Explaining Social Behaviour
6.2 Nature and Component of Attitude
6.3 Attitude Formation And Change
6.4 Prejudice and Discrimination

**YOUR PRACTICE GOAL**

- Objective Type Questions (19 Qs ; MCQs, A-R)
- Subjective Questions (16 VSAs, 19 SAs, 4 LAs, 3 Case Based)

# Attitude and Social Cognition

## 6.1 Explaining Social Behaviour

- Social behaviour is a necessary component of human life, going beyond simply being in the company of others.
- Being social involves engaging in behaviours that are influenced by the presence of other people, whether that presence is actual, imagined or implied.
- Social psychology explores behaviours that occur in these contexts, as seen in studies from previous classes.
- Social psychologists study different types of social behaviour and seek to understand the underlying causes.
- Through social influences, individuals develop perspectives toward people and life issues, creating tendencies in their behaviours.
- To fully comprehend how social contexts shape individual behaviour, it is essential to analyse both social-cognitive processes and social behaviours.
- Social psychologists emphasise the need to move beyond common sense and folk wisdom to explain how individuals interpret their own and others' behaviours.

## 6.2 Nature and Components of Attitude

Attitudes are states of mind or sets of views concerning a topic (or attitude object). They include an evaluative component (positive, negative or neutral), accompanied by an emotional component and a tendency to act in certain ways toward the attitude object.

### Components of Attitude

- The thought component, representing beliefs or views is known as cognitive aspect.
- The emotional response associated with the attitude is known as affective aspect.
- The tendency to act in a particular way regarding the attitude object is known as behavioural (conative) aspect.
- These three aspects have been referred to as the A-B-C components i.e. Affective Behavioural and Cognitive components of attitude.
- Attitudes themselves are not behaviours but indicate a tendency to behave in certain ways. They cannot be directly observed, as they are cognitive states with emotional aspects.
- Attitudes provide a mental framework, that helps decision-making in new situations. For instance, a person's attitude towards foreigners may guide their behaviour when interacting with them.

### Features of Attitudes

#### Valence

- The **valence of an attitude**[1] indicates whether it is positive or negative towards the attitude object.
- Attitudes can be measured on a 5-point scale: 1 (Very bad), 2 (Bad), 3 (Neutral—neither good nor bad), 4 (Good), and 5 (Very good).
- A rating of 4 or 5 towards nuclear research reflects a positive attitude, indicating that the person likes the idea of nuclear research and considers it good.
- Conversely, if the rating is 1 or 2, the attitude is negative, meaning the person dislikes the idea of nuclear research and views it as bad.
- A neutral attitude towards nuclear research would be indicated by a rating of 3 on the same scale, signifying that the individual has neither positive nor negative valence towards nuclear research.

#### Extremeness

- The **extremeness of an attitude**[2] indicates how positive or negative the attitude is.
- In the context of nuclear research, a rating of 1 is as extreme as a rating of 5, as they represent opposite directions in terms of valence.
- Ratings of 2 and 4 are considered less extreme compared to the extremes of 1 and 5.
- A neutral attitude, represented by a rating of 3, is the lowest on the extremeness scale.

#### Simplicity/Complexity

- **Simplicity or Complexity (multiplexity)**[3] refers to number of attitudes exist within a broader attitude.
- An attitude can be thought of as a family containing several 'member' attitudes.
- For topics like health and world peace, individuals often hold multiple attitudes rather than a single attitude.

1 **Valence of an Attitude** The intrinsic attractiveness or aversiveness of an attitude, determining whether it is positive or negative.
2 **Extremeness of an Attitude** The intensity or polarisation of an attitude, ranging from mid to strong.
3 **Simplicity or Complexity (multiplexity)** The degree to which an attitude is straightforward or multifaceted, affecting how it is expressed and understood.

- An attitude system is considered simple if it contains only one or a few attitudes and complex if it is made up of many attitudes.
- For example, an attitude towards health and wellbeing likely consists of several 'member' attitudes, including concepts of physical and mental health, views about happiness, and beliefs about achieving health and happiness.
- In contrast, an attitude towards a specific person typically consists of mainly one attitude.
- The multiple member-attitudes within an attitude system should not be confused with the three components described earlier, as each member attitude also has its own **A-B-C components**.

### Centrality

- Centrality refers to the role of a particular attitude within the attitude system.
- An attitude with greater centrality has a significant influence on other attitudes in the system compared to non-central (or peripheral) attitudes.
- For example, in the context of attitudes towards world peace, a negative attitude towards high military expenditure may serve as a core or central attitude that impacts all other attitudes within the multiple attitude system.

#### Quick Test 1

1. What is the study of behaviours influenced by social contexts called?
2. What do individuals form through social influences toward people and life issues?
3. What is the focus of social psychologists in studying social behaviour?
4. How do social psychologists move beyond common sense in their analysis?

## 6.3 Attitude Formation and Change

- Attitudes towards various topics, things and people are formed as we interact with others.
- There are specific conditions that contribute to the formation of specific attitudes.
- Generally, attitudes are learned through personal experiences and social interactions.
- Although some research studies indicate that there may be an inborn aspect to attitudes, such genetic factors typically influence attitudes only indirectly, in conjunction with learning.
- Consequently, most social psychologists concentrate on the conditions that facilitate the learning of attitudes.

### Process of Attitude Formation

The processes of learning can vary leading to different attitudes among individuals.

### Learning Attitudes by Association

- Learning attitudes by association is a common phenomenon where students often develop a liking for a particular subject due to the influence of the teacher.
- This occurs because students perceive many positive qualities in the teacher.
- These positive qualities become linked to the subject that the teacher teaches.
- Ultimately, this connection manifests as a liking for the subject.
- In other words, a positive attitude towards the subject is learned through the positive association between the teacher and the student.

### Learning Attitudes by Being Rewarded or Punished

- If an individual is praised for demonstrating a particular attitude, there is a high likelihood that they will further develop that attitude.
- For example, if a teenager regularly practices yogasanas and is honoured as 'Miss Good Health' in her school, she may cultivate a positive attitude towards yoga and health in general.
- Conversely, if a child frequently falls ill due to consuming junk food instead of proper meals, the child is likely to develop a negative attitude towards junk food and a positive attitude towards eating healthy food.

### Learning Attitudes through Modelling (Observing Others)

- We learn attitudes by observing others being rewarded or punished for specific behaviours or thoughts.
- For example, children may develop a respectful attitude towards elders by observing that their parents show respect for them and are appreciated for their respectful behaviour.

### Learning Attitudes through Group or Cultural Norms

- We often learn attitudes through the norms of our group or culture.
- Norms are unwritten rules about behaviour that individuals are expected to follow under specific circumstances.
- Over time, these norms may become integrated into our social cognition as attitudes.
- Learning attitudes through group or cultural norms can exemplify all three forms of learning: association, reward or punishment and modelling.
- For instance, offering money, sweets, fruit and flowers in a place of worship is considered normative behaviour in some religions.
- When individuals observe this behaviour being practiced by others and recognise it as expected and socially approved, they may ultimately develop a positive attitude towards such behaviour and the associated feelings of devotion.

### Learning through Exposure to Information

- Many attitudes are learned in a social context, but not necessarily in the physical presence of others.
- With vast access to information *via* various media contributes to the formation of both positive and negative attitudes.
- For instance, reading biographies of self-actualised individuals, can lead to the development of a positive attitude towards hard work and other qualities as means of achieving success in life.

## Factors that Influence Attitude Formation

The following factors influence the learning of attitudes

### 1. Family and School Environment

- Parents and family members play an essential role in shaping attitudes in a child's early years, as children model attitudes and beliefs displayed by family members.
- Later, the school environment plays a crucial role, where attitudes are learned through structured associations, rewards, punishments and modelling from teachers and peers.

### 2. Reference Groups

- Reference groups provide norms for acceptable behaviour and ideas, influencing attitudes toward social topics, such as politics, religion and national issues.

- The impact of reference groups is especially strong in adolescence, as individuals seek belonging and social acceptance.
- Attitudes in these groups often develop through reward and punishment systems, where alignment with group norms is rewarded, while divergence may lead to social penalties.

## 3. Personal Experiences

- Some attitudes are formed through direct personal experiences that significantly change one's perspective on life and people.
- Critical life events can reshape attitudes and behaviours, often leading to strong, deeply held beliefs.
- For instance, an individual facing life-threatening situations might develop an intense appreciation for life, leading to positive attitudes toward social causes or community work.

## Media-related Influences

- Advances in technology have made audio-visual media and the Internet powerful source that lead to attitude formation by continuously providing information.
- Media strengthens cognitive and affective components of attitudes, which can then impact behaviour, creating both positive and negative attitudes.
- School textbooks also play a role in shaping young minds by reinforcing social, moral and educational values.
- The media can, however, create unregulated attitudes or foster consumerist mindsets but also has the potential to encourage social harmony and positive attitudes by disseminating constructive information.

# Attitude Change

- During and after the process of attitude formation attitudes may be changed and modified due to various influences.
- Some attitudes are more susceptible to change than others.
- Formative attitudes that resemble opinions are more flexible and likely to change, compared to attitudes that have become firmly established as part of an individual's core values.
- Community leaders, politicians, advertisers and manufacturers have a strong interest in influencing attitude changes for their objectives.

## Process of Attitude Change

Three major concepts of processes in attitude change are described below

### 1. The Concept of Balance

- The concept of Balance was proposed by Fritz Heider.
- He described using the P-O-X triangle, which represents relationships between three components of an attitude.
- P is the person whose attitude is being studied, O is another person and X is the topic or attitude object being studied.
- For example, if dowry is the attitude topic (X), P has a positive attitude towards dowry (P-X positive) and O has a negative attitude towards dowry (O-X negative).
- If O initially has a positive attitude towards P (O-P positive), the situation becomes unbalanced with P-X positive, O-P positive, but O-X negative.
- To achieve balance, one of the three attitudes (P-O, P-X, or O-X) must change.
- Attitude changes in the direction of balance because imbalance is logically uncomfortable.

- Imbalance occurs when all three sides of the P-O-X triangle are negative or two sides are positive and one side is negative.
- Balance is achieved when all three sides are positive or two sides are negative and one side is positive.
- In some situations, all three components (P, O, X) could represent persons, making this model adaptable.

### 2. The Concept of Cognitive Dissonance

- The concept of cognitive dissonance[4] was proposed by Leon Festinger.
- It emphasises that the cognitive components of an attitude must be consonant (aligned and logically in line), rather than dissonant (misaligned).
- Festinger and Carlsmith, two social psychologists, conducted an experiment demonstrating cognitive dissonance in action.
- Both balance and cognitive dissonance are forms of cognitive consistency which implies that components of an attitude must align logically with one another.
- When cognitive components do not align, the person experiences mental discomfort, feeling that 'something is not quite right'.
- To relieve this discomfort, an aspect of the attitude system changes to restore consistency, as the cognitive system seeks logical coherence.

### 3. The Two-Step Concept

- The two-step concept was proposed by **S.M. Mohsin**, an Indian psychologist according to him, attitude change occurs in two steps.
- In the first step the target of change identifies with the source, who influences the change.
- The target is the individual whose attitude is to be changed, while the source is the one facilitating this change.
- Identification[5] occurs when the target has liking and regard for the source.
- The source must also possess a positive attitude towards the target, creating mutual regard and attraction.
- In the second step the source demonstrates an attitude change by actually altering their behaviour towards the attitude object.
- As the target observes the source's changed attitude and behaviour, they also exhibit an attitude change through their own behaviour.
- This process is characterised as a form of imitation or observational learning.

## Factors that Influence Attitude Change

Following are the major factors that influence attitude change

### Characteristics of the Existing Attitude

- All four features valence, extremeness, simplicity and centrality of attitudes[6] determine attitude change.
- In general, positive attitudes are easier to change than negative attitudes.
- Extreme attitudes and central attitudes are more difficult to change than less extreme and peripheral (less significant) attitudes.
- Simple attitudes are easier to change than multiple attitudes.
- An attitude change may be congruent, meaning it changes in the same direction as the existing attitude; for example, a positive attitude may become more positive or a negative one becomes more negative.

4 Cognitive Dissonance A psychological discomfort arising from holding conflicting beliefs or attitudes, prompting a change to restore consistency.
5 Identification A psychological process where individuals associated themselves with a group, adopting its attitudes and behaviours.
6 Centrality of Attitudes The importance of an attitude within an individual's belief system, influencing behaviour significantly.

- Conversely, an attitude change may be incongruent, meaning it changes in a direction opposite to the existing attitude; for instance, a positive attitude may become less positive or negative or a negative attitude may become less negative or positive.
- Additionally, an attitude may change in the direction of the information that is presented or in a opposite direction.

## Source Characteristics

- Source credibility and attractiveness are two features that affect attitude change.
- Attitudes are more likely to change when the message comes from a highly credible source rather than a low-credible source.
- For example, adults planning to buy a laptop are more convinced by a computer engineer who highlights the special features of a particular brand than by a schoolchild giving the same information.
- However, if the buyers are school children themselves, they may be more convinced by another school child advertising a laptop than by a professional.
- In the case of certain products, such as cars, sales may increase if they are publicised by popular public figures rather than solely by experts.

## Message Characteristics

- The message is the information presented to induce attitude change.
- Attitudes will change when the amount of information given about the topic is just enough, neither too much nor too little.
- Whether the message contains a rational or an emotional appeal makes a difference in its effectiveness.
- For example, an advertisement for cooking food in a pressure cooker may highlight its fuel saving and is economical.
- The motives activated by the message determine attitude change; for instance, drinking milk may be associated with becoming healthy, good-looking, energetic and successful.
- The mode of spreading the message is crucial; the benefits of taking ORS can be effectively communicated through visual media like posters and advertisements on television.
- Face-to-face transmission of the message is usually more effective than indirect transmission, which includes methods such as letters, pamphlets or even mass media.

## Target Characteristics

- Qualities of the target, such as **persuasibility**[7], strong prejudices, selfesteem and intelligence, influence the likelihood and extent of attitude change.
- People with a more open and flexible personality change more easily, benefiting advertisers.
- Individuals with strong prejudices are less prone to attitude change than those who do not hold such prejudices.
- Persons with low self-esteem and less confidence, change their attitudes more easily than those with high self-esteem.
- More intelligent people may change their attitudes less easily than those with lower intelligence; however, sometimes, they may change their attitudes more willingly due to broader base of information and deeper thinking.

# Relationship between Attitude-Behaviour

- An individual's attitudes may not always be exhibited through behaviour.
- One's actual behaviour may be contrary to one's attitude towards a particular topic.

7 **Persuasibility** The degree to which an individual can be influenced to change their attitudes or beliefs.

- Psychologists have found consistency between attitudes and behaviour when the following conditions are met
  - The attitude is strong and occupies a central place in the attitude system.
  - The person is aware of their attitude.
  - There is very little or no external pressure for the person to behave in a particular way, such as group pressure to follow a norm.
  - The person's behaviour is not being watched or evaluated by others.
  - The person believes that the behaviour would have a positive consequence and intends to engage in it.

### Quick Test 2

1. Which groups significantly affect attitudes by offering standards of behaviour?
2. What characteristic refers to how relevant an attitude is to the individual?
3. How does learning through modeling influence attitude formation?
4. What is the role of personal experiences in shaping attitudes?
5. What theory explains attitude change through internal inconsistency?
6. How does the credibility of the source influence attitude change?

## 6.4 Prejudice and Discrimination

- **Prejudice**[8] are examples of attitudes directed towards a particular group, typically characterised as negative.
- In many cases, prejudices may be based on stereotypes, which are the cognitive component of attitudes concerning specific groups.
- A stereotype is defined as a cluster of ideas regarding the characteristics of a specific group.
- Often, stereotypes include undesirable characteristics about the target group, leading to negative attitudes or prejudices towards its members.
- Prejudice can lead to discrimination, which is the behavioural component, resulting in less positive behaviour towards a particular target group compared to another group that is favoured.
- For example, the genocide committed by the Nazis in Germany against Jewish people serves as an extreme illustration of how prejudice can lead to hatred, discrimination and mass killing of innocent individuals.
- Prejudices can exist without manifesting as discrimination and similarly, discrimination can occur without underlying prejudice; however, the two often coexist.
- Wherever prejudice and discrimination are present, conflicts are likely to arise between groups within the same society.
- Social psychologists have shown that prejudice has the following sources

### Learning

- Like other attitudes, prejudices can be learned through association, reward and punishment, observing others, group or cultural norms and exposure to information that promotes prejudice.
- The family, reference groups, personal experiences and the media may all contribute learning prejudices.
- Individuals with prejudiced attitudes may develop a **prejudiced personality**, characterised by low adjusting capacity, anxiety and feelings of hostility towards the outgroup.

8 Prejudice A preconceived negative judgement or attitude towards a group or its members.

### A Strong Social Identity and Ingroup Bias

- Individuals with a strong sense of social identity tend to hold a very positive attitude towards their own group, often enhanced by maintaining negative attitudes towards other groups.
- Such negative attitudes manifest as prejudices against those outside their group.

### Scapegoating

- Scapegoating is a phenomenon where the majority group blames a minority outgroup for its own social, economic or political problems.
- The minority group is often too weak or small in number to effectively defend itself against such accusations.
- This behaviour serves as a group-based expression of frustration and often leads to the development of negative attitudes or prejudice against the weaker group.

### Kernel of Truth Concept

- The **kernel of truth**[9] concept suggests that people may persist in holding stereotypes because they believe there is some underlying truth in what is commonly said about the other group.
- Even a few examples can be enough to reinforce this 'kernel of truth' belief.

### Self-fulfilling Prophecy

- The self-fulfilling prophecy occurs when the group targeted by prejudice inadvertently reinforces that prejudice through its own behaviour.
- The target group may act in ways that align with the negative expectations set by the prejudiced views.
- For example, if a target group is labelled as 'dependent' and incapable of progress, its members might behave in a manner that confirms this label.
- Consequently, this behaviour strengthens the existing prejudice against them.

## Strategies for Handling Prejudice

- Understanding the causes or sources of prejudice is the first step in handling it and effective strategies should minimising opportunities for learning prejudices and change attitudes to reduce prejudice in society.
- De-emphasising a narrow social identity based on the ingroup bias.
- Discouraging the tendency towards **self-fulfilling prophecy**[10] among the victims of prejudice is crucial in breaking the cycle of prejudice.
- These goals can be accomplished through education and information dissemination, which helps correct stereotypes related to specific target groups and tackle the problem of strong ingroup bias.
- Increasing intergroup contact allows for direct communication, removes mistrust between groups and facilitates the discovery of positive qualities in the outgroup.
- However, these strategies only successful if the two groups meet in a cooperative rather than competitive context. Close interactions help them know each other better. Both groups have similar power or status.
- Highlighting individual identity rather than group identity weakens the importance of group affiliations, fostering a more inclusive environment.

---

9 **Kernel of Truth** The notion that stereotypes may contain some factual basis, leading individuals to hold on to these generalisations.

10 **Self-fulfilling Prophecy** A phenomenon where expectations about a group lead to behaviours that confirm those expectations.

## Quick Test 3

1 What is the cognitive component of prejudice called?
2 What concept suggests that stereotypes may have some feactual basis?
3 Which term describes blaming a minority group for broader societal issues?
4 How can prejudice translate into discrimination?
5 What is the self-fulfilling prophecy in the context of prejudice?
6 How does increasing intergroup contact hlep reduce prejudice?
7 What is the significance of de-emphasising social identity in handing prejudice?

# NCERT Folder

**1. Define attitude. Discuss the components of an attitude.**

*Or* **What is attitude? Explain its various components.** **CBSE 2020**

**Ans.** An attitude is a state of the mind, a set of views or thoughts, regarding some topic (called the 'attitude object'), which have an evaluative feature (positive, negative or neutral quality).

Attitude have three components. There are

(i) The thought component, referred to as the cognitive aspect, consists of belief, ideas, values and other information that a person may possesses or believe in. It does not matter if the information is correct or incorrect.

(ii) The emotional component is known as the affective aspect. It is related to a person's feelings about an attitude object, which may be positive, negative or neutral.

(iii) The tendency to act is called the behavioural (or cognative) aspect. It is related to impact of various situations or objects that lead to individual's behaviour based on cognitive and affective components. Only this component of attitude is visible.

**2. Are attitudes learnt? Explain how.**

*Or* **Explain the conditions which lead to the learning of attitudes.**

**Ans.** Yes, attitudes are learnt. It can be explained as follows

- **Learning Attitudes by Association** A positive attitude towards the subject is learned through the positive association between a teacher and a student.

  Students often develop a liking for a particular subject because of the positive qualities of the teacher.

- **Learning Attitudes by Being Rewarded or Punished** If an individual is praised for showing a particular attitude, chances are high that she/he will develop that attitude further.

  For example, if a child gets the honour of being 'Miss Good Health' in her school by practising yoga, she will develop a positive attitude toward yoga.

- **Learning Attitudes through Modelling** (observing others) We learn attitudes by observing others being rewarded or punished for expressing thoughts, or showing behaviour of a particular kind towards the attitude object.

  For example, children may develop respect for elders by observing that their parents show respect to elders.

- **Learning Attitudes through Group or Cultural Norms** Norms are unwritten rules about behaviour that everyone is supposed to show under specific circumstances. Over time, these norms may become part of our social cognition in the form of attitudes.

  For example, by seeing the offerings of money, sweet, fruits in religious places, individual develops a positive attitude towards such behaviour and the associated feeling of devotion.

- **Learning through Exposure to Information** Many attitudes are learned in a social context, but not necessarily in the physical presence of others. By reading the biographies of self-actualised persons, an individual may develop a positive attitude towards hard work and other aspects as the means of achieving success in life.

**3. What are the factors that influence the formation of an attitude?**

*Or* **Discuss the factors that influence attitude formation.**

*Or* **Describe four methods through which attitudes are formed.** **CBSE 2025**

**Ans.** Attitude formation is influenced by several factors, including

- **Family and School Environment** The family and school significantly shape attitudes, primarily through association, rewards, punishments and modelling. Early socialisation within these settings plays a crucial role in developing foundational attitudes.

- **Reference Groups** Reference groups provide norms regarding acceptable behaviour and influence attitudes toward political, social, religious and occupational matters. During adolescence, these groups are particularly impactful as individuals seek belonging and identity, reinforcing attitudes through social approval or disapproval.

- **Personal Experiences** Direct personal experiences can drastically alter attitudes. For example, someone who survives a traumatic event may change their outlook on life or shift careers, illustrating how experiences can reshape one's perspectives and beliefs.
- **Media-related Influences** Media, including television, the internet and textbooks, shape attitudes by providing information and emotional appeal.

  Media can influence attitudes both positively and negatively, fostering consumerism or promoting social harmony, depending on the messages portrayed.

**4. Is behaviour always a reflection of one's attitude? Explain with a relevant example.**

**Ans.** An individual's attitudes may not always be exhibited through behaviour. One's actual behaviour may be contrary to one's attitude towards a particular topic. Attitudes may not always predict actual pattern of one's behaviour. Sometimes, it is behaviour that decides the attitude.

Psychologists have found that there would be consistency between attitudes and behaviour when

- The attitude is strong, and occupies a central place in the attitude system.
- The person is aware of her/his attitude.
- There is very little or no external pressure for the person to behave in a particular way.
- The person's behaviour is not being watched or evaluated by others.
- The person thinks that the behaviour would have a positive consequence and therefore, intends to engage in that behaviour.

In a time when Americans were said to be prejudiced against the Chinese, Richard La Piere, an American social psychologist, conducted the following study. He asked a Chinese couple to travel across the United States, and stay in different hotels. Only once during these occasions they were refused service by one of the hotels.

Sometime later, La Piere sent out questionnaires to managers of hotels and tourist homes in the same areas where the Chinese couple had travelled, asking them if they would give accommodation to Chinese guests. A very large percentage said that they would not do so. This response showed a negative attitude towards the Chinese, which was inconsistent with the positive behaviour that was actually shown towards the travelling Chinese couple. Thus, attitudes may not always predict actual pattern of one's behaviour.

**5. Differentiate between prejudice and stereotype.**

**Ans.** **Prejudices** are examples of attitudes towards a particular group. They are usually negative, and in many cases, may be based on stereotypes (the cognitive component) about the specific group.

Prejudice may also get translated into discrimination, the behavioural component, when people behave in a less positive way towards a particular target group compared to another group which they favour.

**A stereotype** is a cluster of ideas regarding the characteristics of a specific group. Stereotypes consist of undesirable characteristics about the target group, and they lead to negative attitudes or prejudices towards members of specific groups. Thus, prejudice may be based on stereotypes.

**6. Prejudice can exist without discrimination and *vice versa*. Comment.**

***Or*** **Describe the relationship between prejudice and discrimination.** **CBSE 2024 C**

**Ans.** Prejudices can exist without being expressed as discrimination. Similarly, discrimination can be shown without prejudice. Yet, the two go together very often.

- Wherever, prejudice and discrimination exist, conflicts are very likely to arise between groups within the same society.
- Our own society has witnessed many deplorable instances of discrimination, with and without prejudice based on gender, religion, community, caste, physical handicap, and illnesses such as AIDS.
- Moreover, in many cases discriminatory behaviour can be curbed by law. But, the cognitive and emotional components of prejudice are more difficult to change.

**7. Your friend eats too much junk food, how would you be able to bring about a change in her/his attitude towards food?**

**Ans.** I would use the concept of cognitive dissonance, as proposed by Leon Festinger, to bring about a change in their attitude towards food.

The basic idea is that the cognitive components of an attitude must be 'consonant' (opposite of 'dissonant') i.e. they should be logically in line with each other. If an individual finds that two cognitions in an attitude are dissonant, then one of them will be changed in the direction of consonance. Here the cognitions are

- Junk food is bad for health.
- They eat too much junk food.

Holding these two ideas or cognitions will make him feel that something is 'out of tune', or dissonant, in the attitude towards junk food. Therefore, one of these ideas will have to be changed, so that consonance can be attained. To resolve the dissonance, my friend must stop eating too much junk food. This would be the healthy, logical and sensible way of reducing dissonance.

# Exam Pattern Questions

## Objective Type Questions

### Multiple Choice Questions (MCQs)

**1.** **In 1957, Leon Festinger published his theory of**

(a) balance (b) cognitive dissonance
(c) attribution (d) None of these

**2.** **Cluster or ideas regarding the characteristics of a specific group is known as**

(a) progressive (b) stereotype
(c) belief (d) attitude

**3.** **Which of the following is a type of prejudice?**

(a) Attitude (b) Instinct
(c) Emotion (d) Motivation

**4.** **The feature which refers to the number of attributes within a broader attitude is**

(a) valence (b) multiplexity
(c) centrality (d) extremeness

**5.** **Students often develop a liking for a particular subject because of the teacher. This liking is because of**

(a) positive association between a teacher and a student
(b) negative association between a teacher and a student
(c) neutral association between a teacher and a student
(d) Both (a) and (b)

**6.** **Which one of the following is not a factor that will lead to attitude change?** CBSE 2023

(a) Message characteristics
(b) Environmental characteristics
(c) Source characteristics
(d) Target characteristics

**7.** **Which of the following is/are features of attitude?**

**I. Valency** **II. Extremeness**
**III. Complexity** **IV. Singularity**

**Codes**

(a) I and II (b) II and III
(c) I, II and III (d) III and IV

**8.** **Which of the following best defines social behaviour?**

(a) Spending time alone
(b) Engaging in behaviours influenced by the presence of others
(c) Following personal goals without considering others
(d) Ignoring the influence of society on one's actions

**9.** **Which component of attitude involves emotional responses?**

(a) Cognitive (b) Affective
(c) Behavioural (d) Valence

**10.** **The concept of cognitive dissonance was proposed by**

(a) Fritz Heider (b) Leon Festinger
(c) Stanley Milgram (d) Philip Zimbardo

**11.** **The group that is the target of prejudice is sometimes responsible for continuing the prejudice. The members of this target group may behave in a manner that proves the description to be true. This explains the concept of ………. .** CBSE SQP 2024

(a) kernal of truth (b) self-fulfilling prophecy
(c) scapegoating (d) ingroup bias

**12.** **A person dislikes a type of food, expresses negative opinion about it, and avoids it. Which components of the A-B-C model of attitudes are illustrated in this example?** CBSE 2025

(a) Affective and Cognitive
(b) Affective and Behavioural
(c) Cognitive and Behavioural
(d) Affective, Behavioural and Cognitive

**13.** **Mayank helped the victims of the flood-affected region unconditionally, as he understood that they were in need. This is an example of ………. .** CBSE SQP 2024

(a) social cognition (b) social facilitation
(c) pro-social behaviour (d) impression formation

**14.** **Which method of message transmission is likely to be most effective for creating a positive attitude towards Oral Rehydration Salts (ORS) for young children?** CBSE 2025

(a) Mass media advertisements
(b) Pamphlets and brochures
(c) Community social workers and doctors talking to people directly
(d) Radio announcements

## Assertion-Reason Questions

**Direction** (Q. Nos. 15-19) In the following question, a statement of Assertion (A) is followed by a statement of Reason (R). Mark the correct choice.

(a) Both A and R are true and R is the correct explanation of A.
(b) Both A and R are true, but R is not the correct explanation of A.
(c) A is true, but R is false.
(d) A is false, but R is true.

**15.** **Assertion** (A) We assign causes to the behaviour shown in specific social situations. This process is called Attribution.

**Reason** (R) We are also interested in why people behave in ways they do. Therefore, we assign a cause to a behaviour. **CBSE SQP 2022**

**16.** **Assertion** (A) Social psychologists focus on understanding the underlying causes of social behaviours.

**Reason** (R) Social behaviours are influenced by the actual, imagined or implied presence of others.

**17.** **Assertion** (A) The A-B-C model of attitude formation suggests that attitudes are solely formed based on beliefs.

**Reason** (R) Attitudes also contain affective and behavioural components along with beliefs.

**18.** **Assertion** (A) A person's attitude towards an object is only influenced by personal experiences.

**Reason** (R) Family, reference groups and media also shape attitudes by exposing individuals to social norms and values.

**19.** **Assertion** (A) Cognitive dissonance occurs when there is alignment between different cognitive components of an attitude.

**Reason** (R) Cognitive dissonance is the mental discomfort that arises from conflicting elements within an attitude.

# Answers

1. (b) cognitive dissonance
2. (b) stereotype
3. (a) attitude
4. (b) multiplexity
5. (a) positive association between a teacher and a student
6. (b) Environment characteristics
7. (c) I, II and III
8. (b) Engaging in behaviours influenced by the presence of others
9. (b) Affective
10. (b) Leon Festinger
11. (b) self-fulfilling prophecy
12. (d) Affective, Behavioural and Cognitive
13. (c) pro-social behaviour
14. (c) Community social workers and doctors talking to people directly
15. (a) Both A and R are true and R is the correct explanation of A.
16. (a) Both A and R are true and R is the correct explanation of A.
17. (c) A is true, but R is false.
18. (d) A is false, but R is true.
19. (c) A is true, but R is false.

# Subjective Questions

## Very Short Answer Type Questions

**1. Define the term attitude.**

**Ans.** An attitude is a state of the mind, a set of views, or thoughts, regarding some topic (called the 'attitude object'), which have an evaluative feature (positive, negative or neutral quality).

**2. What are values?**

**Ans.** Values are attitudes or beliefs that contain a 'should' or 'ought' aspect, such as moral or ethical values. Values are formed when a particular belief or attitude becomes an inseparable part of the person's outlook on life.

**3. What is valence?**

**Ans.** The valence of an attitude is positive or negative towards the attitude object. A neutral attitude would have neither positive nor negative valence.

**4. Explain the characteristics of an attitude in terms of complexity and centrality.** **CBSE Term II 2022**

**Ans.** **Complexity or Multiplicity** Refers to how many attitudes are there within a broader attitude. An attitude system is said to be simple if it contains only one or a few attitudes and complex if it is made up of many attitudes.

**Centrality** This refers to the role of a particular attitude in the attitude system. An attitude with greater centrality would influence the other attitudes in the system much more than non-central (or peripheral) attitudes.

**5. What do you know about centrality?**

**Ans.** This refers to the role of a particular attitude in the attitude system. An attitude with greater centrality would influence the other attitudes in the system much more than non-central (or peripheral) attitudes.

**6. Define learning attitudes by association.**

**Ans.** Students often develop a liking for a particular subject because of the positive qualities in that teacher. These positive qualities get linked to the subject that she/he teaches, and ultimately get expressed in the form of liking for the subject. In other words, a positive attitude towards the subject is learned through the positive association between a teacher and a student.

**7. Define attitude change.**

**Ans.** During and after the process of attitude formation attitudes may be changed and modified through various influences. Attitudes that are still in the formative stage, are much more likely to change compared to attitudes that have become firmly established, and have become a part of the individual's values.

**8. Define the role of message to bring attitude change.**

**Ans.** The message is the information that is presented in order to bring about an attitude change. Attitudes will change when the amount of information that is given about the topic is just enough, neither too much nor too little. Whether the message contains a rational or an emotional appeal, also makes a difference.

**9. What do you understand by prejudice?**

**Ans.** Prejudices are examples of attitudes towards a particular group. They are usually negative, and in many cases, may be based on stereotypes (the cognitive component) about the specific group.

**10. Define the term discrimination.**

**Ans.** Behaviour that shows a distinction being made between two or more persons, often on the basis of the person's membership of a particular group. In discrimination when people behave in a less positive way towards a particular target group compared to another group which they favour.

**11. Discuss the difference between a simple and a complex attitude system using the example of attitude towards health and well-being versus attitude towards a particular person.** CBSE 2025

**Ans.** A simple attitude system involves consistent beliefs, emotions and actions, like prioritising health. A complex attitude system includes conflicting elements, such as mixed feelings towards a person, showing inconsistency.

**12. Differentiate between congruent and incongruent changes in attitude.**

**Ans.** An attitude change may be congruent when it change in the same direction as the existing attitude. On the other hand, an attitude change may be incongruent when it may change in a direction opposite to the existing attitude.

**13. Assess and write the impact of family and school environment on attitude formation.** CBSE 2025

**Ans.** Family influences attitudes through values and behaviour modelling, while schools shape them by teaching societal norms, promoting interactions and encouraging critical thinking, which significantly impacts personality and beliefs

**14. Suppose you are a college student who wants to contribute towards the country's economy. Suggest a process that you will use to bring an attitude change amongst your peers towards buying only Indian goods to support the nation's economy.** CBSE 2023

**Ans.** To bring an attitudinal change among peers towards buying only Indian goods, Two-Step Concept can be used. According to the Two-Step Concept (SM Mohsin), attitude change takes place in the form of two steps

(i) The target of change (person whose attitude is to be changed) identifies with the source (person through whose influence the attitude is to be changed).

(ii) The source himself/herself shows an attitude change, by actually changing him/her behaviour towards the attitude object. Observing the source's changed attitude and behaviour, the target also shows an attitude change through behaviour.

**15. Explain any two factors that influence attitude formation.** CBSE SQP Term II 2021

**Ans.** The factors that influence attitude formation are as follows

(i) **Reference Groups** It indicates to an individual the norms regarding acceptable behaviour and ways of thinking reflecting learning of cultural norms.

(ii) **Personal Experiences** Many attitudes are formed through direct personal experiences which bring about a drastic change in our attitude towards people and our own life.

**16. Explain any two components of attitudes.** CBSE SQP Term II 2021

**Ans.** There are three components of attitudes as referred to A-B-C components i.e. Affective-Behavioural and Cognitive.

**'A' Component** You feel sad and angry when you see tree being cut down. These aspects reflect the affective (emotional) or 'A' component.

**'B' Component** Suppose you participate in the tree plantation campaign. These aspects shows the behaviourial or 'B' component towards a 'green environment'.

## Short Answer Type Questions

**1. Elaborate the A-B-C component of attitude.**

**Ans.** An attitude is a state of the mind, a set of views, or thoughts, regarding some topic (called the 'attitude object'), which have an evaluative feature (positive, negative or neutral quality).

It is accompanied by an emotional component and a tendency to act in a particular way with regard to the attitude object. If our views are not merely thoughts, but also have emotional and action components, then these views exemplify of attitudes.

The thought component is referred to as the cognitive aspect, the emotional component is known as the affective aspect, and the tendency to act is called the Behavioural (or conative) aspect. These three aspects have been referred to as the A-B-C components (Affective- Behavioural Cognitive components) of attitude.

**2. Discuss the two step concept for attitude change.**

**Ans.** It was proposed by SM Mohsin, an Indian psychologist. According to him, attitude change takes place in the form of two steps

(i) In the first step, the target of change identifies with the source. The target is the person whose attitude is to be changed. The source is the person through whose influence the change is to take place. Identification means that the target has liking and regard for the source.

The source must also have a positive attitude towards the target, and the regard and attraction becomes mutual.

(ii) In the second step, the source herself/himself shows an attitude change, by actually changing her/his behaviour towards the attitude object. Observing the source's changed attitude and behaviour, the target also shows an attitude change through behaviour. This is a kind of imitation or observational learning.

**3. Distinguish between belief and values.**

**Ans.** Attitudes must be distinguished from two other closely related concepts, namely, beliefs and values. Beliefs refer to the cognitive component of attitudes and form the ground on which attitudes stand, such as belief in God or belief in democracy as a political ideology.

Values are attitudes or beliefs that contain a 'should' or 'ought' aspect, such as moral or ethical values. Values are formed when a particular belief or attitude becomes an inseparable part of the person's outlook on life. Consequently, values are difficult to change.

**4. Rakesh regularly takes pan masala. He knows that it causes mouth cancer which is fatal. Explain the process Rakesh wants to take for changing his attitude towards pan masala.** **Competency Based Que.**

**Ans.** Rakesh thinks about the two ideas, viz,

(i) **Cognition I** Pan mansala causes mouth cancer which is fatal.

(ii) **Cognition II** He eats pan masala.

These two ideas or cognitions make Rakesh feels that something is 'out of tune' or dissonant in the attitude towards pan masala.

Cognitive dissonance is the state of an attitude system in which two congitive elements are logically contradictory or inconsistent.

Thus, one of these ideas will have to be changed, so that consonance (opposite of dissonance) can be attained. In order to remove or reduce the dissonance, Rakesh will stop eating pan masala. This would be the healty, logical and sensible way of reducing dissonance.

**5. "Advertisers benefit most from such people." Explain which type of people are prone to attitude change.**

**Ans.** People with strong prejudices are less prone to any attitude change than those who do not hold strong prejudices. Persons who have a low self-esteem, and do not have sufficient confidence in themselves, change their attitudes more easily than those who are high on self-esteem.

More intelligent people may change their attitudes less easily than those with lower intelligence. However, sometimes more intelligent persons change their attitudes more willingly than less intelligent ones, because they base their attitude on more information and thinking.

**6. Discuss how media can influence the attitude change.**

**Ans.** Technological advances in recent times have made audio-visual media and the internet very powerful sources of information that lead to attitude formation and change. In addition, school level textbooks also influence attitude formation.

These sources first strengthen the cognitive and affective components of attitudes, and subsequently may also affect the behavioural component. The media can exert both good and bad influences on attitudes. On one hand, the media and internet make people better informed than other modes of communication. On the other hand, there may be no check on the nature of information being provided.

**7. "Attitude are learned through one's own experience." Critically examine this statement.**

**Ans.** Attitudes are formed as we interact with others. However, there are specific conditions that lead to the formation of specific attitudes. In general, attitudes are learned through one's own experiences and through interaction with others.

There are a few research studies that show some sort of inborn aspect of attitudes, but such genetic factors influence attitudes only indirectly, along with learning. Therefore, most social psychologists have focused on the conditions which lead to the learning of attitudes.

**8. You have been given the responsibility of changing the attitude of your school mates towards food wastages. Identify any three factors that you need to keep in mind while bringing in this attitude change and explain it with the help of an example.**

**Ans.** For the change of attitude of my school mates towards food wastage I must identify the following factors

(i) I must observe how much food in being wasted by them daily.

(ii) I need to identify the preference of the foods of my school mates, i.e. whether they prefer regular meal like Rajma-Chawal or junk foods like burger, pasta etc.

(iii) With the help of teacher I will arrange a seminar on why food in not to be wasted and nutritious food should be taken. The message of "Nutritious food only can give health and energy" can bring a significant changes in the attitude of my school mates. In this way I can change the attitude of my school mates towards food wastages.

**9. A person eats pan masala. However, he reads on the packet of pan masala that it causes mouth cancer which is fatal. What do you think how does it will affect his attitude change?**

**Ans.** Holding the two ideas or cognitions i.e., eating pan masala and it causes mouth cancer will make the person feel that something is 'out of tune', or dissonant, in the attitude towards pan masala. Therefore, one of these ideas will have to be changed, so that consonance can be attained. In the example given above, in order to remove or reduce the dissonance, the person will stop eating pan masala. This would be the healthy, logical and sensible way of reducing dissonance and to bring about attitude change.

**10. Anshu feels that assertive and successful women might become too powerful and neglect their family responsibilities. Explain the factors that will help in changing Anshu's attitude towards assertive and successful women.** **CBSE SQP Term II 2021**

*Or* **State the factors that influence attitude change.**

**Ans.** The major factors that help in changing Anshu's attitude towards assertive and successful women are as follows

- **Characteristics of the Existing Attitude** All four features (valence, extremeness, simplicity and centrality) of attitudes determine attitude change. In general, positive attitudes are easier to change than negative attitudes. Simple attitudes are easier to change than multiple attitudes. An attitude change may be congruent (favourable) or incongruent (not favourable).
- **Source Characteristics** Source credibility and attractiveness are two features that affect attitude change. Attitudes are more likely to change when the message comes from a highly credible source rather than from a low-credible source.
- **Message Characteristics** The message is the information that is presented in order to bring about an attitude change. Attitudes will change when the amount of information that is given about the topic is just enough, neither too much nor too little.
- The message contains emotional appeal, motives and moods of it also play significant role. Face-to-face transmission of the message is usually more effective than indirect transmission i.e. through letters and pamphlets or even through mass media.
- **Target Characteristics** Qualities of the target, such as persuasibility, strong prejudices, self-esteem and intelligence influence the likelihood and extent of attitude change.

  People who have a more open and flexible personality, change more easily. People with strong preconceptions are less prone or inclined to any attitude change. More intelligent people may change their attitudes less easily than those with lower intelligence.

**11. An attitude towards recycling and reuse needs to be encouraged to conserve the environment. Examine the factors that will influence attitude change towards this.** **CBSE SQP 2022**

**Ans.** Attitude change towards recycling and reuse is influenced by several factors

- **Characteristics of the Existing Attitude** Simpler, more positive attitudes are easier to change. The existing attitude's valence (favourable or unfavourable) and extremeness play a role. A positive, simple attitude towards recycling is easier to shift.
- **Source Characteristics** Credible and attractive sources are more persuasive. Messages from environmental experts or well-known figures can motivate attitude changes.
- **Message Characteristics** The information should be balanced–neither too much nor too little. Emotional appeals and face-to-face communication are more effective in fostering attitude change.
- **Target Characteristics** Individuals with open, flexible personalities and lower prejudices are more likely to adopt new attitudes. Intelligence and self-esteem can also impact the ease with which one changes their attitude.

**12. Discuss the four significant features of attitude.**

**Ans.** Four significant features of attitudes are

(i) **Valence (Positivity or Negativity)** The valence of an attitude tells us whether an attitude is positive or negative towards the attitude object. A neutral attitude would have neither positive nor negative valence.

(ii) **Extremeness** The extremeness of an attitude indicates how positive or negative an attitude is.

They are only in the opposite directions (valence). A neutral attitude is lowest on extremeness.

(iii) **Simplicity or Complexity (Multiplicity)** This feature refers to how many attitudes are there within a broader attitude.

In case of various topics, such as health and world peace, people hold many attitudes instead of single attitude. An attitude system is said to be simple if it contains only one or a few attitudes and complex if it is made up of many attitudes.

(iv) **Centrality** This refers to the role of a particular attitude in the attitude system. An attitude with greater centrality would influence the other attitudes in the system much more than non-central (or peripheral) attitudes.

**13. Discuss the concept of balance in attitude change.**

**Ans.** The concept of balance was proposed by Fritz Heider. It is also described in the form of the 'P-O-X' triangle, which represents the relationships between three aspects or components of the attitude.

P is the person whose attitude is being studied, O is another person and X is the topic being studied (attitude object). It is also possible that all three are persons.

An attitude changes if there is a state of imbalance between the P-O attitude, O-X attitude, and P-X attitude because imbalance is logically uncomfortable.

Therefore, the attitude changes in the direction of balance. Imbalance is found when all three sides of the P-O-X triangle are negative, or two sides are positive, and one side is negative.

Balance occurs when all three sides are positive, or two sides are negative and one side is positive.

**14. Discuss cognitive dissonance component in attitude change process.**

**Ans.** Cognitive dissonance was proposed by Leon Festinger. It emphasises that the cognitive components of an attitude must be 'consonant' (opposite of dissonant) i.e. they should be logically in line with each other.

Festinger and Carlsmith, two social psychologists, conducted an experiment that showed the working of cognitive dissonance. Both balance and cognitive dissonance are examples of cognitive consistency.

Cognitive consistency means that two components, aspects or elements of the attitude or attitude system, must be in the same direction. Each element should logically fall in line with other elements.

If this does not happen, then the person experiences a kind of mental discomfort. In such a state, some aspect in the attitude system changes in the direction of consistency, because our cognitive system requires logical consistency.

**15. Discuss the attitude-behaviour relationship.**

**Ans.** An individual's attitudes may not always be exhibited through behaviour. One's actual behaviour may be contrary to one's attitude towards a particular topic. Attitudes may not always predict actual pattern of one's behaviour. Sometimes, it is behaviour that decides the attitude. Psychologists have found that there would be consistency between attitudes and behaviour when

- The attitude is strong and occupies a central place in the attitude system.
- The person is aware of her/his attitude.
- There is very little or no external pressure for the person to behave in a particular way.
- The person's behaviour is not being watched or evaluated by others.
- The person thinks that the behaviour would have a positive consequence and therefore, intends to engage in that behaviour.

**16. State the strategies for overcoming prejudice.**

**Ans.** The first step in handling prejudice is to know about its causes or sources. Thus, the strategies for handling prejudice would be effective if they aim at

- Minimising opportunities for learning prejudices.
- Changing such attitudes.
- De-emphasising a narrow social identity based on the ingroup.
- Discouraging the tendency towards self-fulfilling prophecy among the victims of prejudice.

These goals can be accomplished through

- Education and information dissemination, for correcting stereotypes related to specific target groups, and tackling the problem of a strong ingroup bias.
- Increasing intergroup contact allows for direct communication, removal of mistrust between the groups, and even discovery of positive qualities in the outgroup.These strategies are successful only if
  (a) The two groups meet in a cooperative rather than competitive context.
  (b) Close interactions between the groups helps them to know each other better.
  (c) The two groups are not different in power or status.
- Highlighting individual identity rather than group identity, which weaken the importance of group (both ingroup and outgroup) as a basis of evaluating the other person.

**17. How do you explain prejudice and discrimination in the genocide committed by the Nazis in Germany against the Jewish People?**

**Ans.** Prejudices are examples of attitudes towards a particular group. These are usually negative in nature. Sometimes these are based on stereotypes. Stereotype is an overgeneralised and unverified prototype about a particular group. It is a cluster of ideas regarding the characteristics of a specific group. All members belonging to this group are assumed to possesses these characteristics.

In Nazi Germany Jews remained the worst sufferers. Jews had been stereotyped as killers of Christ and money lenders. Jews lived in separately marked areas called 'ghettos'. They were persecuted through periodic organised violence and expulsion from the land. In Nazism the Jews were terrorised, pauperised and segregated. Large scale genocide was committed by the Nazis against the Jews.

This is an extreme example of how prejudice can lead to hatred, discrimination and mass killing of innocent people. The cognitive component of prejudice is accompanied by dislike or hatred generally. Thus, prejudice may transformed into discrimination. Here, people behave in a less positive way toward a particular group than others. Exactly this was happened in Nazi Germany where prejudice and discrimination led to mass killings of innocent Jewish people.

**18. Mother Teresa believed that she had a mission to fulfill and did what came natural to her, loving others and serving them. Identify the trait being referred to here by Gordon Allport and how it affects a person's behaviour. Distinguish it from other traits given by him.** **CBSE SQP 2022**

**Ans.** Allport thinks that the way a person reacts to given situations depends on his traits, although people sharing the same traits might express them in different way. Any variation in trait may result a different response to the same situation. The trait here referred is cardinal traits.

Cardinal Traits are highly generalised in nature. They indicate the goal around which a person's entire life seems to revolve. Mahatma Gandhi's non-violence and Hitler's Nazism are examples of cardinal traits. Such traits often get associated with the name of the person so strongly that they derive such identities as the 'Gandhian' or 'Hitlerian' trait.

Other traits mentioned by Allport are as follows

- **Central Traits** These are less broad in effect but still quite generalised in nature. These traits (e.g. warm, sincere, diligent, etc) are often used in writing a testimonial or job recommendation for a person.
- **Secondary Traits** These are the least generalised characteristics of a person .Traits such as 'likes mangoes' or 'prefers ethnic clothes' are examples of secondary traits. Quite often we see people getting themselves photographed while helping.

**19. Quite often we see people getting themselves photographed while helping others or even when they are offering donations to the needy. Can we identify the attitudes of these people through their behaviour. When would there be consistency between attitude and behaviour ? Explain.** **CBSE Term II 2022**

**Ans.** Psychologists have found that there would be consistency between attitudes and behaviour when

- the attitude is strong and occupies a central place in the attitude system.
- the person is aware of her/his attitude.
- there is very little or no external pressure for the person to behave in a particular way.
- the person's behaviour is not being watched or evaluated by others.
- the person thinks that the behaviour would have a positive consequence and therefore, intends to engage in that behaviour.

## Long Answer Type Questions

**1. What is attitude? Explain how attitudes are formed.**

**Ans.** An attitude is a state of the mind, a set of views or thoughts, regarding some topic (called the 'attitude object'), which have an evaluative feature (positive, negative or neutral quality).

The processes and conditions of learning may be different, resulting in varying attitudes among people.

- **Learning Attitudes by Association** A positive attitude towards a subject is learned through the positive association between a teacher and a student.
- **Learning Attitudes by Being Rewarded or Punished** If an individual is praised for showing a particular attitude, they are more likely to develop and reinforce that attitude.
- **Learning Attitudes through Modelling** (observing others) We learn attitudes by observing others being rewarded or punished for expressing thoughts or showing behaviour of a particular kind towards the attitude object.
- **Learning Attitudes through Group or Cultural Norms** We learn attitudes through the norms of our group or culture. Norms are unwritten rules about behaviour that everyone is supposed to show under specific circumstances. Over time, these norms become integrated into our social cognition as attitudes.

- **Learning through Exposure to Information** Many attitudes are learned in a social context but not necessarily in the physical presence of others. Today, with the huge amount of information that is being provided through various media, both positive and negative attitudes are being formed.

**2. State the factors that lead to the formation of attitudes. Explain the process of attitude change by giving examples from daily life.**

**Ans. Factors that Influence Attitude Formation are**

(i) **Family and School Environment** Family and school environments play a crucial role in shaping attitudes. Through rewards, punishments and modelling, individuals learn attitudes from both. For example, children often mirror the values and behaviours of their parents or teachers.

(ii) **Reference Groups** Reference groups, such as peer groups, social or cultural groups, help individuals understand acceptable behaviours and beliefs. For instance, adolescents are highly influenced by their peer group in shaping attitudes towards politics or social issues.

(iii) **Personal Experiences** Personal experiences significantly impact attitude formation. A dramatic change in experience can lead to a shift in attitude. For example, a driver who survived a deadly accident may change his profession and become a community leader to help others.

(iv) **Media-related Influences** Media, including social platforms and television, are powerful in shaping attitudes. They affect individuals' cognitive, emotional and behavioural components of attitudes. For instance, media campaigns can change societal attitudes towards smoking or environmental conservation.

**Attitude Change Process**

Attitude change occurs through various processes, such as persuasion, exposure to new experiences and the influence of new information. For example, someone who has a negative attitude toward a specific culture may change their view after learning about its history and contributions to society, thus shifting their perception based on new knowledge and experiences.

**3. Explain prejudice and discrimination with examples also. Discuss any two sources of prejudices.**

**Ans** Prejudice refers to negative attitudes or beliefs about a particular group, often based on stereotypes. These stereotypes involve generalised ideas about the characteristics of a group, which lead to unfair attitudes toward its members. For instance, racial prejudice often stems from the belief that certain races possess undesirable traits. Discrimination, on the other hand, involves actions that treat people unfairly based on such prejudices. While prejudice can exist without discrimination, the two often go hand in hand, leading to conflict and societal divisions.

An example of prejudice leading to discrimination is the Holocaust, where Nazi Germany's prejudice against Jewish people resulted in systematic discrimination, persecution and genocide. Similarly, caste-based discrimination in India has its roots in longstanding prejudices against certain lower castes.

Two sources of prejudice are

(i) **Learning** Prejudices can be learned through socialisation within family, media or peer groups. For example, children may adopt prejudiced attitudes by observing discriminatory behaviour at home or in their communities.

(ii) **Strong Social Identity and Ingroup Bias** Individuals with a strong attachment to their own group often develop negative attitudes towards others to maintain group identity. This ingroup favouritism can lead to prejudice against outgroups, reinforcing division and discrimination.

Addressing prejudice requires education, intergroup contact and highlighting individual identity over group affiliation.

**4. A driver in the army went through a certain experience that transformed his life. On one mission, he narrowly escaped death although all his companions got killed. Wondering about the purpose of his own life, he gave up his job in the army, returned to his native village in Maharashtra, and worked actively as a community leader. Identify the factor that affected the attitude formation in army driver. Also, give a brief about other factors that shapes the attitude formation.**

**Ans.** In the given case study, army driver transformed his life through a purely personal experience when he narrowly escaped death. This individual evolved a strong positive attitude towards community upliftment and evolved as a community leader. As a community leader, his efforts completely changed the face of his village. Many attitudes are formed, not in the family environment or through reference groups, but through direct personal experiences which bring about a drastic change in our attitude towards people and our own life as it happened in this case.

Other factors that shape the attitude formation are as follows

- **Family and School Environment** In the early years of life, parents and other family members play a significant role in shaping attitude formation. Later, the school environment becomes an important background for attitude formation.
  Learning of attitudes within the family and school usually takes place by association, through rewards and punishments, and through modelling.
- **Reference Groups** Reference groups indicate to an individual the norms regarding acceptable behaviour and ways of thinking. Thus, they reflect learning of attitudes through group or cultural norms.

- **Media-Related Influences** Technological advances in recent times have made audio-visual media and the Internet very powerful sources of information that lead to attitude formation and change.

## Case Based Questions

**1. Read the case and answer the questions that follow.**

Mr. Anshul has a positive attitude towards dowry. He is planning to get his son married to the daughter of Mr. Hemant who has a negative attitude towards dowry. If Mr. Hemant has a positive attitude towards Mr. Anshul, the situation is considered as unbalanced.

(i) **Identify the concept of social attitude and cognition that operates in this case. Also discuss it.**

(ii) **Identify some of the possible outcomes in the given case.**

**Ans.** (i) The concept of social attitude and cognition that operates in this case is balance.

The concept of balance was proposed by Fritz Heider. It is also described in the form of the P-O-X triangle, which represents the relationships between three aspects or components of the attitude that are

- P is the person whose attitude is being studied.
- O is another person.
- X is the topic towards which the attitude is being studied (attitude object).

(ii) Some possible outcomes in the given passage can be

- Mr. Anshul will start disliking dowry
- Mr. Hemant will start liking dowry
- Mr. Hemant will start disliking Mr. Anshul

**2. Read the case and answer the questions that follow.**

Ankita reads in the newspapers that a particular soft drink that she enjoys is extremely harmful. But Ankita sees that her favourite sportsperson has been advertising the same soft drink. She has identified herself with the sportsperson, and would like to imitate him. Now, suppose the sportsperson wishes to change people's attitude towards this soft drink from positive to negative. The sportsperson must first show positive feelings for his fans, and then actually change his own habit of consuming that soft drink perhaps by substituting it with a health drink. If the sportsperson actually changes his behaviour, it is very likely that now Ankita will also change her attitude and behaviour, and stop consuming the harmful soft drink.

(i) **What should the sportsperson do to help change Ankita's attitude towards the soft drink?**

(ii) **How might Ankita's identification with the sportsperson influence her behaviour?**

**Ans.** (i) The sportsperson should first express positive feelings for his fans and then change his own behaviour by substituting the harmful soft drink with a health drink. This action could encourage Ankita to follow his lead and stop consuming the harmful beverage.

(ii) Ankita's identification with the sportsperson creates a desire to imitate his actions. If he changes his behaviour by avoiding the harmful soft drink, Ankita is likely to be influenced to do the same, shifting her attitude and behaviour.

**3. Read the case and answer the questions that follow.** **CBSE SQP 2024**

Sophia Duleep Singh was the daughter of Maharaja Duleep Singh- the last Sikh emperor of Punjab. Sophia was a long-time supporter of the Women's Suffrage Movement (right to vote) and a leading campaigner for changing attitudes about women's rights in Britain. However, she remains a little-known figure. In 1910, she was part of a delegation of 300 suffragettes who marched towards the Parliament in London. The Prime Minister refused to meet the women and the demonstration turned violent as policemen and men in the crowd outside the building beat them. Many of the demonstrators were seriously injured and the day came to be called Black Friday in the UK. Sophia was among the 119 women who were arrested. Sophia transcended her heritage to devote herself to battling injustice and inequality. Her main causes were the struggle for Indian Independence, the welfare of Indian soldiers in the First World War and above all the fight for female suffrage. Princess Sophia supported Indians, particularly women, throughout her life.

(i) **"Her causes were the struggle for Indian independence, the welfare of Indian soldiers in the First World War and above all the fight for female suffrage". All of these attitudes were present without a broader attitude, i.e. the attitude against injustice and inequality. Explain the features specified here.**

(ii) **The characteristics of the existing attitude (towards women's right to vote) influence the attitude change. To what extent could these have helped Sophia bring about the change in attitude towards women's right to vote?**

**Ans.** (i) The feature specified is the presence of a broader attitude against injustice and inequality, encompassing various specific causes such as Indian independence, the welfare of Indian soldiers and female suffrage.

(ii) Sophia's existing attitude against injustice and inequality likely provided her with the determination, passion and resilience needed to advocate for women's right to vote, despite facing opposition and adversity.

## SELF ASSESSMENT TEST

### Objective Type Questions

**1.** The thought component is referred to as

(a) the cognitive aspect (b) the affective aspect (c) the behavioural aspect (d) None of these

**2.** The tendency to act is known as

(a) the Cognitive aspect (b) the Behavioural aspect (c) the Affective aspect (d) None of these

**3.** Which is a significant feature of attitudes?

(a) Valence (b) Extremeness (c) Simplicity (d) All of these

**4.** Which of the following indicates how positive or negative an attitude is?

(a) Centrality (b) Valence (c) Extremeness (d) All of these

**5.** **Assertion** (A) Attitude extremeness refers to how simple or complex an attitude is within a broader attitude system.

**Reason** (R) Extremeness measures the level of positive or negative intensity in an attitude.

(a) Both A and R are true and R is the correct explanation for A.

(b) Both A and R are true, but R is not the correct explanation for A.

(c) A is false, but R is true.

(d) A is true, but R is false.

### Very Short Answer Type Questions

**1.** Why values are difficult to change?

**2.** Define discrimination.

### Short Answer Type Questions

**1.** Define the various types of attitude.

**2.** What are the causes of emergence of prejudice?

**3.** Briefly elaborate the process of impression formation.

**4.** State the sources of prejudice.

**5.** Explain P-O-X triangle in attitude change.

### Long Answer Type Questions

**1.** What are the important process of attitude change?

**2.** Discuss the characteristics of prejudice.

### Case Based Questions

**Read the case and answer the questions that follow.**

Adults who are planning to buy a laptop are more convinced by a computer engineer who points out the special features of a particular brand of laptop.

On the other hand, if the buyers are school children, they may be convinced more by another school child advertising a laptop.

In the case of some products such as cars, sales may increase if they are publicised, not necessarily by experts, but by popular public figures.

(i) Why are adults more convinced by a computer engineer's opinion when buying a laptop?

(ii) What influences school children more when it comes to buying a laptop?

07

CHAPTER

A group may be defined is an organised system of two or more interdependent individuals who share common motives and norms to guide member behaviour. Groups provide essential support and comfort, contributing to individual growth.

**YOUR STUDY GOALS**

7.1 Nature and Formation of Groups
7.2 Types of Groups
7.3 Influence of Group on Individual Behaviour

**YOUR PRACTICE GOAL**

- Objective Type Questions (15 Qs ; MCQs, A-R)
- Subjective Questions (21 VSAs, 16 SAs, 2 LAs, 2 Case Based)

# Social Influence and Group Processes

## 7.1 Nature and Formation of Groups

- Groups play a significant role in our lives by providing essential support and fostering growth.
- Groups differ from casual collections of people, such as spectators at a cricket match, as these gatherings lack **interdependence**[1], defined roles and mutual expectations.
- Examples of groups include families, classes and playgroups, where members interact, share responsibilities and rely on each other.
- A group is an organised system of two or more individuals who are interdependent, share common motives, have structured role relationships and follow norms regulating member behaviour.

### Characteristics of Group

Groups have the following salient characteristics

- Groups consist of two or more individuals who identify as belonging to the group, giving it a unique identity.
- Group members share common motives and goals, working either towards a goal or away from threats.
- Members are interdependent, meaning one person's actions impact the entire group (e.g. a fielder dropping a catch in cricket affects the team).

1 **Interdependence** The reliance of group members on each other to achieve common goals.

- Individuals join groups to satisfy personal needs and through this association, they influence one another.
- Group members interact, either directly or indirectly and follow structured roles and norms for behaviour and expected conduct.

Groups can be differentiated from other collections of people, such as

### Crowd

- A crowd is a collection of people gathered by chance.
- Their behaviour is often irrational and there is no interdependence among members.
- For example, if you are walking on the road and an accident occurs, a large number of people may gather, forming a crowd. There is no feeling of belongingness or interdependence among crowd members.

### Teams

- Teams are special kinds of groups where members often possess complementary skills and are committed to a common goal or purpose.
- Team members are mutually accountable for their activities.
- In teams, positive synergy (teamwork) is achieved through the coordinated efforts of members.

### Audience

- An audience is a collection of people assembled for a special purpose, such as watching a cricket match or a movie.
- Generally, audiences are passive; but can become frenzied, turning into mobs.
- Mob behaviour is characterised by homogeneity of thought and behaviour, as well as impulsivity.

### Differences between Groups and Teams

- In groups, performance depends on individual contributions.
- In teams, both individual contributions and teamwork matters. However, in teams, although there is a leader, members hold themselves responsible.
- In groups, the leader holds responsibility for the work.

## Reasons of Joining Groups

People join groups to satisfy a range of needs. Following are reasons to join groups

### Security

- Security groups help reduce the feeling of insecurity experienced when individuals are alone, providing comfort and protection.
- This collective presence fosters a supportive environment, enhancing emotional well-being makes individuals feel stronger.
- This increased sense of strength makes them less vulnerable to perceived threats.

### Status

- When individuals belong to a group perceived as important by others, they experience recognition and validation.
- This recognition leads to a heightened sense of power and self-worth among the group members.
- For instance, when a school wins an inter-institutional debate competition, students feel a sense of pride in their affiliation with the victorious group.

- This pride contributes to their belief that they are better than others, reinforcing their self-esteem and group identity.

### Self-esteem

- Groups contribute to feelings of self-worth among their members and help establish a positive social identity.
- Membership in prestigious groups enhances one's self-concept.

### Satisfaction of One's Psychological and Social Needs

- Groups satisfy individual's social and psychological needs.
- They provide a sense of belongingness, allowing members to feel connected to others.
- They also fulfill the need for love and emotional support within a community.

### Goal Achievement

- Groups help achieve goals that cannot be attained individually.
- There is power in the majority.

### Provide Knowledge and Information

- Group membership offers access to knowledge and information that broadens individual perspectives.
- Individuals may lack comprehensive information on certain topics when acting alone.
- Being part of a group allows members to share insights, experiences and expertise.
- Groups serve as a resource for learning, where members can exchange ideas and information.
- This collective knowledge deepens individuals understanding of various subjects.
- Ultimately, groups enhance awareness and inform their decision-making processes.

## Group Formation

- Groups are formed through interactions between people.
- This interaction is facilitated by the following conditions

### 1. Proximity

- **Proximity**[2] plays a significant role in group formation, as it leads to repeated interactions among individuals.
- These repeated interactions provide opportunities to get to know one another better.
- Through these interactions, individuals can learn about each other's interests and attitudes.
- Common interests and shared attitudes increase the level of liking and attention among many group members.
- Additionally, similar backgrounds can strengthen the bonds within the group.
- Overall, the combination of common interests, attitudes and backgrounds enhances the connection among group members.

### 2. Similarity

- Similarity is a key in group formation, as prolonged exposure helps evaluate commonalities.
- People generally prefer consistency in their relationships, which encourages them to connect with those who share similar traits or interests.
- Liking develops more readily when there is consistency between individuals.

---

2 **Proximity** The physical closeness or distance between group members, influencing interaction.

- For instance, if I enjoy playing football and one of my batchmates shares the same interest, it increases the likelihood that we will become friends.
- Similarity in interests, such as playing football, serves as a strong basis for establishing a friendship.
- Therefore, similarity plays a significant role in building connections and forming groups.

### 3. Common Motives and Goals

- Common motives and goals are essential for group formation, as they bring individuals together.
- When people share similar objectives, they can collaborate effectively to facilitate goal attainment.
- For instance, if I have a desire to teach children in a slum area who cannot attend school, this motive can drive me to form a group.
- By gathering like-minded friends passionate about education, can collectively work towards goal of teaching these children.
- Through collaboration, I can achieve my objective more effectively with the support and resources provided by others in the group.
- This illustrates how common motives and goals can unite individuals and enhance their ability to accomplish shared aspirations.

## Stages of Group Formation

Tuckman suggested that groups pass through five developmental sequences. These are as follows

**1. Forming**

- The forming stage occurs when group members meet for the first time.
- During this initial interaction, there is uncertainity regarding the achievement of group goals.
- Individuals attempt to get to know one another, assessing their compatibility and whether they will fit into the group.
- This stage is characterised by both excitement and apprehension as members learn about each other's interests and backgrounds while simultaneously feeling nervous about the new dynamics.
- The forming stage sets the foundation for future interactions and relationships within the group.

**2. Storming**

- After the forming stage, there is a stage of intragroup conflict[3] which is referred to as Storming.
- In this stage, there is conflict among members about targets, processes, performance and control of resources.
- When this stage is complete, some sort of hierarchy of leadership in the group develops.

**3. Norming**

- The storming stage is followed by another stage known as Norming, where group members develop norms related to group behaviour.
- These norms leads to the development of a positive group identity.

**4. Performing**

- By this stage, the structure of the group has evolved and is accepted and the group focuses on achieving its goal.
- For some groups, this may be the last stage of group development.

**5. Adjourning**

- In this stage, the group may be disbanded once its function is complete.
- However, not all groups proceed from one stage to the next in the same manner.

3 **Conflict** Disagreements or clashes that occur within a group, often about goals, processes or roles.

## Group Structure

- During the process of group formation, groups develop a structure as members interact.
- Over time, this interaction reveals regularities in the distribution of tasks to be performed.
- Responsibilities are assigned to members based on their roles within the group.
- The structure also reflects the prestige or relative status of members in relation to one another.

Four important elements of group structure are

### 1. Roles

- Roles are socially defined expectations that individuals must fulfill in a given situation.
- They refer to the typical behaviour that depicts a person in a specific social context.
- Every individual plays a role within their social environment.
- For example, as a daughter or son, one is expected to respect elders, and be responsible for their studies.
- There are certain role expectations that outline the behaviours expected of someone in a particular role.

### 2. Norms

- Norms are the expected standards of behaviour and beliefs within a group.
- They are established, agreed upon and enforced by group members.
- For example, every family has norms that guide the behaviour of its members.
- These norms represent the family's views of the world and influence how members interact with one another.

### 3. Status

- Status refers to the relative social position assigned to group members by others.
- Status can be either ascribed or achieved.
- Ascribed status is given based on factors such as seniority.
- Achieved status is obtained through personal accomplishments, expertise or hard work.
- For example, the captain of a cricket team holds a higher status compared to other team members but all players are equally important for the team's success.

### 4. Cohesiveness

- Cohesiveness refers to the togetherness, binding or mutual attraction among group members.
- As a group becomes more cohesive, its members start to think, feel and act as a social unit.
- In highly cohesive groups, members feel like part of a collective rather than isolated individuals.
- Members of a highly cohesive group have a greater desire to remain in the group compared to those in low cohesive groups.
- Cohesiveness embodies the team spirit, often described as the 'we feeling' or a sense of belongingness to the group.
- Psychologists suggest that **groupthink**[4] can occur because of extreme cohesiveness.

---

4 **Groupthink** A phenomenon where the desire for consensus within a group leads to irrational decision-making.

### Group Think

- Irving Janis discovered a process known as 'groupthink', in which a group prioritises its concern for unanimity.
- This concern for consensus can lead the group to override the motivation to realistically appraise different courses of action.
- As a result, groupthink creates a tendency for decision-makers to make irrational and uncritical decisions.
- Groupthink gives the appearance of consensus or unanimous agreement within a group.
- In this state, all members agree upon a particular decision and no one expresses dissenting opinions, as doing so may threaten the cohesion of the group.
- There are several ways to prevent groupthink, which include
  - Encouraging and rewarding critical thinking among group members.
  - Encouraging groups to present alternative courses of action to consider different perspectives.
  - Inviting outside experts to evaluate the group's decisions to gain fresh insights.
  - Encouraging members to seek feedback from trusted individuals outside the group for a more balanced view.

### Quick Test 1

1. What term is used to describe socially defined expectations within a group?
2. What are the stages of group formation as per Tuckman?
3. What does cohesiveness in a group indicate?
4. What motivates individuals to join a group?
5. What does the term 'norms' refer to in group behaviour?

## 7.2 Types of Groups

- Groups can vary in numerous respects, leading to different classifications.
- Some groups have many members, such as a country.
- Other groups are small in size, like a family.
- Certain groups are short-lived, such as a committee formed for a specific purpose.
- In contrast, some groups remain together for many years, like religious organisations.
- Some groups are highly organised, exemplified by the army or police forces.
- Conversely, other groups are informally organised, such as spectators at a sports match.

Major types of groups are enumerated below

### Primary and Secondary Groups

- Primary groups are pre-existing formations that are usually assigned to the individual, such as family, caste and religion.
- In a primary group, members interact face-to-face and maintain close physical proximity.
- These groups share warm emotional bonds, fostering strong relationships among members.
- Primary groups are crucial to an individual's functioning, playing a significant role in shaping their values and ideals during early development.
- In primary groups, boundaries are less permeable, meaning that members do not choose their membership.
- In contrast, secondary groups are formed by choice, such as membership in a political party.
- Relationships in secondary groups are typically more impersonal, indirect and less frequent compared to primary groups.
- Joining or leaving secondary groups is generally easier, providing greater flexibility in membership.

## Formal and Informal Groups

- Formal groups are formed based on specific rules or laws and members have clearly defined roles within the group.
- These groups operate according to established norms that help maintain order and structure.
- An example of a formal group is a university, where the functions and responsibilities of members are explicitly stated.
- In the context of an office organisation, the roles and expectations of formal group members are clearly defined.
- On the other hand, informal groups are not based on formal rules or laws.
- Members of informal groups often share close relationships, leading to more personal interactions and connections.

## Ingroup and Outgroup

- The term ingroup refers to one's own group, while the term outgroup refers to another group.
- For members of the ingroup, the pronoun 'we' is used, whereas for members of the outgroup, the pronoun 'they' is used.
- The use of 'we' and 'they' categorises individuals as either similar or different.
- Ingroup members are generally seen as similar, favourable and possessing desirable traits.
- In contrast, outgroup members are often perceived negatively.
- Perceptions of ingroup and outgroup dynamics can significantly affect our social lives and interactions.
- In cultures, like India, plurality is celebrated and embraced.
- This celebration of diversity is reflected in the unique composite culture, which influences various aspects of life, including art, architecture and music.

### Quick Test 2

1. What are primary groups characterised by?
2. What defines secondary groups compared to primary groups?
3. What is the key distinction between formal and informal groups?
4. How is an ingroup different from an outgroup?
5. What type of groups often lack structured rules formal or informal?
6. What role do formal groups play in organisational structure?

# 7.3 Influence of Group on Individual Behaviour

- Groups have a significant impact on individual behaviour and are considered powerful influencers.
- Two key situations help illustrate the nature and impact of group influence
  - (i) An individual performing an activity alone in the presence of others is referred to as social facilitation.
  - (ii) An individual performing an activity alongside others as part of a larger group is known as **Social loafing**[5].

5 **Social Loafing** The tendency of individuals to exert less effort when working as part of a group.

## Social Loafing

- Social loafing refers to the reduction in individual effort when working on a collective task, where outputs are combined with those of other group members.
- They allows group members to relax and take advantage of other's efforts, leading to a phenomenon known as Being a free rider.
- This was demonstrated in various experiments conducted by Latane and his associates where groups of male students were asked to clap or cheer as loudly as possible to measure the noise levels in social settings.
- The results revealed that although the total amount of noise increased, the amount of noise produced by each participant decreased.
- Some reasons for social loafing include
  - Group members feel less responsible for the overall task, leading them to exert less effort.
  - Motivation decreases among members since contributions are not evaluated on an individual basis.
  - The performance of the group is not compared to other groups, reducing competitiveness.
  - There is improper coordination or no coordination among members.
  - Belonging to the same group is not deemed important by members, viewing it merely as an aggregate of individuals.
- To reduce social loafing, the following measures can be implemented
  - Make the efforts of each person identifiable.
  - Increase pressure to work hard by making group members committed to successful task performance.
  - Enhance the apparent importance or value of the task.
  - Ensure that individuals feel their contributions are significant.
  - Strengthen group cohesiveness to boost motivation for achieving successful group outcomes.

## Group Polarisation

- Group polarisation focuses on how groups often make decisions that are more extreme than the original thoughts and views of individual team members.
- For example, if you support capital punishment for heinous crimes and discuss this issue with like-minded people, your views may become more entrenched after the interaction.
- This strengthening of conviction can be attributed to the following three reasons
  (i) In the company of like-minded people, you are likely to hear newer arguments favouring your viewpoints.
  (ii) When you find others also favouring capital punishment, you feel that this view is validated by the public. This is a sort of bandwagon effect.
  (iii) When you find people having similar views, you are likely to perceive them as ingroup. You start identifying with the group, begin showing conformity and as a consequence your views become strengthened.

### Quick Test 3

1. Who conducted experiments demonstrating social loafing?
2. What strategy can help reduce social loafing by making individual efforts clear?
3. What effect does improper coordination have on group performance?
4. What is the term for the tendency of a group to make more extreme decisions than the initial inclinations of its members?
5. What term describes the alignment of personal beliefs with group beliefs leading to strengthened views?
6. Which concept explains decision-making in groups becoming more extreme over time?

# NCERT Folder

**1. Compare and contrast formal and informal groups and ingroups and outgroups.**

**Ans. Formal Groups** We can compare formal group with informal group and ingroup with outgroup in the following ways

(i) The functions of a formal group are explicitly stated an in the case of an office organisation.

(ii) The roles of its group members are well defined.

(iii) The formal groups are based on some specific rules or law. For example, a university.

**Informal Groups**

(i) Informal decision-making process may exist as parallel mechanism.

(ii) Members of this group have a close relationship and take decision in informal settings.

(iii) There are no strict rules and regulation for this group.

**Ingroups**

(i) It is generally considered as me, my, we or our group.

(ii) People in ingroup are viewed as having desirable behaviour and admirable traits.

(iii) It is always good, strong, cohesive.

**Outgroup**

(i) It is considered as 'they' group.

(ii) Members are often perceived negatively.

(iii) It is always people with damaging, dangerous and negative emotions.

**2. Are you a member of a certain group? Discuss what motivated you to join that group.**

*Or* **Discuss the significance of group.**

**Ans.** Being a part of a group fulfills several essential needs and provides numerous benefits that enhance an individual's personal and social life. I join group because this group satisfy a range of needs such as

- **Security** Groups offer a sense of security, reducing feelings of vulnerability and anxiety. Being around others creates a sense of comfort and safety, making people feel stronger and more capable of handling challenges.
- **Status** Membership in a prestigious or influential group can confer a sense of importance and recognition from others. It can elevate a person's social status, giving them a feeling of power and respect.
- **Self-Esteem** Groups contribute positively to our self-image by enhancing our sense of self-worth. When we are part of a valued group, it boosts our confidence and strengthens our self-concept.
- **Psychological and Social Needs** Groups fulfill psychological needs like belongingness, acceptance and connection. They allow us to give and receive affection, attention and support, which are critical for emotional well-being.
- **Goal Achievement** Groups enable us to achieve goals that may be challenging to accomplish individually. Collective efforts are often more powerful and effective, highlighting the value of collaboration.
- **Knowledge and Information** Membership in a group broadens our perspectives by providing access to diverse information, insights and experiences. Group interactions contribute to a richer understanding and make us more informed.

**3. How does Tuckman's stage model help you to understand the formation of groups?**

*Or* **What are the stages of group formation? Explain with examples.**

**Ans.** Tuckman's model explains group formation through five stages, each essential for group cohesion and effectiveness

(i) **Forming** Members meet and explore the group's purpose, experiencing excitement and uncertainty. They assess their roles and compatibility within the group. For example, in a new workplace team, members introduce themselves and discuss initial goals.

(ii) **Storming** Conflicts arise as members express differing opinions and vie for roles or resources. This stage is often marked by disagreements over goals or procedures. For instance, team members may debate task assignments or leadership roles. Resolving these conflicts clarifies expectations.

(iii) **Norming** The group begins to establish norms and mutual respect. Members agree on rules, responsibilities and communication methods. In a project group, for example, members might agree on regular meetings and role assignments, creating a cooperative atmosphere.

(iv) **Performing** The group becomes fully functional and works effectively towards its goals. Collaboration is smooth and productivity is high. For example, a sports team may work seamlessly during a game, focused on winning.

(v) **Adjourning** When the task is complete, the group disbands. Members reflect on their accomplishments and experiences. For instance, after a successful project, team members may move to new assignments.

**4. How do groups influence our behaviour?**

**Ans.** Groups strongly influence our behaviour through social influence, which involves adapting to the expectations or imagined presence of others. This influence shapes our actions daily, sometimes pushing us to do things we would not typically do, while in other cases, we may resist or even sway others to our viewpoint. There are three main processes by which groups influence behaviour

(i) **Conformity** This means aligning one's behaviour with group norms or expectations. People who conform tend to blend in, while those who do not–called 'deviants' or 'non-conformists'–stand out. For example, a person may adopt a group's dress code to fit in.

(ii) **Compliance** Here, individuals act in a particular way due to external pressures or requests, even if no norm requires it. For instance, someone may donate to a cause after being requested, even without feeling a personal obligation.

(iii) **Obedience** This is compliance to an authority figure's direct command, like following a teacher's or police officer's instructions. Obedience is distinct in that it specifically responds to authority, often overriding personal preferences.

**5. How can you reduce social loafing in groups? Think of any two incidents of social loafing in school. How did you overcome it?**

**Ans.** Social loafing occurs when individuals put in less effort in group tasks than they would on their own. This phenomenon, identified in experiments by Latane, shows that as group size increases, individual contributions often decrease. In one study, participants cheered and clapped less loudly in larger groups, showing reduced individual effort.

Two common incidents of social loafing in school include

(i) **Group Projects** Some students contribute very little, letting others carry the workload.

(ii) **Sports Teams** Certain players may skip practice or underperform, affecting team outcomes.

To address social loafing, several strategies can be applied

- **Make Individual Efforts Identifiable** Track each person's contributions to encourage accountability.
- **Increase Commitment** Encourage group members to be invested in the task's success.
- **Emphasise Task Importance** Highlighting the significance of the task can inspire more dedication.
- **Value Individual Contributions** Ensure each member feels their input matters.
- **Strengthen Group Cohesion** Building unity can motivate members to work harder for the group's success.

By using these techniques, social loafing can be minimised, leading to more effective teamwork and better results.

# Exam Pattern Questions

## Objective Type Questions

### Multiple Choice Questions (MCQs)

**1.** **A collection of people around a road side performer is an example of**

(a) crowd (b) group (c) mob (d) audience

**2.** **Working together to achieve a shared goal is called**

(a) co-operation (b) compliance
(c) conformity (d) obedience

**3.** **Membership of a club is an example of**

(a) primary group (b) secondary group
(c) outgroup (d) large group

**4.** **We all belong to different types of groups. What type of group will the armed forces be if you join it?** CBSE 2023

**I. Primary II. Secondary III. Formal IV. Informal**

Codes

(a) I, III and IV (b) III and IV
(c) II and III (d) I, II and IV

**5.** **A working group was formed to organise the annual sports competition in a school. At a particular stage, there was a lot of conflict in the group. Identify this stage and the stage that is likely to follow it.** CBSE SQP 2023

(a) The group was at the storming stage followed by the norming stage.
(b) The group was at the norming stage followed by the forming stage.
(c) The group was at the storming stage followed by the performing stage.
(d) The group was at the forming stage followed by the norming stage.

**6.** **The relative social position given to group members by others is known as** CBSE SQP 2024

(a) roles (b) norms (c) status (d) structure

**7.** **The stage in which there is conflict among members about how the target of the group is to be achieved is called the stage.** CBSE SQP 2024

(a) Forming (b) Storming (c) Norming (d) Performing

**8.** **Akhil caught his taking bribes. Akhil's staff supported his decision to terminate the services of his employee. This extreme action could be taken because of …… .** CBSE SQP 2024

(a) group polarisation (b) storming
(c) social loafing (d) social facilitation

**9.** **A peaceful audience at a sports event suddenly turns into a frenzied mob following a controversial decision by the referee. Which factors are likely responsible for this transformation?** CBSE 2025

(a) The audience's initial passive nature
(b) The presence of clear and enforced rules
(c) The polarisation of attention and shared emotions among the audience
(d) The diverse opinions and behaviours within the crowd

**10.** **A company is forming a new committee to plan a major event. To ensure effective collaboration, they want the committee to function as a primary group. Which of the following strategies would best support this goal?** CBSE 2025

(a) Assigning clear roles and tasks to each member
(b) Encouraging frequent, informal interactions among members
(c) Setting strict rules and guidelines for all meetings
(d) Limiting communication to official emails and reports

### Assertion-Reason Questions

**Direction** (Q. Nos. 11-15) Two statements are given in the question below as Assertion (A) and Reason (R). Read the statements and choose the appropriate option.

(a) Both A and R are true and R is the correct explanation of A.
(b) Both A and R are true, but R is not the correct explanation of A.
(c) A is true, but R is false.
(d) A is false, but R is true.

**11.** **Assertion** (A) People join groups to enhance their sense of self-worth and social identity.

**Reason** (R) Belonging to a group that is regarded positively by others can improve an individual's self-esteem.

**12.** **Assertion** (A) Crowds are a type of group with high interdependence among members.

**Reason** (R) Crowds are typically formed by people who come together by chance and often lack a shared purpose or structure.

**13.** **Assertion** (A) Similarity among individuals is essential for group formation.

**Reason** (R) People are more likely to form connections with those who share common interests and values.

**14.** **Assertion** (A) During the 'storming' stage of group formation, members experience harmony and high levels of cooperation.

**Reason** (R) The storming stage is characterised by conflicts and disagreements as members try to establish roles and goals.

**15.** **Assertion** (A) In primary groups, relationships are usually indirect and impersonal.

**Reason** (R) Primary groups are small, closely knit groups where members have face-to-face interactions and warm emotional bonds.

## Answers

1. (a) crowd
2. (a) co-operation
3. (b) secondary group
4. (c) II and III
5. (d) The group was at the forming stage followed by the norming stage.
6. (c) status
7. (b) Storming
8. (b) storming
9. (c) The polarisation of attention and shared emotions among the audience
10. (b) Encouraging frequent, informal interactions among members
11. (a) Both A and R are ture and R is the correct explanation of A.
12. (d) A is false, but R is true.
13. (a) Both A and R are true and R is the correct explanation of A.
14. (d) A is false, but R is true.
15. (d) A is false, but R is true.

# Subjective Questions

## Very Short Answer Type Questions

**1. What do you understand by group?**

**Ans.** A group may be defined as an organised system of two or more interdependent individuals, who have common motives and norms to regulate the behaviour of its members.

**2. What is meant by mob?**

**Ans.** In mobs, there is a definite sense of purpose. There is polarisation in attention, and actions of persons are in a common direction. Mob behaviour is characterised by homogeneity of thought and behaviour as well as impulsivity.

**3. How group help to improve self-esteem?**

**Ans.** Groups provide feelings of self-worth and establish a positive social identity. Being a member of prestigious groups enhances one's self-concept.

**4. Define the role of group in providing knowledge and skill.**

**Ans.** Membership provides knowledge and information and thus broadens our view. As individuals, we may not have all the required information. Groups supplement this information and knowledge.

**5. What do you know about proximity?**

**Ans.** Repeated interactions with the same set of individuals give us a chance to know them and their interests and attitudes. This is known as Proximity.

**6. Define formation stage in group.**

**Ans.** When group members first meet, there is a great deal of uncertainty about the group, the goal and how it is to be achieved. People try to know each other and assess whether they will fit in. There is excitement as well as apprehensions. This stage is called the Forming stage.

**7. What do you understand by group structure?**

**Ans.** During the process of group formation, groups also develop a structure as members interact. Over the time, this interaction shows regularities in distribution of task to be performed, responsibilities assigned to members and the prestige or relative status of members.

**8. Mention the different types of groups.**

**Ans.** Major types of groups are enumerated below

- Primary and secondary groups
- Formal and informal groups
- Ingroup and outgroup

**9. Define the term social facilitation.**

**Ans.** When an individual performs an activity alone in the presence of others, it is called social facilitation.

**10. What do you understand by group polarisation?**

**Ans.** Group polarisation focuses on how groups usually make decisions that are more extreme than the original thoughts and views of the individual team members. It refers to the tendency for a group to make decisions that are more extreme than the initial inclination of its members.

**11. What is Bandwagon effect?**

**Ans.** The Bandwagon effect is a psychological phenomenon whereby people do something primarily because other people are doing it, regardless of their own beliefs, which they may ignore or override.

**12. Define how groups fulfill psychological needs.**

**Ans.** Groups satisfy one's social and psychological needs such as sense of belongingness, giving and receiving attention, love and power through a group.

**13. Enumerate the five stages of group formation.**

**Ans.** The five stages of group formation are

(i) **Forming** Members get to know each other.

(ii) **Storming** Intragroup conflicts arise.

(iii) **Norming** Group norms develop.

(iv) **Performing** Focus on achieving goals.

(v) **Adjourning** Group disbands after completing its task.

**14. Sometimes popular brands announce special discount for their products and declare the last date for it. They want to make people hurry to purchase their product. Which technique is adopted here?**

**Ans.** The technique used by brands offering discounts with a specified deadline is called the Deadline technique. It creates urgency, encouraging people to purchase before the offer expires, leveraging the fear of missing out.

**15. Explain any two characteristics of a group.** CBSE 2020

**Ans.** Two characteristics of a group are

(i) Group as a social unit distinguishes from other groups which gives its unique identity.

(ii) Group has common motives and goals. It functions either working towards a given goal or away from certain threats facing the group.

**16. Explain any two differences between primary and secondary groups.** CBSE 2020

**Ans.** Two differences between primary and secondary groups are

(i) Primary groups are pre-existing (e.g., family, caste), while secondary groups are formed by choice (e.g., political party).

(ii) Primary groups have close, emotional bonds; secondary groups have impersonal, indirect relationships.

**17. We are members of a number of groups at any given time. Explain the reasons that make people join groups.** CBSE SQP Term II 2021

**Ans.** People join groups for reasons like

- **Security** Groups provide comfort and protection, reducing feelings of insecurity.
- **Status** Being part of an important group gives recognition and a sense of power.

**18. Groups differ in many respects. Identify the characteristics that distinguish primary groups from secondary groups.** CBSE SQP Term II 2021

**Ans.** Primary groups are pre-existing and involve close, emotional relationships, like family, with face-to-face interactions.

Secondary groups are voluntary, with impersonal, goal-oriented relationships, like workplaces or clubs.

**19. Explain any two elements of a group structure.** CBSE SQP 2022

**Ans.** Two important elements of group structure are

(i) **Roles** Socially defined expectations of behaviour in a given context.

(ii) **Norms** Shared standards of behaviour and beliefs that guide group members.

**20. Identify and explain two strategies to reduce social loafing within a group.** CBSE 2025

**Ans.** The two strategies to reduce social loafing within a group are

(i) **Assign individual tasks** This ensures accountability and motivates members to contribute equally.

(ii) **Set clear goals** Unified objectives inspire teamwork, which reduces chances of loafing.

**21. Evaluate the role of common motives and goals in forming and maintaining a cohesive group, with an example.** CBSE 2025

**Ans.** Common motives and shared goals unite individuals, which fosters teamwork and reduces conflicts. For example, sports teams work cohesively to win matches, showcasing aligned efforts for mutual success and bonding.

## Short Answer Type Questions

**1. Why do people behave according to the group norms?**

**Ans.** Norms are expected standards of behaviour and beliefs established, agreed upon and enforced by group members. They may be considered as a group's unspoken rules. In a family, there are norms that guide the behaviour of family members. These norms represent shared ways of viewing the world. If people do not follow group norm, they feel uncomfortable. People see norms as the reflecting view of majority.

**2. Explain how crowd is different from the groups.**

**Ans.** A group is an organised system with interacting, interdependent members who share common goals and follow norms. It has structured relationships and roles. In contrast, a crowd is a spontaneous gathering of people, often with no pre-defined structure, roles or norms. Crowds form by chance and behaviour is often irrational and not interdependent.

**3. Distinguish between audience and mob.**

**Ans.** An audience is also a collection of people who have assembled for a special purpose, may be to watch a cricket match or a movie. Audiences are generally passive but sometimes they go into a frenzy and become mobs. In mobs, there is a definite sense of purpose.

There is polarisation in attention and actions of persons are in a common direction. Mob behaviour is characterised by homogeneity of thought and behaviour as well as impulsivity.

**4. Differentiate between ingroup and outgroup.** CBSE 2023

**Ans.** An ingroup refers to one's own group, where members are perceived positively and share common traits, often referred to as 'we'. An outgroup is a group perceived as different, often viewed negatively, using 'they'. These perceptions influence social dynamics, and in diverse cultures like India, pluralism is celebrated, reflecting unique cultural aspects in art, architecture and music.

**5. Cricket team in Ranjan's locality is very famous. Ranjan and his group of friends are active members in this team. What is the main difference between their group and team?**

**Ans.** The main differences between group of Ranjan and his friends and their cricket team are

- In their group, performance is dependent on contributions of individual members. In cricket team both individual contributions and teamwork matter.
- In group, Ranjan is the leader who is heading the group and taking the responsibility for the work of the group. However, in cricket team, although there is a captain (leader), members hold themselves responsible for the performance of the team.

**6. A person 'X' was caught taking a bribe and her/his colleagues were asked to decide on what punishment she/he should be given. They could either let her/him go with just a warning or decide to terminate her/his services. After a discussion with other employees of the organisation, an extreme decision was taken to terminate this person's services. Identify this phenomenon and explain why it occurs.** CBSE SQP Term II 2021

**Ans.** The phenomenon described is group polarisation, where group discussions lead to more extreme decisions than individuals initially considered. This occurs because

- In like-minded groups, arguments reinforcing personal viewpoints emerge.
- The bandwagon effect validates opinions as popular.
- Identifying with the ingroup increases conformity, strengthening individual views, leading to a more extreme decision like termination in this case.

**7. Ananya had been trying to learn a new form of dance to win a competition. She decided to join a dance group which was also practicing the same dance form. Identify the reason for Ananya wanting to join the dance group. Explain some of the other reasons that make people join groups.** CBSE SQP 2022

**Ans.** Ananya joined the dance group to improve her skills and increase her chances of winning the competition, as groups can aid in achieving goals that are hard to reach alone. Other reasons people join groups include

- **Security** Groups provide comfort, reducing feelings of vulnerability.
- **Status** Being in respected groups boosts recognition and a sense of power.
- **Self-esteem** Membership enhances self-worth and social identity.
- **Psychological and Social Needs** Groups fulfill needs for belonging, attention and connection.
- **Knowledge and Information** Groups offer additional knowledge and broaden perspectives.

**8. Mary found herself very lonely when she joined a new college, but soon felt at ease when she made friends and became a member of a hobby group too. With the help of this example, discuss the conditions that lead to group formation.** CBSE Term II 2022

**Ans.** Mary's experience illustrates key conditions for group formation

- **Proximity** Regular interactions with peers helped Mary become familiar with her new college mates.
- **Similarity** Shared interests in the hobby group created bonds.
- **Common Goals** Mary's desire for companionship aligned with the group's focus, leading to a sense of belonging and easing her loneliness.

**9. Describe the characteristics of the group.**

**Ans.** Groups have the following characteristics

- **Social Unit** Comprising two or more individuals who identify as part of the group.
- **Common Goals** Members work toward shared objectives.
- **Interdependence** Member's actions affect one another.
- **Influence** Individuals satisfy needs through interaction.
- **Interaction** Members engage directly or indirectly.
- **Roles and Norms** Interactions are governed by structured roles and expectations.

**10. Describe the element of group structure.**

**Ans.** The four elements of group structure are

(i) **Roles** Socially defined expectations guiding individual behaviour in specific contexts.

(ii) **Norms** Unspoken standards of behaviour and beliefs, shaped by group members.

(iii) **Status** The relative social position of individuals, either ascribed or achieved.

(iv) **Cohesiveness** The mutual attraction and sense of unity that binds group members together, encouraging continued participation.

**11. What is meant by social loafing? Give suitable examples.**

***Or*** **Explain the phenomenon of 'social loafing' by giving examples.**

**Ans.** Social loafing refers to the tendency of individuals to exert less effort when working in a group than when working alone. It occurs in tasks where individual contributions are pooled. For example, in a tug-of-war, team members may not be aware of others' efforts, leading some to relax and contribute less, relying on others to exert more force.

**12. What is polarisation? Explain with examples.**

**Ans.** Polarisation refers to the tendency of a group to adopt more extreme views than initially held. For example, if someone supports capital punishment and discusses it with like-minded individuals, their stance may become more rigid. This happens due to hearing supportive arguments, perceiving the view as popular (bandwagon effect) and identifying with the group, leading to stronger convictions.

**13. Distinguish between primary and secondary group.**

**Ans.** Primary and secondary groups differ in several ways

(i) **Formation** Primary groups are pre-existing, while secondary groups are chosen.

(ii) **Examples** Family, caste and religion are primary, while political parties are secondary.

(iii) **Interaction** Primary groups have close, emotional bonds; secondary groups are impersonal.

(iv) **Membership** Primary group membership is fixed, while secondary groups allow easier joining and leaving.

**14. In school, Puja joins the dance group. What are the reasons that led her to join this group?**

**Ans.** Puja joins the dance group for several reasons

(i) **Security** It provides comfort and protection.

(ii) **Status** Being in the group gives recognition and power.

(iii) **Self-esteem** The group enhances her self-worth.

(iv) **Psychological needs** It satisfies her sense of belonging and emotional needs.

(v) **Goal Achievement** It helps achieve goals she cannot alone.

(vi) **Knowledge** The group provides valuable information.

**15. How does the group structure develop? Identify any three elements of group structure.** **CBSE 2019**

**Ans.** Group structure develops as members interact and establish regularities in task distribution, responsibilities and status. Three elements of group structure are

(i) **Roles** Expectations for behaviour in specific contexts.

(ii) **Norms** Standardised behaviours and beliefs upheld by group members.

(iii) **Status** The relative social position of members, either ascribed or achieved.

**16. "Groupthink have no tradition of considering alternatives and that face a decision with high costs or failures." Examine this statement with relevant example.**

**Ans.** Groupthink occurs when a group prioritises consensus over critical evaluation, leading to poor decisions. It happens in cohesive, isolated groups facing high-stakes decisions without considering alternatives.

An example is the Vietnam War (1964-67), where despite warnings, the U.S. escalated the war to maintain group unity, resulting in massive loss of life and financial deficits.

## Long Answer Type Questions

**1. Explain group polarisation. Give reasons for occurrence of group polarisation.** **CBSE 2018**

**Ans.** Group polarisation refers to the tendency of groups to make decisions or adopt views that are more extreme than the initial positions of individual members. When individuals discuss an issue with others who hold similar opinions, the group's final stance often becomes more intensified than each member's original viewpoint.

For example, if someone supports capital punishment for serious crimes, discussing this stance with like-minded people can lead to even stronger support for it, as members reinforce each other's beliefs.

**Reasons for Group Polarisation**

Group polarisation typically occurs due to the following factors

- **Exposure to New Arguments** In a group setting, individuals hear additional arguments supporting their views, which strengthens their original stance.
- **Social Validation (Bandwagon Effect)** When others in the group also favour a position, individuals feel their views are validated, leading them to adopt an even stronger stance.
- **Ingroup Identification** Identifying with like-minded individuals fosters a sense of belonging and conformity, reinforcing each person's views, resulting in a more extreme group consensus.

Group polarisation demonstrates how social interaction and shared identity within groups can escalate initial inclinations into more extreme viewpoints.

**2. Explain the reasons why individuals join groups and the types of groups they may belong to. Illustrate your answer with examples.**

**Ans.** A group is a collection of individuals who interact and share common goals or interests. It plays a crucial role in fulfilling personal and social needs such as security, status and self-esteem.

**Reasons Individuals Join Groups**

(i) **Security** Groups provide protection and a sense of safety. For example, family groups offer emotional security and support.

(ii) **Status** Joining prestigious groups enhances one's sense of recognition and self-worth. For example, becoming part of a successful sports team or student council.

(iii) **Self-Esteem** Being part of a respected group boosts personal identity and confidence. Academic clubs, for instance, help individuals feel valued for their intellectual abilities.

(iv) **Satisfaction of Social Needs** Groups fulfill the need for love, attention and emotional support, as seen in friendship circles or community groups.

(v) **Goal Achievement** Groups enable collective goal accomplishment that might be difficult alone. For instance, work teams collaborating on projects.

(vi) **Access to Knowledge and Information** Group interactions provide insights and broaden perspectives, as seen in professional development groups.

**Types of Groups**

- **Primary Groups** Small, close-knit groups with long-lasting relationships, such as families.
- **Secondary Groups** Larger, goal-oriented and often temporary groups, such as workplace teams.
- **Formal Groups** Organised and structured groups with defined roles and rules, like company departments.
- **Informal Groups** Spontaneous and flexible groups formed based on social bonds, such as a group of friends.

## Case Based Questions

**1. Read the case and answer the questions that follow.**

Mr. Anshul has a positive attitude towards dowry. He is planning to get his son married to the daughter of Mr. Hemant who has a negative attitude towards dowry. If Mr. Hemant has a positive attitude towards Mr. Anshul, the situation is considered as unbalanced.

(i) **Identify the concept of social attitude and cognition that operates in this case. Also discuss it.**

(ii) **Identify some of the possible outcomes in the given case.**

**Ans.** (i) The concept of social attitude and cognition that operates in this case is balance. The concept of balance was proposed by Fritz Heider. It is also described in the form of the P-O-X triangle, which represents the relationships between three aspects or components of the attitude that are

- P is the person whose attitude is being studied.
- O is another person.
- X is the topic towards which the attitude is being studied (attitude object).

(ii) Some possible outcomes in the given passage can be

- Mr. Anshul will start disliking dowry
- Mr. Hemant will start liking dowry
- Mr. Hemant will start disliking Mr. Anshul

**2. Read the case and answer the questions that follow.**

The annual snake boat race in the Southern Indian State of Kerala is a unique sporting spectacle because of its scale and popularity. Each team has many players. The participants practice for weeks before the race. On the day of the event, they bring down their oars in perfect harmony with frenzied beats of drums, creating a drizzle in mid-air as spectators go wild during the race. The boat that springs forward is one of the biggest in a water sport anywhere in the world. When it comes to a task like rowing, does everyone perform their share of the work? When several people work together to accomplish a task, it is probable that everyone will not exert the same amount of effort. Some will work very hard others will do less, and perhaps a few will do nothing at all, while pretending to work hard! This pattern is quite common in situations where groups perform what are known as additive tasks - ones in which the contributions of each member are combined into a single group output. Some will contribute by taking on as much of the load as they can, while some will pretend to be working as hard as they can when, in fact, they are not. Social psychologists are interested in studying this phenomenon.

(i) **'Social psychologists are interested in studying this phenomenon.' Which phenomenon is being talked about here? State a characteristic feature of this phenomenon.**

(ii) **Will this phenomenon occur more on practice days or on the day of the final race? Give reasons for your answer.**

**Ans.** (i) The phenomenon being discussed is social loafing. A characteristic feature of social loafing is that some individuals in a group exert less effort, relying on others to compensate for their lack of contribution, particularly in additive tasks where the final output is the sum of all contributions.

(ii) Social loafing is likely to occur more on practice days. On practice days, the pressure to perform is lower, and individuals may feel they can slack off without significant consequences, assuming that others will carry the load. However, on the day of the final race, the stakes are higher, and individuals are more likely to give their best effort due to the competitive nature of the event.

# SELF ASSESSMENT TEST

## Objective Type Questions

**1.** Which of the following is an example of a group?
(a) Family (b) Class (c) Playground (d) All of these

**2.** People join group for the reason of
(a) security (b) status (c) self-esteem (d) All of these

**3.** Which of the following are not the element of group structures?
(a) Role (b) Norms (c) Status (d) Expectations

**4.** What is one of the main distinctions between a 'group' and a 'crowd'?
(a) A group lacks interdependence among members.
(b) A crowd consists of people who share common motives and structured roles.
(c) A group includes members who are interdependent and have common goals.
(d) A crowd provides essential support and fosters individual growth.

**5.** **Assertion** (A) Group cohesiveness refers to the level of emotional attachment and unity among group members.

**Reason** (R) High cohesiveness in a group often leads to groupthink, where members prioritise harmony over critical thinking.
(a) Both A and R are true and R is the correct explanation of A.
(b) Both A and R are true, but R is not the correct explanation of A.
(c) A is true, but R is false.
(d) A is false, but R is true.

## Very Short Answer Type Questions

**1.** Define group.

**2.** Who was Tuckman?

**3.** What are the stages of group formation?

**4.** State some examples of primary groups.

## Short Answer Type Questions

**1.** Differentiate between primary and secondary group.

**2.** Find the relationship between group and team.

**3.** Briefly discuss determinants of cooperation and competition.

**4.** A person is suffering from conflict. He approached a psychologist to seek resolution from the conflict. Enumerate the strategies that would have been suggested by psychologists.

## Long Answer Type Questions

**1.** Define Group. Mention its characteristics.

**2.** Describe conditions for the formation of group.

## Case Based Questions

**Read the case and answer the questions that follow.**

Anika has joined a new workplace where her colleagues regularly engage in discussions about various social issues. Anika notices that everyone in her team shares similar opinions on these issues. She initially disagrees with some of their views but, over time, begins to align her thoughts and opinions with those of her team to feel included. This change in her perspective reflects the influence of her group.

(i) Identify the concept of social influence demonstrated in this scenario and briefly discuss it.

(ii) Suggest one possible outcome if Anika continues to conform to the group's views.

SAMPLE PRACTICAL FILE

SAMPLE QUESTION PAPERS (1–3)

CBSE SOLVED PAPER 2025

# PRACTICAL FILE ON DEVELOPMENT OF CASE PROFILE AND FIVE PSYCHOLOGICAL TESTS

Name : .................................................

Class : .................................................

Roll No. : .................................................

Subject : .................................................

School : .................................................

*Submitted by ............*

*Submitted to ............*

**Sample Project**

# Acknowledgement

I would like to extend my sincere and heartfelt obligation towards all those who have helped me in making this project. Without their active guidance, help, cooperation and encouragement, I would not have been able to present the project on time.

I am extremely thankful and pay my gratitude to my teacher Mr/Ms ........... for his/her valuable guidance and support for completion of this project.

I extend my gratitude to my Principal Mr/Ms ........... for the moral support extended during the tenure of the project.

I also acknowledge with a deep sense of reverence, my gratitude towards my parents, other faculty members of the school and friends for their valuable suggestions given to me in completing this project.

Date...........

....................

Name of Student

# Certificate

This is to Certify that the project work

.............................................................................. is the bonafide

work of .................................... (Name of the student) who

carried out the work under my supervision

................................

Name and Signature of
Teacher/Supervisor

# Contents

# GUIDELINES FOR PRACTICALS IN PSYCHOLOGY

Psychological tools and techniques help to uncover the latent aspects of an individual's behaviour. Practicals in psychology are intended to provide students with requisite knowledge and skills in psychological tools and techniques to gain an understanding of human behaviour. They attempt to provide hands-on experience to the students with both quantitative tools of measurement (standardised psychological tests) and qualitative tools (interview and observation).

Before undertaking practical work, it is important to ensure that the students have knowledge about various methods of research in psychology and their merits and demerits, the behavioural characteristics being assessed, the nature and uses of psychological tests, and the ethical guidelines to avoid their misuse.

Keeping in view the syllabus of psychology for Class XII, the students would undertake practicals in psychological testing which would involve using standardised psychological tests in different domains, e.g. intelligence, personality, aptitude, adjustment, attitude and self-concept and anxiety, etc.

**Note :** A psychological test can be administered only by a professionally qualified person. A student of psychology at 12th level would not have reached the stage of a professionally qualified person. Therefore, she/he is not fully equipped to interpret the scores of a psychological test for any conclusive purpose, e.g. selection, prediction, diagnosis, etc. For this purpose, the test administration may be broken into small components/activities.

# CASE PROFILE

Developing a case profile would primarily involve the use of qualitative techniques, such as observation, interview, survey, etc. During the course of preparing a case profile, the students would gain a first-hand experience in the use of these qualitative techniques.

## Objective of Preparing Case Profile

The main objective of preparing a case profile is to understand the individual in totality. This would further help in establishing the cause and effect relationship more accurately.

## Suggested Format for Preparing a Case Profile

A format for case presentation covering broad aspects is given below. It is suggested that the case be developed in a narrative format along the following points.

1. **Introduction**
   - A brief introduction of about one or two pages presenting the nature of the problem, its incidence, likely causes, and possible counselling outcomes.
2. **Identification of Data**
   - Name (may be fictitious)
   - Diagnosed Problem
   - Voluntary or Referral (i.e., by whom referred – such as teacher, parent, sibling, etc.)
3. **Case History**
   - A paragraph giving age, gender, school attended, class (grade) presently enrolled in, etc.
   - Information about socio-economic status (SES) consisting of information about mother's/father's education and occupation, family income, house type, number of members in the family— brothers, sisters and their birth order, adjustment in the family, etc.
   - Information about physical health, physical characteristics (e.g., height and weight), any disability/illness (in the past and present), etc.
   - Any professional help taken (past and present), giving a brief history of the problem, attitude towards counselling (indicating the motivation to seek help, etc.).
   - Recording signs (i.e., what is observed in terms of facial expressions, mannerisms, etc.) and symptoms (i.e., what the subject reports, for example, fear, worry, tension, sleeplessness, etc.).
4. **Concluding Comments**

## Different Methods for Development of Case Profile

### Interviews

An interview is different from a survey in the way that it is always conducted in person and usually involves much fewer persons (as few as 5, 20, or 40, usually not much more than that). Interviews may be structured, and follow a predetermined pattern of questions or unstructured, where only a set of topics is pre-decided, and the actual questions emerge as part of a conversation.

Interviews may be more or less intensive, in the sense that one may interview a person for a long time (2-3 hours) or in repeated visits to get a really detailed version of their story. Interviews have the advantage of being flexible in that promising topics may be pursued in greater detail, questions may be refined or modified along the way, and clarifications may be sought. The disadvantage of the interview method is that it cannot cover a large number of people and is limited to presenting the views of a selected group of individuals.

### Observation

Observation is a method where the researcher must systematically watch and record what is happening in whatever context or situation that has been chosen for the research. This sounds simple but may not always be easy to do in practice. Careful attention has to be paid to what is happening without pre-judging what is relevant to the study and what is not. Sometimes, what is not happening is as important or interesting as what does actually happen. For example, if your research question is about how different classes of people use specific open spaces, then it is significant that a given class or group of people (say poor people, or middle class people for example) never enter the space, or are never seen in it.

## Case Profile on Specific Learning Disorder

Specific Learning disorder is a classification that includes several areas of functioning in which a person has difficulty in learning basic skills in reading, writing and mathematics.

## Causes of Learning Disorder

The causes for learning disabilities are not well understood, and sometimes there is no apparent cause for a learning disability. However, some causes of neurological impairments include

### Heredity and Genetics

Learning disabilities often run in the family. Children with learning disabilities are likely to have parents or other relatives with similar difficulties.

### Problems during Pregnancy and Birth

Learning disabilities can result from anomalies in the developing brain, illness or injury, fetal exposure to alcohol or drugs, low birth weight, oxygen deprivation, or by pre-mature or prolonged labour.

### Accidents after Birth

Learning disabilities can also be caused by head injuries, malnutrition, or by toxic exposure (such as heavy metals or pesticides).

## Symptoms of Learning Disability

- Short attention span
- Poor memory
- Difficulty in following directions
- Inability to discriminate between/among letters, numerals or sounds
- Poor reading and/or writing ability
- Eye-hand coordination problems; poorly coordinated
- Difficulties with sequencing

## Sample Case Study on Learning Disorder

**Rohan** was a 2nd grade student. He found it difficult to match alphabets to their sounds or combine alphabets to create words. This led him to be a little frustrated and disturbed in class and he had difficulty completing his class work. When the class teacher informed Rohan's parents, they replied that their son was intelligent and would gradually pick these things as time passed.

However, when the results came, Rohan had received C and D grades in various subjects and this got the parents worried. This time, the teacher gently insisted that the parents approach a clinical psychologist for an evaluation of his learning difficulties.

The psychologist educated the parents about Learning Disability (LD) and explained that there are standardised assessments available for assessing this condition. He explained the various tests and the functions they measure. As the tests were administered and the results emerged, the parents were able to obtain a better understanding of the difficulty Rohan faced.

This psychological assessment proved that Rohan has a mild level of LD. The details of the type of LD were also evident on these tests. A detailed assessment was done by the psychologist and a psychiatrist to rule out other medical, neurological and psychological disorders commonly associated with LD. Fortunately, in Rohan's case there was no evidence of any such associated condition.

Parents were advised to take help from a special educator. As time passed, with the help of the special educator, Rohan made substantial progress. Presently he is almost at par with his peers. He is motivated to put in the extra work and his grades have improved.

Among children with normal intelligence, as many as 1 out of every 5 children have some degree of learning difficulty that may need additional training or special education. The following terms are used in the context of Learning Disability, but most children have a combination of these difficulties

- Dyslexia – is the difficulty to read
- Dysgraphia – is the difficulty to write
- Dyscalculia – is the difficulty with arithmetic skills

# Test Administration

In this process, it is expected that students will develop skills to establish rapport (relation) with the test takers to make them comfortable in a relatively new and different context. Establishing rapport involves the test administrator's efforts to arouse the test takers' interest in the test, elicit their cooperation, and encourage them to respond in a manner appropriate to the objectives of the test.

The main objective of establishing rapport is to motivate the respondents to follow the instructions as fully and meticulously as they can. It may be noted that the nature of the test (e.g., individual or group, verbal or non-verbal, etc.), and the age and other characteristics of the test takers determine the use of specific techniques for the establishment of rapport.

## Points to be Kept in Mind While doing a Test

The following points may be kept in mind while doing a test

### Uniform Testing Conditions

Basically, the function of psychological tests is to measure differences between individuals or between the responses of the same individual on different occasions. If the scores obtained by different individuals are to be compared, testing conditions must obviously be the same for all. Attention should be given to the selection of a suitable testing room, which should be free from undue noise and distraction. This room should provide adequate lighting, ventilation, seating facilities, etc. for test takers.

### Standardised Instructions

In order to secure uniformity of testing conditions, the test constructor provides detailed directions for administering the test. Standardised instructions include the exact materials used, time limit (if any), oral instructions to subjects, preliminary demonstrations, ways of handling queries from subjects, and other possible details of the testing situation.

### Training of Test Administrator

The test administrator is the person who administers and scores the test. The importance of a trained test administrator is evident. The test administrator also provides test takers with appropriate and understandable explanations of test results and of any recommendations stemming from them.

## Suggested Format for Writing a Psychological Testing Report

1. **Problem/Title of the Study** (e.g., to study the level of adjustment/personality/aptitude of students).
2. **Introduction**
   - Basic Concepts
   - Variables
3. **Method**
   - Subject
   - Name
   - Age
   - Gender
   - Class
   - Material
   - Brief description of the test (name of the test, author, year, psychometric properties, etc.).
   - Other materials (e.g., stop watch, screen, etc.).
   - Procedure
   - Process of test administration, such as rapport formation, instructions, precautions, actual conduct of test, etc.
   - Scoring of the test
   - Preparation of graph, psychogram, etc. (if required).
4. **Results and Conclusions**
   - Describing subject's scores in terms of norms and drawing conclusions.
5. **References**
   - List the books, manuals and materials consulted on the topic.

## Different Psychological Test

### Test 1 : Intelligence Test

Intelligence tests are of several types. On the basis of their administration procedure, they can be categorised as individual or group tests. They can also be classified as either verbal or performance tests on the basis of the nature of items used. Depending upon the extent to which an intelligence test favours one culture over another, it can be judged as either culture-fair or culture-biased.

## Types of Intelligence Tests

### Individual or Group Tests

An individual intelligence test is one which can be administered to one person at a time. A group intelligence test can be administered to several persons simultaneously. Individual tests require the test administrator to establish a rapport with the subject and be sensitive to her/his feelings, moods and expressions during the testing session. Group tests, however, do not allow an opportunity to be familiar with the subjects' feelings. Individual tests allow people to answer orally or in a written form or manipulate objects as per the tester's instructions. Group tests generally seek written answers usually in a multiple choice format.

### Verbal, Non-Verbal, or Performance Tests

An intelligence test may be fully verbal, fully non-verbal or fully performance based, or it may consist of a mixture of items from each category. Verbal tests require subjects to give verbal responses either orally or in a written form. Therefore, verbal tests can be administered only to literate people. The non-verbal tests use pictures or illustrations as test items. **Raven's Progressive Matrices** (RPM) Test is an example of a non-verbal test.

### Raven's Progressive Matrices (RPM) Test

Raven's Progressive Matrices (often referred to simply as Raven's Matrices) are multiple choice intelligence tests of abstract reasoning, originally developed by Dr. John C. Raven in 1936. In each test item, the subject is asked to identify the missing item that completes a pattern.

### Objective

In this test, the subject examines an incomplete pattern and chooses a figure from the alternatives that will complete the pattern.

### Material Required for the Test

RSPM Manual, RSPM Test Booklet, RSPM Answer sheet, RSPM Scoring Key, Eraser and Pencil.

### Basic Concept of the Test

As a non-verbal measure of mental ability, the RPM provides three ability levels to minimise the effect of language skills and cultural bias. The matrices require the examinee to solve problems presented in abstract figures and designs. The test is designed to help measure an individual's ability to form perceptual relations and to reason by analogy, independent of language and formal schooling, by offering insight about a person's capacity to observe, solve problems, and learn.

The test offers three progressively more difficult forms intended for different populations. Items on all forms ask the examinee to identify the missing component in a series of figural patterns. Grouped in sets, the items require increasingly greater skill in encoding and analysing information. The test can be individually or group administered. The three forms are: Coloured Progressive Matrices (CPM), Standard Progressive Matrices (SPM), and Advanced Progressive Matrices (APM).

The Raven's APM measures high-level observation skills, clear thinking ability, and intellectual capacity. This test is designed to differentiate between people at the high end of intellectual ability. When administered under timed conditions, the APM can also be used to assess intellectual efficiency – quick and accurate high-level intellectual work. The Raven's APM produces a single raw score as well as percentile rank to indicate the candidate's educative ability or the ability to make sense of complex situations, compared to a norm group. The Raven's APM provides 'Difficult' level tests that spread scores of the top 20% of the population.

#### Areas of Application

The Raven's APM score can be used as

- An indication of a candidate's potential for success in high-level technical, professional, and executive positions that require high levels of clear and accurate thinking, problem identification, holistic situation assessment, and monitoring of tentative solutions for consistency with all available information.
- For developmental purposes in occupational and advanced educational settings.

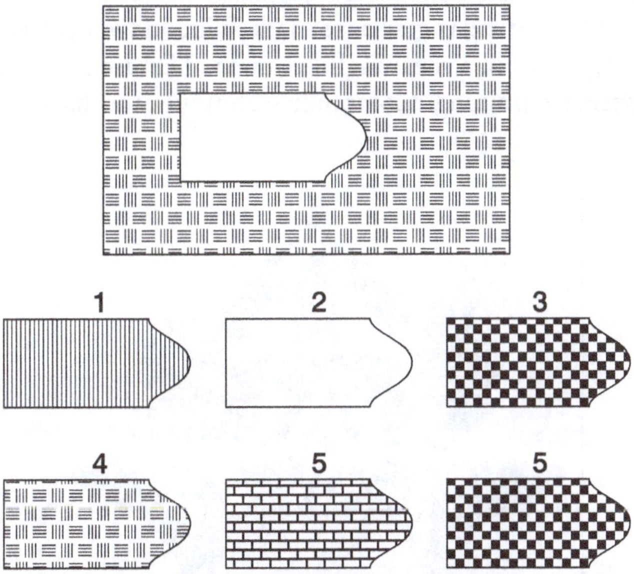


**Raven's Progressive Matrices (RPM) Test**

### Precautions

- Before starting the practical proper bond or rapport should be established.
- There is no time limit and seating arrangement should be comfortable.
- Lighting conditions and ventilation should be proper in the room.
- No item should be left unanswered by the candidate.
- Instructions about the test and subject should be very clear.

## Test 2 : The Rorschach Inkblot Test (Based on Personality)

This test was developed by Hermann Rorschach. Hermann Rorschach was a Swiss Freudian psychiatrist and psychoanalyst, best known for developing the Rorschach test.

### Description of the Test

The test consists of 10 inkblots. Five of them are in black and white, two with some red ink, and the remaining three in some pastel colours. The blots are symmetrical in design with a specific shape or form. Each blot is printed in the centre of a white cardboard of about 7″ to 10″ size. The blots were originally made by dropping ink on a piece of paper and then folding the paper in half (hence called inkblot test). The cards are administered individually in two phases.

In the first phase, called performance proper, the subjects are shown the cards and are asked to tell what they see in each of them. In the second phase, called inquiry, a detailed report of the response is prepared by asking the subject to tell where, how, and on what basis was a particular response made. Fine judgement is necessary to place the subject's responses in a meaningful context. The use and interpretation of this test requires extensive training. Computer techniques too have been developed for analysis of data.

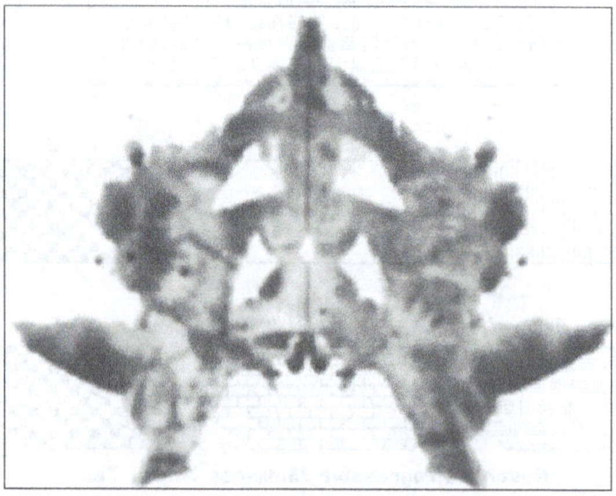

**An example of the Rorschach Inkbolt**

## Test 3 : The Thematic Apperception Test (TAT)

This test was developed by Morgan and Murray. Henry Alexander Murray was an American psychologist at Harvard University. He was Director of the Harvard Psychological Clinic in the School of Arts and Sciences after 1930. Christiana Drummond Morgan was an artist, writer and lay psychoanalyst at Harvard University best known for her work co-authoring the Thematic Apperception Test, one of the most widely used projective psychological tests.

### Description of the Test

It is a little more structured than the Inkblot test. The test consists of 30 black and white picture cards and one blank card. Each picture card depicts one or more people in a variety of situations. Each picture is printed on a card. Some cards are used with adult males or females. Others are used with boys or girls. Still others are used in some combinations. Twenty cards are appropriate for a subject, although a lesser number of cards (even five) have also been successfully used. The cards are presented one at a time. The subject is asked to tell a story describing the situation presented in the picture: What led up to the situation, what is happening at the moment, what will happen in the future, and what characters are feeling and thinking? A standard procedure is available for scoring TAT responses. The test has been modified for children and for the aged.

**An Illustration Showing the Drawing of a Card of TAT**

### **Test 4 : Group Pressure and Conformity** (The Asch Experiment)

Asch examined how much conformity there would be when one member of a group experiences pressure from the rest of the group to behave in a specific way, or to give a particular judgement.

#### Description of Test

A group of seven persons participated in an experiment that was a 'vision test'. There was actually only one true subject. The other six participants were associates of the experimenter, or 'confederates' as they are called in social psychology. These confederates were given instructions to give specific responses. Of course, this was not known to the true subject. All participants were shown a vertical line (standard line) that had to be compared with three vertical lines of different lengths, A, B, and C (comparison lines). Participants had to state which of the comparison lines, A, B, or C, was equal to the standard line.

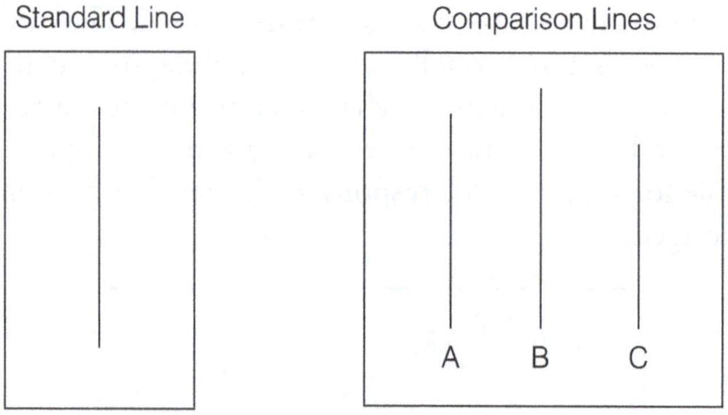


When the experiment began, each participant, by turn, announced her/his answer. The first five persons gave wrong answers (as they had been instructed to do so). The true subject's turn came last but one in each round. So the true subject had the experience of 5 persons giving incorrect answers before her/him. The last person (also a confederate) gave the same incorrect answer as the first five persons. Even if the true subject felt that these answers were incorrect, a norm had been presented to her/him. There were twelve trials. Did the true subject conform to the majority answer, or did she/he give her/his own judgements? It was observed that 67 per cent subjects showed conformity, and gave the same incorrect answer as the majority. Remember that this was a situation in which the answers were to be given publicly.

## Test 5 : Draw-a-Person Test (Based on Personality)

It is a simple test in which the subject is asked to draw a person on a sheet of paper.

### Description of the Test

A pencil and eraser is provided to facilitate drawing. After the completion of the drawing, the subject is generally asked to draw the figure of an opposite sex person. Finally, the subject is asked to make a story about the person as if she/he was a character in a novel or play.

Some examples of interpretations are as follows

- Omission of facial features suggests that the person tries to evade a highly conflict-ridden interpersonal relationship.
- Graphic emphasis on the neck suggests lack of control over impulses.
- Disproportionately large head suggests organic brain disease and preoccupation with headaches.

The analysis of personality with the help of projective techniques appears fairly interesting. It helps us to understand unconscious motives, deep-rooted conflicts, and emotional complexes of an individual. However, the interpretation of the responses requires sophisticated skills and specialised training. There are problems associated with the reliability of scoring and validity of interpretations. But, the practitioners have found these techniques quite useful.

# Viva Voce Questions

**1.** ***What is the use of psychological tools and techniques?***

***Ans.*** Psychological tools and techniques help to uncover the latent aspects of an individual's behaviour.

**2.** ***What is the fundamental aim of psychology?***

***Ans.*** Understanding, predicting, and controlling the human behaviour is the fundamental aim of psychology.

**3.** ***Name two qualitative tools used in psychological experiments.***

***Ans.*** Interview and observation are qualitative tools used in psychological experiments.

**4.** ***What should students known before conducting practical work of psychology?***

***Ans.*** Students should be aware of merits and demerits of methods used in psychological research, behavioural characteristics, the nature and uses of psychological tests and ethical guidelines.

**5.** ***What is the main objective of establishing rapport in test administration?***

***Ans.*** The main objective of establishing rapport is to motivate the respondents to follow the instructions as fully and meticulously as they can.

**6.** ***What does establishing rapport involve?***

***Ans.*** Establishing Rapport involves the test administrator's efforts to arouse the test takers' interest in the test, elicit their cooperation, and encourage them to respond in a manner appropriate to the objectives of the test.

**7.** ***What is the function of psychological tests?***

***Ans.*** The function of psychological tests is to measure differences between individuals or between the responses of the same individual on different occasions.

**8.** ***What do non-verbal tests use?***

***Ans.*** The non-verbal tests use pictures or illustrations as test items.

**9.** ***Given an example of non-verbal test.***

***Ans.*** Raven's Progressive Matrices test.

**10.** ***Who is Hermann Rorschach?***

***Ans.*** Hermann Rorschach was a Swiss Freudian psychiatrist and psychoanalyst, best known for developing the Rorschach test.

**11.** ***Who was Morgan and Murray?***

***Ans.*** Morgan and Murray developed the psychological test called The Thematic Apperception test.

**12.** ***Which test is more structured between Inkblot and Thematic Apperception test?***

***Ans.*** Thematic Apperception test is more structured.

**13.** ***What is Asch experiment?***

***Ans.*** Asch examined how much conformity there would be when one member of a group experiences pressure from the rest of the group to behave in a specific way, or to give a particular judgement.

**14. *Discuss about Draw-a-person test.***

***Ans.*** It is a simple test in which the subject is asked to draw-a-person on a sheet of paper.

**15. *What interpretation is for omitting the facial features in Draw-a-Person Test?***

***Ans.*** Omission of facial features suggests that the person tries to evade a highly conflict-ridden interpersonal relationship.

**16. *What in draw a person test suggests about lack of control over impulses?***

***Ans.*** Graphic emphasis on the neck suggests lack of control over impulses.

**17. *What does disproportionately large head in draw a person test describe?***

***Ans.*** Disproportionately large head suggests organic brain disease and preoccupation with headaches.

**18. *How does projective techniques help to analyse a personality?***

***Ans.*** It helps us to understand unconscious motives, deep-rooted conflicts, and emotional complexes of an individual.

**19. *What do you know about Raven's Progressive Matrices?***

***Ans.*** Raven's Progressive Matrices are multiple choice intelligence tests of abstract reasoning, originally developed by Dr. John C. Raven in 1936.

**20. *How is Raven's Progressive Matrices test done?***

***Ans.*** In this test, the subject examines an incomplete pattern and chooses a figure from the alternatives that will complete the pattern.

**21. *What is the material that is required for Raven's Progressive Matrices test?***

***Ans.*** RSPM Manual, RSPM Test Booklet, RSPM Answer Sheet, RSPM Scoring Key, Eraser and Pencil.

**22. *Name the three forms of Raven's Progressive Matrices test.***

***Ans.*** Coloured Progressive Matrices (CPM), Standard Progressive Matrices (SPM), and Advanced Progressive Matrices (APM).

**23. *What does Raven's APM measure?***

***Ans.*** The Raven's APM measures high-level observation skills, clear thinking ability, and intellectual capacity.

**24. *What is Raven's test designed for?***

***Ans.*** This test is designed to differentiate between people at the high end of intellectual ability.

**25. *What happens when Raven's test is conducted under timed conditions?***

***Ans.*** When administered under timed conditions, the APM can also be used to assess intellectual efficiency – quick and accurate high-level intellectual work.

**26. *How can be Raven's APM score used?***

***Ans.*** It can be used as an indication of a candidate's potential for success in high-level technical, professional, and executive positions that require high levels of clear and accurate thinking, problem identification, holistic situation assessment, and monitoring of tentative solutions for consistency with all available information.

**27. *List two precautions to be taken in Raven's APM test.***

***Ans.*** Some of the precautions to be taken in Raven's APM test are

(i) Lighting conditions and ventilation should be proper in the room.

(ii) No item should be left unanswered by the candidate.

**28.** *What is the objective of preparing case profile?*

***Ans.*** The main objective of preparing a case profile is to understand the individual in totality.

**29.** *How is an interview different from survey?*

***Ans.*** An interview is different from a survey in that it is always conducted in person and usually involves much fewer persons.

**30.** *What is the difference between the structured and unstructured interviews?*

***Ans.*** Structured interviews follow a predetermined pattern of questions, while unstructured interview has only a set of topics, and actual questions emerge as a part of a conversation.

**31.** *How are interviews more flexible?*

***Ans.*** Interviews have the advantage of being flexible in that promising topics may be pursued in greater detail, questions may be refined or modified along the way, and clarifications may be sought.

**32.** *What is the disadvantage of interview method?*

***Ans.*** The disadvantage of the interview method is that it cannot cover a large number of people and is limited to presenting the views of a select group of individuals.

**33.** *What is observation method?*

***Ans.*** Observation is a method where the researcher must systematically watch and record what is happening in whatever context or situation that has been chosen for the research.

**34.** *Tell about Learning disability?*

***Ans.*** Learning disability is a classification that includes several areas of functioning in which a person has difficulty learning in a typical manner, usually caused by an unknown factor or factors.

**35.** *Name some causes of neurological impairments.*

***Ans.*** Some causes of neurological impairments include - heredity and genetics, problems during pregnancy and birth and accidents after birth.

**36.** *Name some anomalies that cause learning disabilities.*

***Ans.*** Learning disabilities can result from anomalies in the developing brain, illness or injury, fetal exposure to alcohol or drugs, low birth weight, oxygen deprivation, or by premature or prolonged labour.

**37.** *List some symptoms of learning disabilities.*

***Ans.*** Some of the symptoms of learning disabilities are short attention span, poor memory and difficulty in following directions etc.,

**38.** *What is dyslexia about?*

***Ans.*** Dyslexia is the difficulty to read.

**39.** *What is dysgraphia?*

***Ans.*** Dysgraphia is the difficulty to write.

**40.** *What is dyscalculia?*

***Ans.*** Dyscalculia is the difficulty with arithmetic skills.

# SAMPLE QUESTION PAPER 1

## A Highly Simulated Sample Question Paper for CBSE Class XII

# PSYCHOLOGY

### General Instructions

- All questions are compulsory except where internal choice has been given.
- Question Nos. 1-14 in Section A carry 1 mark each.
- Question Nos. 15-19 in Section B are Very Short Answer Type-I questions carrying 2 marks each. Answer to each question should not exceed 30 words.
- Question Nos. 20-23 in Section C are Short Answer Questions Type-II carrying 3 marks each. Answer to each question should not exceed 60 words.
- Question Nos. 24-27 in Section D are Long Answer Type-I questions carrying 4 marks each. Answer to each question should not exceed 120 words.
- Question Nos. 28-29 in Section E are Long Answer Type questions carrying 6 marks. Answer to this question should not exceed 200 words.
- Question Nos. 30-33 in Section F are based on two cases given. Answer to each one-mark question should not exceed 20 words. Answer to each two-mark question should not exceed 30 words.

**Time : 3 hours** **Max. Marks : 70**

**1.** Which of the following personalites gave the conecpt of logotheraphy? (1)

(a) Victor Frankl (b) Sigmund Freud
(c) Ivan Pavlov (d) Carl Rogers

**2.** Rahul, a 14-year-old, excels in multiple subjects at school and participates in various extracurricular activities. He often comes up with creative solutions to problems. His teacher notices his consistent dedication and exceptional performance across different areas. Based on the provided information, how would you classify Rahul's abilities? (1)

(a) Talent (b) Giftedness
(c) Prodigy (d) High creativity

**3.** Mithu, a final year college student of Delhi University, is known as a 'problem solver' in her college. She not only understands student's emotions but also helps them in taking right decisions about courses and job placements. Which of the following traits do you think Mithu possess? (1)

(a) Emotionally Intelligent Person
(b) Emotionally Creative Person
(c) Powerful Influential Person
(d) Socially Influential Person

**4.** Sam is 19-year old athletic built ambitious swimmer. He has been selected for upcoming Asian Games and for that he is preparing hard. However, his coach has found that Sam is bit distressed and not properly taking food or sound sleep. What is the best therapy suitable for him? (1)

(a) Humanistic-existential therapy
(b) Psychoanalytical therapy
(c) Behaviour therapy
(d) Cognitive therapy

**5.** In the following question, a statement of Assertion (A) is followed by a statement of the Reason (R). Read the statements and choose the appropriate option. (1)

**Assertion** (A) Children learn to respect elders by observing their parents.

**Reason** (R) Learning attitudes through modeling involves observing others being rewarded or punished for certain behaviour.

**Codes**
(a) Both A and R are true and R is the correct explanation of A
(b) Both A and R are true, but R is not the correct explanation of A
(c) A is true, but R is false
(d) A is false, but R is true

**6.** Which of the following statements best describes the nature of the therapeutic relationship in psychotherapy? (1)
(a) The therapeutic relationship is a causal and lifelong bond between the therapist and the client.
(b) The therapist dominates the client in all forms of therapy and makes decisions on their behalf.
(c) The therapeutic relationship is a professional, confidential, and dynamic alliance aimed at helping the client overcome psychological issues.
(d) The therapist shares the client's personal information to encourage open discussions.

**7.** Name the Psychologist who proposed the Two-Step Theory of attitude change. (1)
(a) Sigmund Freud (b) Ivan Pavlov
(c) SM Mohsin (d) Fritz Heider

**8.** Suryakant Nayar, a trained Ayurveda Doctor lives in Kerala is known for his knowledge of ancient medicines and always encourages people to opt for traditional methods of medicines and treatment, as mentioned in 'Charak Samhita'.
According to Ayurveda, which of the following is not a 'dosha' for classification of people? (1)
(a) Vamdosha (b) Pittadosha
(c) Vatadosha (c) Kaphadosha

**9.** Which among the following is a dynamic situation-specific reaction to stress? (1)
(a) Stressor (b) Coping
(c) Avoiding (d) Relieving

**10.** Which of the following is not one of the ABC components of an attitude? (1)
(a) Affective–emotional reactions
(b) Behavioural–tendency to act
(c) Cognitive–thoughts and beliefs
(d) Reactive–immediate responses

**11.** Match List I with List II. (1)

| List I (IQ Range) | | List II (Descriptive Label) | |
|---|---|---|---|
| 1. | Above 130 | I. | Average |
| 2. | 120–130 | II. | Superior |
| 3. | 110–119 | III. | Very superior |
| 4. | 90–109 | IV. | High Average |

| | 1, | 2, | 3, | 4 |
|---|---|---|---|---|
| (a) | III, | II, | IV, | I |
| (b) | III, | II, | I, | IV |
| (c) | IV, | I, | III, | II |
| (d) | II, | IV, | I, | III |

**12.** Ramya while facing a job interview, was asked numerous questions regarding her qualifications, likes and dislikes, etc. She confidently gave answers regarding her qualities and skills and other characteristics. The type of identity Ramya possesses is called ............ . (1)
(a) interpersonal identity
(b) ideal self
(c) personal identity
(d) social identity

**13.** Which of the following life skill helps us to communicate, clearly and confidently, our feelings, needs, wants and thoughts? (1)
(a) Time management
(b) Rational thinking
(c) Self-care
(d) Assertiveness

**14.** Radhika, a middle-aged housewife, started hearing voices and became paranoid, believing someone was watching and plotting against her. She withdrew from social interactions, appeared disconnected from reality, and had difficulty following conversations. These symptoms impacted her daily life. Identify the disorder. (1)
(a) Schizophrenia disorder
(b) Anxiety disorder
(c) Neurodevelopmental disorder
(d) Major depressive disorder

FULLY SOLVED

**15.** Do you agree with the statement "Psychological disorders develop when a diathesis is set off by a stressful situation"? Give reasons in support of your answer. (2)

**16.** Vaani is not just smartest girl but also requires less command by her teachers and parents to accomplish any given tasks. She analyse problems and arrives at solutions quickly. Identify the type of intelligence Vaani has. (2)

**17.** Jatin, a college student, often feels anxious and loses his temper quickly. He prefers to stay in his room rather than join social events. Based on HJ Eysenck's personality dimensions, how would you classify Jatin's traits? Explain. (2)

**18.** Tanya is always does some unique activities to get herself physically and mentally fit every day. Why is creative visualisation important in physical fitness? (2)

**19.** What do you know about centrality? (2)

*Or*

Analyse, in which stage a male child experiences the Oedipus complex.

**20.** Ankit rarely does his homework regularly. Her mother promised him to prepare his favourite dish whenever he does homework at the designated time. Identify the reinforcement given by Ankit's mother. How does it benefit the Ankit? (1.5+1.5)

**21.** Explain the 'four Ds' of abnormality? How do these criteria help in identifying psychological disorders? (3)

*Or*

Can heroin intake significantly interfere with social and occupational functioning? What risks are associated with developing a dependence on heroin? (3)

**22.** Ankita, a 17-year-old high school student, has been increasingly withdrawn from her friends and family. Her marks have been dropping, and her parents have noticed that she often refuses to eat meals with them. They have also found large quantities of laxatives and diuretics hidden in her room. Her parents are concerned and suspects that she might have an eating disorder. Based on Ankita's situation, describe the symptoms and behaviours associated with bulimia nervosa. How might her distorted body image and secretive behaviour impact her relationships and daily life? (3)

**23.** Ankit rarely does his homework regularly. Her mother promised him to prepare his favourite dish whenever he does homework at the appointed time. Identify the reinforcement given by Ankit's mother. How does it benefit the person? (3)

**24.** Seema Rajput, a Hindi literature teacher, is renowned in her school, with many students choosing Hindi as a subject due to her warmth and soft-spoken skills. How do students often develop a preference for a specific subject based on their perception of the teacher? Explain this process of attitude formation through association. (4)

*Or*

Priyanka frequently indulges in junk food despite knowing its harmful effects on her health. She desires to give it up but struggles due to guilt.

Describe the psychological process that could lead to a change in her attitude.

**25.** Bhavna, a high school student, who believes in her ability to study effectively and perform well in her final exams. Identify and explain which aspect of self is related to Bhavna's belief and explain which factors can help in the develop- ment of this aspect of self. (4)

**26.** Describe the link between positive thinking and positive attitude in personality trait. (4)

**27.** Explain the PASS Model of Intelligence. (4)

**28.** Describe in-group and out-group bias in social psychology. (6)

*Or* Explain the major characteristics of group formation.

FULLY SOLVED

29. Describe the basic premise of Allport's trait approach to personality. Explain the three categories of traits proposed by Allport-cardinal, central, and secondary traits. Provide examples for each type. (6)

*Or*

Explain Sigmund Freud's concept of ego defence mechanisms and their role in dealing with anxiety. Additionally, evaluate the potential impact of excessive use of these mechanisms on an individual's perception of reality and overall adjustment.

Read the case study given below and answer the questions that follow.

Technologically advanced societies adopt child rearing practices that foster skills of generalisation and abstraction, speed, minimal moves, and mental manipulation among children.

These societies promote a type of behaviour, which can be called technological intelligence. In these societies, persons are well-versed in skills of attention, observation, analysis, performance, speed and achievement orientation. Intelligence tests developed in Western cultures look precisely for these skills in an individual.

30. What is technological intelligence? (1)

31. Why is technological intelligence not valued in many Asian and African societies? (2)

Read the case study given below and answer the questions that follow.

The Humanistic-existential model focuses on broader aspects of human existence. Humanists believe that human beings are born with a natural tendency to be friendly, cooperative and constructive, and are driven to self-actualise, i.e. to fulfil this potential for goodness and growth. Whereas Existentialists believe that from birth we have total freedom to give meaning to our existence or to avoid that responsibility.

Those who shirk from this responsibility would live empty, inauthentic and dysfunctional lives.

In addition to the biological and psychosocial factors, socio-cultural factors such as war and violence, group prejudice and discrimination, economic and employment problems, and rapid social change, put stress on most of us and can also lead to psychological problems in some individuals.

32. How is Humanistic-existential model is useful in the study of human behaviour? (1)

33. Why self-actualisation is necessary according to, Humanistic-existential theory? (2)

FULLY SOLVED

# Answers

1. (a) Victor Frankl
2. (b) Giftedness
3. (a) Emotionally Intelligent Person
4. (c) Behaviour therapy
5. (a) Both A and R are true and R is the correct explanation of A
6. (c) The therapeutic relationship is a professional, confidential, and dynamic alliance aimed at helping the client overcome psychological issues.
7. (c) SM Mohsin
8. (a) Vamdosha
9. (b) Coping
10. (d) Reactive–immediate responses
11. (a) III, II, IV, I
12. (c) personal identity
13. (d) Assertiveness
14. (a) Schizophrenia disorder
15. Yes, I agree with the statement. The diathesis-stress model effectively explains how a combination of biological vulnerability (diathesis) and exposure to stressors can lead to psychological disorders.

    These disorders include anxiety, depression, and schizophrenia, emphasising the interplay between genetics and environment.
16. Vaani has componential or analytical intelligence, where person analysis the given information and quickly solve problems. Persons high on this ability think analytically and critically and succeed in schools.
17. Jatin's traits align with Eysenck's dimensions of neuroticism and introversion. As he has anxiety and quick temper, he exhibits high neuroticism. Additionally, he exhibits high introversion, as he prefers solitude over social activities.

**18.** Creative visualisation is important as it reduces the risk of interference from unbidden thoughts and provides the creative energy needed for turning an imagined scene into reality.

**19.** Centrality pertains to the role of a specific attitude with in the attitude system. An attitude of higher centrality would exert a greater influence on the other attitudes in the system compared to non-central attitudes.

*Or*

The male child experiences the Oedipus complex in Phallic stage. It involves love for the mother, hostility towards the father, and the consequent fear of punishment or castration by the father. A major developmental achievement of this stage by accepting his father's relationship with his mother, and modelling his own behaviour after his father.

**20.** In the given case, Ankit's mother is giving positive reinforcement. Positive reinforcement is a process that strengthens the likelihood of a particular response by adding a stimulus.

The positive reinforcement of making favourite dish will increase the Ankit's behaviour of doing homework at the appointed time. Persons with behavioural problems can be given a token as a reward every time a wanted behaviour occurs. Thus, a positive reinforcement is given to increase the deficit.

**21.** The 'four Ds' of abnormality are deviance, distress, dysfunction, and danger.

(i) Deviance refers to behaviour that is different or extreme.

(ii) Distress refers to behaviour that is unpleasant or upsetting.

(iii) Dysfunction refers to behaviour that interferes with daily activities.

(iv) Danger refers to behaviour that is potentially harmful.

These criteria help in identifying psychological disorders by highlighting key aspects of behaviour that are considered abnormal.

*Or* Yes, heroin intake can significantly interfere with social and occupational functioning. Heroin abusers often develop a dependence on the drug, leading them to prioritise its use above other responsibilities. This can result in neglect of relationships, work, and other important aspects of life. Additionally, heroin abuse can lead to tolerance, withdrawal symptoms, and the danger of overdose, which can be life-threatening.

**22.** Bulimia nervosa is characterised by episodes of binge eating followed by purging behaviours, such as using laxatives or vomiting, to prevent weight gain.

Ankita's secretive behaviour and refusal to eat meals with her family are indicative of possible bulimia nervosa.

Her distorted body image may cause her to perceive herself as overweight despite evidence to the contrary. This can lead to feelings of shame and disgust. This impacts her relationships and daily life as she becomes increasingly withdrawn and preoccupied with food and weight.

**23.** In the given case, Ankit's mother is giving positive reinforcement. Positive reinforcement may be used by the child's mother by preparing the child's favourite dish whenever he does homework at the appointed time.

The positive reinforcement of food will increase the behaviour of doing homework at the appointed time. Persons with behavioural problems can be given a token as a reward every time a wanted behaviour occurs. Thus, appositive reinforcement is given to increase the deficit.

**24.** The process described is known as "Learning attitudes by association." Students often develop a liking for a subject based on the positive qualities they associate with the teacher. When a teacher is perceived as warm, knowledgeable and engaging, students may develop a positive attitude towards the subject they teach. This occurs through a process of association, where the positive qualities of the teacher become linked to the subject itself. As a result, students are more likely to enjoy and engage with the subject. This process highlights the role of teachers in shaping students' attitudes towards learning and the importance of positive teacher-student relationships in education. Thus, attitudes can be shaped by associating one positive notion with a person or object.

*Or* The process that could lead to a change in Priyanka's attitude is cognitive dissonance. This psychological concept, proposed by Leon Festinger, suggests that when there is inconsistency between a person's beliefs or attitudes and their behaviour, it creates a state of discomfort or dissonance. In Priyanka's case, her knowledge of the harmful effects of junk food conflicts with her frequent consumption of it, leading to guilt. To reduce this dissonance, Priyanka may alter her attitude towards junk food, recognising it as harmful and reducing her consumption. This change in attitude would align her beliefs and actions, reducing the psychological discomfort associated with the inconsistency.

**25.** Bhavna's belief in her ability to study effectively and perform well is related to the aspect of self-efficacy. Self-efficacy refers to an individual's belief in their ability to succeed in specific situations or accomplish a task. Factors that can help develop self-efficacy include social modeling (observing others similar to oneself succeed), social persuasion (encouragement and feedback from others), mastery experiences (successes in similar tasks), and psychological responses (emotional and physical states). Our society, parents, and our own positive experiences can help in the development of a strong sense of self-efficacy by presenting positive models during the formative years of children. This belief in one's capabilities can enhance motivation, resilience and overall well-being.

**26.** There is strong correlation between positive thinking and positive attitude. People who inherent consistently positive attitudes can expect great results, which are likely to achieve by them. On the other hand, positive thinking is developed when we have a positive attitude.

Positive attitude included positive health and well-being can be realised by having a positive attitude. Some of the factors leading to a positive attitude are having a fairly accurate perception of reality, a sense of purpose in life and responsibility, acceptance and tolerance for different viewpoints of others, etc.

On the other hand, the power of positive thinking has been increasingly recognised in reducing and coping with stress. Optimism, which is the inclination to expect favourable life outcomes, has been linked to psychological and physical well-being.

**27.** The knowledge base of the PASS Model represents all information obtained from the cultural and social background and throws light on various parts of behaviour. Simultaneous processing is essential for organisation of information into groups or a coherent whole. Knowledge base is closely associated with the Planning, Attention-Arousal, Simultaneous and Successive (PASS) theory of intelligence model and all processes are found within this framework.

The PASS Model of Intelligence, has been developed by JP Das, Jack Naglieri and Kirby in 1994. According to this model, intellectual activity involves the interdependent functioning of three neurological systems, called the functional units of brain.

**28.** In-groups are groups to which a person belongs, and out-groups are groups to which a person does not belong which could therefore become target for in-group bias. In psychology terms, when we develop a strong identity with our own group, the categorisation as in-group and out-group emerges and becomes salient. Gender, ethnicity, occupation, economic and social position are all meaningful dimensions by which a person can define him or herself and others in terms of in-groups and out-groups; this is a process of social (and self) categorisation.

The in-group bias refers to a form of favouritism toward one's own group or criticism of another group. The in-group bias can take many forms and on many dimensions, both evaluative and behavioural. Evaluative in-group bias refers to the rating of one's own group as better (more positive, less negative) on dimensions of judgement, and as such, it is closely related to the concept of prejudice.

Contemporary theorists have been proposing that people may have good reasons to trust and reward those within their in-group, who may in turn help them in the future. This may explain in-group favouritism but may less easily explain evidence of maximum differentiation or out-group derogation. Clearly in-group bias is not just a matter of rational self-interests but may also include more symbolic and emotional benefits to the group.

*Or*

The major characteristics of a group formation are as follows

**Common Motive** The members of a group shares a common outcome with other members. The group may disintegrate when the common motive is satisfied. This refers to a temporary group like a party or groups formed to collect money for relief fund or to celebrate Ganesh Puja. But a group can also have permanent motive or purpose like family, religious groups and clubs which are formed to fulfil some permanent purposes.

**Mutual Benefit** There is a rewarding experience associated with group membership, the mutual benefit. The group provides not only the sense of security to its members but also various benefits and roles to participates certain tasks.

**Social Structure** The group provides a stable organisation of relationships among members, it also provides interaction and communication among members, the group basically act as an idea exchange platform for its members and self-categorisation. The group also provides one as a member of the group.

**Fate Interdependence** Events that affect one group member affects other group members and can affect the ability of the group to meet the goals for which it may have been formed. If a football team is successful, all members share in the glory. But when the team loses, it is a loss for the whole group.

**29.** Gordon Allport's trait approach to personality emphasises that individuals possess a number of traits that are dynamic in nature and determine their behaviour consistently across different situations. According to Allport, traits integrate stimuli and responses, giving coherence to an individual's actions. This approach suggests that people approach varied situations with similar behavioural patterns due to their underlying traits.

Allport categorised traits into three types as follows

(i) **Cardinal Traits** These are highly generalised dispositions that dominate an individual's entire life, often becoming synonymous with their identity.

For example, Mahatma Gandhi's dedication to non-violence and Adolf Hitler's association with Nazism are examples of cardinal traits, leading to terms like "Gandhian" or "Hitlerian."

(ii) **Central Traits** These are less pervasive but still generalised dispositions that are fundamental to an individual's personality. These traits, such as being warm, sincere, or diligent, are typically highlighted in testimonials or job recommendations. They provide a broad description of an individual's core characteristics.

(iii) **Secondary Traits** These are the least generalised characteristics, often seen in specific preferences or attitudes. Examples include a liking for mangoes or a preference for ethnic clothes. These traits do not significantly define a person's overall personality but reflect more situational aspects of behaviour.

*Or*

Sigmund Freud's concept of ego defence mechanisms revolves around the idea that these psychological strategies are employed by the ego to manage anxiety and protect itself from distressing thoughts and feelings.

Freud proposed that when individuals face anxiety-provoking situations or impulsive desires that threaten their sense of self, they unconsciously develop defence mechanisms to distort reality and reduce anxiety.

Few common defence mechanisms includes

- **Repression**, where anxiety-inducing thoughts are pushed out of conscious awareness. For example, a person may completely forget a traumatic event from childhood.
- **Projection** involves attributing one's own unacceptable traits to others, such as a person with aggressive tendencies perceiving others as overly aggressive.
- **Reaction formation** involves adopting behaviours opposite to one's true feelings, such as a person with strong sexual urges exhibiting extreme piety.
- **Rationalisation** makes unreasonable behaviour seem reasonable, like a student buying new pens to improve exam performance.

Excessive reliance on these mechanisms can lead to a significant distortion of reality and various forms of maladjustment. Individuals may struggle to face and resolve their true feelings, leading to persistent anxiety and dysfunctional behaviour patterns. Consequently, their overall psychological health and ability to adapt to reality can be severely compromised.

**30.** Technological intelligence refers to the set of skills and behaviours that are fostered in technologically advanced societies. These skills include generalisation, abstraction, speed, minimal moves and mental manipulation. People with this type of intelligence are proficient in paying attention, observing, analysing, performing tasks, working quickly, and having a strong focus on achievement.

**31.** Technological intelligence is not highly valued in many Asian and African societies because the qualities and skills considered intelligent in these cultures are different from those emphasised in Western cultures. Asian and African cultures value self-reflection and a collectivistic orientation, which focuses on the well-being and harmony of the group, rather than personal achievement and an individualistic orientation.

**32.** The Humanistic-existential model is useful in the study of human behaviour because it emphasises self-acceptance, personal values, personal meaning and individual choice.

**33.** According to Humanistic-existential theory, self-actualisation is necessary because it helps individuals achieve a sense of wholeness and integration, leading to personal growth and fulfillment.

This theory suggests that psychological distress arises from feelings of loneliness, alienation, and a lack of meaning in life. Human beings have an innate desire for personal growth and self-actualisation, and when these needs are suppressed by societal or familial pressures, they experience psychological distress.

# SAMPLE QUESTION PAPER 2

## A Highly Simulated Sample Question Paper for CBSE Class XII

# PSYCHOLOGY

### General Instructions

- All questions are compulsory except where internal choice has been given.
- Question Nos. 1-14 in Section A carry 1 mark each.
- Question Nos. 15-19 in Section B are Very Short Answer Type-I questions carrying 2 marks each. Answer to each question should not exceed 30 words.
- Question Nos. 20-23 in Section C are Short Answer Questions Type-II carrying 3 marks each. Answer to each question should not exceed 60 words.
- Question Nos. 24-27 in Section D are Long Answer Type-I questions carrying 4 marks each. Answer to each question should not exceed 120 words.
- Question Nos. 28-29 in Section E are Long Answer Type questions carrying 6 marks. Answer to this question should not exceed 200 words.
- Question Nos. 30-33 in Section F are based on two cases given. Answer to each one-mark question should not exceed 20 words. Answer to each two-mark question should not exceed 30 words.

**Time : 3 hours** **Max. Marks : 70**

**1.** Saima, an illustrator in newspaper agency is known for her ability to draw satire cartoon on various issues. Her cartoon strikes into the minds of reader with great message. Which type of intelligence she has? (1)

(a) Logical Intelligence
(b) Spatial Intelligence
(c) Imaginative Intelligence
(d) Linguistic Intelligence

**2.** Despite of the fact Renuka couldn't clear NEET exam this time, she doesn't seems shaken. Instead, she has started preparing hurriedly for the upcoming exams with same amount of motivation and spirit. Name the trait she possess as per Friedman and Rosenman. (1)

(a) Type-A Personality
(b) Type-B Personality
(c) Type-C Personality
(d) Type A-B Personality

**3.** Karan, who was suffering from depression and mental health issues, suggested to visit psychotherapist, who suggested Karan to adopt logotherapy, which helped him in finding meaning in every aspect of life. It also encouraged him to deal positively with good and bad experiences.

Who propounded the logotherapy concept? (1)

(a) Sigmund Freud (b) Victor Frankl
(c) Ivan Pavlov (d) BF Skinner

**4.** Sanya, a 35-year-old woman, has been experiencing severe anxiety and panic attacks for the past few months. She reads about different therapeutic approaches including, Cognitive Behaviour Therapy (CBT). Which of the following statements about CBT is most accurate? (1)

(a) CBT focuses solely on addressing biological aspects of distress.
(b) CBT combines cognitive therapy with medication for treating psychological disorders.

(c) CBT is not effective for treating anxiety, depression or panic attacks.
(d) CBT is a comprehensive technique that addresses biological, psychological, and social aspects of distress through relaxation procedures, behaviour therapy and cognitive therapy techniques.

**5.** Raghav, with a high level of self-esteem, is less likely to change his attitude towards a political issue compared to Mary, who has lower self-esteem. In the context of attitude change, this is an example of ......... characteristics. (1)

(a) source (b) target
(c) message (d) mode

**6.** Emily, a student, often finds herself thinking, "I'll never be good enough for anything." According to Aaron Beck, such persistent negative thoughts are characterised by (1)

(a) emotional regulation
(b) cognitive distortions
(c) behavioural reinforcements
(d) social conformity

**7.** Pooja a class 2 student in Delhi faces problems in basic skills in reading, writing and mathematics, but her teachers says that she do better with additional efforts. The disorder she is facing called as ...... . (1)

(a) specific mental disorder
(b) specific learning disorder
(c) common learning disorder
(d) cognitive disorder

**8.** Which of the following attributes, assesses an individual's preference for engaging in specific activities relative to others? (1)

(a) Intelligence (b) Aptitude
(c) Interest (d) Personality

**9.** Which of the following combinations correctly matches the factor influencing attitude formation with its effect? (1)

(a) Personal Experiences – Attitudes are formed only by observing others in society.
(b) Reference Groups – Indicate norms that influence thinking and acceptable behaviour, especially during adolescence.
(c) Family and School Environment – Influence attitudes only through reading and media exposure.
(d) Media-related Influences – Only reinforce behaviour, not cognitive or affective components of attitudes.

**10.** Which of the following statements best explains why defining abnormality is complex? (1)

(a) All psychological disorders have a fixed and universal definition.
(b) Abnormal behaviour is always easily distinguishable from normal behaviour.
(c) Definitions of abnormality depend on various factors such as statistical rarity, societal norms, and individual distress, making it a complex process.
(d) There is complete agreement among professionals on what constitutes abnormality.

**11.** In this question, a statement of Assertion (A) is followed by a statement of the Reason (R). Read the statements and choose the appropriate option. (1)

**Assertion** (A) Freud proposed a five-stage theory of personality development, where problems encountered at any stage can have long-term effects on a person's life.

**Reason** (R) According to Freud, the core aspects of personalaity are established early, remain stable throughout life, and can be changed only with great difficulty.

**Codes**

(a) Both A and R are true and R is the correct explanation of A
(b) Both A and R are true, but R is not the correct explanation of A
(c) A is true, but R is false
(d) A is false, but R is true

**12.** The term 'Dissociation' in psychology can be viewed as severance of the connections between ideas and emotions. Which among the following conditions are associated with it? (1)

(a) Associative Amnesia
(b) Depersonalisation and Dissociative Identity Disorder
(c) Personalisation
(d) All of the above

13. Emma recently experienced the sudden breakup of a long-term relationship and had to move to a new house due to a job transfer. Consequently, she finds it challenging to cope with the changes and experiences symptoms of stress. Which category of stressors does Emma's situation best exemplify? (1)

(a) Life Events
(b) Hassles
(c) Traumatic Events
(d) None of these

14. Which of the following statements is not true about self-esteem? (1)

(a) Self-esteem refers to a person's value judgement about themselves.
(b) High self-esteem is associated with better school performance and peer acceptance.
(c) Self-esteem cannot be measured through self-reports.
(d) Warm and positive parenting helps develop high self-esteem in children.

UNSOLVED

15. Radhika comes from a family where members are overly involved in each other's activities and emotions, leading to her struggle with independence. Despite having friends, Radhika often feels isolated. Explain how socio-cultural factors contribute to Radhika's difficulties in becoming independent and maintaining fulfilling relationships. (2)

16. According to Erikson's theory, why is ego identity considered crucial in personality development, particularly during adolescence? Provide a brief explanation of Erikson's concept of identity crisis and its significance in the developmental process. (2)

17. Esha is always eager to help others and share her toys with her friends. Her parents often praise her for being kind and generous. As Esha grows older, she continues to exhibit these behaviours, seeking approval and appreciation from others. Over time, her behaviour becomes a consistent part of her personality. Which is the structural unit of personality according to many behaviourists? (2)

18. Rohan has been diagnosed with Obsessive-Compulsive Disorder (OCD). He feels compelled to check the locks on his door repeatedly before leaving the house, fearing that the door might be left unlocked. This checking behaviour is driven by obsessive thoughts of someone breaking in, despite knowing it's unlikely. What is Obsessive-Compulsive Disorder (OCD)? (2)

19. Kriti has been experiencing setbacks in work life and she is also facing trouble in her friendships. She reaches out to a therapist who tells her that she has been under a lot of stress lately. What are the common signs of stress? (2)

*Or*

Jatin has always struggled with maintaining healthy relationships. He often finds himself in conflicts with friends and family due to his inability to communicate effectively and manage his emotions. After realising the impact this has on his life, Jatin decides to work on his life skills. Describe the meaning and importance of life skills.

20. Alternative therapies, including yoga and meditation, have gained popularity as treatment options for psychological distress in the past few decades. How do alternative therapies such as yoga and meditation contribute to mental health treatment, according to the passage? (3)

21. Jahnvi, a young woman, experiences persistent feelings of sadness and loss of interest in her usual activities. She also struggles with changes in appetite, constant sleep problems, and feelings of worthlessness. Identify the disorder Jahnvi is suffering from. Additionally, discuss in brief, the predisposing factors contributing to her symptoms. (1.5+1.5)

22. Explain unconditional positive regards for others in the context of counselling. (3)

*Or* Explain negative reinforcement and positive reinforcement for behaviour modification.

**23.** Radhika has been diagnosed with generalised anxiety disorder. Explain the development of this disorder with the help of the diathesis-stress model. (3)

**24.** Explain Allport's Self-report measures in assessment of personality. (4)

**25.** In the field of psychology, intelligence is a complex and multifaceted concept that has been studied through various theories. Two major approaches to understanding intelligence are the psychometric/structural approach and the information-processing approach. What do you understand by the psychometric approach and the information-processing approach? (4)

**26.** Rehana is always worried about her children's future. Due to family pressure to have a boy child, she became the mother of six girls. Her in-laws always taunt her and don't treat her equally in the family. She remains under great stress all day long. Explain the psychological meaning and process of stress in this context. (2+2)

**27.** Sarah is a 10 year old girl who has been struggling in school. Despite receiving extra help and support from her teachers, she has difficulty in learning even basic skills like reading and math. Sarah also struggles with tasks that require independence, such as dressing herself or following simple instructions. Her parents are concerned and have noticed that she seems to be significantly behind her peers in terms of her intellectual development. Based on Sarah's difficulties and the criteria for intellectual disability, how would you assess her situation? (2+2)

*Or*

Maya is a very bright student. She always gets top grades in her class and is very good at solving math problems and understanding difficult concepts in science. However, Maya struggles with making friends and often feels lonely. She finds it hard to understand how others are feeling and sometimes says things that hurt their feelings without meaning to. Maya also gets very nervous before exams and finds it hard to calm down. Based on Maya's experiences, how would you explain the concept of emotional intelligence?

How do you think improving emotional intelligence could help Maya in her school and personal life?

**28.** Who discovered the process of groupthink? Also discuss about the process of groupthink. (1+5)

*Or*

Summarise the meaning of 'group polarigation'. Explain the factors which contribute to its occurrence.

**29.** Describe attitudes and write about formation of attitudes. (1+5)

*Or*

Identify the factors that affect the attitude formation.

Read the case study given below and answer the questions that follow.

On the one hand, there are the gifted and creative persons. On the other hand, there are children who face enormous difficulty in learning even very simple skills. Those children who show intellectual deficiency are termed as 'intellectually disabled'. As a group, there is wide variation among the intellectually disabled. The American Association on Mental Deficiency (AAMD) views intellectual disability as "significantly sub-average general intellectual functioning existing concurrently with deficits in adaptive behaviour and manifested during the developmental period". Individuals who are categorised as having intellectual disability show significant variation in their abilities, ranging from those who can be taught to work and function with special attention, to those who cannot be trained and require institutional care throughout their lives.

**30.** What symptoms are associated with intellectual disability disorder? (1)

**31.** Explain intellectual giftedness. (2)

Read the case study given below and answer the questions that follow.

Gary is a 19 year old, who withdrew from college after experiencing a manic episode during which he was brought to the attention of the Campus Police. He had changed his stream from engineering to philosophy. He spends his nights on phone, talking to his friends about life and reality. He had been convinced about the importance of his ideas, stating frequently that he was more learned and advanced than all his professors.

He also increased a number of high-risk behaviours - drinking and engaging in sexual relations in a way that was unlike his previous history. At the present time, he has returned home and has been placed on a mood stabiliser (after a period of time on an antipsychotic), and his psychiatrist is requesting adjunctive psychotherapy for his disorder. The patient's parents are somewhat shocked by the diagnosis, but they acknowledge that Gary had early problems with anxiety during pre-adolescence, followed by some periods of withdrawal and depression during his adolescence. His parents are eager to be involved in treatment, if appropriate.

**32.** Identify the disorder with which Gary has been diagnosed. (1)

**33.** What is Bipolar disorder? Mention few symptoms of it. (1+1)

# Answers

**1.** (b) Spatial Intelligence

**2.** (a) Type-A Personality

**3.** (b) Victor Frankl

**4.** (d) CBT is a comprehensive technique that addresses biological, psychological, and social aspects of distress through relaxation procedures, behaviour therapy, and cognitive therapy techniques.

**5.** (b) target

**6.** (b) cognitive distortions

**7.** (b) specific learning disorder

**8.** (c) Interest

**9.** (b) Reference Groups – Indicate norms that influence thinking and acceptable behaviour, especially during adolescence.

**10.** (c) Definitions of abnormality depend on various factors such as statistical rarity, societal norms, and individual distress, making it a complex process.

**11.** (a) Both A and R are true and R is the correct explanation of A

**12.** (b) Depersonalisation and Dissociative Identity Disorder

**13.** (a) Life Events

**14.** (c) Self-esteem cannot be measured through self-reports.

# SAMPLE QUESTION PAPER 3

## A Highly Simulated Sample Question Paper for CBSE Class XII

# PSYCHOLOGY

### General Instructions

- All questions are compulsory except where internal choice has been given.
- Question Nos. 1-14 in Section A carry 1 mark each.
- Question Nos. 15-19 in Section B are Very Short Answer Type-I questions carrying 2 marks each. Answer to each question should not exceed 30 words.
- Question Nos. 20-23 in Section C are Short Answer Questions Type-II carrying 3 marks each. Answer to each question should not exceed 60 words.
- Question Nos. 24-27 in Section D are Long Answer Type-I questions carrying 4 marks each. Answer to each question should not exceed 120 words.
- Question Nos. 28-29 in Section E are Long Answer Type questions carrying 6 marks. Answer to this question should not exceed 200 words.
- Question Nos. 30-33 in Section F are based on two cases given. Answer to each one-mark question should not exceed 20 words. Answer to each two-mark question should not exceed 30 words.

**Time : 3 hours** **Max. Marks : 70**

**1.** In the ......... stage, the parasympathetic nervous system calls for more cautious use of the body's resources. (1)

(a) alarm reaction (b) resistance
(c) exhaustion (d) adaptation

**2.** Which of the following psychologists proposed the Rational Emotive Therapy (RET)? (1)

(a) Abraham Maslow
(b) Albert Ellis
(c) Aaron Beck
(d) Carl Rogers

**3.** Kanika is a 35-year-old woman who feels overwhelmed by her emotions but finds it difficult to express them. She feels disconnected from herself and struggles to understand why she reacts to situations the way she does. Despite her successful career, Kanika feels a sense of emptiness and dissatisfaction in her life. She might benefit from a therapy that focuses on increasing self-awareness and self-acceptance. Identify the type of therapy which can help her. (1)

(a) Cognitive Behavioral Therapy
(b) Gestalt Therapy
(c) Psychodynamic Therapy
(d) Existential Therapy

**4.** Which of the following statements best describes the concept of attitude valence? (1)

(a) It refers to the number of beliefs a person holds about a topic.
(b) It shows how strongly a person behaves towards something.
(c) It reflects whether an attitude is positive, negative, or neutral towards an object.
(d) It measures how often a person changes their mind.

**5.** In this question, a statement of Assertion (A) is followed by a statement of Reason (R). Read the statements and choose the appropriate option. (1)

**Assertion** (A) The basis of meaning making is a person's quest for finding the spiritual truth of one's existence.

**Reason** (R) Therefore Frankl emphasised the role of spiritual anxieties in leading to meaninglessness.

**Codes**

(a) Both A and R are true and R is the correct explanation of A
(b) Both A and R are true, but R is not the correct explanation of A
(c) A is true, but R is false
(d) A is false, but R is true

**6.** Name the psychologist who experimented the prejudices and attitude - behaviour relationship survey by American towards Chinese. (1)

(a) Abraham Maslow (b) Joseph E. McGrath
(c) Richard LaPiere (d) B F Skinner

**7.** Shrishti is elder daughter of Gupta family. She is considered as the most introverted person in the family who doesn't mix up with people and loves to remain busy in her own projects and studies. Which among the following are not introversion personality traits? (1)

(a) Impulsive
(b) Solitary
(c) Socially withdrawn
(d) Cautious and passive

**8.** Which among the following is a dynamic developmental process that involves maintenance of positive adjustment under challenging life conditions? (1)

(a) Positive attribute (b) Resilience
(c) Free spirit (d) Stress management

**9.** Which of the following therapies adopts a bio-psychosocial approach to understanding of psychopathology? (1)

(a) Alternative Therapy
(b) Cognitive Behaviour Therapy
(c) Humanistic Therapy
(d) Therapeutic Alliance

**10.** Which of the following is not a part of Thurstone's Primary Mental Abilities? (1)

(a) Verbal comprehension
(b) Musical ability
(c) Word fluency
(d) Inductive reasoning

**11.** Despite experiencing strong feelings of anger towards her colleague, Jane always goes out of her way to be excessively kind and helpful to him. Which defense mechanism is Jane exhibiting if she feels strong anger towards her colleague but acts excessively kind and helpful towards him? (1)

(a) Sublimation (b) Denial
(c) Reaction formation (d) Projection

**12.** Name the skill that has a positive effects on reducing tension, anxiety and depression. (1)

(a) Physical exercise
(b) Social alienation
(c) Excessive eating
(d) Excessive sleeping

**13.** According to the classification of symptoms in schizophrenia, which of the following combinations is correctly matched? (1)

(a) Positive symptoms–Poverty of speech, social withdrawal, avolition
(b) Negative symptoms–Delusions, hallucinations, inappropriate affect
(c) Psychomotor symptoms–Catatonic stupor, rigidity, posturing
(d) Positive symptoms–Catatonia, blunted affect, apathy

**14.** Rahul, a 35-year-old man with schizophrenia, often hears voices speaking to him, telling him to do things or commenting on his actions. All of this is distressing and confusing for him, as the voices sometimes argue with each other or make derogatory remarks about him. In this example, Rahul's experience of hearing voices is an example of ..................... . (1)

(a) Visual hallucinations
(b) Auditory hallucinations
(c) Tactile hallucinations
(d) Olfactory hallucinations

**15.** Swarnalipi is an organised girl who does everything according to her own schedule and planning. She also motivates others to do the same. Identify and define the type of her intelligence. (2)

**16.** Urmila has enrolled in a new skill development course to further enhance her career. She never hesitate to expand her knowledge. What does Carl Rogers says about people like Urmila? (2)

*Or*

Parents of Sonam are really proud of her daughter as she is the youngest Youtuber with

UNSOLVED

5 million strong followers. She is just 7 but has memorised various facts and figures.

Explain the two characteristics of her personality.

**17.** Explain any two features of Self-report Measures Test. (2)

**18.** Rahul has a positive attitude towards foreigners, believing they are interesting and friendly. This attitude provides him with a mental framework that guides his behaviour, making him more open and welcoming whenever he meets someone from another country. What is the purpose served by an attitude (2)

**19.** Name the psychological disorder where an individual behaves temporarily in two different or opposite ways at the same time. (2)

**20.** Mandy is an emerging and promising Radio Jockey (RJ) who hosts a Q&A session every Saturday from 9 to 10 PM. He addresses common problems and issues related to difficult married life over the phone. Do you believe he possesses certain personality traits? (3)

**21.** Rani, a 10 years girl has been diagnosed with moderate level of self-skill and speech-related problem. Medical treatment proved unsuccessful to bring her into mainstream life. Describe some characteristics of individuals with varying levels of intellectual disability. (3)

**22.** How Electro-Convulsive Therapy (ECT) is used in biomedical therapy? (3)

*Or*

How is psychotherapy proving helpful through its different therapeutic approaches? Describe five goals and aims of Psychotherapy.

**23.** "Attitude are learned through one's own experience." Critically examine this statement. (3)

**24.** Why modern thinkers and psychologists gives utmost importance to Emotional Intelligence? Mention some of its attributes. (1+3)

*Or*

What is the role of 'Arousal-Attention' in PASS Model of Intelligence? Explain with some of its characteristics.

**25.** Sanya, a psychology student, is conducting a study on personality assessment techniques. She decides to use projective techniques to uncover unconscious motives and feelings in her participants. How do projective techniques differ from direct methods of personality assessment, and what advantage do they offer in understanding an individual's personality? (4)

**26.** Ravi is known for his imaginative and curious nature. He enjoys exploring new ideas and engaging in cultural activities. He is also very social, outgoing, and assertive, often taking the lead in social situations. However, he tends to be emotionally unstable, often feeling anxious and distressed. Despite this, he is highly dependable, responsible, and hardworking, always striving to achieve his goals. Additionally, he is very friendly and cooperative, always willing to help others. Based on the Five-Factor Model of Personality, identify and describe the five personality traits that characterise Ravi. (4)

**27.** Define disruptive, impulse-control and conduct disorders? (4)

**28.** "The Group satisfies one's psychological and social needs." Elaborate. (6)

*Or*

Explain the major advantages and disadvantages by group formation.

**29.** How does stress impact the immune system and health? (3+3)

UNSOLVED

*Or*

Given what you know about coping strategies, what suggestion would you give to your friends to avoid stress in their everyday lives.

Read the case study given below and answer the questions that follow.

Interpersonal intelligence is an ability to understand to subtle aspects of others' behaviours. Psychologists, counsellors, politicians, social workers, and religious leaders are likely to possess high interpersonal intelligence. On the other hand, intrapersonal is an ability to understand of one's own feelings, motives, and desires.

This refers to the knowledge of one's internal strengths and limitations and using that knowledge to effectively relate to others. Persons high on this ability have finer sensibilities regarding their identity, human existence, and meaning of life. Philosophers and spiritual leaders present examples of this type of intelligence.

**30.** Psychologist, counsellors, politicians, social workers, and religious leaders are likely to posses high interpersonal intelligence. Why? (1)

**31.** Describe any two methods to enhance one's interpersonal intelligence. (2)

Read the case study given below and answer the questions that follow.

Children with autism spectrum disorder experience profound difficulties in relating to other people. They are unable to initiate social behaviour and seem unresponsive to other people's feelings. They are unable to share experiences or emotions with others. They also show serious abnormalities in communication and language that persist over time. Many of them never develop speech and those who do, have repetitive and deviant speech patterns.

Such children often show narrow patterns of interests and repetitive behaviours such as lining up objects or stereotyped body movements such as rocking. These motor movements may be self-stimulatory such as hand flapping or self-injurious such as banging their head against the wall.

**32.** What challenges do children face in autism spectrum disorder ? (1)

**33.** Describe some of the signs of self-stimulatory behaviour of child autism. (2)

UNSOLVED

# Answers

**1.** (b) resistance

**2.** (b) Albert Ellis

**3.** (b) Gestalt Therapy

**4.** (c) It reflects whether an attitude is positive, negative, or neutral towards an object.

**5.** (b) Both A and R are true, but R is not the correct explanation of A

**6.** (c) Richard LaPiere

**7.** (a) Impulsive

**8.** (b) Resilience

**9.** (b) Cognitive Behaviour Therapy

**10.** (b) Musical ability

**11.** (c) Reaction formation

**12.** (a) Physical exercise

**13.** (c) Psychomotor symptoms–Catatonic stupor, rigidity, posturing

**14.** (b) Auditory hallucinations

# BOARD QUESTION PAPER 2025

# PSYCHOLOGY

## General Instructions

- All questions are compulsory except where internal choice has been given.
- Question Nos. 1-14 in Section A carry 1 mark each.
- Question Nos. 15-19 in Section B are Very Short Answer Type-I questions carrying 2 marks each. Answer to each question should not exceed 30 words.
- Question Nos. 20-23 in Section C are Short Answer Questions Type-II carrying 3 marks each. Answer to each question should not exceed 60 words.
- Question Nos. 24-27 in Section D are Long Answer Type-I questions carrying 4 marks each. Answer to each question should not exceed 120 words.
- Question Nos. 28 & 29 in Section E are Long Answer Type questions carrying 6 marks. Answer to this question should not exceed 200 words.
- Question Nos. 30-33 in Section F are based on two cases given. Answer to each one-mark question should not exceed 20 words. Answer to each two-mark question should not exceed 30 words.

**Time : 3 hours** **Max. Marks : 70**

**1.** Madhu is a student who excels in remembering facts and figures but struggles when it comes to solving complex problems that require critical thinking and creativity. According to Arthur Jensen, which level of abilities does Madhu possess? (1)

(a) Level II, associative learning
(b) Level I, cognitive competence
(c) Level I, associative learning
(d) Level II, observational learning

**2.** Match the following. (1)

| | Rearing Practices | Correlation | |
|---|---|---|---|
| 1. | Identical twins reared in different environment | I. | 0.50 |
| 2. | Fraternal twins reared together | II. | 0.60 |
| 3. | Brothers and sisters reared together | III. | 0.72 |
| 4. | Siblings reared apart | IV. | 0.25 |

| | 1 | 2 | 3 | 4 |
|---|---|---|---|---|
| (a) | I, | II, | III, | IV |
| (b) | III, | II, | I, | IV |
| (c) | IV, | I, | III, | II |
| (d) | II, | IV, | I, | III |

**3.** A researcher is conducting a survey to assess the personality traits of participants. One of the items in the survey asks, "( always help others when they are in need." Which of following biases is most likely to attect the response to this item? (1)

(a) Non-response bias (b) Acquiescence
(c) Random responding (d) Social desirability

**4.** Which of the following best describes the nature of creativity tests where there are no specified answers to questions or problems, allowing for freedom to use one's imagination and express it in original ways? (1)

(a) Divergent (b) Convergent
(c) Analytical (d) Structured

**5.** Which of the following is not a major criticism of Psychodynamic theories? (1)

(a) They are largely based on case studies and lack a rigorous scientific basis.
(b) They use small and a typical individuals as samples for advancing generalisations.

(c) The concepts are well defined and easily submitted to scientific
(d) They face criticism for using non-representative samples

**6.** In the following question, a statement of Assertion (A) is followed by a statement of Reason (R). Read the statements and choose the appropriate option. (1)

**Assertion (A)** Psychological tests are widely used for clinical diagnosis, guidance, personnel selection, placement and training.

**Reason (R)** Objective tests provide a standardised and reliable measure of an individual's psychological attributes.

(a) Both (A) and (R) are true, and (R) is the correct explanation of (A).
(b) Both Assertion (A) and (R) are true, but (R) is the correct explanation of (A)
(c) (A) is true, but (R) is false.
(d) (A) is false, but (R) is true.

**7.** A study finds that individuals who are regularly exposed to high stress levels have a higher incidence of infections. This observation can be explained by. (1)

(a) Enhanced production of antibodies during stress.
(b) Increased white cell count due to stress.
(c) Impaired immune response due to stress.
(d) Reduced need for sleep due to stress.

**8.** A person dislikes a type of food, expresses negative opinion about it, and avoids it. Which components of the A-B-C model of attitudes are illustrated in this example? (1)

(a) Affective and Cognitive
(b) Affective and Behavioural
(c) Cognitive and Behavioural
(d) Affective, Behavioural and Cognitive

**9.** Which method of message transmission is likely to be most effective for creating a positive attitude towards Oral Rehydration Salts (ORS) for young children? (1)

(a) Mass media advertisements
(b) Pamphlets and brochures
(c) Community social workers and doctors talking to people directly
(d) Radio announcements

**10.** A peaceful audience at a sports event suddenly turns into a frenzied mob following a controversial decision by the referee. Which factors are likely responsible for this transformation? (1)

(a) The audience's initial passive nature
(b) The presence of clear and enforced rules
(c) The polarisation of attention and shared emotions among the audience
(d) The diverse opinions and behaviours within the crowd

**11.** According to Sheldon's typology, which of the following combinations correctly matches the body build with the associated temperament? (1)

(a) Endomorphs–Thin, long, fragile, brainy, artistic, introvert
(b) Mesomorphs–Strong musculature, strong body build, rectangular, energetic, courageous
(c) Ectomorphs–Fat, soft, round, relaxed, sociable
(d) Endomorphs–Strong musculature, rectangular, energetic, courageous

**12.** A company is forming a new committee to plan a major event. To ensure effective collaboration, they want the committee to function as a primary group. Which of the following strategies would best support this goal? (1)

(a) Assigning clear roles and tasks to each member
(b) Encouraging frequent, informal interactions among members
(c) Setting strict rules and guidlines for all meetings
(d) Limiting communication to official emails and reports

**13.** Ravi constantly believes he is a failure because he once performed poorly on a test. Which cognitive problem is he exhibiting according to the Cognitive Model? (1)

(a) Accurate self-assessment
(b) Overgeneralisation

(c) Rational thinking
(d) Logical reasoning

**14.** Which of the following statements best describes how societal norms influence the perception of abnormal behaviour? (1)

(a) Societal norms are universally consistent and do not change over time.
(b) Behaviours, thoughts and emotions that align with societal norms are always considered abnormal.
(c) Societal norms are derived from society's culture, including its history, values and institutions and these norms can change over time.
(d) Aggressive behaviour is universally accepted as normal behaviour across all cultures.

**15.** A teacher notices that Neeraj, one of her class 5 students, learns new languages very easily, loves new subjects, and is very sensitive to changes in the classroom. Comment on the intellectual abilities of Neeraj. (2)

**16.** (a) Discuss the difference between a simple and a complex attitude system using the example of attitude towards health and well-being versus attitude towards a particular person. (2)

*OR*

(b) Assess and write the impact of family and school environment on attitude formation.

**17.** Identify and explain two strategies to reduce social loafing within a group. (2)

**18.** How can assertiveness impact an individual's response to stress? (2)

**19.** Evaluate the role of common motives and goals in forming and maintaining a cohesive group, with an example. (2)

**20.** You are working with a client who handles high stress well and remains healthy. How would you evaluate and support their ability to manage stress effectively? (3)

**21.** Explain how the Age of Reason and Enlightenment influenced the treatment and perception of psychological disorders in the seventeenth and eighteenth centuries. (3)

**22.** (a) Analyse the relationship between intelligence and creativity, based on Terman's research findings. (3)

*OR*

(b) Evaluate how Gardner's view of intelligence as an independent and interactive type challenges the traditional notions of a singular, unified intelligence.

**23.** Ashok, who suffers from Obsessive Compulsive Disorder (OCD), is considering alternative therapies to complement his current treatment. Recommend and justify which approach might be most beneficial for Ashok. (3)

**24.** (a) Compare and contrast technological and integral approaches to intelligence. Also discuss the cultural factors that may influence these perspectives. (4)

*OR*

(b) Manoj and Sunil are two managers in a company. State four reasons how Manoj's higher emotional intelligence contributes to his popularity with colleagues as compared to Sunil, who lacks these qualities.

**25.** Describe four methods through which attitudes are formed. (4)

**26.** You are a psychologist assessing the personality and emotional state of a new client using projective techniques. You decide to use the Sentence Completion Test and Draw-a-Person Test. Describe how you would use these tests and explain what kind of information you might gain from each test. (4)

**27.** Meera has an intense irrational fear of spiders and experiences sudden episodes of intense terror with breathlessness and dizziness. Identify the two types of anxiety disorders she might be suffering from and suggest one coping strategy for each. (4)

**28.** (a) How does Freud explain the stability and potential changes in personality over a person's lifetime? Provide an overview of each stage and discuss the impact of encountering problems at any stage on personality development. (6)

*OR*

(b) How do ecological and cultural environments influence personality development? Provide concrete examples from hunting-gathering and agricultural societies to illustrate your answer.

**29.** (a) Discuss the role of core schemas, negative automatic thoughts, cognitive distortions and irrational beliefs in cognitive therapies. (6)

*OR*

(b) Discuss six key ethical standards that professional psychotherapists must adhere to. Explain how each standard contributes to the effectiveness of psychotherapy and ensures the well-being of clients.

**(Case Study–1)**

**Read the case study given below and answer the questions (Q. 30 and 31) that follow.**

Social stress can be broadly defined as a situation which threatens one's relationships, esteem, or sense of belonging within a dyad group, or larger social context. Social stress, can emerge in a number of situations.

Social stress can stem from difficult social interactions, for example, a conflictual or tumultuous marital or family relationship. Social stress can also emerge in the context of evaluated performance situations, where others could be judgemental or critical, or in contexts in which one feels rejected, ostracised, or ignored. Social stress can also be more broadly construed, representing perceptions of one's lower role or standing within a group or community. Social stress can lead to a range of observable and measurable responses related to health outcomes.

**30.** What impact can social stress have on an individual? (1)

**31.** State two causes of social stress in day-to-day life. (2)

**(Case Study - 2)**

**Read the case study given below and answer the questions (Q. 32 and 33) that follow.**

At any one time, a diverse set of individual, family, community and structural factors may combine to protect or undermine mental health.

Although most people are resilient, people who are exposed to adverse circumstances–including poverty, violence, disability and inequality–are at higher risk of developing a mental health condition. Protective and risk factors include individual, psychological and biological factors, such as emotional skills as well as genetics. Many of the risks and protective factors are influenced through changes in brain structure and/or function.

People with mental disorders also require social support, including support in developing and maintaining personal, family and social relationships. People with mental disorders may also need support for educational programmes, employment, housing and participation in other meaningful activities.

**32.** According to the above paragraph, what type of people are more likely to have a psychological disorder? (1)

**33.** State two steps which are helpful in addressing the concerns of mentally-ill people. (2)

# Answers

**1.** (c) Level I, associative learning

**2.** (b) III, II, I, IV

**3.** (d) Social desirability

**4.** (a) Divergent

**5.** (c) The concepts are well defined and easily submitted to scientific testing.

**6.** (a) Both (A) and (R) are true, and (R) is the correct explanation of (A).

**7.** (c) Impaired immune response due to stress

**8.** (d) Affective, Behavioural and Cognitive

**9.** (c) Community social workers and doctors talking to people directly

**10.** (c) The polarisation of attention and shared emotions among the audience

**11.** (b) Mesomorphs–Strong musculature, strong body build, rectangular, energetic, courageous

**12.** (b) Encouraging frequent, informal interactions among members

**13.** (b) Overgeneralisation

**14.** (c) Societal norms are derived from society's culture, including its history, values and institutions and these norms can change over time.

**15.** Neeraj shows high intellectual abilities, including quick learning, curiosity for new knowledge and heightened sensitivity to his environment, suggesting giftedness and potential for exceptional cognitive and emotional growth.

**16.** (a) A simple attitude system involves consistent beliefs, emotions and actions, like prioritising health. A complex attitude system includes conflicting elements, such as mixed feelings towards a person, showing inconsistency.

*OR*

(b) Family influences attitudes through values and behaviour modelling, while schools shape them by teaching societal norms, promoting interactions and encouraging critical thinking, which significantly impacts personality and beliefs.

**17.** The two strategies to reduce social loafing within a group are

(i) **Assign Individual Tasks** This ensures accountability and motivates members to contribute equally.

(ii) **Set Clear Goals** Unified objectives inspire teamwork, which reduces chances of loafing.

**18.** Assertiveness helps manage stress by enabling individuals to express feelings, set boundaries and resolve conflicts effectively, which reduces the emotional burden and fostering control over challenging situations. It promotes healthier coping mechanisms.

**19.** Common motives and shared goals unite individuals, which fosters teamwork and reduces conflicts. For example, sports teams work cohesively to win matches, showcasing aligned efforts for mutual success and bonding.

**20.** To evaluate stress management, we need to observe the client's coping skills, resilience and emotional stability in challenging situations. There is a need to check their use of strategies like relaxation techniques, problem-solving and maintaining healthy habits.

Support their stress-handling ability by encouraging mindfulness practices, regular physical activity and positive social interactions. Provide constructive feedback and set achievable goals to enhance resilience and overall well-being effectively.

**21.** The Age of Reason and Enlightenment shifted views on psychological disorders. People began seeing mental illness as a medical issue, not supernatural. Compassionate care replaced harsh treatments. Shelters were established to provide humane environments. This era emphasised therapy, social interaction, and recovery-focused approaches, laying the foundation for modern mental health care

**22.** (a) Terman's research suggests a positive relationship between intelligence and creativity, but only to a certain extent. High intelligence often supports creativity by providing problem-solving skills and knowledge. However, creativity also involves originality and divergent thinking, which are not entirely dependent on intelligence.

Thus, although intelligence helps creativity but being highly creative doesn't always require exceptional intelligence. Both are distinct but connected traits.

*OR*

(b) Gardner's view challenges traditional ideas of intelligence by proposing multiple intelligences, for example, linguistic, spatial, interpersonal, etc., instead of a single IQ. He argues these intelligences are independent yet interact to solve problems.

His approach of multiple intelligences highlights diverse talents and abilities, emphasising creativity, emotional skills, and practical knowledge, showing intelligence as a broader and more dynamic concept beyond standardised tests.

**23.** Ashok can try Cognitive Behavioural Therapy, especially Exposure and Response Prevention because this therapy helps him to face his fears and reduce compulsive behaviours gradually.

CBT and ERP therapies are effective because they teach Ashok to manage anxiety without relying on rituals and improve his daily life. Combining this with mindfulness can further enhance his emotional control and well-being.

**24.** (a) Technological approaches to intelligence focus on measuring cognitive skills through tests and algorithms, which emphasise problem-solving and logical reasoning. In contrast, Integral approaches view intelligence holistically and incorporate emotions, creativity and social interactions alongside cognition.

Cultural factors shape these perspectives. Western cultures value analytical thinking and favouring technological approaches. In contrast, Eastern cultures prioritise harmony and relationships, supporting integral approaches. Societal norms also influence the acceptance of multiple intelligences, such as musical or kinesthetic skills.

*OR*

(b) Manoj's higher emotional intelligence makes him more popular with colleagues because of the following reasons

(i) **Better Communication** He understands others' feelings and expresses himself clearly, which builds trust.

(ii) **Conflict Resolution** He handles disagreements calmly, ensuring positive relationships.

(iii) **Empathy** He listens and shows care, creating strong bonds.

(iv) **Team Motivation** He encourages and supports others, boosting teamwork and morale.

In contrast, Sunil lacks these qualities and he may struggle with understanding or connecting with colleagues, which leads to misunderstandings and weak relationships. This shows how emotional intelligence plays a vital role in creating a harmonious workplace.

**25.** The four methods through which attitudes are formed are

(i) **Direct Experience** Personal experiences can strongly shape attitudes. For example, a bad meal might make someone dislike a certain food.

(ii) **Social Learning** Observing others, especially family or friends influences attitudes. For instance, children often adopt their parents' beliefs.

(iii) **Cultural Influence** Traditions and societal norms guide attitudes, such as respect for elders in certain cultures.

(iv) **Media Impact** Advertisements and movies can shape attitudes by presenting information or values in appealing ways.

**26.** In the Sentence Completion Test, psychologists ask the client to finish sentences. For example, I feel happy when ......... . or I get scared of ......... . Their responses reveal their emotions, desires, conflicts and personality traits, which helps to understand their mental state.

In the Draw-a-Person Test, psychologists ask the client to draw a person. Details in the drawing, like size, placement and features, which offer insights into their self-image, emotions or concerns. For example, a small figure might suggest low self-esteem.

These tests are projective, so they help to uncover unconscious thoughts and feelings, which makes them helpful for exploring deeper aspects of personality and emotional well-being.

**27.** Meera's intense and irrational fear of spiders indicates a specific phobia, while the sudden episodes of terror, breathlessness and dizziness suggest she might also experience panic disorder.

Coping strategies for both the disorders are given below

(i) **Coping with Phobia** Gradual exposure therapy can help to cope up with phobia. By slowly facing her fear of spiders in a controlled way, she can reduce her anxiety over time.

(ii) **Coping with Panic Disorder** Deep breathing exercises and relaxation techniques can help her to manage sudden panic attacks and restore calmness. Seeking therapy can also provide additional support.

**28.** (a) Sigmund Freud explained personality development through his psychosexual stages theory, where personality is shaped by managing conflicts between biological drives and societal expectations. He described five stages which are

(i) **Oral Stage (0-1 year)** Focus is on the mouth, like sucking and biting. If needs aren't met, it may lead to dependency or oral habits.

(ii) **Anal Stage (1-3 years)** Focus shifts to bowel control. Problems here can result in traits like being overly tidy or messy.

(iii) **Phallic Stage (3-6 years)** Attention centers on genital awareness. Issues with the Oedipus or Electra complex could affect confidence and relationships.

(iv) **Latency Stage (6-12 years)** Sexual energies are dormant and focus moves to social and intellectual skills. Trouble here may hinder social abilities.

(v) **Genital Stage (12 years onwards)** Sexual energies return, focusing on relationships. Unresolved earlier conflicts can cause difficulties in intimacy.

Problems at any stage can lead to fixation where personality traits remain tied to that stage. According to Freud, resolving these challenges is crucial for healthy personality development.

*OR*

(b) Ecological and cultural environments play a vital role in shaping personality development. They influence behaviours, values and social norms by determining daily survival needs and societal structures.

- **In hunting-gathering societies,** individuals live close to nature and rely on teamwork for survival. Traits like cooperation, adaptability and sharing become essential because people hunt in groups and share food. For example, in such societies, children learn to work collaboratively and develop trust within their community.
- **In agricultural societies,** dependence on stable land and long-term planning fosters traits like diligence, patience and responsibility. Children often assist in farming tasks, learning values like hard work and discipline. In these societies people develop a sense of belonging to a larger community with roles and responsibilities defined by their place in agriculture.

**29.** (a) Cognitive therapies focus on understanding how thoughts influence emotions and behaviours. The four key concepts in cognitive therapies are

(i) **Core Schemas** These are deep-rooted beliefs about oneself, others or the world. For example, a person may believe 'I'm not good enough.' Such schemas can shape how individuals interpret situations and impact their self-esteem.

(ii) **Negative Automatic Thoughts** These are quick, unconscious thoughts that occur in response to events. They're often pessimistic, like 'I'll fail this exam' or 'Nobody likes me'. Cognitive therapy works to make people aware of these thoughts and challenge their validity.

(iii) **Cognitive Distortions** These are faulty thinking patterns, such as overgeneralisation. Identifying and correcting these distortions helps people think more rationally.

(iv) **Irrational Beliefs** These are unrealistic, rigid beliefs like 'I must be perfect' or 'Life must always be fair'. Such beliefs create stress and therapists help individuals to replace them with balanced and flexible beliefs.

*OR*

(b) Psychotherapists follow six key ethical standards to ensure effective therapy and client well-being and these are

(i) **Confidentiality** Therapists must keep client information private, which creates trust and a safe space for sharing thoughts and feelings.

(ii) **Informed Consent** Clients must understand the therapy process, including its goals and methods. This empowers clients to make informed decisions about their treatment.

(iii) **Competence** Therapists should possess adequate knowledge and skills in their field. Competent therapists provide high-quality care and help clients achieve positive outcomes.

(iv) **Non-Maleficence** Therapists avoid causing harm to clients by practicing responsibly and ensuring their methods do not worsen the client's condition.

(v) **Beneficence** Therapists actively work for the client's well-being, designing therapy plans that address their specific needs and improve their mental health.

(vi) **Professional Boundaries** Therapists maintain clear boundaries, such as avoiding dual relationships, to ensure ethical and effective interactions.

**30.** Social stress negatively affects health, causing anxiety, depression, weakened immunity, high blood pressure, sleep problems and poor social relationships.

**31.** Two common causes of social stress in daily life are

(i) Conflicts in personal relationships, like family disputes fear of judgement.

(ii) Criticism during performance evaluations or social interactions.

**32.** People exposed to poverty, violence, disability, inequality or adverse circumstances are more likely to develop psychological disorders.

**33.** Two steps which are helpful in addressing the concerns of mentally-ill people include

(i) Providing social support for maintaining relationships.

(ii) Offering access to educational programmes, employment opportunities, housing and other meaningful activities to improve their quality of life.